Politics of Change in Middle East and North Africa since Arab Spring

A Lost Decade?

Politics of Change in Middle East and North Africa since Arab Spring

A Lost Decade?

Edited by
MD. MUDDASSIR QUAMAR

KNOWLEDGE WORLD
KW Publishers Pvt Ltd
New Delhi

MEI@ND

Series: MEI-KW Middle East Series

ISBN 978-93-91490-76-8 Hardback
ISBN 978-93-91490-82-9 ebook

Published in India by Kalpana Shukla

KNOWLEDGE WORLD
KW Publishers Pvt Ltd
4676/21, First Floor, Ansari Road
Daryaganj, New Delhi 110002
Phone: +91 11 43528107
Marketing: kw@kwpub.in
Editorial: production@kwpub.in
Website: www.kwpub.in

Printed and Bound in India

To

My parents

Md. Jameel Akhter

&

Shireen Rafat Jahan

Contents

About MEI@ND

Launched in February 2010, the Middle East Institute, New Delhi seeks to promote the understanding of contemporary Middle East. It is India-based but not India-centric. Its main research focus is the geopolitical dynamics of the Middle East including, but not limited to, military matters, economy, energy security, political system and institutions, society, culture and religion, and conflicts in the region. The institute also encourages research on bourgeoning Asian interest in and engagements with the Middle East. MEI@ND documents bilateral relations amongst the Middle Eastern states and strives to produce an updated analysis of the region's changing strategic landscape. Besides a host of web-based activities, the premier publications of MEI include, *Contemporary Review of the Middle East* (a quarterly by Sage) and *Persian Gulf: India's Relations with the Region* (an annual by Palgrave). Professor P R Kumaraswamy is the Honorary Director of MEI@ND.

MEI-KW Middle East Series is the latest step in promoting Middle Eastern studies in India and seeks to be a platform for younger scholars to develop and showcase their academic pursuits. Books both edited and authored of about 75,000 words on contemporary Middle Eastern developments will be published under the series. Fresh Ph.D. holders are especially encouraged to convert their doctoral theses into books as part of the series. The MEI@ND has partnered with KW Publishers, New Delhi to publish books under this series, and strives to publish 2-4 books annually. The Honorary Director of MEI is the editor of the Series. Queries and proposals should be addressed to mei.newdelhi@gmail.com

The edited volume *Politics of Change in Middle East and North Africa since Arab Spring: A Lost Decade?* is the first in the series and presents a constellation of essays on political, economic and social developments in MENA since Arab Spring.

Acknowledgements

Editing a volume presents its own set of challenges. Besides the need for delicate planning and coordination, striving to remain honest to the theme without compromising on the quality becomes sacrosanct. Between conceiving the idea and finalizing the manuscript, one goes through various emotions of ecstasy and despair depending on the ups and downs in the response of the prospective contributors. Eventually, it is the contributors who carry the day when the chips are down. I am therefore most thankful to each one of the contributors to this volume for not only agreeing to write a chapter despite their busy schedule and the challenges posed by the Covid-19 pandemic but also for reposing their faith in me.

Preparing a manuscript, whether authored or edited, is a demanding job and requires discipline, and dedication but above all inspiration and guidance. I am thankful to MEI@ND for giving me the opportunity to edit this volume.

I am thankful to Manohar Parrikar IDSA, its Director-General, Ambassador Sujan R. Chinoy, all the senior colleagues and members of the West Asia centre for helping me in various ways to develop my understanding of the region and its various nuances and complexities. Teachers, mentors and friends in academia and beyond have at different times and in various ways inspired me to strive for excellence in academics and I am thankful to each of them for their faith and encouragement. The list is long and it is impossible to name everyone but I must mention Professor Girijesh Pant, Professor Gulshan Dietl, Commodore C. Uday Bhaskar, Dr. Sreeracha Dutta and Dr. Sameena Hameed, for their constant support and encouragement.

The MEI@ND was kind enough to accept the idea of publishing a volume to commemorate the decade since Arab Spring and I am thankful to all the friends of the MEI@ND for their constant support and encouragement and for helping it produce quality academic work and promoting younger scholars to pursue Middle East studies. I am also thankful to Ms. Kalpana Shukla and her team at KW for agreeing to launch the *MEI-KW Middle East Series* with this volume.

Lakshmi has been a pillar of support to me ever since I first met her on those rainy August days of 2002 in Jawaharlal Nehru University. Her unconditional love and support through the ups and downs of the years of togetherness, despite all my eccentricities, has given me the strength to continue and helped me grow into a better human being.

Finally, I am thankful to my family for bearing with me in my academic pursuit, to my late father for inspiring me to pursue higher studies, and to my mother for all her care, adulation and endorsement of my life choices. I, therefore, dedicate this volume to my parents.

I am grateful to all those mentioned here and others who helped in the completion of this manuscript. All omissions and errors are mine and mine alone.

New Delhi
31 July 2021

Md. Muddassir Quamar

Contributors

Md. Muddassir Quamar is Associate Fellow at Manohar Parrikar Institute for Defence Studies and Analyses, New Delhi and holds a Ph.D. in Middle East studies from Jawaharlal Nehru University. He has a wider interest in politics and societies in the Arabian Gulf, political Islam, Middle East strategic affairs and India's relations with the Middle East. Dr. Qumar is the author of *Education System in Saudi Arabia: Of Change and Reforms* (2021), and co-author *India's Saudi Policy: Bridge to the Future* (2019) and *Persian Gulf: India's Relations with the Region* (2018, 2019 and 2020). He has published several research papers in reputed international journals and contributed chapters for edited volumes. He was Visiting Fellow at the King Faisal Center for Research and Islamic Studies, Riyadh. Dr. Quamar has been associated with the MEI@ND in various capacities since its inception in 2010.

Hussein Solomon is Academic Head of the Department of Political Studies and Governance at the University of the Free State, South Africa. He is also a Senior Research Associate of the Jerusalem-based think tank Research on Islam and Muslims in Africa (RIMA) as well as a Visiting Professor at the Osaka School of International Public Policy, Japan. His research focus has been on the Middle East and North Africa region as well as on issues of global security.

Joseph A. Kéchichian is Senior Fellow at the King Faisal Center for Research and Islamic Studies in Riyadh, Saudi Arabia. He held the post of Senior Writer with the Dubai-based *Gulf News* between 1 January 1995 and 31 August 2017, and served as the Honorary Consul of the Sultanate of Oman in Los Angeles, California, between 2006 and 2011.

Kéchichian received his doctorate in Foreign Affairs from the University of Virginia in 1985, where he also taught (1986-1988), and assumed the assistant deanship in international studies (1988-1989). Between 1990 and 1996, he laboured at the Santa Monica-based RAND Corporation as an Associate Political Scientist, and was a lecturer at the University of California in Los Angeles. The author of sixteen published books, his latest titles are *Sa'udi Policies Towards Migrants and Refugees: A Sacred Duty* (with Fahad L. Alsharif) Sussex Academic Press, September 2021; *The Attempt to Uproot Sunni-Arab Influence: A Geo-Strategic Analysis of the Western, Israeli and Iranian Quest for Domination*, Sussex, January 2017; *From Alliance to Union: Challenges Facing Gulf Cooperation Council States in the Twenty-First Century*, Sussex, 2016; *'Iffat Al Thunayan: An Arabian Queen*, Sussex, 2015; and *Legal and Political Reforms in Sa'udi Arabia*, Routledge, 2013.

Joseph Alagha is Professor of Political Science and Intercultural Studies at Haigazian University, Beirut, Lebanon. He is a prolific author in humanities and social sciences. Alagha is the author of four peer-reviewed university press books, two monographs, three books in Arabic, and more than one hundred refereed publications (Journal Articles; Festschriften/ Book Chapters; Review essays, Book Reviews and Commentaries) in four languages: Arabic, English, French, and Dutch, but mostly in English. As attested by his publications, Alagha is a subject matter expert (SME) in four disciplines: (1) Contemporary Islamic Movements; (2) Islamism and post-Islamism; (3) Political Mobilisation and Performing Arts in the Middle East and North Africa (MENA)\West Asia; and (4) Prevention of Violent Extremism (PVE): Gender-based Violence.

Krzysztof Strachota is Head of Department for Turkey, Caucasus and Central Asia (since 2001) at the Ośrodek Studiów Wschodnich (Centre for Eastern Studies; OSW)—a think tank in Warsaw, Poland that he joined in 1999. Since 2018, he is also coordinator of OSW's China Research Programme, and since 2019, of the Israel Research Programme. He has coordinated a number of OSW research projects, including studies on the evolution of Islam in the Post-Soviet space, the 'war on terror' after 2001, the military operations in Afghanistan and Iraq and the Arab

Spring. He focuses on security issues and political, cultural and identity changes in the Greater Middle East, based on both web source analysis and regular study trips to areas of interest, using anthropological field research methods. He is regularly published in the Polish press and participates in debates. Dr. Strachota is also Visiting Fellow at the University of Warsaw. His select major publications include *The Middle East in the Shadow of the Islamic State*; *China vs. Central Asia: The Achievements of the Past Two Decades* (co-author A. Jarosiewicz); *Turkey and the Kurdish Problem: New Approaches in the Face of the Middle East Crises*; *Jihad vs. The New Great Game: Paradoxes of Militant Islamic Threats in Central Asia* (co-author M. Falkowski); *Reintegration or Reconquest? Georgia's Policy towards Abkhazia and South Ossetia in the Context of the Internal and International Situation* (Co-Author W. Bartuzi).

Lakshmi Priya is Research Analyst at the Manohar Parrikar Institute for Defence Studies and Analyses, New Delhi. She has a Ph.D. in West Asian studies from Jawaharlal Nehru University. Prior to this, she was associated with the Indian Social Institute and Office of the Cultural Attaché, Embassy of the Kingdom of Saudi Arabia, as a researcher. She completed her masters in the Arabic language from the School of Languages, Jawaharlal Nehru University. In addition to area studies, she also has an interest in international relations and political theory. She has published a research article on the legitimacy of the Ba'ath in Syria and the Gramscian idea of Cultural Hegemony.

Maria Elizabeth Joseph earned her Masters in Middle Eastern and African History from Tel Aviv University in 2021. She was awarded the Middle Eastern Studies thesis grant in 2019 for her dissertation on *The Islamic Republic of Iran's State Policy towards the Baluch and Kurdish National Movements from 1979–1999.* Her research interests include the development of Baluch identity and nationalism and minority movements in the Middle East. Her doctoral research will focus on the significance of the Baluch and its contribution to oceanic Islam.

Michael Barak is a lecturer at the Lauder School of Government Diplomacy and Strategy at The Interdisciplinary Center (IDC), Herzliya where he teaches courses on Terrorism, Middle East studies, and Spoken and Colloquial Arabic. He is a senior researcher at the Institute for Counter-Terrorism (ICT) where he serves as the head of radical Islam and global jihad desk. Dr. Michael also serves as a senior researcher at The Moshe Dayan Center for Middle Eastern and African Studies (MDC). His main fields of research are radical Islam, global jihad (AQ & ISIS), modern Egypt, Sufi & Salafi movements, and social media networks in the Arab world. He has been publishing articles on these topics. His new book *The Islamic State Vision* is under production.

Mona Ali is the chief editor of the website for the Interregional Center for Strategic Analysis, an Emirati think tank that provides decision-making support. Mona has also previously worked at a number of think tanks in the Gulf and Middle East, including Future for Advanced Research and Studies (FARAS) in Abu Dhabi and the Regional Center for Strategic Studies (RCSS) in Cairo. Her research is interdisciplinary in nature, blending comparative politics with strategic studies. More specifically, she focuses on the impact of domestic state/society transformations on national security policies in Middle East countries.

Mordechai Chaziza holds a Ph.D. from Bar-Ilan University and is a senior lecturer at the Department of Politics and Governance and the division of Multidisciplinary Studies in Social Science, at Ashkelon Academic College (Israel). Dr. Chaziza is the author of *China and the Persian Gulf: The New Silk Road Strategy and Emerging Partnerships* (2019), and *China's Middle East Diplomacy: The Belt and Road Strategic Partnership* (2020). His current research focuses on China's foreign policy in the Middle East-North Africa (MENA), and China's Non-intervention policy in intrastate wars.

Nina Slama is a guest lecturer and teaching assistant at the Interdisciplinary Center (IDC) Herzliya. She holds a M.A. in International Relations from Bar-Ilan University (BIU). Her thesis focuses on "Foreign Policy Turning Points: India's Israel Policy 1948-2018". She also holds a B.A. in Government, Diplomacy and Strategy, and a Certificate in European Studies from IDC Herzliya. Her areas of interest and research are international relations, India's politics and foreign policy, India-Israel relations, Israel's foreign policy, and the European Union. She is fluent in English, French and Hebrew.

P. R. Kumaraswamy teachers contemporary Middle East at Jawaharlal Nehru University (JNU), New Delhi. From 1992-1999 he was a research fellow at the Harry S., Truman Research Institute for the Advancement of Peace, Jerusalem. Since joining JNU in September 1999, he has been researching, teaching, and writing on various aspects of the contemporary Middle East. His works include *Squaring the Circle: Mahatma Gandhi and the Jewish National Home* (2018), *India's Israel Policy* (2010), and *Historical Dictionary of the Arab Israeli Conflict* (2015, second edition). In February 2010, he set up the virtual Middle East Institute, New Delhi and serves as its honorary director. He is the editor of *Contemporary Review of the Middle East* (Sage India) and the series editor of *Persian Gulf: India's Relations with the Region* (Palgrave Macmillan).

Rohit Sharma is a Ph.D. Candidate in Centre for West Asian Studies, Jawaharlal Nehru University (JNU), New Delhi. He is a law graduate and holds a master's in international relations from South Asian University. He also holds a Postgraduate Diploma in Human Rights, International Humanitarian and Refugee Laws from The Indian Society of International Law, New Delhi. Currently, he is working on the Evolution of Cyber Security in Israel for his Ph.D.

Sameena Hameed is Assistant Professor in Middle Eastern studies at Jawaharlal Nehru University, New Delhi. Her areas of specialisation include the Middle Eastern economy, India's economic relations with the Middle East and energy security issues and has contributed monographs, journal articles and chapters to edited volumes. She has prepared research papers and study reports for the Ministry of External Affairs (MEA), Government of India and other Indian trade and commerce organisations like ASSOCHAM. She has been a member of the MEA-constituted Select Group on Gulf and West Asia. She was also a member of the Indian team for 'India—GCC Strategic Partnership' project and the Indo-Saudi Dialogue.

Simone Bekker is a postgraduate student in the Department of Political Studies and Governance at the University of the Free State. She has also published on gender issues in the Middle East which is her research focus.

Sinem Cengiz, born and raised in Kuwait, is a Ph.D. Candidate at the Department of Area Studies at Middle East Technical University in Ankara, where she also earned her Master's Degree at the Department of International Relations. She has several peer-reviewed journal articles and book chapters published on Gulf affairs and Turkey's relations with the broader Middle East. She is also the author of the book titled *Turkish-Saudi Relations: Cooperation and Competition in the Middle East* published by Gerlach Press in 2020. Besides her academic track, she worked as a diplomatic correspondent covering the post-2011 Middle East through fieldwork in the regional countries (2012-2014). Based in Athens, she contributed to *Al Arabiya* as a weekly columnist (2014-2015). She also worked at the Embassy of State of Kuwait in Turkey (2015-2018) at the department of press and political affairs. Lastly, she was affiliated with Kuwait University with a government scholarship (2018-2019). She is currently a weekly columnist in the *Arab News*, a Saudi newspaper, since 2016.

Uma Purushothaman teaches International Relations at the Central University of Kerala. She is a Non-Resident Fellow at the Middle East Institute, New Delhi. She was earlier associated with the Observer Research Foundation and the United Service Institution of India. Her areas of interest include great power politics, Russian foreign policy, soft power, Middle East politics, and US domestic and foreign policies. She serves as a reviewer to several international and national journals. She has published in national and international journals and presented papers at national and international conferences.

1. Introduction

Md. Muddassir Quamar

The Arab Spring protests were historic in many ways. The uprisings that began in Tunisia were unprecedented because they affected the whole region and no country in the Middle East and North Africa (MENA) remained completely untouched by the protest movements. No aspects of life—political, economic, strategic, social and cultural—remained immune from its impacts. The protests set off a series of events in the region and shook the foundations of many long-serving dictatorial regimes forcing leaders such as Zein El Abidine Ben Ali in Tunisia, Hosni Mubarak in Egypt, Ali Abdullah Saleh in Yemen and Muammar Gaddafi in Libya to either step down or flee. Syria's Bashar al-Assad, faced mounting internal and external pressure to abdicate but managed to survive but not without triggering a decade-long and ongoing civil war.

The early successes of the uprisings generated hopes for democratic transformations in the Arab world. However, ten years later, the hopes have given way to despair, death and destruction. The optimism of the early days of Arab Spring was crushed by the deep state's propensity to survive and reinvent accompanied by the vagaries of realpolitik and the rise of radical ideologies. Powerful regimes or their remnants found ways to fight back and cling to power enlisting support from their regional or external benefactors. This has nonetheless sharpened the geopolitical tensions and rivalries.

The limitations of the uprisings had become evident in the first two years (2011-2012). Except for Tunisia, wherein the local actors preferred to accommodate differences and committed to electoral politics, and for an interim period in Egypt, with its short-lived experiment with an elected government led by Mohammed Morsi (June 2012- July 2013), no country showed any promise for political change. The refusal of Assad and Gaddafi to heed the people's demand for political change, and the use of force to crush the budding opposition, led to bloody civil wars in Syria and Libya, causing unforeseen death and destruction. In Libya, an ill-conceived North Atlantic Treaty Organization (NATO)-led military intervention forced Gaddafi to relinquish power and go into hiding, only to meet a violent death in October 2011. The vacuum fuelled the tribal infighting to control the vast mineral and hydrocarbon resources and proliferation of Islamist terrorists resulting in a prolonged civil war. In Syria, due to the Iranian and Russian military interventions, the Assad regime survived but not before the ensuing conflict ravaged the country.

Despite early signs of a possible smooth transfer of power from Saleh to his deputy Abdrabbuh Mansur Hadi due to the Gulf Cooperation Council (GCC) mediation, the situation in Yemen deteriorated due to the Houthi rebellion in 2014-15 and the proxy war for regional influence between Iran and Saudi Arabia. In Bahrain, which also witnessed serious protests in early 2011, the monarchy survived due to the GCC's Peninsula Shield Force (PSF). The PSF led by Saudi forces proved instrumental in containing the protests. Nevertheless, the most serious reversal against the hope for democratic change came with the end of the democratic experiment in Egypt after the military takeover in July 2013.

The internal strife and violence faced by several countries after the uprisings raised questions about the future of the Arab Spring. Even as a bigger challenge emerged in the form of *ad-Dawlah al-Islāmiyah fī 'l-'Irāq wa-sh-Shām* (the Islamic State in Iraq and Levant or ISIL), also known as Islamic State in Iraq and Syria (ISIS) or merely as *ad-Dawlah al-Islāmiyah* (Islamic State) and by its Arabic acronym Daesh. The terror spread by the breakaway group of Al-Qaeda in Iraq (AQI) and the pseudo-state it established in Iraq and Syria created havoc in the region, and its ripple effects were felt far and beyond. Temporarily, the international and regional powers came together to fight the challenge, and Daesh was militarily defeated in 2017 with the fall of Mosul and Raqqa. As a result, the threats from Daesh weakened, but the humanitarian crises in Syria, Libya and Yemen continue to pose a challenge for the region and international community.

Despite the failures of the protest movement to bring any significant positive change except in Tunisia, and the violent conflicts and terrorist threats it produced, the hopes for a better future among the people, both men and women, especially among the youths, has not entirely diminished. If at all, those aspiring for participatory politics, a just society and economic prosperity continue to express their demands, grievances and disgruntlement against existing political and social structures as was witnessed in Algeria, Oman, Sudan, Lebanon, Iraq and other countries in 2018 and 2019.

A decade since the eruption of Arab Spring protests in MENA, the region confronts popular disenchantment, protests and mass mobilisation. Unfortunately, a majority of the regimes have refused to heed the demand for democratisation; some have chosen to confront the protestors by sheer use of force, leading the country into civil war and strife, others have found ways to regain power jolting the hopes for democratic transformation. But there are some silver linings such as regular elections in Tunisia, greater political participation in Jordan and Morocco, reduction in violence in Iraq and Syria, military defeat of Daesh, and increased social reforms in Saudi Arabia. There is also greater scrutiny against corruption, for better public services, awareness on the need for women empowerment and the rights of minorities. Simultaneously, debates on terrorism, extremism and radicalism and the interplay of religion, politics and identity have become widespread.

The larger challenges remain. Problems of a closed political system, economic struggles, poverty, unemployment, poor economic opportunities, crony capitalism and rampant corruption, lack of quality education and exclusion of women and minorities are visible throughout the region. On the other hand, every affected country faces a unique challenge that requires specific solutions. For example, Iraq needs to disarm various militias loyal to different tribal, ethnic and sectarian leaders either by disbanding them or bringing them within the fold of the Iraqi security forces. Likewise, Libya requires the exit of all foreign mercenaries to succeed in its national dialogue process to bring a durable political solution. On the other hand, Syria will have to find a way to deal with the Kurdish and Sunni opposition groups and accommodate its huge refugee population in neighbouring counties to end the civil war.

The hopes and despair generated by the Arab Spring protests and its aftermath have underlined some key trends that are likely to define the politics and society of the MENA region in the times to come. Some of these, including demands for democratisation, continuation of old elites, need for economic reorganisation, political Islam including its radical, extremist and jihadist manifestations, women's right and their increased role in public life, transformation of media and communication landscape, regional geopolitical competition and continued influence of external powers are discussed in this volume.

Demands for Democratisation

First and foremost, the Arab Spring underlined the widespread democratic deficit in the region and the surge in demand for participatory politics, democratisation and better governance. The self-immolation by Mohammed Bouazizi on 17 December 2010 that sparked a series of protests in Tunisia underlined the extent of disenchantment among the Arab masses. Regardless of the type of political system, the regional countries, in general, have been ruled by authoritarian leaders who refuse to leave the office until they face a military or palace coup or are assassinated or die of natural causes. The idea of limits on power, division of responsibility, institutional accountability and a smooth transition of power through elections has remained strange to the modern Middle East.

Whether ruled by hereditary monarchies (Morocco, Jordan and the six Gulf Cooperation Council (GCC) countries, namely Saudi Arabia, United Arab Emirates (UAE), Qatar, Bahrain, Kuwait and Oman) or by constitutional republics (Yemen, Iraq, Syria, Lebanon, Egypt, Sudan, Algeria, Tunisia, Libya and Mauritania), democratic governance and leaders have alluded Arab countries. Through the Arab Spring, the one rallying cry that echoed on the Arab streets was for better governance, participatory politics and accountable leadership. The demonstrators who came out on the streets and squares demanded justice and dignity and called for an end of dictatorships.

The protests and demonstrations underlined that the people are fed up with authoritarian regimes. The slogans such as *Ash-sha'b yurīd isqāṭ an-niẓām* (the people want to bring down the regime) underlined the popular resentment against the regimes in Tunisia, Egypt, Libya, Syria, Bahrain and Yemen. The people who came out on the streets raised slogans calling for *hurriyah* (freedom), *masawah* (equality), *huquq al-Insan* (human rights), *huquq al-mara'a* (women's rights), *adl* (justice) and *karamah* (dignity). The Tunisian uprising was termed *Thawrat al-Karāmah* (Revolution for Dignity). The Arab Spring underlined the latent anger against restrictive political systems.

Notably, the violence and civil wars ensued by the protests and crackdown by the regimes have not entirely dampened the people's yearning for change and the end of authoritarian and unaccountable governments. As was witnessed in 2018 and 2019, many countries that had not experienced large-scale protests during the first phase of Arab Spring protests, such as Algeria, Lebanon, Iraq and Oman, saw a series of protests and demonstrations resonating with the spirit of Arab Spring.

Continuation of Old Elites and Structures

The second most important trend is the continuation of old elites and structures. The Arab Spring protests did generate hope and brought positive changes in some cases, but it provoked the regimes, and the deep state patronised by them, to take 'counter-revolutionary' actions to fight, suppress and crush the demands for democratisation. In most cases, the regimes and old structures managed to survive without using coercive force, but when needed, the deep state did not shy away from using the military to survive even at the cost of pushing the country to civil war, death and destruction. In some cases, such as in Syria, the deep state and regime supporters used all possible means to brand the entire opposition as extremists and radical terrorists, thus legitimizing their coercive actions.

It underlined that the old elites and their supporters remain strong and continue to enjoy varying degrees of popularity and legitimacy and will not easily agree to share power. Therefore, the struggle for participatory politics, democratisation and good and accountable governance will be long and arduous. For a better future, the people and groups wanting to see a democratic change will have to find innovative ways and seize relying on violence to end all the problems. The larger concern in the Arab world is the absence of democratic institutions and inclusive civil society, without which democratisation is likely to remain a pipedream. Therefore, a democratic revolution will need to be preceded by a democratic social change. Until then, the old elites and structures will continue to dominate the politics in the region.

Need for Economic Reorganisation

Thirdly, the Arab Spring protests underlined the need for economic reorganisation in the MENA countries. Undoubtedly, besides oppressive political regimes, the grievance that resonated on the Arab streets from Tunisia to Yemen reflected the lack of economic opportunities. The economic situation in the MENA countries was, and continues to be, marked with growing disparity, poverty and inequality. A young demography and a high rate of unemployment are a common thread binding the regional countries. However, oppressive regimes, surrounded by corrupt leaders and crony capitalists, refuse to listen to the mounting economic grievances and brand all voices for economic reorganisation and equitable distribution of wealth as dissent. As a result, voices raising economic grievances are forcefully silenced.

The economic problem in the region is far from over. Regional countries, including those not ravaged by civil war and strife, struggle with varying degrees of economic challenges. Egypt, Tunisia, Lebanon, Jordan, Bahrain and Oman have faced serious economic problems and have struggled to turn around the slowdown. Lebanon has been ravaged by corruption; Egypt and Tunisia have mismanaged resources while Oman, Bahrain and Jordan lack resources. The oil-rich Gulf monarchies have managed the economic grievances by offering financial handouts and bring reforms but continue to face challenges due to declining oil revenues due to depleting production and dropping prices. Though countries like UAE have fared better in initiating reforms to improve economic conditions, the process of economic diversification poses a challenge for other GCC countries. Persistent low economic growth and high unemployment (Figure 1) are chronic problems afflicting the regional countries.

Undoubtedly, these economic challenges emanate from deeper structural problems that the political leaders have continuously ignored. However, with young demography and no serious effort to resolve the economic challenges, seen together with authoritarian regimes, the region is unlikely to resolve the problems echoed through the Arab Spring.

Figure 1: GDP Growth and Rate of Unemployment in MENA, 2001-2019

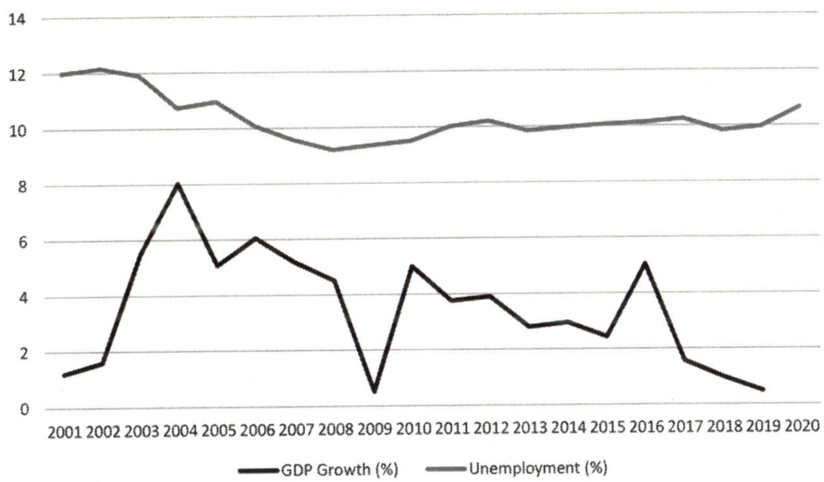

Source: The World Bank, https://data.worldbank.org/region/middle-east and north-africa

Political Islam

Fourthly, a key trend in the region is the rise in political Islam, including its radical, extremist, and jihadist manifestations. Islamist movements did not initiate the Arab Spring protests, but with a notable presence of such movements in almost all Arab countries, the Islamists soon joined the Arab Spring protests. In some countries, such as Egypt and Syria, the youth protests were hijacked by Islamist groups, while in others, such as Tunisia, the Islamists joined hands with youth groups to demand political change. In countries such as Iraq and Yemen, extremist sectarian and terrorist groups like Daesh, Kataib Hezbollah and Houthis have emerged as serious threats to the countries' integrity.

Political Islam is one of the most widespread phenomena in the region, and in one or the other form, its manifestations are visible in all regional countries from Tunisia, Morocco and Algeria to Oman, Saudi Arabia, Iran and Yemen. In their extremist and jihadist form, including Al-Qaeda and Daesh, the Islamist groups have wreaked havoc in the region and beyond, but even in their moderate or pacifist form, Political Islam is increasingly seen as a threat to regional peace and security by many countries, especially the Gulf monarchies and Egypt.

Since the removal of the Morsi government in 2013, Egypt has increasingly cracked down on the Muslim Brotherhood that stood in support of Morsi and demanded his reinstatement. As a result, the group has now largely gone underground, and a majority of its leaders are either in jail or have fled the country to take refuge in Qatar and Turkey. In addition, the UAE and Saudi Arabia have gradually hardened their stand on Islamist groups because of their goal to bring an end to monarchies and the formation of Islamic republics.

In some countries such as Morocco and Jordan, the Islamists, despite sharing complicated relations with the monarchies, have constrained themselves from calling for republican forms of government. Hence, they have avoided serious government scrutiny or have occasionally even shared power. In Turkey and Tunisia, the Islamists have adopted themselves to the secular republican institutions and have shared power with secular groups through electoral victories. In addition to the Sunni Islamists, there are Shia Islamists, such as Hezbollah and Houthis, who look up to the Iranian revolution as an example of successful resistance against domestic, regional and international powers.

Political Islam, despite the reverses the Islamists groups have faced due to the actions taken by the regimes, cannot be written off due to the support enjoyed by them among the masses. The perception of the Islamists being victimised by the ruling class, which many citizens in the region can identify with, help the masses to identify themselves with the Islamist groups.

Greater Role for Women in Public Life

Fifth, the region was witness to greater political participation of women during the protests and demonstrations. The MENA is one of the worst-performing regions globally in female participation in the workforce and politics. One of the key issues that echoed during the uprisings was equal opportunities for women. Women participated in protests in great numbers in Tunisia, Yemen, Egypt and Libya, and in Sudan, Algeria and Lebanon during the second phase. Even the Arab Gulf countries and Iran, which have traditionally imposed a more restrictive socio-political environment on their women, witnessed many women coming out of their homes and voicing demands for better opportunities. Some were even incarcerated for this tenacity, but this did not dampen the popular appeal for a greater role for women in public life.

Some women such as journalist Tawakkol Karman in Yemen, Nadia Morad in Iraq, Loujain al-Hathloul and Samar Badawi in Saudi Arabia and Alaa Salah in Sudan became global youth icons for their leading role in demanding social, political and economic change in their respective countries and were recognised by the international community. For example, Karman was awarded the Nobel Peace Prize for her role in Yemen protests in 2011. Though this has not brought instant changes to the everyday struggle of women for equal opportunities, it has certainly highlighted their ability to voice issues and pressurise the society and its leaders to bring positive change. Thus, countries such as Saudi Arabia have brought incremental changes to create greater economic and social opportunities for women by opening doors for their participation in governance and public life.

Transformation of Media and Communication Landscape

Sixth, the media and communication landscape in the region has significantly changed in the aftermath of the Arab Spring. The protest movement was one of the first transnational movements wherein political groups recognised social media's power for mobilising the masses and wider dissemination of their message. Although the protest movements did not eventually succeed in bringing a significant political change, they certainly revolutionised the way news was created and consumed. Facebook, Twitter and many such social media platforms and applications, played a crucial role in disseminating ideas and information during the Arab Spring. Access to smartphones and the internet played a crucial role in the fast spread of the protests, and hence the Arab Spring protests were often referred to as Facebook or Twitter revolution.

In the decade since then, many new developments have taken place. While the adverse effects of social media in the form of fake news and dissemination of misinformation have been widely recognised, the authorities have caught up with the new medium to use it as an effective tool for spreading propaganda and tracking any form of dissent. Nonetheless, the way social media and the internet have transformed the media and communication landscape is inescapable. There are new innovations taking place in the media and communication landscape every day, enabling people to widely share their ideas not only in written and pictorial forms but also through the broadcast of live videos that have an instant impact on the viewers. Social media, the internet and new technologies are here to stay and will continue to play a significant role in the future of media and civil society movements in the MENA region with a significantly high internet penetration of the internet and wide usage of social media.

Regional Geopolitical Competition

Seventh, the region has witnessed sharpening regional geopolitical competition in the aftermath of the Arab Spring, and with a stalemate in the form of a regional balance of power, it is unlikely to abate anytime soon. Some of the most important regional actors engaged in geopolitical competition and rivalries are Iran, Saudi Arabia, Turkey, Egypt and smaller but influential states such as Israel, Qatar and UAE. Saudi Arabia and Iran, the two regional giants, located across the Persian Gulf, have engaged in gaining strategic depth in the region to counter their mutual threat perceptions. During the Arab Spring protests, Saudi Arabia along with its regional allies, extended support to the protestors in Syria and Libya. On the other hand, Iran supported the protestors' rights in Bahrain and Yemen. In Syria and Yemen, the two have supported rival groups based on their interests fuelling civil wars and causing humanitarian crises.

In addition to Saudi Arabia and Iran, Israel and Iran are locked in geopolitical tensions. The two are engaged in a proxy fight inside Syria and Iraq. Israel feels threatened by the presence of Iranian military personnel and Iranian-trained militias close to its borders and regularly takes military measures to neutralise them by targeting their warehouses, munition factories and transport vehicles. At the same time, Iran, an ardent supporter of the Palestinian right to self-determination, has continued arming militias in Palestinian territories and Lebanon, thereby increasing friction with Israeli security forces. For Iran, which fears the widespread military capability of Israel and the United States, this is a way to take the fight close to enemy borders, thus avoiding fighting inside the Iranian borders.

There is significant rivalry brewing between Egypt and Turkey since 2013, and this has been witnessed in Libya, where the two supported and armed rival factions during the second Libyan civil war (2014-2020). However, the most important component of the Turkish-Egyptian rivalry is ideological support or opposition to Muslim Brotherhood. While Egypt, the birthplace of the group, has become increasingly hostile to it to the extent of terming it a terrorist organisation, Turkey under the Justice and Development Party (AKP) has remained steadfast in supporting and providing refuge to the Muslims Brotherhood and its leaders fleeing from different parts of the region. Thus, Turkey has been trying to regain its lost historical connection and strategic depth in the MENA region, and this has revived the historical Arab-Turkish tensions leading to some calling the Turkish regional activism as 'Neo-Ottomanism.'

The regional rivalries are not confined to bigger powers, even smaller countries such as UAE and Qatar have taken to an activist regional policy. This has not only created friction with bigger powers but also among themselves, as was seen during the 2017-21 GCC crisis wherein Qatar faced a diplomatic, political and economic boycott from the quartet of Saudi Arabia, Egypt, Bahrain and UAE. Both have largely used their deep pockets to advance their regional influence and are key players in the ongoing internal problems in Yemen, Libya, Syria, and Ethiopia and inside Palestinian territories.

The regional rivalries and tensions have manifested in ideological, ethnic and sectarian tensions and are partly responsible for the continued fighting in many regional countries. However, the most important component of the rivalries is geopolitical, with each country acting to enhance its influence. Despite its obvious potency to keep the region on fire, the likelihood of the regional countries agreeing on some form of regional security architecture to resolve problems remains low in the foreseeable future because of the wide differences and conflicting loyalties to their perceived ideals. If at all, the frictions are likely to intensify further with a fragile regional balance of power.

Continued influence of External powers

Finally, the Arab Spring protests underlined that the external powers would continue to remain influential in regional affairs. While the United

States is the only global power with a significant regional presence and influence, countries such as Russia and China have enhanced their strategic, military and economic presence in MENA since 2011. Russia, which had lost its regional presence and influence after the disintegration of the Soviet Union, saw an opportunity in Syria to regain its influence through a military intervention in 2015 and has continued to enhance its strategic engagements with the regional countries since then. On the other hand, China has been involved in mega connectivity and infrastructure projects, making it one of the leading economic partners of regional countries. Even the European countries have become more engaged in the region either to prevent the fires from spreading to their borders or to gain a share in the resources and market offered by the regional countries.

In 2011, when the Arab Spring protests were raging, the United States shifted its focus away from the Middle East to the Asia-Pacific region. However, a decade later as the talk of lesser American involvement in the Middle East became part of the strategic debates; the United States is far from decreasing its regional commitments. This is not only because the region continues to move from one crisis to another but also regional countries constantly seek the United States mediation in their disputes. The large-scale military presence of the United States is also why the fragile regional balance of power has not fallen apart, preventing a wider regional conflict.

The bottom line is that despite the increased involvement of many other globals and rising powers in the region, there is no country with the ability, resources, and influence of the United States to maintain the regional balance of power. This does not mean that other global powers such as Russia, China and European Union or rising powers such as India, Japan, South Korea, Brazil and Australia will not engage and enhance their presence in the regional countries. This would mean that the trend of external involvement in regional affairs in MENA will continue in the foreseeable future.

About the volume

This volume was conceived as a commemoration to mark the first decade of Arab Spring. The idea is to capture some of the political, economic, strategic and social developments in the region through papers either dedicated to examining the situation in an affected country such as Tunisia and Egypt or the regional trends concerning specific issues such as women's rights, radicalisation and so on. Excluding the introduction, the volume comprises 15 chapters. The chapter by Joseph Kéchichian examines the changes in Saudi Arabia in the socio-economic domain and the approach to governance and extremism. Kéchichian, a leading expert on the Gulf, takes a long view of the transformation inside the kingdom since 2011 and underlines the significance of the steps taken by the monarchy as a responsible regional power to the demands of its aspiring youth population. In their chapter, Hussain Solomon and Simone Bekker shed light on the widespread problem of authoritarianism and patriarchy in the region, with Iran and Saudi Arabia as case studies.

Michael Barak's chapter discusses the role of the Al-Azhar as a centre of Sunni Islamic learning and its role in the fight against the jihadist narrative by global terrorist groups, and its significance as a means of soft power for Egypt. In her chapter on the role of think tanks in determining the security policy of Gulf Arab countries, Mona Ali busts the myth that these state-funded organisations are mere mouthpieces. Her systematic study of the publications by Gulf think tanks after 2011 underlines that they have had a profound impact on the security policymaking in the regional countries. Nina Slama's chapter looks at the Tunisian case and how the country has remained committed to the ideals of the Arab Spring despite facing serious political and economic challenges.

Sameena Hameed examines the impact of the real estate boom in Egypt in the wake of the Arab Spring and how that has affected the economy of the country, as well as the kind of impact it had on common Egyptians and their economic aspirations. The chapter by Lakshmi Priya examines the impact of Arab Spring on the arms trade in MENA and underlines that the protests and their aftermath have significantly increased the volume of arms trade and transfer in the region. Joseph Alagha sheds light on the protests in Lebanon during the second phase of Arab Spring. He examines the role of WhatsApp in mass mobilisation while underscoring the deep roots of the tribulations due to the nexus between the corrupt political class, business people and social elites.

Maria Joseph examines the trend of growing radicalisation among Sunni Muslims in Iran.

In his chapter, Rohit Sharma examines the digitalisation of conflict in the region analysing the trend of conflicts and cooperation regarding the digital domain in cyberspace. He underlines that innovation such as Artificial Intelligence (AI) is likely to change the way countries engage with each other both in conflict and cooperation. The chapter by Krzysztof Strachota presents a detailed analysis of the Turkish response to the Arab Spring from the initial enthusiasm to the eventual recognition that the Turkish-Arab relations cannot be fundamentally altered by promoting regime change in the region. Sinem Cengiz also focuses on the Turkish engagement with the Arab world through examining the past publications of government-aligned think tanks in Ankara and how that shaped the Turkish policy toward the Arab world before and after the Arab Spring.

The chapter by Mordechai Chaziza examines the rise of China as a leading external power in the MENA region after the Arab Spring, especially in the economic domain. He underlines that China's policy towards the region has significantly transformed in the wake of the Arab Spring, wherein regional security has emerged as one of the major concerns for Chinese policymakers. Uma Purushothaman examines the contours of Russia's return to the Middle East as a leading external military power facilitated by the events of the Arab Spring. She underlines that though the Russian involvement is relatively small compared to the United States, it is bound to have a serious impact on the regional security situation, especially in the Levant. Finally, the volume ends with a chapter examining the Indian response to Arab Spring by P. R. Kumaraswamy, who identifies some of the broad issues that contributed to India maintaining a stoic silence on the Arab Spring events.

2. Saudi Arabia after the Arab Spring

Joseph A. Kéchichian

Introduction

Arab history's next chapter, which started with the late 2010 uprisings, occurred because of intrinsic failures by several governments throughout the twentieth century. Experimentations with alien ideologies prevented an Arab renaissance until a lone merchant in Tunisia set himself on fire that literally lit the torch of freedom. Regrettably, critics of the so-called Arab Spring have long concluded that timid protests came to nought, as most dissenters allegedly reverted to traditional norms that quickly skirted genuine demands for reforms (Haddad et al., 2012; Alexander, 2012). To be sure, and even if somewhat exaggerated, anti-revolutionary regimes returned, especially in Egypt, Syria and Yemen, although a decade is too short of a time-frame to conclude whether the uprisings failed or whether it was little more than a paragraph in a long chapter of Arab history that was still in progress.

What the decade accomplished was epochal with the removal of ossified authoritarian governments in Tunisia, Egypt, Yemen, Algeria, Iraq, Sudan and, perhaps, in Lebanon, where long-term transformations were underway in 2021 and where challenged establishment figures failed to earn the necessary trust from their populations. In several Arab countries, the spirit of the revolts that lit up in late-2010/early-2011 is still alive, though the health pandemic that gripped the globe in 2020 slowed the process down. Remarkably, the wars in Yemen and Syria taught revolutionary forces a hard lesson—one almost always neglected the military at one's peril. What started out as peaceful protests in Syria and Yemen, in particular, transformed themselves into deadly conflicts, with no ends in sight. Thus, it was eminently straightforward to surmise—perhaps even draw a critical warning from the two wars—

that the only option for success was to keep the movements peaceful and optimistic.

Still, the Arab Spring is truly in its infancy even if the enthusiasm that mobilised millions in 2011 has long since dissipated, while most continued to fear acute chaos and violence (Brynen et al., 2012; Gelvin, 2012). A few believed that time was on their side and that they would, eventually, realise aspirations for justice and freedom. Ironically, this was the case in Egypt, Iraq and elsewhere, though few ventured to make similar predictions about the conservative Arab Gulf monarchies, including Saudi Arabia, allegedly because the Gulf States were immune to such phenomenon. The paradox was visible to students of the Arab Gulf who, more often than not, highlighted how largely paternalistic societies were far more attuned to the needs of their rapidly evolving populations. Such perspectives were usually dismissed, ostensibly because the conservative monarchies, and especially the Kingdom of Saudi Arabia, were non-democratic, led by rulers that seldom reflected popular norms and, worse, that they were both anti-revolutionary and extremist.

As discussed below, nothing could be further from the truth since Saudi Arabia adapted to the repercussions of the Arab Spring far better than Levantine republics, especially as the latter confronted existential struggles that led to renewed authoritarianism. While few Levantines reminisced about the movements that mobilised elements of their societies in 2021, Saudis were not embarrassed to discuss what challenges their country faced and how they ought to address them. In contrast to Egyptians, for example, who lamented their naivety and, perhaps, recklessness as some thought that they could replace a Pharaonic dictatorship with its totalitarian Muslim Brotherhood counterpart, Saudis were realistic and aware of the necessities to usher in fundamental reforms. The fall of the Muslim Brotherhood regime in Cairo demonstrated that one could not have freedom *and* stability in a society that valued authoritarian rule. Riyadh avoided that trap and sought both transformations and steadiness. Ironically, while few Egyptian revolutionaries regretted their actions and most longed for serious economic transformations, most Saudis accepted that only fundamental economic renovations would secure their future.

Arabs everywhere appreciated that peaceful and optimistic options were easy to anticipate, though these necessitated hard work, foresightful leaders who could spare their societies various calamities, and the wisdom to plan for reforms that would benefit dramatically shifting demographics.[1] Importantly, the only places where these three criteria were met were in the Arab Gulf States, even if the conservative societies had their share of problems. Mercifully, Gulf Cooperation Council (GCC) States led by Saudi Arabia displayed the fortitude of alert officials to address various challenges, largely because they were legitimate and far more competent than Levantine merchant-politicians. Of course, the monarchies lacked the modern trappings drawn from elections and representative forms of government, but no persuasive perspectives were available to suggest that kingdoms and shaykhdoms were not as, or perhaps more, representative than so-called democratising societies. It was worth repeating that the monarchies were legitimate because they provided relatively dignified lives for their citizens, and because of the symbiotic tie between ruler and citizen through public majlises, the gatherings that brought them together to share the citizen's concerns and views. Moreover, the Bay'ah—which is the Islamic contract between ruler and citizen where the latter offers allegiance to the former and the former returns the favour with good governance, the rule of law, and protection of property and well-being—further seals such ties. There are inevitable shortcomings for a portion of the population, as in all countries, which emerged due to rapid and haphazard development policies, though the paradigm stood the test of time.

By all accounts, GCC States recorded dramatic changes during the past decade, led by substantive technological advancements and, in the case of the Kingdom of Saudi Arabia, a firm and secure lock on significant economic progress. In 2020, Riyadh hosted a G20 Summit that showcased to the entire world concrete diversification steps favoured by King Salman bin 'Abdul 'Aziz and Heir Apparent Muhammad bin Salman. If the 2010/2011 uprisings ended what was surely a stale regional order, Riyadh forcefully declared its preferences—which certainly required time to mature—as it ushered in bold policies that aimed to empower entrepreneurship and encourage wealth creation. Saudi authorities wanted nothing short of gargantuan, ranging from universal health care to effective education to strong economic initiatives and stable financial returns, precisely to avoid economic precariousness, corruption, and poor governance. In short, what Riyadh aimed for was enhanced competence in the ruling, an end to corruption and nepotism, as well as full employment as soon as possible.

Given Riyadh's rich agendas for the decades to come, what were the specific contemplated and/or applied efforts to date? Have Saudi officials implemented concrete and sufficiently diversified initiatives that either met or could satisfy an increasingly educated population? What were some of the rapidly changing governance features introduced under the *Vision 2030* programs? Was it even possible to conceive steps that could address nepotism and corruption in the Kingdom and through which mechanisms? Finally, what were the ultimate challenges that confronted the monarchy, including an existential threat from extremists? Could Riyadh manage to deal with such destructive elements precisely to deny the latter a platform to ride on the Arab Spring bandwagon?

Arab Spring Challenges to Saudi Arabia: "Day of Rage"

To better answer the questions raised above, and to further underscore the lessons learned by Saudi authorities in the aftermath of the early 2011 massive demonstrations in Cairo and elsewhere, it is crucial to examine the so-called "Day of Rage," which Saudi opposition figures called for and that fizzled faster than a coyote's run in the desert.

The so-called "Day of Rage" scheduled for 11 March 2011 using various social media outlets witnessed no demonstrations against the government, save for a few marches in the Eastern Province. There was no day of rage because there was nothing to be enraged about. Qatif, Hufuf and Awamiyyah witnessed organised marches, but these were nothing new as similar events occurred from time to time in these cities. Even after large-scale protests took place in nearby Bahrain, which prompted the GCC to deploy troops [Saudi, Emirati and Kuwaiti] to assist the overwhelmed Bahraini forces, Riyadh did not fear for its throne though there were serious concerns about the Bahraini monarchy.

Far more critical was the fall of President Hosni Mubarak because Egypt is a leading Arab country whose fate affected everyone. To be sure, and as an astute observer of the Kingdom noted, the country faced problems similar to what many other Arab societies faced, including a youth bulge, unemployment, corruption, as well as a dynamic population that aspired for representation. In other words, "sections of Saudi society felt excluded and discriminated against when it came to the distribution of wealth and allocation of rights, and such sentiments were more palpable among Shias, women, and other minorities," which led to "protests and violence in the Shia-dominated" and oil-rich Eastern Province (Quamar, 2014, p. 143).

How the government responded to these problems was classic. On 22 February 2011, Riyadh announced a series of benefits for citizens amounting to US$36 billion, of which US$ 10.7 billion were earmarked for scarce housing projects. King 'Abdallah bin 'Abdul 'Aziz first authorised this massive package that included numerous benefits, including the release of prisoners indicted for financial crimes, followed on 18 March 2011, by the allocation of an additional US$ 93 billion in grant payments. At least 500,000 new homes were earmarked for construction at the cost of US$ 67 billion, 60,000 new security jobs were created, and scores of smaller grants were announced over several months. Among these were a US$ 500 per month unemployment assistance, a minimum base salary of US$ 750 per month and, in an unprecedented move, generous grants to all public servants of two months' salary bonuses (Fisk 2011; *The Guardian* 2011).

These generous financial packages were meant to prevent a recurrence of any calls to demonstrate, and, extraordinarily, Saudi authorities fared well as they assumed responsibilities and met various expectations. Indeed, the effort was not a theoretical question, as Riyadh addressed many of the undeniable trials that were raised by various groups. To their credit, government officials embarked on a massive socio-economic transformation of the Saudi society that prevented serious clashes, which was no small feat. Simply stated, the monarch did not allow entrenched elites to suppress public voices and participation, especially among recent graduates or youths with vocational training, all of whom wished to join the workforce and earn decent wages. Moreover, Riyadh's responses were not limited to financial packages, as most senior figures rallied around the King who ushered in new socio-political steps.

In addition to financial "investments" in the society, King 'Abdallah announced that women would be allowed to vote and contest in municipal elections scheduled for 2015, and he increased the membership of the

Majlis al-Shura (Consultative Council) to 150, nominating 30 women in the process. Importantly, and this was a critical point to emphasise, these moves were not cosmetic initiatives as the chosen individuals represented a wide spectrum of society. In other words, the initiatives were critical building blocks in the edifice of reforms that illustrated Al Saud preferences for evolutionary steps. They further reaffirmed the results of several National Dialogues that analysed various needs, including women's rights that, at least in the local context (which was what mattered), highlighted yet another feature of democratisation (Kéchichian, 2012, pp. 62-108).

Salman Accedes the Throne

King Salman juggled several challenges as the Kingdom's monarch starting on 23 January 2015, immediately after his accession to the throne. A visionary ruler who came to power when he was already advanced in age and frail health, Salman bin 'Abdul 'Aziz was and remains a man in a hurry, willing and ready to tackle internal pressures for liberalisation to meet the expectations of his country's increasingly educated youths. Often dubbed a pro-fundamentalist leader, an accusation bordered on the comical, the King intended to check pressures as the more conservative religious elements prevented the state from governing according to traditional but evolutionary norms.

A true believer (in his faith as well as his nation), the pious Salman observed how the clerical establishment strangulated Saudi society and admonished them to be vanguards of the faith, not those who derailed it. His economic policies, which entailed diversification, infrastructure construction, education and a move towards a "knowledge economy," were visionary too. What they required was a firm hand that would deliver on so many fronts without neglecting oil and gas, still the Kingdom's bread and butter. These immense tasks were entrusted to Heir Apparent Muhammad bin Salman, who shared his father's vision to reinvent the polity and, over the course of less than a generation, alter a system that served well but needed reforms.

In addition to these internal challenges, and perhaps as important as any of the contentions that Salman's vision confronted, was Saudi Arabia's pivotal role in the Arab and Muslim worlds. Beyond the core concern over Palestine, as well as the need to reach a peaceful settlement in the Middle East along with a two-state solution that restored Palestine while it provided peace to Israel, King Salman was antagonised by Turkey and Persia, along with the latter's Shi'a ideology. Ankara's quest to restore the moribund Ottoman Empire and Iran's anti-Sunni agenda stood as dual threats the likes of which Saudi Arabia seldom experienced. Uprisings and wars in Egypt, Syria, Yemen, Bahrain, Lebanon, and Iraq, all substantiated the monarch's fears.

Muhammad bin Salman understood better than most why the Kingdom had to address popular grievances and reinvest in the country's economic activities. It took several years of preparation, but the *Vision 2030* projects, when revealed, addressed most of the claims made by various observers as to the best ways to deal with core socio-economic challenges. *Vision 2030* was and remains pragmatic as it contemplated genuine reforms that proposed to introduce functional but effective transformations and, a hugely critical point, settle on a less corrupt government.[2] Whether this was a form of authoritarianism or simple pragmatism will largely be determined by historians in a few decades, though few could deny that Riyadh set out to improve the quality of governance, usher in accountability in state services, reinvent the economic model, rebuild the country's infrastructure, and even update several conservative social norms that the clerical establishment monopolised to serve its own narrow interests.

The ultimate goal was how best to serve Saudis, and it was towards that purpose that Muhammad bin Salman loosened numerous social restrictions. Regrettably, the media concentrated on the largely cosmetic initiative to allow women to drive, but the Saudi government perceived the uprisings of young Arabs across the region as a legitimate call for evolutionary transformation that needed urgent answers on many fronts. Both the monarch and his heir apparent, along with scores of senior officials, realised that one simply could not throw money to the public and be inattentive to the aspirations of citizens anxious for long-term changes that improved economic conditions for all. Some even contemplated eventual political representation changes. Others perceived the need to usher ineffective social transformations that would distance the traditional society from extremism, which stifled creativity without protecting conservative values that, truth be told, was a major goal. In short, where Saudi authorities were successful was precisely in introducing effective modernisation schemes, with accountability whenever possible, even if this was easier said than done.

Ultimately, the most valuable recent development in Saudi Arabia was the government's focus on establishing a transparent system of rules and laws to increase confidence and encourage foreign direct investments (FDI). While FDI flows declined when oil prices were low, economic diversification and various new projects outside the oil and gas sector helped reverse the trend. According to the United Nations Conference on Trade and Development (UNCTAD), FDI flows increased by 7 per cent between 2018 and 2019, reaching US$ 4.6 billion (UNCTAD, 2020). This happened because Riyadh "removed the ownership limits for foreign strategic investors." In fact, UNCTAD data confirmed that "the stock of FDI rose in 2019 and reached US$ 236 billion, by far the highest number among Arab countries." According to preliminary data from UNCTAD, inflows to Saudi Arabia in the first half of 2020 rose by 12 per cent on the year to US$ 2.6 billion," which further solidified the outlook, notwithstanding global downturns due to the COVID-19 pandemic. In addition to leading Western economies, the United States, the United Kingdom, France, the United Arab Emirates, Singapore, Japan, Kuwait and Malaysia were the main investors in the Kingdom, with ventures primarily oriented towards the chemical industry, real estate, fossil fuels, automobiles, tourism and machinery.[3]

To its credit, Saudi Arabia adopted seven *Guiding Principles for Investment Policymaking* in 2019, which included non-discrimination clauses, investment protection positions, investment sustainability measures, enhanced transparency rules, protection of public policy concerns, ease of entry for employees to the country, and the transfer of knowledge and technology. In fact, *Vision 2030*'s new investment policy and economic reform programs aim to improve the country's investment environment to promote economic diversification better. In addition, in September 2020, Riyadh announced that it would invest US$ 810 billion over the next few years in tourism projects to open the country beyond pilgrimage.

According to Heir Apparent Muhammad bin Salman, the country was poised to offer a plethora of investment opportunities, which experts he consulted estimated to be worth US$ 6 trillion until 2030. This was a very large package but entirely of the doable variety given the country's potential, requirements for tourism-related employment opportunities, as well as the creation of wealth that defined the official's core economic principles. If obstacles stood in the way in the past, whether of the political and social varieties, new chapters were written to encourage FDIs. Indeed, *Vision 2030* was not only focused on national infrastructure projects that would attract investments under normal circumstances, it also was determined to diversify the economy and provide employment for younger generations.

With that goal in mind, Riyadh authorised 100 per cent foreign ownership of new companies in the retail and wholesale sectors. FDI was further welcomed whenever it facilitated the transfer of technology, employed and trained the national workforce, and fostered economic development. Other measures that further encouraged FDI included the country's relatively successful controls of inflation, stable exchange rates for the national currency, and a slew of privatisation programmes, which included the banking sector—heretofore monopolised—to several non-oil sector projects. These steps send a clear message: Saudi Arabia was open for business, which was reflected in a major World Bank study classification that ranked the Kingdom 62nd out of 190 economies, up by 30 places from 2019 (World Bank Group 2020). The country was also ranked the world's top improver on the list due to significant trading progress and fresh credit lines. The country's overall score rose to 71.6 points (over 100) from 63.5 in 2019 that was certainly good news.

Changing Governance Features

To better achieve their socio-economic objectives, the ruler and his heir apparent wished to promote moderation, with the latter boasting that Saudi Arabia recorded major achievements during the past few years, of which perhaps the most important was Riyadh's successful initiatives to secure a *fatwah* [religious decree] from the Council of Senior Scholars to warn the public about the "Muslim Brotherhood" organisation and its great danger to Islam, Muslims, and the rest of the world.

To be sure, this was a point of contention as some perceived the Brotherhood as local boy scouts whereas, in reality, the organisation boasted an all too real ideology of extremism. Saudi Arabia opposed the Muslim Brotherhood and has identified the group as a terrorist organisation. Riyadh aimed to prevent it from carrying out acts of extremism and succeeded in eliminating acts of terrorism in the Kingdom. For one observer, the Kingdom "has no qualms about admitting and recognising problematic areas and laying out plans and solutions to get rid of them," and "[b]y directing its efforts towards eliminating terrorism and combating extremism, Saudi Arabia has taken it upon itself to rid the world of this affliction as the leader of the Islamic world, the cradle of revelation, and the heart of the Islamic faith" (al-Otaibi, 2020).

Indeed, Riyadh's methodical approach eliminated several extremist groups at home, while the Saudi-Iraq rapprochement, as well as the war against the Iran-backed Houthi militias in Yemen, have all recorded significant gains. Regrettably, Muslim Brotherhood and other extremist groups campaigned in Europe—often supported by Turkey—culminated in acts of terrorism in Vienna, a raid against the Saudi embassy in The Hague, attacks in Canada, as well as high alerts in Germany and other European countries. Riyadh called on its European partners to stiffen their backs and address various fundamentalist groups operating freely on their soil though this recommendation was not always followed. For its part, and unabashedly, Saudi Arabia was determined to fight extremist groups and, unlike leading powers that allowed these groups to operate freely, was dead-set to fight them in toto, precisely to deny them any opportunities to spread the kind of devastation that engulfed several Arab and Muslim countries.

Nepotism and Corruption on the Wane

Equally critical was Riyadh's continued efforts to fight corruption at home, stripping middlemen from their business cloaks, which the monarchy once tolerated for its patronage benefits. By definition, an absolute monarchy conducted its businesses through complex winnowing even if most observers of the Kingdom treated it as a republic that must not protect the ruling family, with some opining that the country "belonged" to the Al Saud who named the land after themselves, even if these were little more than pedantic interpretations. Accusations flew over the very ownership of state assets and the personal wealth of senior princes, as critics of the monarchy alleged that systemic and endemic corruption prevailed, as acknowledged and defended in a 2001 television program by the former Saudi Ambassador to the United States Bandar bin Sultan (Ottaway 2008, pp. 161-163).

Over the years, numerous allegations were made against senior arms merchants and their royal family protectors, implying that substantial financial resources exchanged hands illegally. Western companies, of course, paid commissions to secure lucrative contracts though not a single company seems to have lost monies through these sales. On the contrary, most delighted in their prowess to secure huge projects that bagged billions to wealthy American, British and French companies and their shareholders, among others. In other words, corruption allegations were documented, though few acknowledged that Western companies, and through them democratic governments, were engaged in these bribery schemes.

Be that as it may, both King Salman and Heir Apparent Muhammad bin Salman understood that the time was long overdue to end these arrangements. Under their rule, Riyadh wished to act without intermediaries to meet stricter regulations passed by Washington and London, among other Western partners, and because it wished to eliminate commission-seeking negotiators that sullied the country's reputation. Towards that end, and in a surprise move, Saudi Arabia embarked on an unprecedented sweep of 11 princes and dozens of former ministers, who were detained in a new anti-corruption probe starting on 5 November 2017. Included among those arrested were Prince Al-Walid bin Talal, ostensibly one of the wealthiest Saudis with a global footprint, National Guard Minister Prince Mit'ab bin 'Abdallah, the son of the late King 'Abdallah, and Economy and Planning Minister 'Adil Fakih. Even if those apprehended were housed at the Riyadh Ritz-Carlton Hotel, the purge sent shockwaves throughout the world since many of those arrested had powerful and influential contacts throughout the world.

Of course, critics of the Kingdom saw a vindictive hand behind the apprehensions, allegedly because Prince Muhammad bin Salman was clearly eliminating all putative challengers to his accession to the throne. Few found merit in the state's efforts to end corrupt practices by the accused, and while the anti-corruption committee that investigated financial holdings and froze assets that belonged to the accused, a little over US$ 100 billion was recovered in what an official statement declared came from those who abused the system and placed their interests above those of the public (DiChristopher, 2019).

In addition to senior officials, most of whom were eventually released, Saudi Arabia conducted another mass-detention campaign and arrested 298 government employees out of the 674 people investigated on suspicion of corruption in early March 2020. Detainees included current and retired military officers, security officers assigned to the Ministry of the Interior, health officials and judges, which confirmed that Riyadh was serious in tackling corruption in the Kingdom.

The Decline of Extremism

The need to address extremism, whether associated with terrorist activities or practices that amounted to the brainwashing of gullible souls, stood out as a necessity. Far worse than recruitment, "brainwashing, incitement, training and agitation until an individual harbouring extremist inclination is finally ready to become a true terrorist and commit an act of terror," preoccupied decision-makers everywhere (al-Otaibi, 2020). While few admitted that Saudi Arabia and most Western societies, led by the US, shared values, opposition to extremism certainly topped the list. Of course, and in the aftermath of the 9/11 attacks, Westerners in general and Americans, particularly, paid more attention to the role that religious extremists played in spreading vile ideologies without acknowledging the strides made by the Kingdom to combat the relevant scourge in their society. The facile explanation advanced by analysts was that the US and Saudi Arabia were engaged in a basic security-for-oil agreement, which was a valid formulation in the twentieth century, though one wondered whether anyone was paying attention.

Few noted the Kingdom's domestic governance reforms even if most focused on the War for Yemen—which Riyadh waged under United Nations Security Council Resolution 2216 (2015) passed under the UN Charter's Chapter VII—along with the Jamal Khashoggi assassination by rogue elements.[4]

For no matter how obtuse some wished to interpret Saudi policies, alleging diminished reliance on Riyadh for "outrageous" acts, the trend was towards accountability and not, as conveniently labelled a Trump Administration preference to focus on the economic benefits of jobs produced from arms sales to the Kingdom. Under a Biden Administration, and notwithstanding the late February 2021 release of a skeleton declassified intelligence report that blamed Muhammad bin Salman for authorising the Khashoggi murder (in an assessment that did not provide any evidence), the importance of the Kingdom was underscored by all concerned. Even if there was an appetite to reassess the US-Saudi relationship under a Biden presidency, no one contemplated "ending the alliance or the partnership with Saudi Arabia." In the words of Secretary of State Anthony Blinken, "It [would be about] making sure that the alliance actually reflects our interests and our values [and] not just Saudi Arabia's," which was spot on since Blinken telegraphed what was common to both Riyadh and Washington: a shared visceral opposition to extremism (*CBS News*, 2019).

Of course, the most important extremist challenge that faced Saudi Arabia, one that Western powers presumably did not wish to see, was a nuclear Iran. For no matter how convoluted the logic to restore the so-called Iran deal was, analyses that presented Tehran as a panacea against an increasingly hostile Sunni world failed to come close to the truth. The Iran nuclear agreement, formally known as the Joint Comprehensive Plan of Action (JCPOA), reached between Iran and the five permanent members of the UNSC plus Germany [P5+1] in July 2015, anticipated that Tehran would dismantle much of its nuclear programme and open its facilities to more extensive international inspections in exchange for billions of dollars' worth of sanctions relief. Its complex time frame stretched over a decade, which raised serious questions about long-term compliance, especially given Iran's interest to join the nuclear club. President Donald J. Trump withdrew Washington from the deal in 2018, claiming it failed to curtail Iran's missile programme and regional influence. Remarkably, Tehran began ignoring limitations on its nuclear programme a year later, but President Biden has said that the US would return to the JCPOA if Iran resumed compliance, emphasising diplomacy as the best way to prevent the latter from acquiring nuclear weapons. Still, Iran insisted on full sanctions relief before it would return to the agreement in early 2021, while the US vowed to deny Tehran a nuclear capability. Notwithstanding these steps, Saudi Arabia was and remains the pivotal power to any effective coalition to counter Iran, along with its amply documented destabilising regional influences (Khalifé, 2017).

Conclusion

A different Saudi Arabia came to light in 2015, one that was not bashful about its views and vision in terms of internal, regional and international affairs. For Riyadh, Iran and extremists were existential threats that required determination, but opposing both was not sufficient. An equally critical resolve was to dramatically alter Saudi society through the *National Transformation Program* (NTP) and *Vision 2030*. Both of these blueprints embarked the Kingdom on epochal changes, ranging the gamut from re-writing textbooks to opening up the country to foreign direct investments under legally secure conditions. The break with past policies could not be starker, preferring Saudi nationalism, modernisation, religious tolerance, support for the arts, music and culture to outdated ideological commitments. All of these changes were evolutionary in nature and took several decades to mature but, and this must be acknowledged openly and without any reservations, the individual responsible for accelerating the pace of change was Heir Apparent Muhammad bin Salman.

The Kingdom's *Vision 2030* perspectives, which altered the very conception of socio-economic development towards a far more nationalist and self-reliant model, were and are his. Only antagonists wished to see failures so that Saudi Arabia resembled a radical country that supported extremist views. A nationalist Saudi Arabia defined itself with a more autonomous and less pan-Islamic identity that obviously did not denigrate the faith nor distance itself from every obligation associated with the Custodianship of the Two Holy Mosques. Of course, the value of Saudi nationalism rested on the success of various *Vision 2030* strategies—which will take time even if critics would like to see everything ready and functioning by yesterday. These expensive projects, along with the costs of the War for Yemen, led fault finders to believe that Riyadh would burn through all its foreign exchange reserves by 2019 to disparage the Kingdom and its leaders further. Doomsday predictions and miscalculations came to nought, however, as reserves remained at around US$450 billion in 2020.

Saudi Arabia matured as a legitimate and effective monarchy for decades and is now able to meet its internal duties and global obligations. The Al Saud monarchy and its key decision-makers, the King and his Heir Apparent, were determined to defend the Kingdom from hegemonic neighbours embarked on a suicidal mission to challenge Sunni supremacy. Since Saudi policies were almost always based on interests, one could expect relationships with regional and global powers to flourish when common interests prevailed or when mutually beneficial ones could be devised. Towards that end, few should have any illusions that Riyadh, under King Salman and his successor, will abandon key regional security issues—led by the Iranian threat—to satisfy real-politic requirements. Simply stated, there were existential concerns that could no longer be ignored, including cooperation with Russia, China and even Israel—once it accepts the Arab Peace Initiative—as long as these advanced Saudi interests.

What King Salman and his government shared with allies and partners about these grave concerns cannot, indeed must not be ignored or dismissed as the wishes of a minor regional developing country. On the contrary, as a rising regional power, Saudi assessments of their national security priorities, from security concerns to equally important economic issues defined under *Vision 2030*, were valid matters that allies and partners aimed for security on and around the Arabian Peninsula ought to take into account.

Notes

1. The exception to this was Lebanon, one of the most critical Arab countries as far as democratisation was concerned, since indigenous forces could not agree on the country's "final" status. Even if the country was 100 years old as a republic, such discords perpetuated crises, and ensured the population's miseries. Those who did not accept Lebanon as a true nation-state—both Syria and Israel considered it a geographical error—confronted existential dilemmas too since many Lebanese citizens wished for Beirut to become a functioning free political entity. Their challenge was in persuading a majority to abandon sectarianism, separate church from state, and adopt liberty as the country's distinct character.

Failure to accomplish such a goal meant that on-going confrontations would, inevitably, lead to partition.

2. An analysis of *Vision 2030* is beyond the scope of this essay. What follows are basic observations though readers can easily refer to various sources to avail themselves with the latest developments. See, for example, the dedicated web-page at https://www.vision2030.gov.sa/en as well as the web-page for the National Transformation Program at https://www.vision2030.gov.sa/en/programs/NTP. In 2015, the United Nations Economic and Social Commission for Western Asia issued a seldom quoted report on various development programs that deserved close attention. ESCWA affirmed that: "The Arab region is in crisis and it is easy to succumb to pessimism about its future. This report, however, embraces a vision of hope: one that illustrates the many ways in which the region can act to ensure its future security and prosperity. It envisages a day when authoritarianism, occupation, foreign domination and all forms of discrimination end. A vision of human development and economic prosperity implies that citizens are free to voice their opinions and practice their beliefs without fear, the rule of law applies equally to all, and the basic necessities for a decent life are affordable even for the least fortunate" (United Nations, 2015).
3. Data in this section are drawn from "Foreign Direct Investment (FDI) in Saudi Arabia," *Nordea*, a leading Nordic bank, at https://www.nordeatrade.com/en/explore-new-market/saudi-arabia/investment.
4. Few bothered to read the UN resolution but it was worth recalling that it expanded the sanctions regime through the creation of a targeted arms embargo against Houthi rebels and authorised states to "take the necessary measures to prevent the direct or indirect supply, sale or transfer to, or for the benefit of Ali Abdullah Saleh, Abdullah Yahya Al Hakim, Abd Al-Khaliq Al-Houthi, and the individuals and entities designated by the Committee established pursuant to paragraph 19 of resolution 2140 (2014)." See United Nations Security Council, Resolution 2216 (2015). For a discussion of the Khashoggi case, see Joseph A. Kéchichian (2019), pp. 173-202.

References

Alexander, Anne (2012), "Digital Generation," in Ziauddin Sardar & Robin Yassin-Kassab (eds), *Critical Muslim 1: The Arabs Are Alive,* London: Hurst & Co, pp. 85-104.

al-Otaibi, Abdullah bin Bajad (2020), "The Unyielding Saudi Position Against Terrorism and Extremism," *Al-Arabiya,* 15 November at https://english.alarabiya.net/in-translation/2020/11/15/The-unyielding-Saudi-position-against-terrorism-and-extremism

Brynen, Rex, Pete W. Moore, Bassel F. Salloukh, and Marie-Joelle Zahar (2012), *Beyond the Arab Spring: Authoritarianism and Democratization in the Arab World*, Boulder & London: Lynne Rienner Publishers.

CBS News (2019), "Transcript: Antony Blinken Talks with Michael Morell on 'Intelligence Matters'," 9 January at https://www.cbsnews.com/news/transcript-antony-blinken-talks-with-michael-morell-on-intelligence-mat- ters/

DiChristopher, Tom (2019), "Saudi Arabia says it Raised $106 billion from 'Anti-Corruption' Drive that Swept Up Royals," *CNBC*, 30 January at https://www.cnbc.com/2019/01/30/saudi-arabia-says-it-raised-106-billion-from-anti-corruption-drive.html

Fisk, Robert (2011), "Saudis Mobilise Thousands of Troops to Quell Growing Revolt," *The Independent*, 5 March at https://www.independent.co.uk/news/world/middle-east/saudis-mobilise-thousands-troops-quell-growing-revolt-2232928.html

Gelvin, James L. (2012), *The Arab Uprisings: What Everyone Needs to Know*, New York: Oxford University Press.

Haddad, Bassam, Rosie Bsheer and Ziad Abu-Rish (eds.) (2012), *The Dawn of the Arab Uprisings: End of an Old Order*? London: Pluto Press.

Kéchichian, Joseph A. (2012), *Legal and Political Reforms in Saudi Arabia*, Abingdon, Oxon: Routledge.

Kéchichian, Joseph A. (2019), *Saudi Arabia in 2030: The Emergence of a New Leadership*, Seoul, Korea: Asan Institute for Public Policy, August at http://en.asaninst.org/contents/saudi-arabia-in-2030-the-emergence-of-a-new-leadership/

Khalifé, Nabil (2017), *Istihdaf Ahl al-Sunna*, translated and introduced by Joseph A. Kéchichian as *The Attempt to Uproot Sunni-Arab Influence: A Geo-Strategic Analysis of the Western, Israeli and Iranian Quest for Domination*, Eastbourne: Sussex Academic Press.

Ottaway, David (2008), *The King's Messenger: Prince Bandar Bin Sultan and America's Tangled Relationship with Saudi Arabia*, New York: Walker & Co.

Quamar, Md. Muddassir (2014), "Managing the Arab Spring: The Saudi Way," *Contemporary Review of the Middle East* 1(2): pp. 141–163.

The Guardian (2011), "Saudi Arabia's King Announces Huge Jobs and Housing Package," 18 March at https://www.theguardian.com/world/2011/mar/18/saudi-arabia-job-housing-package

United Nations Conference on Trade and Development (UNCTAD) (2020), *World Investment Report 2020: International Production beyond the Pandemic*, New York: United Nations Publications at https://unctad.org/system/files/official-document/wir2020_en.pdf

United Nations Security Council Resolution 2216 (2015), 14 April at https://documents-dds-ny.un.org/doc/UNDOC/GEN/N15/103/72/PDF/N1510372.pdf

United Nations (2015), *Arab Development Outlook: Vision 2030*, E/ESCWA/EDID/2015/3, Beirut: UN Economic and Social Commission for Western Asia, 2015, at https://www.unescwa.org/sites/www.unescwa.org/files/publications/files/arab-development-outlook-vision-2030-english_0.pdf

World Bank Group (2020), *Economy Profile, Saudi Arabia—Doing Business 2020: Comparing Business Regulation in 190 Economies*, Washington, D.C. at https://www.doingbusiness.org/content/dam/doingBusiness/country/s/saudi-arabia/SAU.pdf

3. Exploring the Nexus between Democratisation, Authoritarianism and Patriarchy in Iran and Saudi Arabia

Hussein Solomon and Simone Bekker

It was in the ancient Near East (specifically Mesopotamia), where patriarchy first developed between 3100 BC and 600 BC (Lerner, 1986, p. 8). It was, however, only in 1947 that Max Weber first used the term "patriarchy" to describe a system of government where men used their positions as heads of households to rule societies. Radical feminists appropriated the term in the 1990s to refer to a "...system of social structures and practices in which men dominate, oppress and exploit women. The use of the term social structure is important here since it implies rejection both of biological determinism, and the notion that every individual man is in a dominant position and every woman in a subordinate position" (ibid., p. 20).

There are three inter-related reasons why identifying patriarchy in this way is important. First, reference to social structures and practices suggests that the practices of patriarchy were constructed and can be deconstructed as the history of Western societies could attest to. Behaviour–both individual and institutional–therefore, can be unlearned (ibid., p. 6). Second, issues of gender are mediated through other variables like class, race, ethnicity, and religious affiliation. Thus, a poor rural woman from a marginalised ethnic or religious group will experience gender discrimination far more intensely than her wealthy, urban counterpart who belongs to the dominant ethnic or religious group. Third, patriarchy viewed systemically allows one to understand the oppression of women from the workplace to the home, from issues of culture and faith to the administration of the state.

Such an expanded view of patriarchy is imperative if one considers the origins of this practice and its institutionalisation. Patriarchy is linked to issues of ownership and domination. Historically, the appropriation of women's sexual and reproductive capacity by men was followed by the institutionalisation of private property and the emergence of class stratification. Similarly, the enslavement of women preceded the enslavement of other groups. The first states, meanwhile, owe their origins to the patriarchal family. Therefore, the earliest states had a vested interest in the subordination of women, and the earliest law codes institutionalised this subordination. By the second millennium BC, Babylon already had legislation controlling women's sexuality (ibid., p. 89).

Attempting to control women's sexuality has been an enduring feature of the Middle East and North Africa (MENA) societies. The most recent survey published by the Arab Barometer (2020), for instance, found that almost a third (32 per cent) of Egyptians approved of the barbaric practice of female genital mutilation. From the foregoing, it would be difficult to dispute the logical conclusion of Gerda Lerner (1986): "Men learned to institute dominance and hierarchy over other people by their earlier practice of dominance over the women of their own group" (p. 9). Conversely, the emancipation of women is intimately associated with true societal emancipation. Therefore, it is not coincidental that the MENA region is characterised by both a democratic deficit and the subjugation of women.

Indeed, authoritarianism and its corollary–the democratic deficit across the region–are intimately connected to the broader politics of exclusion and patriarchy. Therefore, the emancipation of women should lay at the heart of any attempt to secure a more democratic region. This chapter, therefore, seeks to explore the issues of patriarchy and how these intersect with authoritarianism and the dearth of democracy in two country case studies—Iran and Saudi Arabia—two large and influential regional countries representing predominantly Shia and Sunni societies, respectively.

Patriarchy in Iran

Under the governing system in the Islamic Republic of Iran, women are confronted with a systematic and widespread legal discrimination. The law does not treat them as equal citizens with regard to issues such as personal status, including marriage, divorce and inheritance, individual freedom like travel and work, and crime and punishment. Iran is a country where almost half of the population consists of females, and women account for a large portion of university graduates. However, only a minority of women in Iran are employed, and women barely have a presence in the country's political system. In addition, Iranian women are subjected to discriminatory laws and policies (Moghadam, 2018). Regardless of progress in selected fields, like education and healthcare, the issue of Iranian women's human rights continues to be characterised by exclusion and inequality (Minority Rights Group International, 2019).

The "Boys club"

Under public patriarchy, power is distributed amongst all patriarchs according to whatever other principles of stratification operate (Moghadam, 2004). Thus, women do not have access to society's most important institutions since men hold all the power in those institutions. This leads to the notion that it is a "boys club" and women are excluded from the club.

Women and men are required by Iranian law to sit in separate areas in public transportation and university classes. They must attend separate schools and use separate entrances to some airports, public buildings, and universities. One of the best examples of women being excluded from the "boys club" is that female students are banned by more than 30 universities from studying almost 80 different degree courses (Sahraei, 2012). Moreover, women are excluded from everyday activities such as attending sporting events. Shortly after the 1979 Islamic Revolution, a ban was put in place which prohibited women from entering sports stadiums. In 2019, Sahar Khodayari—an Iranian female football fan—faced up to two years in jail for dressing as a man to sneak into a football stadium. Consequently, Khodayari, who was called "blue girl" by Iranians for the colour of her team's jersey, set herself on fire in front of the courthouse (*Al-Jazeera*, 2019). Following some coercion from human rights groups and the Federation Internationale de Football Association (FIFA), Iran granted a 5 per cent quota (4,600) on seats for women in the stadium.

However, although this marks a step forward, Human Rights Watch (HRW) called the cap of 4,600 female fans "discriminatory, deceptive, and dangerous" (Masters, 2019).

Four decades after the Islamic Revolution promised to bring women their human rights, official statistics on Iran indicate a complex reality. Iran's economic participation rate for women is one of the lowest in the world. In 2018, women's economic participation was placed at 15.9 per cent compared to men's at 64.1 per cent. Furthermore, the unemployment rate for women is almost double that of men, with 19.1 per cent for women and 10.1 per cent for men (*Radio Farda*, 2017). Women who hold a university degree are three times more likely to be unemployed than their male counterparts (Minority Rights Group International, 2019). The 2016 Global Gender Gap report estimated that in general, men earn 5.79 times more than women for equal work and on average, women earn 41 per cent less than men (World Economic Forum, 2016). This deep-rooted culture of patriarchy not only disparages women's work but also severely limits women's access to paid work.

According to the 2020 Global Gender Gap Report, produced by the World Economic Forum, Iran ranks among the last ten countries (148 out of 153) for gender equality, including equality in economic participation. It is important to note that an article by Human Rights Watch (2017) asserts that although Iranian law opposes discrimination against women in the workplace, the application of this law is not extended to the hiring process, where it is most crucially needed. Data from Human Rights Watch reveals that government, as well as private sector employers, consistently choose to hire men rather than women, specifically for technical and managerial positions.

When advertising vacancies, employers in both public and private sectors denote gender preferences based on arbitrary and discriminatory criteria. These employers view men as the breadwinners, and as such, they are permitted to exercise authority over their wives. By consistently hiring men over women, employers ensure that men will remain the breadwinners and women will forever be trapped in economic subservience. This not only holds negative consequences for the household economy and the economy at large, but also generates a greater dependency of females on their male family members, such as husbands, fathers and brothers

(Solomon, 2020). In the process, patriarchy, constructed as it is on vertical power relations, is further embedded.

Legislative discrimination

The culture of classic patriarchy in Iran is nothing more than the authoritarian exercise of male power over women. The *Iran Wire* (2015) points out that women are taught by the legal code that their testimony is worth half that of a man's, that she can be stoned to death for her adultery, that legally her children can be taken from her once they reach a certain age, and that the domestic violence she might suffer at the hands of her husband has no legal definition. The limited representation in Iran's politics and judiciary is not the only realm that reflects the secondary status of women, it is also reflected in their homes. By way of law, husbands hold primary control over domestic affairs. Several women across the country (especially in the more remote and impoverished areas) struggle with normalised patterns of coercion, physical violence, and marital rape—a crime which is at this time still unrecognised by Iranian law (Minority Rights Group International, 2019).

As mentioned, citizens are treated differently by Iranian law depending on their gender. An example of Iran's discriminatory laws against women is the issue of travel and passports. The Center for Human Rights in Iran (2017) calls attention to Article 18 of Iran's *Passport Law*, which stipulates that married women require their spouse's permission or the local prosecutor's permission in special cases if they want to travel abroad alone. In 2015, Niloufar Ardalan, a footballer of Iran's women's national team, could not leave Iran to play in the Asian Championship because her husband would not allow her to renew her passport and travel (BBC News, 2015). In the culture of classic patriarchy, a woman's principal obligation is to take care of her children and to obey her husband. In return, the husband is the breadwinner, and he is permitted to exercise authority by confining his wife's movements. He can even prevent her from showing herself in public.

Men in-charge: From the dinner table to the houses of parliament

Patriarchy is about control, traditional gender roles, and the undertaking to guarantee that men remain in charge, from the dinner table to the houses of parliament. The state controls Iranian women via a discriminatory legal code that offers women-only a portion of male citizens' rights. Minority Rights Group International (2019) reports that the participation of women in political life in Iran is extremely limited, particularly at high levels. During the 2017 presidential election, all 137 women who registered to become presidential candidates were disqualified by the Guardian Council. According to the Human Rights Watch (2017), there has never been a woman who the Guardian Council has approved to stand in a Presidential or Assembly of Experts election, despite women registering for both. In February 2020, however, 17 women were elected to serve in parliament. Even though it only represents 5.85 per cent of the total seats, it is the highest number ever in the history of the Islamic Republic (Inter-Parliamentary Union, 2020).

Iranian women are prohibited from being employed in "dangerous, arduous or harmful work" by the Iran Labour Law (1990). Article 5 designates specific professions, such as judge or fire fighter, as unsuitable for women, either because of the authorities' understanding of shari'a on the subject or because of their claims that work conditions are unsuitable for women (Human Rights Watch, 2017). Moreover, the Iranian Civil Code (1928) offers every husband the right to forbid his wife from taking any job that he might consider to be "against family values or inimical to his or her reputation." Certain employers demand that women who are either engaged or married must provide a written statement of permission from their husband/fiancée to be hired. Women often face direct or indirect discrimination from employers in their hiring practices. As a result of cultural norms which specify that men should provide for the family, men are usually seen as more deserving of employment (Iranian Civil Code, 1928).

Violence against women in the Islamic Republic

In a region where religion, tradition, war, social norms, and politics are all fused into powerful and space-based patriarchy, gender-based violence takes on fascinating nuances and wears multiple faces. One of the most common forms of violence inflicted against Iranian women is the state-sponsored measures to enforce the compulsory veil. Iranian women are required by law to cover their hair, arms, and curves in public. Ever since the 1979 Islamic revolution, women have been forced by the compulsory Hijab law to cover up (Mahtan, 2020). The law was initially introduced by the country's 'morality' police and is currently still imposed by authorities. Amnesty International (2019) has made it clear that the Islamic dress code and other standards of conduct that are expected from women are maintained by various institutions.

Under Article 29 of the Criminal Code (adopted in 2014), trained and qualified officers of the Basij Forces (civilian volunteers integrated into the Islamic Revolutionary Guards Corps) are seen as judicial officers with the power to arrest and to perform judicial police tasks (Iran Criminal Code, 1999; Amnesty International, 2019). Additionally, Guidance Patrols, which are known as *Gasht-e-Ershad*, *Ansar-e-Hezbollah*, and vigilante morality police, are all joined in combatting 'bad hijab' (Elmjouie, 2014). Women are also verbally attacked on public transport and in the streets by citizens who have strong ties to the regime for not adhering to the state-sanctioned dress code. As a result, the hijab has become a sign of oppression for several Iranian women who have been protesting for more freedom and independence in the strictly conservative Islamic society.

Iranian Penal Code (2013) stipulates those girls and women who fail to comply with the dress code risk being arrested, fined, lashed, and even imprisoned for committing *haram* (forbidden or outlawed as per Islamic law or custom). Iranian activist Shaparak Shajarizadeh, who has lived in exile in Canada for the past decade, was arrested for the first time in February 2018 when she protested without a hijab. Shajarizadeh is one of the most effective campaigners for ending the compulsory hijab for women. She participated in online protest campaigns like *#WhiteWednesday* and *#TheGirlsofRevolutionStreet,* which encouraged women in Iran to share images and videos of themselves without their hijab (Cooper, 2019).

Patriarchal cultural norms often legitimise the practice of domestic violence. According to the United Nations General Assembly [UNGA] (2016), there are no laws that specifically criminalise domestic violence in Iran. For domestic violence cases to be prosecuted as crimes of bodily assault, two male witnesses are required. Given the absence of such male witnesses, prosecution hardly occurs. Moreover, spousal rape is not a crime in Iran. After the recommendations relating to the criminalisation of spousal rape and other types of domestic violence, made during the

UN's 2014 Universal Periodic Review, the Iranian government responded that "the issue of marital rape was not considered by many countries and cultures" and was mostly raised by extreme feminists (UNGA, 2016).

Under Iranian rules of evidence, a rape victims' testimony is worth half that of a man, and men must corroborate it in order for her to prove her claims (Moradian, 2009). This reinforces the notion that when gender relations are maintained and sanctioned by culture and religion, especially when violence is committed in the name of honour, societal violence becomes naturalised, accepted, and accessible (Salhi, 2013). Zahra Tizro (2012) asserts that women are forced by Iran's patriarchal culture to keep silent about the abuse they suffer from the men in their families. Minor types of violence against women and children are usually tolerated when the acts are perceived as needed for discipline. Tizro (2012) further explains that women tend to only classify exceptionally severe beatings as violence and they regardless forceful hitting or psychological abuse as normal behaviour.

Patriarchal relations within households

In Iran, family law has its roots in a system of male guardianship over women via the institution of marriage and laws that control the family unit. Consequently, women are faced with restrictions of their rights and limitations to their autonomy throughout the processes of marriage, divorce, child custody, etc. Iran's Civil Code authorises husbands as to the head of the family, and thus women are placed under their guardianship. In this scenario, husbands have authority over their wives in an array of matters. Some of these, such as employment, have already been discussed. The Suuntaus Project (2015) noted that in their role as heads of the household, men have particular financial obligations in marriage. This includes *nafage* (spousal support), *mahriye* (dower payment) and *orjat al-mesl* (compensation for domestic work). In exchange for these, it is expected that women abide by the principle of *tamkin* or compliance with the will of their husbands. Women are held responsible by Article 1108 of the civil code for the duty of fulfilling their husbands' sexual needs. If she fails to abide by the principle of *tamkin*, a wife can lose her right to *nafage* (Iranian Civil Code, 1928).

Patriarchy in Saudi Arabia

The Islamic legal codes differ across Muslim countries. Some are informed by secular and liberal ethos, and some strictly follow orthodox and conservative interpretations (Solati, 2018). Valentine M. Moghadam (2003) explains that in Muslim societies, "the status of women is neither uniform nor unchanging, nor is it unique" (p. 6). The reason for this is that Islam is practiced and interpreted in various ways in different Muslim countries and also over time. Saudi women are faced with formal and informal barriers when attempting to make decisions or take action without the presence or consent of a male relative.

The Road to Reforming Patriarchy?

The second-class status of women in Saudi Arabia is caused by the legitimacy of the monarchy as a custodian of religious and tribal values. The Saudi model of citizenship is one where men control women's movements and choices via the guardianship system. Accordingly, men are the main political constituency, and women are citizens only by proxy (Aldosari, 2018). Under Saudi law, females require the approval of a male guardian (*wali*) for various critical decisions. This male figure is generally a father, husband, brother, son or even a minor son. As a result of this fundamental source of gender inequality, Saudi women face crucial barriers to empowerment in their daily experiences. Under the male guardianship system, men can file cases against their daughters, female relatives or wives for "disobedience," which can lead to a forcible return to their male guardian's home or even imprisonment (Human Rights Watch, 2020).

Patriarchy methodically restricts women's empowerment and, in some cases, regards women as perpetual minors who must be provided for by their fathers or husbands. Saudi women were universally treated as legal minors until recently (Chulov, 2019). However, in 2019 the Kingdom partially dismantled guardianship laws that have confined women to narrow gender roles and marginalised their role in society. The decision by the Council of Ministers was published in the *Saudi Gazette* (2020) on 1 August 2020 and it amended the Travel Documents Law, the Civil Status Law, and the Labour Law.

These legal changes now allow women over the age of 21 to obtain passports and travel without needing the permission of a male guardian. Women are now allowed to register their child's birth with the civil status office and are not legally required to stay with their husbands. They are also now allowed to notify the civil status office of a death, marriage, or divorce and get hold of family records. This is a major step towards dismantling the control that previously made women second-class citizens. Moreover, the changes permit women, together with their husbands, to be considered the "head of household" with respect to their children (Said, 2019).

The changes made to the Labour Law will now clarify that the term "worker" can refer to male as well as female persons. Women are also protected from arbitrary dismissal or threat thereof due to pregnancy or during maternity leave or if they have an illness resulting from pregnancy or childbirth. In addition to these changes, there are new protections against discrimination in employment. The new law states: "citizens are equal with respect to the right to work without any discrimination on the basis of sex, disability, age, or any other form of discrimination" (Saudi Gazette, 2020). Furthermore, in 2018, the future seemed a little brighter for Saudi women when the ban which prevented women from driving was lifted. This meant that women were finally free from the need to rely on males for their basic right to move around (*Al-Jazeera*, 2018).

Saudi women can drive, but here is the real roadblock

The above-mentioned legal advances are bitter sweet victories as the courageous Saudi female activists who called for these reforms of the guardianship system and those who fought for decades for the right to drive had to face imprisonment; in some cases, they remain behind bars and face unfair trials (Liloia, 2019). Loujain al-Hathloul, one of the most noticeable and outspoken activists and female right to drive campaigners, for example, together with other prominent Saudi female rights activists, was arrested in May 2018. These brave activists had all been advocating for the right of women to drive, for justice and equality, and an end to the male guardianship system.

In February 2021, Hathloul was released after spending 1,001 days in prison. However, she is banned from travel and has a suspended sentence, which allows the authorities to return her to prison for any supposed criminal activity at any moment in time (Human Rights Watch, 2021). Hathloul was one of at least a dozen women's rights activists detained in the country in 2018. Samar Badawi, Nassima al-Sadah and Mayaa al-Zahrani are believed to remain in prison until mid-2021 (*Al-Jazeera*, 2021). Although Muhammad Bin Salman (MbS), the powerful crown prince, has tried to present himself as a modernist reformer, the arrests of dissidents and activists suggest that the regime only wants change on its terms. The silencing of feminists may slow the momentum for pushing the Saudi regime into making more meaningful changes.

Violence against women in Saudi Arabia

Violence cannot be identified as merely a form of physical harm that targets women's bodies, but rather it comprises numerous forms of violence aimed at women because of their gender. These include male guardianship and rigid restrictions on the mobility of women. Cultural rules which are deeply rooted in a system of values and which maintain that it is acceptable for men to control women and guard their female kin are prevalent in many societies in the MENA region. This is the case with Saudi Arabia; certain cultural norms infer the cycle of gender inequality and violence against women as an illustration of social power used to control and dominate women; wives are controlled by their husbands, sisters controlled by their brothers, all within "legitimate" social acceptance.

Although Saudi laws clearly state that a guardian may be guilty of abuse, the definition of abuse disregards certain forms of harm by stating that abuse is only that which "exceeds the bounds of the guardianship" (Human Rights Watch, 2016). Saudi Arabia fails to define the bounds of guardianship clearly, and this has been problematic for a country where male relatives can bring legal claims against "disobedient" female dependents based on *uquq* (disobedience to parents) or *inqiyad* (submission to a guardian's authority). Men can bring claims ordering their wives to be returned to the marital home, and a *mahram* (male unmarriageable relative) can request his female relative be returned to him (Zayadin, 2020).

Throughout the patriarchal cycle, life options for women are exceedingly limited, and it is expected that women value their roles first and foremost as mothers and wives. In return, the male is the breadwinner and is permitted to exercise his authority by preventing her from showing herself in public. Under the umbrella of patriarchal culture, together with the misinterpretations of religious rules, the human rights of women are removed and violated. Although all versions of Islam indicate that women should dress modestly, often suggesting covering their hair and body, Saudi Arabia is one of the two Muslim-majority countries that legally imposes a dress code (Iran is the other). Depending on the particular region of Saudi Arabia, Saudi women and foreign women are required when they are in public places to wear *abayas*, usually paired with either a *hijab* (headscarf), *niqab* (veil, which leaves a slit for the eyes) or a *burqa* (which covers the body from head to toe, with a mesh for the eyes) (*The Economist*, 2015).

Nonetheless, the internet has enabled women to interact with the rest of the world, and as a result, they more clearly understand the extent of their oppression and are demanding equal rights and better representation. Donna Abdulaziz (2019) explains that today women are starting to abandon the plain black version of the traditional *abaya*. In its place, they are opting for conservative but creative alternatives, experimenting with different styles of the traditional robe even though they all still wear the *abaya*. However, women outside of the relatively cosmopolitan cities like Jeddah or Riyadh could still face harassment for violating dress codes deeply rooted in Saudi traditions.

Patriarchal relations within paid work

Saudi Arabia continues to rank near the bottom of the list for its progress towards gender equality across various metrics. According to the World Economic Forum's (2019) Global Gender Gap Report, Saudi Arabia has a remarkably high gender gap index, ranking 146 out of 153. This represents a drop of more than 30 rankings (from 114) from its 2006 position. According to the World Bank (2020a), in 2016, only 22 per cent of Saudi women were employed outside of their homes, compared to 78.7 per cent of the male population.

Nonetheless, as noted earlier in this chapter, the Kingdom recently enacted new reforms to improve its record of female and gender equality–ultimately, abstaining from the "patriarchal gender contract". The patriarchal gender contract, which Moghadam (2002) describes as where the female is the dependent homemaker and male the breadwinner. This contract is incorporated into law, specifically in family laws, by which women are compelled to have permission from a male such as their fathers and husbands for education, employment, travel, etc. Saudi Arabia has been recognised as the top reformer globally in 2019 by the World Bank in their report *Women, Business, and the Law 2020.* The Kingdom has implemented historic reforms to advance the economic participation of women in the country. The bold reforms discussed earlier fundamentally changed the legal rights of Saudi women. There are already 5.5 million Saudi women above the age of 21 who benefit from the reforms, and women will continue to reap the benefits for generations to come (The World Bank, 2020b). Thomas Lippman (2012) notes that Saudi Arabia has been gradually moving up the United Nation's Development Programme's Gender Empowerment Measure index as a result of reforms.

Patriarchal relations within households

Anya van Wagtendonk (2019) asserts that the guardianship system has not completely been abolished, and some elements of the system remain. Various aspects of women's life such as obtaining approval to get married or exiting prison and continue to be governed by guardianship rules. Additionally, women still require the permission of a male guardian to enter or leave a domestic violence shelter. Under the male guardianship system, women who have escaped abuse in shelters may, and in prisons do, require a male relative to agree to their release before they may exit state facilities. Women are kept in jail by authorities until their legal guardian comes to claim her, even if he is the one who put her in jail (Human Rights Watch 2016). This means that it is almost impossible for domestic violence victims to independently pursue protection or gain legal redress.

As noted earlier, language requiring women to live with their husbands has been removed from official documents by the government. However, Nabih Bulos (2019) notes that amendments like this require changes in other legal processes. The new regulations state that a woman is no longer forced to live with her husband, but theoretically, he can still claim disobedience against his wife in court. The question raised here is whether the judge will cite this change to the civil status law and say, "you have no right to demand this," or will his judgment be based on shari'a law, where a woman must obey her husband?

It was noted earlier that one of the new reforms allows women above the age of 21 to obtain passports and travel without approval from their male guardians. Yet, it should also be noted that women who are forced to flee due to abuse and the oppressive guardianship system are in many cases under the age of 21. Eighteen-year-old Rahaf Muhammad al-Qunun gained significant attention after she fled to Thailand and barricaded herself in a Bangkok hotel room after she was threatened by Thai authorities with deportation back to Saudi Arabia. Muhammad, who has since learned that her family disowned her, has dropped "al-Qunun" from her name. She has revealed that she was locked in the house for six months because she cut her hair short and was beaten up for not praying (*Al-Jazeera*, 2019).

Analysis

Although governments in the Middle Eastern region advocate female advancement abroad, they still enforce traditional gender roles, which means that many Arab Muslim women face extensive social and legal inequalities. This Muslim-majority region demonstrates that authoritarian figures and societies of the region are not progressing towards gender equality at the same pace as other regions. Social indicators and statistics mentioned in this chapter illustrate that women within the region tend to be more disadvantaged economically, politically, and socially than women in other regions.

True democracy is cantered on the attainment of human rights and gender equality. To flourish, women possibly need democracy, but conversely, democracy requires women if it is to be inclusive, representative and enduring. Feminist social scientists believe that if there is no proper representation of women, a polity will not be fully democratic (Moghadam, 2012). Taking this into consideration, according to Hannah Ritchie (2019), women account for 49.6 per cent of the world population, yet they are challenged by a wide range of restrictions to efficient engagement as candidates, voters, and elected officials, the most basic democratic exercises. John Walker (2015) points out that 80 per cent or more of the populace in 36 countries worldwide is made up of

Muslims. Walker further notes that only two of these are ranked as free according to Freedom House's definition, which refers to respect for civil liberties and political rights.

The MENA region, which is a Muslim-majority region, has struggled to make progress towards gender equality. As noted in a study led by the United Nations Development Programme (UNDP), Muslim majority countries have the second-lowest percentage in women's rights (Tailassane, 2019). Zahia Smail Salhi (2013) further indicated that unequal power relations between men and women continue to prevail in the MENA region and have been prolonged by both patriarchy and the rise of Islamism in the last few decades.

The political discourse of the ruling elite is structured by patriarchy, which is anchored in control. Islamist discourses, in turn, have reinforced patriarchal norms as well as emphasising leaders' control over their populations. The politics of control and patriarchy have their foundation in how family laws are constructed and how gender and violence are identified and dealt with. It is a regular occurrence in the MENA region that women's human rights are removed and violated under the umbrella of patriarchal culture and misinterpretations of religion. As pointed out by Salhi (2013), patriarchy in the MENA region thrives on the instrumentalisation of religion and politics, which are frequently used to preserve males' control over women. Patriarchy persists for several convoluted social and political reasons. Its institutional and economic arrangements provide certain benefits and some people have a united interest in upholding those (Gilligan & Snider, 2018, p. 27).

Nonetheless, as a result of urbanisation, greater education, globalisation and the internet, women are able to mobilise more easily, and attitudes towards them are changing. According to a study conducted by Kathrin Thomas (2019) for Arab Barometer, the level of acceptance regarding female heads of state is, on average, nearly 18 points higher among women than among men. Women seem to be significantly more accepting of this right than men. The survey further illustrates that 75 per cent of people in the region support women obtaining tertiary education, and 84 per cent believe women should be allowed to work.

Hussein Solomon (2020) asserts that the reason for these attitude changes is that the younger population tends to hold less patriarchal views. This is good news for women in the region since the Saudi General Authority for Statistics (2020) indicate that in Arab countries' populations, young people are the fastest-growing segment; some 60 per cent of the population is under the age of 25, making this one of the most youthful regions in the world, with a median age of 22 years compared to a global average of 28.

Conclusion

The dramatic events of the 'Arab Spring' have demonstrated how women are actively involved in the "new wave of demands for political dignity and freedoms" (Bachelet, 2011). Kim Ghattas (2019) notes that women were at the forefront of protests in Libya, and Yemen, with one woman, Tawakkol Karman, going on to win a Nobel Peace Prize. Women were central to the activism that assisted the protests and civilian resistance against Syrian President Bashar al-Assad, with hundreds, if not thousands, landing in government jails. The 2011 mass social protests for democratisation and justice in the MENA region led to increased prospects for female mobilisation. Ten years after the Arab Spring, the system of patriarchy is slowly but surely starting to erode due to the great determination and courage of the very females suppressed by the system. If women continue to be as courageous as those before them and resume the fight against patriarchy, one will continue to see some forms of changes in these age-old patriarchal systems.

References

Abdulaziz, Donna (2019), "Saudi Women are Breaking Free from the Black Abaya," *The Wall Street Journal*, 2 October at https://www.wsj.com/articles/saudi-women-are-breaking-free-from-the-black-abaya-11570008601

Aldosari, Hala (2018), "Saudi Women can Drive Now: Will that Hurt Saudi Women?" *The New York Times*, 22 June at https://www.nytimes.com/2018/06/22/opinion/saudi-arabia-salman-women-driving.html?searchResultPosition=2

Al-Jazeera (2018), "Saudi Women Hit the Road as Driving Ban is Lifted," 24 June https://www.aljazeera.com/news/2018/6/24/saudi-women-hit-the-road-as-driving-ban-is-lifted

Al-Jazeera (2019), "'Nothing to Lose': Saudi Teen Rahaf Mohammed Details Family Abuse," 15 January at https://www.aljazeera.com/news/2019/1/15/nothing-to-lose-saudi-teen-rahaf-mohammed-details-family-abuse

Al-Jazeera (2019b), "'Blue Girl': Iran's Football Fan, Denied Stadium Entry, Dies," 10 September at https://www.aljazeera.com/sports/2019/9/10/blue-girl-irans-football-fan-denied-stadium-entry-dies

Al-Jazeera (2021), "The Saudi Women's Rights Activists who Remain Behind Bars," 11 February at https://www.aljazeera.com/news/2021/2/11/saudi-arabia-women-rights-activists-that-are-still-in-jail

Amnesty International (2019), "Iran: Pro-Government Vigilantes Attack Women for Standing Up Against Forced Hijab Laws," https://www.amnesty.ca/news/iran-pro-government-vigilantes-attack-women-standing-against-forced-hijab-laws

Amnesty International (2020), "Saudi Arabia: Women's Rights Campaigner Loujain Al-Hathloul Due in Court," 9 March at https://www.amnesty.org/en/latest/news/2020/03/saudi-arabia-womens-rights-campaigner-loujain-alhathloul-due-in-court/

Arab Barometer (2020), "Do Citizens of Egypt and Iraq Approve of Female Circumcision?" Factsheet, 30 January at https://www.arabbarometer.org/2020/01/fact-sheet-do-citizens-of-egypt-and-iraq-approve-of-female-genital-mutilation/

Bachelet, Michelle (2011), "Democracy and Gender Equality," Speech delivered by Under-Secretary-General and Executive Director of UN Women at the Democracy and Gender Equality Roundtable, United Nations Headquarters, New York on May 4, 2011, UN Women, 5 May at https://www.unwomen.org/en/news/stories/2011/5/democracy-and-gender-equality

BBC News (2015), "Iran: Footballer Calls for Easing of Women's Travel Laws," 15 September at https://www.bbc.com/news/blogs-news-from-elsewhere-34258286

Bulos, Nabih (2019), "Saudi Arabia Adopts Landmark Changes for Women, Including an End to Travel Restrictions," *Los Angeles Times*, 2 August at https://www.latimes.com/world-nation/story/2019-08-02/saudi-women-travel-guardianship

Center for Human Rights in Iran (2019), "Blood Money Paid for a Woman in Iran is Still Half That Paid for a Man, Despite New Ruling," 2 August at https://www.iranhumanrights.org/2019/08/blood-money-paid-for-a-woman-in-iran-is-still-half-that-paid-for-a-man-despite-new-ruling/

Chulov, Martin (2019), "'We Feel Empowered': Saudi Women Relish their New Freedoms," *The Guardian*, 3 August at https://www.theguardian.com/world/2019/aug/03/we-feel-empowered-saudi-women-relish-new-freedoms

Cooper, Celine (2019), "Shaparak Shajarizadeh and the Fight for Women's Rights in Iran," *Open Canada*, 3 January at https://www.opencanada.org/features/shaparak-shajarizadeh-and-fight-womens-rights-iran/

Elmjouie, Yara (2014), "Iran's Morality Police: Patrolling the Streets by Stealth," *The Guardian*, 19 June at https://www.theguardian.com/world/iran-blog/2014/jun/19/iran-morality-police-patrol

Finnish Immigration Service (2015), "Violence against Women and Honour-related Violence in Iran," Suuntaus Project, 26 June at https://migri.fi/documents/5202425/5914056/61597_Suuntaus-raportti_VakivaltaIran_finalFINAL_kaannosversio_EN.pdf/04123eff-529a-457a-aa0d-d5218d046ffe

Freedom House (2020), "Saudi Arabia: Joint Statement Denounces the Detention of Human Rights Defenders," 31 July at https://freedomhouse.org/article/saudi-arabia-joint-statement-denounces-detention-human-rights-defenders

General Authority for Statistics, Kingdom of Saudi Arabia (2020), "Saudi Youth in Numbers: A Report for International Youth Day, 2020," https://www.stats.gov.sa/sites/default/files/saudi_youth_in_numbers_report_2020en_0.pdf

Ghattas, Kim (2019), "Arab Women are Tired of Talking about Just 'Women's Issues,'" The Atlantic, 24 August at https://www.theatlantic.com/international/archive/2019/08/arab-women-media-literature/596455/

Gilligan, Carol and Snider, Naomi (2018), Why Does Patriarchy Persist? Cambridge: Polity Books.

Human Rights Watch (2016), "Boxed In," 16 July at https://www.hrw.org/report/2016/07/16/boxed/women-and-saudi-arabias-male-guardianship-system

Human Rights Watch (2017), "It's a Men's Club," 25 May at https://www.hrw.org/report/2017/05/25/its-mens-club/discrimination-against-women-irans-job-market

Human Rights Watch (2020), World Report 2020: Rights Trends in Saudi Arabia, https://www.hrw.org/world-report/2020/country-chapters/saudi-arabia

Human Rights Watch (2021), "Saudi Arabia: Prominent Women's Rights Activist Released," 10 February at https://www.hrw.org/news/2021/02/10/saudi-arabia-prominent-womens-rights-activist-released

Inter-Parliamentary Union (2020), "Data on Women in National Parliament," https://data.ipu.org/node/79/dataonwomen?chamber_id=13421 https://data.ipu.org/node/79/data-on-women?chamber_id=13421

Iran Wire (2015), "Hijab: The Most Cherished of Weapons," January 4, https://iranwire.com/en/features/422.

Iranian Civil Code (1928), "The Civil Code of the Islamic Republic of Iran," 23 May 1928 [Unofficial Translation], https://www.refworld.org/docid/49997adb27.html

Iranian Criminal Code (1999), "Criminal Code of Procedure for Public and Revolutionary Courts Approved on September 19, 1999 with Amendments,"

Unofficial Translation by Iran Human Rights Documentation Center, https://www.refworld.org/docid/517fb0994.html

Iranian Labour Code (1990), "Iran: Labour Code," English Translation from Persian Published by Rouznameh Rasmi on 17 February 1991 at https://www.refworld.org/docid/4c35e7802.html

Iranian Penal Code (2013), "Iran: Islamic Penal Code," [Persian] Reproduced by Iran Human Rights Documentation Center, at https://www.refworld.org/docid/518a19404.html

Lerner, Gerda (1986), *The Creation of Patriarchy*, New York: Oxford University Press.

Liloia, Alainna (2019), "Saudi Women are Fighting for Their Freedom—And Their Hard-Won Victories are Growing," The Conversation, 9 August at https://theconversation.com/saudi-women-are-fighting-for-their-freedom-and-their-hard-won-victories-are-growing-121610

Lippman, Thomas W. (2012), *Saudi Arabia on the Edge: The Uncertain Future of an American Ally*, New York: Council on Foreign Relations and Potomac Books.

Mahtani, Melissa (2020), "Iranian Women's Rights Activist: 'Don't Wait for Anyone to Hand You Your Rights,'" CNN, 25 February at https://edition.cnn.com/2020/02/25/world/iranian-womens-rights-shapark-2020-geneva-prize-intl/index.html

Masters, James (2019), "Iranian Women Finally Allowed to Officially Watch Soccer Match After 40 Years," CNN, 10 October at https://edition.cnn.com/2019/10/10/football/iran-soccer-women-cambodia-spt-intl/index.html

Minority Rights Group International (2019), "Fact Sheet on Discrimination Against Women in Iran," Factsheet, October at https://minorityrights.org/wp-content/uploads/2019/09/FACTSHEET-Discrimination-against-women-in-Iran-October-2019.pdf

Moghadam, Valentine M. (2003), *Modernising Women: Gender and Social Change in the Middle East*, Boulder: Lynne Rienner Publishers.

Moghadam, Valentine M. (2012), "Patriarchy Challenged: Women and the Changing Family in the Middle East," in Hans Bertram and Nancy Ehlert (eds.), *Family, Ties, and Care: Family Transformation in a Plural Modernity*, Berlin: Barbara Budrich Publishers, pp. 587-609.

Moghadam, Valentine M. (2018), "Iranian Women, Work, and the Gender Regime," The Cairo Review of Global Affairs, 16 May at https://www.thecairoreview.com/essays/iranian-women-work-and-the-gender-regime/

Moradian, Michael Azad (2009), "Domestic Violence against Single and Married Women in Iranian Society," *The Iranian*, 9 September at https://iranian.com/2009/09/10/domestic-violence-against-single-and-married-women-in-iranian-society/

Radio Farda (2017), "Women's Unemployment in Iran Twice That of Men," 17 August at https://en.radiofarda.com/a/iran-women-unemployment-twice/28681903.html.

Ritchie, Hannah and Roser, Max (2019), "Gender Ratio," Our World in Data, June at https://ourworldindata.org/gender-ratio

Sahraei, Fariba (2012), "Iranian University Bans on Women Causes Consternation," BBC News, 22 September at https://www.bbc.com/news/world-middle-east-19665615

Said, Summer (2019), "Saudi Arabia to Allow Women to Travel Abroad without Permission," *The Wall Street Journal*, 2 August at https://www.wsj.com/articles/saudi-arabia-to-allow-women-to-travel-abroad-without-permission-11564693852

Salhi, Zahia Smail (2013). *Gender and Violence in Islamic Societies*. London: I. B. Tauris.

Saudi Gazette (2020), "Cabinet Decisions Approving the Amendment of the System of Travel Documents, Civil Status, and the System of Work and Social Insurance," https://www.uqn.gov.sa/articles/1564686389678699500/

Solati, Fariba (2018), *Women, Work, and Patriarchy in the Middle East and North Africa*, New York: Palgrave Macmillan.

Solomon, Hussein (2020), "Women in the Middle East North African Region Pushing Back Against Patriarchy," *Mail & Guardian*, 14 March at https://mg.co.za/article/2020-03-14-women-in-the-middle-east-north-african-region-pushing-back-against-patriarchy/

Solomon, Hussein and Tausch, Arno (2020), *Islamism, Crisis and Democratization: Implications of the World Values Survey for the Muslim World, Cham*, Switzerland: Springer.

Tailassane, Roumaissane (2019), Women's Rights and Representation in Saudi Arabia, Iran, and Turkey: The Patriarchal Domination of Religious Interpretations, International Relations Honors Paper. Ursinus College, 29 April at https://digitalcommons.ursinus.edu/int_hon/5/

The Economist (2015), "Saudi Arabia's Dress Code for Women," 28 January at https://www.economist.com/the-economist-explains/2015/01/28/saudi-arabias-dress-code-for-women

The World Bank (2020b), "Saudi Women Rising Up in Business in Line with Vision 2030," 11 March at https://www.worldbank.org/en/news/feature/2020/03/11/saudi-women-rising-up-in-business-in-line-with-vision-2030

The World Bank (2020a). *Women, Business and The Law 2020*. Washington: World Bank Group.

Thomas, Kathrin (2019), "Women's Rights in the Middle East and North Africa," Arab Barometer, August, https://www.arabbarometer.org/wp-content/uploads/AB_Women_August2019_Public-Opinion_Arab-Barometer.pdf

Tizro, Zahra (2012), *Domestic Violence in Iran: Women, Marriage and Islam*. London: Routledge.

United Nations General Assembly (UNGA) (2016). "Situation of Human Rights in the Islamic Republic of Iran," Report of the Special Rapporteur, No. A/71/418, https://undocs.org/pdf?symbol=en/A/71/418

van Wagtendonk, Anya (2019), "Saudi Arabia Changed Its Guardianship Laws, but Activists Who Fought Them Remain Imprisoned," 3 August at https://www.vox.com/world/2019/8/3/20752864/saudi-arabia-guardianship-laws-women-travel-employment-mbs

Walker, John (2015), "Islam and Political Freedom," Fourmilab, 22 November at http://www.fourmilab.ch/documents/islam_freedom

World Economic Forum (2016). Global Gender Gap Report 2016, http://www3.weforum.org/docs/GGGR16/WEF_Global_Gender_Gap_Report_2016.pd

World Economic Forum (2019). Global Gender Gap Report 2020, http://www3.weforum.org/docs/WEF_GGGR_2020.pdf

Zayadin, Hiba (2020), "Saudi Women Are Speaking Up Online," Human Rights Watch, 14 April at https://www.hrw.org/news/2020/04/14/saudi-women-are-speaking-online

4. Al-Azhar as a Key Player in Countering the Radical Ideology of Global Jihad

Michael Barak

One of the contemporary challenges that the world is facing for over two decades is the threat of global jihad's extremist ideology. Since 2014, Al-Azhar University, the most prestigious centre for Sunni Islamic learning in the world, has been bearing the burden of countering radical ideologies, especially of Al-Qaeda and the Islamic State (ISIS). Al-Azhar has played a significant role in promoting a moderate interpretation of Islam, producing counter-narratives against ISIS and Al-Qaeda, cultivating tolerance and coexistence, building interdisciplinary channels and strengthening relations with the Vatican.

Although Al-Azhar plays a key role in the issue, its position in the eyes of the Egyptian regime appears to be eroding. This is due to rising tensions in the relationship between the two characterised by power struggles in the face of the centralised policy of the Egyptian regime which seeks to impose full authority on the religious establishment. Ahmad al-Tayeb, the Grand Sheikh of Al-Azhar, however, has thus far been successful in maintaining Al-Azhar's independence and has refused to succumb to the dictates of the regime, even at the cost of confronting it.

Al-Azhar was founded in 972 CE by the Ismaili Fatimid dynasty for the propagation of Ismaili Shiism. In the 12th century CE, it became a Sunni institution thanks to the conquest of Egypt by the Ayyubid dynasty. Under the rule of the Mamluks (1252-1517) and the Ottomans (1517-1805), it consolidated a reputation as a centre for Qur'anic teaching and Shafi'i jurisprudence and attracted many Sunni 'ulama and students from across the Muslim world. Over the years, Al-Azhar has become a leading religious authority in the Sunni Muslim world (Nanji, 2006). Al-Azhar currently has more than two million students and 4,000 teaching institutes across Egypt (Sofuoglu, 2020) and several official branches abroad.

Al-Azhar under Sisi's rule

'Abd al-Fatah al-Sisi's rise to power in July 2013 significantly strengthened al-Azhar's status. The Egyptian regime's decision to exclude the Muslim Brotherhood from the public sphere, designate it as a terrorist organisation and outlaw it in December 2013 reduced the public criticism of the Muslim Brotherhood towards Al-Azhar which they had termed as "a fossilised institution and a tool in the hands of the regime" (Barak, 2016). For example, the Brotherhood accused Al-Azhar of supporting Sisi's military coup and ousting President Morsi–a member of the Brotherhood. Sheikh Yusuf al-Qaradawi, the spiritual leader of the movement, expressed his disappointment with the stance taken by al-Tayeb, and accused him of abusing his position:

> I would like for Sheikh Al-Azhar to confront the Army and all of the people who suggested that he support the idea of a revolt against the President who was legitimately elected ... but my hopes have been dashed ... your role, Sheikh Al-Azhar, is to represent all of the Muslims, in addition to the Muslim inhabitants of Egypt, and not to be satisfied with representing only a small group within the Egyptian population (Al-Qaradawi, 2013).

The strategic partnership formed between Al-Azhar and Sisi also contributed to the consolidation of its status. In December 2014, at a conference hosted by Al-Azhar on the fight against terrorism, Sisi entrusted Al-Azhar with an important national mission: creating a tolerant ideological climate in which Al-Azhar was required to reform the religious discourse, to produce counter-narratives condemning the Muslim Brotherhood's thinking and the Islamic terrorist organisations especially ISIS and Al-Qaeda and cultivate a moderate interpretation of the religion of Islam. Sisi called as well on Al-Azhar to carry out a "religious revolution" which would adapt the religious discourse to the modern era (Cook, 2015). At the end of the conference, al-Tayeb noted that "the young people of the nation have been and still are exposed to brainwashing" by the spread of a radical interpretation of the Holy Scriptures, which requires the 'Ulema and intellectuals to take responsibility and reveal their true meaning (*al-Masry al-Youm*, 2014). In the following years, Al-Azhar established various mechanisms to deal with the issue and engaged vigorously in the task, although not fully.

Since the beginning of 2015, Al-Azhar has carried out extensive propaganda activities in Egypt and around the world against the radical thinking of Islamist terrorist organisations. Special emphasis was placed on educating the younger generation on the values of tolerance, acceptance of the "other" and attachment to the homeland. In 2015, the World Association for Al-Azhar Graduates (WAAG) launched the *Al-Nur* magazine for children and youth aged 8-18. Sheikh al-Azhar explained that the magazine served as an important channel for the transmission and assimilation of humane values among the younger generation that would help form a strong Muslim identity and strengthen the young people's connection to the Egyptian homeland. Sisi gave his blessing to the new magazine and in November 2015 pledged to increase its budget (Barak, 2016). The magazine was later translated into foreign languages and is also distributed among Muslim communities in the West (Barak, 2016).

In 2014, Al-Azhar established a centre for the dissemination of fatwas in which several hundred clerics are active, who have been assigned the job of providing immediate and direct theological answers to Muslims Egypt and other countries round the clock. In this way, Al-Azhar strives to present a legitimate alternative to the religious authority that radical Islamist and jihadist groups, such as ISIS, claim to have. In June 2015, Al-Azhar set up a centre to monitor propaganda materials of jihadist organisations distributed on social networks to refute them in Arabic and other languages such as French, German and Swahili (Barak, 2016). Tareq Sha'aban, the director of the Monitoring Center noted that "We have established collaborations with several EU governments and international organizations such as the United Nations and the European Union on the subject of terrorist groups and how they recruit young people" (Eltoham, 2019).

In addition, Al-Azhar has translated from Arabic into English and French to date more than 1,000 fatwa issued by it. It chose rulings that debunked claims made by the extremists and published a series of books in several languages about the latent danger in classifying any Muslims as apostates. Another example of Al-Azhar's external activity can be seen in the sermons given by representatives of the institute to young Muslims living in the West, and in the scholarships awarded to them for studying Islamic sciences and Arabic at Al-Azhar. The goal is to expose the students to moderate interpretation of the Islamic holy sources, and to create "ambassadors" who will return to their native countries in order to preach those modern interpretations (Barak, 2016).

The year 2020 was characterised by impressive activity by Al-Azhar in which it published more than 756,000 fatwas on questions from Muslims around the world, broadcasted 248 programmes in Arabic, English, French and German on issues related to religion and society, and conducted 67 social media campaigns on various topics such as the illness inherent in extremist ideology etc. (*Sawt al-Azhar*, 2020). At the end of December 2020, al-Tayeb even ruled on a ban on joining the ranks of the Muslim Brotherhood (*Asharq al-Awsat*, 2020).

Al-Azhar has been cultivating the social resilience of the Egyptian society as well by strengthening the bonds of brotherhood between various strata. For example, al-Tayyeb has emphasised many times that the Coptic Christians in the country (who account for about 10 per cent of the total population) are an integral part of Egypt's social fabric and have a significant contribution to Egypt's development. In January 2019, during the inauguration of a new church and mosque in the new administrative city, al-Tayeb emphasised that the two places of worship stand as a symbol for those who "try to undermine the stability of the state by sectarianism" (*The Times of Israel*, 2019). At the end of 2020, al-Tayeb ruled that Muslims can celebrate with Christians the birth of Jesus, eat their dishes, and shake their hand. This ruling was given against the background of a heated debate with some members of the Salafi stream in Egypt opposing congratulating Christians on the occasion of the holiday. Al-Tayeb stressed that the key to the revival of the Egyptian people lies in renouncing radical rulings and cultivating good neighbourly relations and unity among all sectors of the Egyptian people (*Al-Watan*, 2020).

Cultivating relationships with the Christian world

An important milestone in strengthening Al-Azhar's international prestige is related to cultivating its ties with the Christian world, especially with the Vatican. In 2016, Al-Azhar renewed its ties with the Vatican and agreed to tighten cultural ties and conduct inter-religious discourse after a five-year hiatus due to sharp criticism by Pope Benedict XVI of the Egyptian regime's oppressive and discriminatory treatment of the Coptic Christian minority in Egypt (*France24*, 2017). The appointment of Francis to the Pope in 2013 and Sisi's plan to include Al-Azhar in the fight against Islamic terrorism as he declared in December 2014 were the main factors in restoring relations between the two. In May 2016, al-Tayeb visited the Vatican and at the end of April 2017, the Pope visited Cairo. It was an important historical landmark in relations between the Christian and the Muslim worlds.

The Pope's visit to Cairo emphasised the message that the two religions were not hostile to each other but share values of tolerance and acceptance of the "other" while at the same time being determined to lead a common fight against terrorists who exploit religion to justify violence. The climax of the relationship between the two occurred on 4 February 2019 with the signing of a historic agreement called the "Document on Human Fraternity for World Peace and Living Together" by Pope Francis and Sheikh al-Azhar al-Tayeb designed to promote a peaceful interfaith dialogue (The Higher Committee of Human Fraternity, 2019). The UN General Assembly adopted the document, thanks to the involvement of the Kingdom of Saudi Arabia, UAE, Bahrain and Egypt, and stated that as of 4 February 2021, the International Day of Human Fraternity will be marked every year on this date (*Al-Ahram Weekly*, 2020).

Al-Azhar's channels of influence

Al-Azhar dominates an extensive cross-continental social network through which it promotes its worldview and influence around the world. This network contributes to strengthening its position in the world as a leading Sunni religious authority. The network includes the WAAG which has several official affiliates in Asia, Africa and Europe, a wide range of Muslim scholars from dozens of countries around the world who come to Cairo every year to receive training at Al-Azhar, and so do

Muslim clerics around the world who identify with Al-Azhar's agenda (*Al-Watan*, 2019).

The WAAG is an umbrella organisation established in 2006 with the aim of strengthening Al-Azhar's ties with its alumni around the world. In a report published on the organisation's activities for 2020, it was noted that its graduates were taking part in promoting the agenda of Al-Azhar and Sheikh al-Tayeb (WAAG 2020). Moreover, it underlined that the students were trained and equipped with knowledge that would help them upon their return to their homeland to become a "wall against the spread of extremist thought" and disseminators of the moderate thinking of Al-Azhar (ibid). Jamia al-Karam, a College of Islamic Studies at Retford in Nottinghamshire which became an official branch of WAAG in the UK since 2011, has been teaching Al-Azhar's curriculum in the UK (Jamia al-Karam, n.d.). In January 2018, many of its members wrote a letter to the Egyptian regime praising the historic role played by Al-Azhar and al-Tayeb in promoting moderate Islam and building bridges with the Vatican, the Anglican Church and the Coptic Church (Thomas-Johnson, 2018).

Another channel of influence which has been consolidating Al-Azhar's status is the "Academy for the Training of Imams and Preachers" which is founded on 16 January 2019 with the aim of training Muslim clerics from around the world. Since its opening, Al-Azhar has trained hundreds of scholars, and in the shadow of the COVID-19 pandemic, it continues to do so through distance learning. For example, in January 2021, Al-Azhar began training 85 Muslim clerics from Sweden, France, Slovenia, India, Pakistan, Cameroon, Nigeria, Central Africa and Gambia (*Akhbar al-Yawm*, 2021). This training is welcomed by some world leaders such as Emanuel Macron, President of France, who called on all Imams in France already in early 2019 to undergo training at the Al-Azhar Institute (*Middle East Monitor*, 2019). Muslim religious leaders in the West are urging their governments to allow Al-Azhar to be more involved in the religious life of the local Muslim population to counter radical Islamic ideologies. For example, in February 2019, Muwaffiq al-Rifai—Imam of the Lausanne Mosque in Switzerland—emphasised that Al-Azhar played an important role in curbing the influence of the Muslim Brotherhood in Switzerland and in improving the image of the

Islamic religion. Therefore, he claimed that the Swiss authorities should strive for cooperation with Al-Azhar (*Al-Ahram*, 2019).

It seems that the UAE has a contribution as well to the consolidation of Al-Azhar's status. As part of the fight against the extremist ideology of the global jihadist organisations, the Emirates has established several institutions designed for this goal. In July 2014, it founded the Council of Muslim Elders based in Abu Dhabi headed by Sheikh al-Tayeb. It includes many other eminent religious figures and scholars from around the Muslim world, including Sheikh Bin Bayyah, a distinguished leading religious authority who heads the Emirates' Fatwa Council. Sheikh Bin Bayyah and other religious authorities such as Sheikh Ali Jifri, a prominent Yemeni Sufi sheikh who heads the Taba Institute in Dubai, who are being part of the social network that the emirate regime has weaved (al-Anani, 2020) have repeatedly emphasised the significant contribution of the al-Azhar to creating a healthy society, building bridges with other religions and being a religious authority (*Ṣada al-Balad*, 2020). Moreover, the UAE's General Authority Islamic Affairs and Endowment signed an agreement in 2015 to open al-Azhar's first abroad branch in the UAE. The UAE has also built new centres for al-Azhar (Amasha, 2020).

Al-Azhar a "Soft Power" or a Stumbling Block to the Egyptian regime?

Against the background of this extensive activity, Al-Azhar strengthens its image in the eyes of the Egyptian regime and Egyptian society as a significant component in the "soft power" of Egypt. Dr. Osama al-'Abd, head of the Waqf and Religious Affairs Committee in the Egyptian Parliament and former head of Al-Azhar University stressed that Al-Azhar is "Egypt's most important soft power over the world. The esteemed al-Azhar [is considered] the national security of Egypt. [...] there is no other way that all the religious institutes should be under al-Azhar's umbrella" (al-Bawaba, 2020). Muhammad al-Mahrasawi, director of Al-Azhar University, stressed that tens of thousands of students who come to Egypt from more than a hundred countries to study in Al-Azhar are helping to strengthen Egypt's "soft power" (*Al-Masri Al-Yawm*, 2020). In 2018, Egyptian Foreign Minister Sameh Shukri praised Al-Azhar for its contribution to cultivating Egypt's "soft power" in Southeast Asian countries following the positive impression al-Tayeb left on his visits to Indonesia (State Information Service, 2018).

The extensive activity and hard-working social network that Al-Azhar has built can attribute it important role in the "soft power" of Egypt. However, it is clear that Al-Azhar and the Egyptian regime do not always see things eye to eye due to power struggles that obscure the equation between them. In 2015, al-Tayeb repeatedly refused to plead with the Egyptian regime to rule that ISIS members were considered infidels. Al-Tayeb and his colleagues explained that Al-Azhar would not be different from ISIS if it also used *takfir*. Furthermore, a Muslim cannot be labelled as an infidel as long as he says the *shahadah,* even if his way is wrong (Al-Azhar Observatory for Combating Extremism, 2015).

In 2016, Sisi sought to establish unified written Friday sermon prayers in mosques to monitor the contents and prevent incitement sermons, but this initiative was rejected by Al-Azhar, who refused the plan. This was on the grounds that it harms the self-judgment of the preachers and restricts the religious discourse (*Daily News Egypt*, 2016). In January 2017, al-Tayeb refused to change the procedure of divorce after Sisi sought to apply the divorce proceedings only in writing with the intention of halting the high divorce rate in Egyptian society (Brown, 2017). In November 2018, the tension between the two reached a boiling point when Sisi expressed resentment over Sheikh Al-Azhar and stressed that he had asked him four or five times to reform the religious discourse, but in practice, no real results were seen (*Al-Jazeera*, 2019).

Egyptian intellectuals also express disappointment at Al-Azhar's level of commitment to real reform in the religious discourse and question whether it intends to carry it out. At a conference held in July 2020 on behalf of members of the Egyptian Human Rights Organization in Cairo, The Egyptian Initiative for Personal Rights, participants discussed Al-Azhar's contribution to building bridges between the various segments of Egyptian society through examining its religious discourse. Some of the participants claimed that Al-Azhar speaks with a double tongue. On the one hand, an official line that portrays Al-Azhar as a religious authority that advocates religious pluralism, freedom of expression and improving the status of women in society. On the other hand, statements by Al-Azhar's members that indicate intolerance towards non-Christian religious minorities such as the Baha'is and Shiites, and an unwillingness to advance the status of women (al-Mubādara al-Misriyya lil-Huqūq al-Shakhṣiyya, 2020).

Ahmad Abduh Mahir, an Egyptian thinker and veteran critic of Al-Azhar, said in December 2018 that after examining Al-Azhar's changes in its curriculum he realised that Al-Azhar's people "laughed at Egypt. They teach the same content and the same books. They changed the books' titles and corrected only a little [...] in practice no corrections were made". Furthermore, he added that Al-Azhar continued to be a major source of bloodshed and the expansion of the circle of terrorism in the Arab world (*Raseef 22*, 2020).

Although Al-Azhar has the support of many Sufis in Egypt, criticisms can also be found among them. Abdallah Nasir, Secretary-General of the Union of Sufi Forces, accused Al-Azhar of unwillingness to denounce sources of infidelity, especially the rulings of the 14th-century Hanbali scholar Ibn Tayymiyya and the 18th century Najdi puritanical scholar, Muhammad 'Abd al-Wahhab. According to him, as long as such rulings exist, terrorism will continue around the world. Moreover, he claimed that Al-Azhar's curriculum adversely affects the minds of students and has the potential to produce candidates for ISIS. In view of this, he called for the abolition of Al-Azhar's role in renewing the religious discourse and limiting its activities to teaching religion and language only (*Infirād*, 2016).

Sisi, desperate from Al-Azhar's unwillingness to advance his plans, turned to Dar al-Aftaa, an Egyptian Islamic advisory, justiciary and governmental body established as a centre for Islam and Islamic legal research and thinking. On 3 August 2018, Dar al-Ifta launched an Imam Training Academy like the one of Al-Azhar Institutes. Although this was a duplication, it expressed the regime's desire to cultivate an alternative religious authority that will completely follow the regime's dictates. In July 2020, the Egyptian parliament approved a bill that gives Dar Al-Ifta independent status and abolishes its subordination to al-Azhar. Eventually, however, al-Tayeb did not allow Dar al-Ifta to become independent of Al-Azhar on the ground that bill violated Article 7 of the Egyptian constitution, which states that Al-Azhar is an independent Islamic Institute that serves as the central authority in interpreting the holy sources of Islam and that Sheikh Al-Azhar is independent (BBC, 2020).

Al-Azhar and the Palestinian issue

Even if there is justice in some of the criticism directed to Al-Azhar it has not eroded Al-Azhar's global reputation. Al-Azhar continues to be courted around the world since it is perceived as a moderate religious actor that cultivates tolerance and co-existence. However, this is not the case in the case of the Palestinian-Israel conflict.

Since the appointment of al-Tayeb as the grand sheikh of Al-Azhar in 2010, he has used harsh polemic against Israel and its sovereignty over Jerusalem aiming to promote the Palestinian issue to the top of the international community's agenda. On 20 November 2011, Al-Azhar published the "Al-Azhar Convention on the Honorable Jerusalem", which emphasised that the identity of Jerusalem was originally Arab founded by the ancient Jebusites in the fourth millennium BC long before Judaism. In the mentioned convention, Al-Azhar argued that the Jews, like other nations throughout history, invaded Jerusalem but did not manage to control it for a long time. For Al-Azhar, history teaches any foreign domination including Jewish in Jerusalem is temporary. In the convention, Al-Azhar accused the Zionists of "relying on the oppressive forces of Western imperialism in their attempts to Judaise Jerusalem [...]". In this regard, Al-Azhar mentioned a letter written by the famous 12th-century leader Salah al-Din al-Ayyubi to King Richard I of England emphasising that he would not be able to build a single stone in Jerusalem as long as jihad continued. Moreover, Al-Azhar has called "all the freemen around the globe [...] to assist in the liberation of Jerusalem and Palestine" (Al-Azhar, 2011). In the following years, the convention was published several more times to emphasise that Al-Azhar's position on the issue had not changed.

The announcement by US President Donald Trump to recognise Jerusalem as the capital of Israel and to transfer the US embassy to it provoked a sharp reaction from Al-Azhar which in response re-published its convention on Jerusalem. In December 2017, al-Tayyeb refused to meet with Mike Pence, US Vice-President, claiming that "how can I sit with someone who gives something without having it to someone we are not entitled to receive [...]" (al-Bawaba, 2017). Moreover, he called on the Arab residents of Jerusalem to protest against US policy on Jerusalem and supported launching a third intifada (Al-Ahram, 2017). In January 2018, he hosted an international conference in Cairo in the presence of Palestinian Authority Chairman Mahmoud Abbas and representatives from 86 countries including diplomats and religious leaders, in protest of Trump's decision. At the end of the conference, the Al-Azhar Aid Charter for Jerusalem was published. It included 13 clauses emphasising the Arabness of Jerusalem, its sanctity to Islam and Christianity, being the eternal capital of the independent state of Palestine, support in the struggle of the Palestinians, and strengthening the scale of a public campaign in front of the international in this regard (*Al-Yawm Al-Sabi*, 2018).

In late 2020, in an article published in al-Azhar's mouthpiece *Sawt al-Azhar*, al-Tayeb was portrayed as a scholar whose approach to Jerusalem traditionally continued the path of his predecessors in office. In 1929, Sheikh al-Azhar at that time warned of the British occupation and the Jewish takeover of the Western Wall; in 1935, two Al-Azhar scholars, Sheikh Muhammad Rashid Rida and Sheikh Amin al-Husayni, issued a jurist ruling banning the sale of land to Jews; in 1936, Al-Azhar's senior scholars committee supported the Great Arab Revolt; in 1937 Al-Azhar protested against the British Peel Commission that decided to divide Palestine to Jewish and Arab states; in 1938, Al-Azhar's senior scholars' committee called for preserving the Arab identity of Jerusalem; in 1948, Sheikh Hassanein Makhlouf issued a fatwa requiring defending Palestine, be it through sacrificing selves or money etc. (*Sawt al-Azhar*, 2020). Al-Tayyeb was described as a Al-Azhar scholar who has to broaden the scale of al-Azhar's activity on the Palestinian issue facing threats and challenges to the Arabs and Muslims (*Sawt al-Azhar*, 2020).

Summary and Conclusion

The global warfare against the Global Jihad cannot be limited only to "boots on the ground." It requires a determined global counter ideological campaign as well. The Egyptian Al-Azhar University has been playing an important and central role in countering the extremist ideology of global jihad organisations. Its status as a prominent Sunni religious authority, the high prestige it enjoys in the Muslim and non-Muslim world and its link to an extensive social network that stretches from east to west can help in countering radical Islamic ideologies. Nonetheless, Al-Azhar shares a complicated equation with the Sisi regime and this impedes the regime's efforts to control the religious sector in Egypt.

It is difficult to estimate the scale of Al-Azhar's success in countering radical ideologies. As long as there are conflict zones, corruption, poverty, ungoverned territories and foreign support in militant Islamic groups it becomes more difficult. Al-Azhar is not the only actor which is investing efforts to win the heart and minds of Muslims over the world. There are other actors as well such as the Muslim Brotherhood movement, Turkey, Iran, Qatar and others who strive to increase their religious influence. Moreover, the hostile attitude of Al-Azhar towards Israel does not fit its image of a peaceful religious actor that is interested to cultivate co-existence with other faiths and groups and therefore may fuel unrest and encourage radicalisation. Nevertheless, Al-Azhar is carrying on to fulfil a very important role in countering the ideology of global jihad.

References

Cook, Steven A. (2015), "Revolutionizing Religion in Sisi's Egypt," Council for Foreign Relations, 2 February at https://www.cfr.org/blog/revolutionizing-religion-sisis-egypt

Akhbar al-Yawm (2021), "Acadimiyyat al-Azhar Tuwāsilu Dawrāt 'Idād al-Dā'iyyah al-Mu'āsir bi-T'alīm 'an Bu'd," (Al-Azhar is not the only actor which is investing efforts to win the hearts and minds of Muslims over the world), 31 January at https://m.akhbarelyom.com/news/newdetails/3244557/1/أكاديمية-الأزهر-تواصل-دورات--إعداد-الداعية-المعاصر--بالتعليم-عن-بعد

Al-Ahram (2017), "Al-Imam al-Akbar li-Ahali al-Quds: la-Takun Intifadatukum bi-Qadr Imanikum bi-Qadiyyatikum wa-Mahhabatikum li-Watanikum.. wa-Nahnu ma'kum wa-lan Nakhdulukum," (The Grand Imam to the citizens of Jerusalem: Let your uprising be as much as your faith in your cause and your love for your country ... and we are with you and will not let you down), 8 December at https://gate.ahram.org.eg/News/1693057.aspx

Al-Ahram (2019), "Imām Masjid LūzānL al-Azhar al-Marj'aiyyah al-Awla lil-Muslimīn.. wa-Swīsra al-Afḍal fi al-Ta'āyush al-Dīnī—Hiwār" (Imam Lausanne Mosque: Al-Azhar The First Authority of Muslims.. Switzerland is the one best for Religious Coexistence—An Interview), 17 February at https://gate.ahram.org.eg/News/2110407.aspx

Al-Ahram Weekly (2020), "UN Approves Egypt-backed Proposal Declaring 4 February International Day of Human Fraternity," 24 December at http://english.ahram.org.eg/NewsContent/1/64/397386/Egypt/Politics-/UN-approves-Egyptbacked-proposal-declaring--Februa.aspx

Al-Anani, Khalil (2020), "The UAE's Manipulative Utilization of Religion," Arab Center Washington DC, 29 September at http://arabcenterdc.org/policy_analyses/the-uaes-manipulative-utilization-of-religion/

Al-Azhar (2011), Wathīqat al-Azhar 'an al-Quds al-Sharīf (Al-Azhar Convention on the Honorable Jerusalem), 20 November at https://drive.google.com/file/d/1HMDMFy1vOg0QGzwm2yD5TGrI2bAPvbOZ/view

Al-Azhar Observatory for Combating Extremism (2017), "Al-Azhar rejects Takfir … Won't You understand?!" 7 December at https://www.azhar.eg/observer-en/details/ArtMID/1153/ArticleID/1984/Al-Azhar-rejects-Takfir-%E2%80%A6-Won%E2%80%99t-You-understand

Al-Bawaba (2017), "Shaykh al-Azhar Yarfaḍ Liqa Nāib al-Raīs al-Amrīki wayubāriku Intifāḍat al-Filastīnīn," (Al-Azhar Chief Refuses Meeting with US Vice President, Blesses Palestinian Intifada), 8 December at https://www.albawaba.com/ar/أخبار/شيخ-الأزهر-يرفض-لقاء-نائب-الرئيس-الأمريكي-مايك-بنس-1058510

Al-Bawaba (2020), "Al-Azhar al-Quwwah al-Nā'imah al-Al-Aham li-Misr wala Khilaf 'ala Qayyimatihi," (Al-Azhar Most Important Soft Power of Egypt and there is not Dispute on its Value), 19 July at https://www.albawabhnews.com/4088107

Al-Jazeera (2019), "al-Tayyib.. Sheikh al-Azhar aldhi Ja'alathu al-Thawra Za'īma Siyāssiyya," (al-Tayyib: Sheikh al-Azhar who became a Political Leader following the Revolution), 19 March at https://www.aljazeera.net/news/politics/2019/3/19/ت□ع-□نوات-على-الطيب-شيخا-للأزهر

Al-Masry al-Yawm (2014), "Mutamar al-Azhar li-Muwājat al-Tattaruf: Shabāb al-Ummah yata'araduna li-Ghasl al-Admigha," (Al-Azhar's Conference against Extremism: the Nation's Youth are Exposed to Brain Washing), 5 December at https://today.almasryalyoum.com/article2.aspx?ArticleID=446344

Al-Masry al-Yawm (2020), "Al-Mahrasawi: al-Azhar a-Sharif al-Quwwa al-Nā'imah li-Misr Mahaliyya wa-Dawaliyya wa-Yahtaḍinu 33 Alf Tālib Wāfid," (The Distinguished al-Azhar is the Local and International Soft Power of Egypt and it Cultivates 33,000 Coming Students), 29 December at https://www.almasryalyoum.com/news/details/2201200

Al-Qardawi, Yusuf (2013), "Waqafat ma' Sheikh al-Azhar wa Qadiyyat al-Inqilab ala al-Shariyya" (Observation on Sheikh al-Azhar and the Coup Issue as viewed by the Islamic Law), Website of Sheikh Yusuf al-Qardawi, Commentaries, 4 September at https://www.al-qaradawi.net/node/2848

Asharq al-Awsat (2020), "Al-Azhar Bans Joining the Muslim Brotherhood," 21 December at https://english.aawsat.com/home/article/2695296/al-azhar-bans-joining-%E2%80%98muslim-brotherhood%E2%80%99

Al-Watan (2019), "Tadrīb al-Aima Dākhil wa-Khārij Misr.. 'Ansar Jadīd lil-Quwwa al-Na'ima," (Training the Imams in Egypt and Abroad: A New Component in the Soft Power), 24 December at https://www.elwatannews.com/news/details/4497930

Al-Watan (2020), "Sheikh al-Azhar yufannidu Asbāb Intishār Khitāb al-Tattaruf fi al-Ta'āmul ma' al-Aqbāt," (Sheikh of Al-Azhar refutes the causes of the spread of extremist discourse in dealing with Copts), 25 December at https://www.elwatannews.com/news/details/5170208

Amasha, Muhammad (2020), "The UAE-Sponsored 'Islams': Mapping the Terrain," *Maydan*, 15 September at https://themaydan.com/2020/09/the-uae-sponsored-islams-mapping-the-terrain/

Al-Yawm al-Sabi (2018), "Naṣṣ 'Ilān al-Azhar al-'Ālami li-Nuṣrat al-Quds.. al-Imām al-Akbar: 2018 'Ama lil-Madīna al-Muqadassa," (Text of Al-Azhar's declaration to support Jerusalem ... The Grand Imam: 2018 is the year of the Holy City), 18 January at https://www.youm7.com/story/2018/1/18/3607362نص-إعلان-الأزهر-العالمى-لنصرة-القدس-الإمام-الأكبر-2018-عاما

Barak, Michael (2016), "The Al-Azhar Institute—A Key Player in Shaping the Religious and Political Discourse in Egypt," *ICT Insights*, The International Institute for Counter-Terrorism, March at https://www.ict.org.il/UserFiles/JWMG-Al-Azhar-Institute-Mar-16.pdf

BBC Arabic (2020), "Qanūn dār al-Iftā': Khilāf bayna Majlis al-Nuwwāb wal-Azhar fi Misr hawla Mashrū' Qanūn Tanẓim Dār al-Iiftā," (Dar Al Iftaa Law: A dispute between the Parliament and al-Azhar in Egypt over a draft law organizing the Dar al-Iftaa), 24 August at https://www.bbc.com/arabic/middleeast-53894466

Brown, Nathann J. and Mariam Ghanem (2017), "Why is a Marriage Question Dividing Abdel-Fattah al-Sisi and Sheikh Ahmad al-Tayyib?" *Diwan*, Carnegie Middle East Center, 15 February at https://carnegie-mec.org/diwan/68001_

Daily News Egypt (2016), "Al-Azhar Rejects Unified Written Friday Sermon," 27 July at https://dailynewsegypt.com/2016/07/27/al-azhar-rejects-unified-written-friday-sermon/

Eltoham, Amr (2019), "Sisi Keeps Watchful Eye on Al-Azhar's Growing Role Abroad," *Al-Monitor*. Retrieved 18 March 2021 at https://www.al-monitor.com/originals/2019/04/azhar-grand-imam-moderate-islam terrorism-organizaitons.html

France24 (2017), "Pope Heads to Egypt to Mend Ties with Islam, Reassure Christians," 28 April at https://www.france24.com/en/20170427-pope-francis-meet-with-christian-muslim-leaders-egypt

Infirād (2016), "Al-Quwwa al-Sufiyya: Tajdīd al-Khitāb al-Dīni Maswuliyyat al-Jamī' fi Misr wak-'Alām," (The Sufi Forces: Renewing the Religious Discourse is the Responsibility of Everyone in Egypt and the World), 26 July at http://www.innfrad.com/News/54/304106/-القوى-الصوفية-تجديد-الخطاب-الدينى-م□ئولية-الجميع-فى-مصر-والعالم

Jamia al-Karam (n.d.), "WAAG-UK," at https://alkaram.org/resources/waag-uk/

Middle East Monitor (2019), "Macron: French imams should be trained at Egypt's Al-Azhar," 30 January at https://www.middleeastmonitor.com/20190130-macron-french-imams-should-be-trained-at-egypts-al-azhar/

Al-Mubādara al-Misriyya lil-Huqūq al-Shakhṣiyya (2020), "Muntada al-Dīn wal-Hurrīyyāt Yunāqishu 'Sawt al-Azhar," (The Religion and Freedom Forum is discussing with Sawt al-Azahr), 21 July at https://eipr.org/press/2020/07/منتدى-الدين-والحريات-يناقش-صوت-الأزهر-احتفاء-برفض-تبرير-التحرش-ومطالبة-بمزيد-من

Nanji, Azim (2006), "Al-Azhar", in *Medieval Islamic Civilization: An Encyclopaedia*, The Institute of Ismaili Studies, at https://prod-static-iis.s3.eu-west-2.amazonaws.com/s3fs-public/al-azhar_logo-135308194.pdf

Raseef22 (2020), "Ahmad 'Abdu Māhir li-Rasif22: Fuqahāa al-Islām Ṣan'aū min al-Ṣahāba Aṣnāma," (Ahmad Abdu Mahir to Rasif22: the Islamic Jurists made the Companions [of Muhammad) to Idols," 20 December at https://raseef22.net/article/133420-أحمد-عبده-ماهر-لرصيف22-فقهاء-الإ□لام-صن

Ṣada al-Balad (2020), "Al-Habīb al-Jifri: al-Azhar al-Ṣarh al-Marja'ī al-A'ẓam li-Ahl al-Sunna fi al-'Ālim," (al-Habib al-Jifri: al-Azhar is the True Greatest Authority for the Sunnis in the World), 22 November at https://www.elbalad.news/4583650

Sawt al-Azhar (2020), "Mawāqif Tarihīyya lil-Azhar wa-Imāmihi al-Tayyib li-Da'm wa-Nuṣrat al-Qaḍiyya al-Filastīnīyya," (An Historic stance of al-Azhar and its Imam for supporting and helping to the Palestinian issue), 2 December, p. 2.

Sawt al-Azhar (2020), "2020 al-Hiṣād al-Tayeb," (2020: The Best Harvest), 30 December, pp. 1 and 6.

State Information Service (2018), "FM: We Respect Al-Azhar's Message in Strengthening Egypt's Soft Power," 28 May at https://www.sis.gov.eg/Story/130762/FM-We-respect-Al-Azhar's-message-in-strengthening-Egypt's-soft-power?lang=en-us

TRT World (2020), "Sisi's Era Seen as 'One of the Worst Ages' for Famed Al Azhar," 17 June at https://www.trtworld.com/magazine/sisi-s-era-seen-as-one-of-the-worst-ages-for-famed-al-azhar-37349

The Higher Committee of Human Fraternity (2019), "Document on Human Fraternity for World Peace and Living Together," 4 February at https://www.forhumanfraternity.org/document-on-human-fraternity-detail

The Times of Israel (2019), "Egypt's Sisi Inaugurates Cathedral, Mosque in New Capital," 6 January at https://www.timesofisrael.com/egypts-sissi-inaugurates-cathedral-mosque-in-new-capital/

Thomas-Johnson, Amandla (2018), "UK Imams Back Leading Egyptian Cleric amid Rift with Sisi," *Middle East Eye*, 16 January at https://www.middleeasteye.net/news/uk-imams-back-leading-egyptian-cleric-amid-rift-sisi

The World Organization for al-Azhar Graduates (WAAG) (2020), "Munaẓamat Kharijī al-Azhar Tu'linu Hisad Abraz Anshita Idarat al-Wafidin li-'Ām 2020," (The World Organization for al-Azhar Graduates Announces the Harvest of the Most Prominent Activities for Visitors Management for the year 2020), 19 November at https://azhargraduates.org/waag_new/19689/

5. Gulf Think Tanks and Regional Security Policy after 2011

Mona Ali

The existing literature has long overlooked the influence of Gulf Cooperation Council (GCC) think tanks in formulating security policy. Eurocentric tendencies in the analysis of the foreign and security policies of developing countries in general and the Arab world, in particular, led to a focus on official decision-making institutions that ignored the rapid development of think tanks in some GCC countries. Think tanks in GCC countries challenge the paradigms presented by Western schools of thought on this matter, such as the pluralistic school, which argues that think tanks are only as effective as they are independent (Nicander, 2015, p. 498). In this case, the lack of independence on the part of Gulf think tanks enables them to receive necessary government funding to continue their work.

The Arab uprisings of 2011 restructured the regional landscape and changed the balance of power in the Middle East, which increased demand for new and unconventional policy proposals to address the challenges that arose in the wake of the revolutions. As a result, this led to a remarkable boom in think tank momentum and activities. The volume of publications produced by these newly-established think tanks doubled in a short time, while their networking efforts also gained momentum to reach leading researchers and experts worldwide. GCC think tanks held multiple mega-events with active participation from officials and experts worldwide, such as the Abu Dhabi Strategic Forum that the Emirates Policy Center (EPC) holds annually. The think tanks' interests varied widely and included proposals to restore regional stability following the Arab Spring.

Despite this expansion, the impact of GCC think tanks on regional security has been complicated by their lack of transparency about their funding sources and networks. Moreover, many think tanks have stated vaguely that they carry out projects to support the decision-making process without clarifying their relationship with decision-makers. Hence, analysing some of the GCC think tanks' publications offers a potential opportunity for tracking their influences and connections. In this regard, this paper argues that despite the difficulty of measuring the extent of think tanks' influence on formulating regional security policies, there are non-coincidental similarities between the policy proposals that think tanks present and the policies later executed by decision-makers in this field. This reflects the implicit influence of think tanks in GCC countries.

The Influence of Think Tanks on Regional Security

Despite some differences in perspective, there is a consensus that think tanks play a central role in security policy-making in many countries worldwide. This growing global phenomenon is closely related to the increasing demand for knowledge and expertise to deal with complex foreign policy and security affairs issues and the emergence of unprecedented threats that require non-traditional solutions. According to James G. McGann (2018), think tanks are policy-oriented research organisations that provide decision-makers with consultancy, advocacy, public relations, and research services to support their ability to reach rational and efficient decisions on public policy issues. McGann argues that think tanks are non-profit institutions that carry out research and publish studies in a particular field of public policy to support the decision-making process by generating a wide range of policy options, alternatives and non-traditional ideas (McGann, 2018, pp. 8-12).

Other scholars have asserted that the defining characteristics of think tanks are their independence and non-profit status. For example, James McGann and R. Kent Weaver (2000, p. 4) argue that think tanks must be non-governmental and non-profit organisations that work independently from the influence of governments, corporations, pressure groups, lobbies, and political parties (as cited in Pautz, 2011, p. 421). However, this definition excludes many think tanks, especially in developing countries funded by governments and other political agents in the political system.

Regardless of the debate on the independence of think tanks, they function as a bridge between governments and the private sector, universities, the media, and society, as they attempt to help governments formulate more responsive public policies.

According to Diane Stone (2013), think tanks perform many vital functions, such as setting the public policy agenda, producing policy papers, strengthening communication between citizens and decision-makers, developing the leadership skills of political officials, launching public dialogues between political actors on public policies and influencing debates in the public sphere (pp. 113-132). In addition, think tanks carry out relevant research that can be easily transformed into public policies to solve real-world problems. They also focus on generating creative and out-of-the-box alternatives to offer decision-makers a wider array of options. The "elitist" approach sees think tanks as an integral part of the power structure of the state, concerning their role in providing knowledge and consulting to decision-makers, while the "pluralist" approach concentrates on competition between think tanks to influence decision-makers (Nicander, 2015, pp. 484-485).

The effect of think tanks on regional security extends beyond their role in the decision-making process to include a wide array of interrelated influences. Olivier Urrutia (2013) argues that think tanks can define and implement defence policies and strategies. He affirms that the most important role that think tanks play in formulating and implementing defence policy is in framing strategic inputs, mapping threats, determining national security priorities and providing policy options to decision-makers. The difficulty of measuring the influence of think tanks on regional security stems from the ambiguous nature of the ties between think tanks and decision-makers. In many cases, independent think tanks use networking and other similar channels to communicate with decision-makers to demonstrate that they are trustworthy and dependable. Lars Nicander (2015) concludes that the most effective think tanks use personal ties to interact with political officials and disseminate their ideas and recommendations on national security policy (pp. 480-501).

The influence of think tanks extends beyond their connections to decision-makers and security professionals; they also play a role in shaping public opinion and citizens' perceptions and attitudes about the regional environment, including threats to national security. Think tanks also use the media to promote security policies in the public sphere. One of the think tanks' main strategies in regional security policy is to form public coalitions to ensure certain issues are treated as priorities within the national agenda (Youness, 2018, pp. 137-139). According to Zeev Ma'oz (1997), regional security depends upon perceived freedom from external threats on the national level over a certain period of time (pp. 6-7). These perceptions correlate to national measures to ensure independence and security. In this regard, think tanks shape decision-makers' threat perceptions and propose policies to achieve national security through building alliances, allocating resources and engaging with regional conflicts.

Think tanks also play a regional role in promoting dialogue between key regional security powers through tracking bilateral diplomacy, building regional think-tank networks and hosting international security conferences. One such conference is the annual Munich Security Conference, which is attended by political and military leaders worldwide to discuss regional and international security threats.

The Evolution of Think Tanks in the Gulf

The number of think tanks in GCC countries has risen substantially between 2008 and 2020. The increasing number of Gulf think tanks included in the Global Go To Think Tank Index Reports, published by the Think Tanks and Civil Societies Program at the University of Pennsylvania, attests to this surge (McGann, 2021, p. 47). The index shows that the number of think tanks in Bahrain has grown from three in 2008 to 15 in 2020. During the same period, Kuwait jumped from eight to 16, while in Oman, there were three think tanks listed in the 2020 UPenn index, up from zero in 2008. In Qatar, the index recorded 15 think tanks in 2020, up from a single think tank in 2008. In Saudi Arabia, the number rose from three to 13 think tanks during the same period. According to the index reports, the UAE saw a surge from four think tanks in 2008 to sixteen in 2020. Thus, Gulf countries' total number of think tanks increased from 19 in 2008 to 78 in 2020 (McGann, 2008, p. 14; McGann, 2021, p. 47).

Figure 1: Think Tanks in the Gulf: 2008-2020

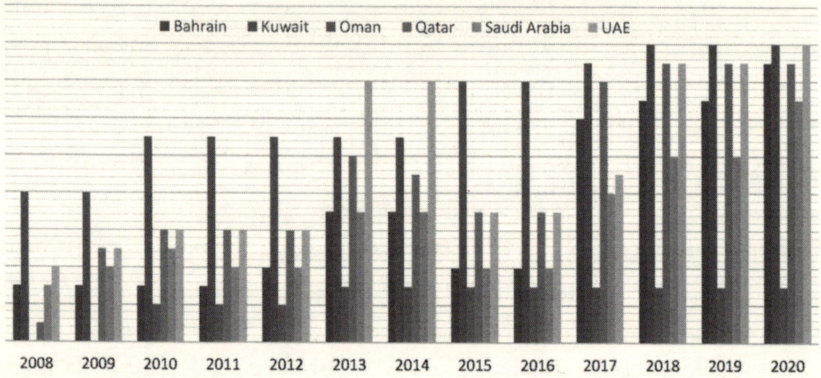

Source: This figure draws on data from James G. McGann (2008-2021), *Global Go To Think Tanks index reports,* University of Pennsylvania, Think Tanks and Civil Societies Program (2021, p. 47; 2020, p. 45; 2019, p. 39; 2018, p. 40; 2017, p. 29; 2016, p. 33; 2015, p. 56; 2014, p. 23; 2012, p. 38, 2011, p. 31, 2010, p. 25; 2009, p. 17; 2018; p. 15).

Think tanks in the GCC countries are a relatively recent phenomenon. It is only in the last few years that Gulf think tanks have seen significant developments in their role and influence. This is because think tanks require relative autonomy, channels of communication with decision-makers and direct engagement with public opinion and intellectual/political elites. Moreover, given the absence of organised legal frameworks in which think tanks can operate in GCC countries, they are required to register as non-profit organisations with a commercial license.

The first wave of think tanks in GCC countries emerged in the 1990s when several research centres funded by state institutions were established. During this phase, strategy-oriented think tanks were also set up, such as the Emirates Center for Strategic Studies and Research (ECSSR). These developments were connected to the communication and information revolution and the expansion of educated intellectual elites in these countries (Koch, 2014, pp. 162-163). In addition, the transformations in the Gulf region following the Iraqi invasion of Kuwait in August 1990 also led to an increased demand for think tanks and security/political consulting firms.

The second wave of think tanks in the new millennium saw the emergence of quasi-independent think tanks. There was also a growing trend towards opening branches of global think tanks in the Gulf, such as the RAND-Qatar Policy Institute in coordination with the Qatar Foundation in 2003 (RAND, n.d.). The Brookings Institution opened an office in Doha in 2007 (Brookings, 2007), known as the Brookings Doha Center, while the International Institute for Strategic Studies (IISS) opened a branch in Bahrain in 2009 (*IISS*, 2009). In addition, with the turn of the new millennium, some new Gulf think tanks have sprung up to support civil society and human rights, such as the Tawasul Center, founded in August 2008 in Oman (Tawasul, n.d., b). It aims to empower civil society organisations, publish various policy papers on societal issues and organise conferences and seminars to raise public awareness on civil society matters (Tawasul, n.d., a).

In 2002, the Bahrain Center for Human Rights was established as a non-profit, non-governmental organisation after registering with the Ministry of Labour and Social Development. Although the authorities decided to shut down the centre in November 2004, it continues to carry on its work through foreign and domestic support (Bahrain Center for Human Rights, n.d.). This second wave was connected to several political and economic transformations taking place in the Middle East. First, the increasing pressure on governments, as unemployment rates among educated youth soared, while satellite dishes and foreign television channels provided platforms for oppositional voices from outside the region to influence it from within. Moreover, the US invaded Iraq in 2003 amidst increasing US pressure to promote democracy in the region, and there were also marked changes in the threats surrounding the Gulf. This was evident both in terms of escalating terrorist threats within countries in the region and the growing spectre of Iran and rising Iranian interference in the internal affairs of neighbouring Arab countries (Bensahel et al., 2004, pp. 299-308). These factors produced a state of uncertainty and spurred efforts to formulate new proposals for achieving stability, both within the Gulf and among regional allies.

The third wave of think tanks, which began in 2011, saw a trend in the opposite direction towards national think tanks in GCC countries. The branch offices of the German Konrad Adenauer Foundation (KAS) and US-based National Democratic Institute in the UAE were both shut down in 2012. The reason given for the closures was alleged licensing violations

(Abdurabb, 2012). The branch office of the RAND Corporation in Abu Dhabi was also shut down in December 2012, though RAND declined to provide a reason for the closure at the time (Kasolowsky, 2012). In December 2013, the contract between the Qatar Foundation and RAND was terminated. In this case, the stated cause was RAND's failure to carry out a development project in the education sector in Qatar, which it had launched in 2003 (Khatri, 2013).

A limited number of foreign think tanks could hold on, especially those with established connections to ruling regimes. A report in *The Guardian* in December 2016 noted that it had found documents indicating that the IISS had received £25 million in donations from governmental institutions in Bahrain since 2011. These donations had been used to fund the IISS branch in Bahrain, while the Manama Dialogue received £14.9 million in funding between 2011 and 2016. The IISS stated that its agreement with Bahrain "expressly gives the IISS full freedom to develop the agenda [of the Manama Dialogue] and invite participants in line with priorities it judges to be important to encourage strong debate on regional issues and facilitate important diplomatic contacts" (Evans, 2016, para 18).

Meanwhile, many national think tanks were launched, most of which published their materials in both English, Arabic, as well as in other languages, such as Persian (Farsi). These think tanks included the Orient Research Center, which opened in mid-2011 in Dubai (Orient Research Center, n.d.), the Emirates Policy Center in September 2013 in Abu Dhabi (Emirates Policy Center, n.d.), and TRENDS Research and Advisory in 2014 in Abu Dhabi (TRENDS, n.d.). There were other think tanks founded in Saudi Arabia, such as Rasanah: the International Institute for Iranian Studies, which opened in 2016 in Riyadh, and the King Abdullah Petroleum Studies and Research Center in 2013, also in Riyadh (KAPSARC, n.d.).

During this period, the surge in think tanks is tied to the Arab Spring uprisings, the political transformations in the Middle East, and escalating internal conflicts in certain countries, such as Syria, Iraq, Yemen, and Libya. There have also been growing threats from terrorist organisations, especially ISIS, which in 2014 had declared the establishment of its own quasi-state within areas under its control in Syria and Iraq. During this time, GCC countries also announced that they would help organise some global events, such as Qatar hosting the 2022 FIFA World Cup (Government Communications Office, n.d.). Similarly, the UAE announced in February 2012 that it had formed a Higher Committee for Hosting the World Expo in 2020 (*The National,* 2012). The fast-paced and unexpected changes in the region during these years led to an increased demand for think tank services.

Security Parameters for the Region

The views of Gulf think tanks about regional security can be analysed by conducting a sample analysis of think tank materials published between 2011 and 2020. To conduct this analysis, think tanks were selected based on two main criteria: (1) proximity to centres of power (this could be determined by looking at the "About us" section of the think tank's website and ascertaining whether there was some kind of official cooperation with government agencies or joint activities with government ministries); and (2) an actively-updated website with readily-accessible publications. Gulf think tanks broadly define the geographic parameters of Gulf security. Security concerns extend into Asia and the Horn of Africa due to their geographical proximity and the potential security threats. Any upheaval in these regions could lead to instability in the Gulf and vice versa. For example, an analysis published by Rasanah indicated that Iran was attempting to expand its influence in the Maldives and in so doing, it would pose a threat to peace and stability in the Middle East (al-Maraghi, 2016).

An analysis published by the ECSSR suggested that Gulf countries could be seen as part of the "Greater Indian Ocean region" (ECSSR, 2013) as has also been argued in pieces published by the Emirates Policy Center. One such article claimed that Afghanistan's stability had a direct impact on regional security for Gulf countries. Thus, this prompted both Saudi Arabia and the UAE to help maintain peace and work towards achieving security, stability, and development in Afghanistan (Emirates Policy Center, 2013).

Other analyses indicated that instability in the Gulf would likewise have negative implications for Asia and the Horn of Africa. Many studies produced by Qatari think tanks, for example, have examined the rivalries between Qatar, the UAE, and Saudi Arabia to exert influence over the Horn of Africa, especially after the Gulf crisis, which had implications for Qatar's national security. For example, Al-Jazeera Center for Studies in Qatar published articles warning against efforts to shift the Gulf crisis from the Middle East to the Horn of Africa or clamp down Qatar in that region (Al-Jazeera Center for Studies, 2016a; Arab, 2017).

Threats to Regional Security

Recent publications of Gulf think tanks demonstrate a growing emphasis on traditional security threats, with a lesser focus on non-traditional threats, due to lingering concerns over non-state actors, such as terrorist organisations. For example, the Emirates Policy Center stated that the 2011 Arab Spring revolutions created an environment conducive to the spread of terrorist organisations (Emirates Policy Center, 2015). Most Gulf think tanks expressed concerns that the coronavirus pandemic would provide an opportunity for terrorist organisations to spread. It was argued that some terrorist groups, such as the Houthis and Hezbollah, have offered medical services and aid to their countries' citizens and this could help improve their image and bolster legitimacy (Mohamed, 2020; ECSSR, 2020; Abdo, 2020).

A majority of the Gulf think tanks agree that Iran poses a growing threat to regional security. Some analyses from Qatari think tanks blame the UAE and Saudi Arabia for the spread of Iranian influence in the region. For example, one analysis published by the Al-Jazeera Center for Studies stated that "Saudi policies are at odds with the process of democratic transition and paved the way for the Iranian-aligned Houthis to carry out a coup against the transitional government in fall 2014" (Al-Jazeera Center for Studies, 2019). Although Qatari think tanks have opposed Iran's support for the Houthis, Iran's support for Qatar after the Gulf boycott led to stronger relations between the two sides. On this note, one Al-Jazeera Center for Studies analysis stated that "Iran's opposition to the Qatar boycott, including opening its airspace to Qatari planes, as well as Kuwait and Oman's anxieties about Saudi aggression, have resulted in friendlier relations between Tehran, Doha, Kuwait, and Muscat" (Al-Jazeera Center for Studies, 2019).

While Qatari think tanks have held certain reservations about Iran's policies, especially its policy on Syria, Yemen, and Bahrain, they have underlined that there is also a serious possibility for normalised relations with Iran considering common religious, cultural, and political grounds (Al-Jazeera Center for Studies, 2016b). The Gulf Center for Studies and Research in Kuwait has adopted a similar approach, arguing that Gulf countries want peaceful coexistence with Tehran, as is evident in the levels of commercial exchange already taking place between them. However, there have also been some disputes, as Tehran's interests in Yemen, Iraq, and Syria are at odds with the Gulf's (Gulf Center for Studies and Research, 2019).

Many Gulf think tanks believe in the need for a new strategy in dealing with Tehran. The strategy of extreme pressure on Iran has only led to greater Houthi threats in the region. Counter attacks are a central part of the strategy of Iranian deterrence (Maloncy, 2019). Tehran may also counter this pressure in other ways, such as increasing attacks on Saudi infrastructure or US interests in the Gulf or offensives at sea using its navy or the Iranian Revolutionary Guard Corps (Raine, 2019). Therefore, some Emirati think tanks have called for developing a unified Arab strategy against the Iranian threat. This, according to them, would start gradually with a partial boycott and then lead to the formation of a joint Arab force to preserve Gulf security, in cooperation with Western allies, but without fully relying upon them. These think tanks have also called for resolving conflicts among Arab states and maintaining a united Gulf front to ensure the success of this strategy (Emirates Policy Center, 2018b; ECSSR, 2019a).

On the other hand, some Saudi think tanks hold that Iran cannot have a seat at the negotiation table until after ratcheting up pressures and regional/international isolation against Iran, or even perhaps after the US launches a military campaign against it (Abo El-Kasem, 2020, p. 26). Some Gulf think tanks are also concerned about the rising Turkish influence in the region after 2011. Analyses published by IISS Bahrain and the Al-Jazeera Center for Studies suggest that the Syrian crisis was a turning point for Turkey's role in the region (Raine, 2017; Özkizilcik & Yeşiltaş, 2019). Emirati think tanks have warned that the growing Turkish influence may undermine regional stability. For example, the

ECSSR stated that Ankara was supplying arms and equipment to the National Unity Government in Libya in its struggle against the UAE-backed Libyan National Army. This analysis argued that Turkey's intervention was part of a foreign policy to interfere in all regional conflicts to broaden its regional influence and secure its interests, thereby undermining stability (ECSSR, 2019d). The Emirates Policy Center also cautioned about Qatari-Turkish axis, as well as the mutual understandings and visits happening to covertly pursue this agenda (Emirates Policy Center, 2018c, p. 14).

Meanwhile, Qatari think tanks do not seem concerned about Turkish expansion in the region. For example, an analysis published by the Arab Center for Research and Policy Studies in Qatar (2018) highlighted Turkish support for Doha after the Gulf crisis, arguing that the "involvement of an important regional player like Turkey in the crisis will force the countries imposing the blockade and trying to isolate Qatar to rethink their calculations." An analysis published by Brookings Doha also claimed that Ankara posed a threat to the UAE and Saudi Arabia's interests, but not to Qatar's (Vertin, 2019). This is because, it argued, that Ankara funds the Muslim Brotherhood, which the UAE considers to be an "existential threat." It further highlighted that Ankara competes with the UAE and Saudi Arabia over regional influence in the Middle East, Horn of Africa, Red Sea and the western Indian Ocean. The analysis additionally underlined that the "Turkish model," which combines Islamic values and democratic elections, poses an existential threat to Gulf monarchies (Vertin, 2019).

The Role of International Actors

Despite the relative drop in US interest in the Middle East, most publications from both national and foreign think tanks in GCC countries have emphasised the American role in protecting the Gulf from various threats, especially the threat of terrorism and Iran. Emirati and Saudi think tanks see the US as a bulwark against terrorist threats (ECSSR, 2019c). They believe that US involvement in Syria and Iraq also prevents the spread of Iranian influence either south to the Gulf or west to Jordan and Syria. Washington, therefore, has the power to counter any sudden Iranian movement in the region (Iraqi Studies Unit, 2018; Rasanah,

2019b). An article published by the Brookings Doha affirmed that the US still has the power to impose the rules and parameters of war. The symbolic weight of US presence in the Middle East should not be underestimated; without it, the ISIS threat could resurface again, and Iran could establish a land bridge from Iran to Lebanon and the Mediterranean Sea (Alaaldin, 2019).

Although Qatari think tanks agree about the importance of the US role in the region, they had some reservations about Washington's stance towards Saudi Arabia and the UAE during the Gulf crisis. For example, a seminar held by the Al-Jazeera Center for Studies, in cooperation with Georgetown University in Qatar and the Al-Jazeera Network, suggested that Washington was one of the key actors in the Gulf crisis and was demonstrably biased towards Saudi Arabia and the UAE. This had negative ramifications on Washington's role in the region and resulted in greater influence for other international and regional forces, such as Russia, Iran and Turkey (Al-Jazeera Center for Studies, 2018a). It is, therefore, not surprising that Qatari think tanks seemed relieved about Biden's victory since they saw this as an opportunity to resolve Gulf disputes (Al-Jazeera Center for Studies, 2020). Furthermore, an analysis published by the Arab Center for Research and Policy Studies stated that "Saudi Arabia tried to preempt any potential pressures that the new US administration might exert upon it…and made clear that the decision to resolve the crisis with Qatar was its own sovereign choice" (Arab Center or Research and Policy Studies, 2021).

Meanwhile, Emirati and Saudi think tanks discussed potential regional security arrangements in the Biden era, especially given the likelihood of returning to the negotiation table with Iran. There is a general understanding that the return of the nuclear deal with Iran will inevitably occur. The Saudi and UAE think tanks thus provided recommendations to mitigate losses and reduce threats that might result from such an agreement. Mohammed bin Saqr al-Sulami, head of Rasanah, indicated that the US administration needed to focus on negotiating three issues simultaneously: Iran's support of Houthi militias, its support for Hamas and Islamic Jihad in Palestine, and uranium enrichment. He stated that the US should consult countries in the region, involve them throughout the resolution process and that they should have representatives present at the negotiations (Al-Sulami, 2020). The head of the Emirates Policy Center, Ebtesam al-Ketbi, wrote in a joint article with Amos Yadlin, executive director of the Institute for National Security Studies at Tel Aviv University that:

> If Washington insists on bringing back the agreement of 2015, ignoring the concerns of its regional allies, then we would advise our governments to not get involved in a vicious fight to oppose a policy that the US intends to pursue. Instead, governments should focus on opening back channels of communication with the White House in order to be able to ensure that their opinions, concerns, and interests are taken into account (Yadlin and Ketbi, 2021, para 11)

Most Gulf think tanks do not see an alternative to the US role in the Middle East. Russia is trying to broaden its influence in the region to counter NATO's expansion in Eastern Europe, prevent the spread of terrorism in those areas, and circumvent the sanctions imposed upon it (ECSSR, 2016). However, Moscow is aware of the limits of the role it can play and the rules of engagement—it will not cross certain red lines that could provoke Washington's ire (North African Studies Unit, 2017).

The European position in the Middle East does not diverge significantly from that of Russia; in both cases, pragmatic concerns are at the forefront. Most European Union (EU) countries want to promote their economic interests, prevent the spread of terrorist threats to Europe, and stop the waves of illegal immigration and refugees. There are also concerns about European support for Iran, especially from Emirati, Saudi, and Bahraini think tanks (Rasanah, 2019a, pp. 206-219). The role of Asian countries usually only pertains to development and economic issues in the Middle East, and rarely with regards to their impact on regional security. However, some think tanks expect to see China become more involved in Middle East security affairs in the future, as Beijing's economic interests in the region expand, in addition to its Belt and Road Initiative (BRI). The Emirates Policy Center argues that China will need to protect the huge investments made through the BRI, which will require greater military involvement beyond its borders (Emirates Policy Center, 2017).

Andrew Scobell, a senior political scientist at the RAND Corporation, made a similar argument in a study published by the Center for Regional and International Studies at Georgetown University in Qatar during his involvement with the China and Middle East working group at Georgetown University in Qatar. He agreed that China would seek to protect its investments in light of escalating traditional and non-traditional security threats (Scobell, 2018, pp. 3-4). Some Gulf think tanks also point to India's future role in the region's security. An analysis by Brookings Doha mentioned the possibility of India becoming involved in security discussions about Iran, as it tries to pursue policies that balance between the Gulf and the US on the one hand and Iran on the other (Pethiyagoda, 2018).

Regional Security Arrangements

Most Gulf think tanks are on the same page regarding the central role of Gulf countries in formulating any future regional security agreements while also including some other regional forces in these arrangements. However, some Qatari think tanks have expressed doubts about the possibility of resolving conflicts in the region in the light of disputes within the Gulf, as well as the growing power of Saudi Arabia and the UAE, which have developed goals at odds with GCC objectives (Al-Jazeera Center for Studies, 2018b). Meanwhile, Emirati think tanks have affirmed the importance of the alliance with Saudi Arabia in maintaining security and stability in the region. The two states previously worked together in the US-led international coalition against ISIS. Additionally, Saudi Arabia is trying to establish a unified Arab position against the threats that the region faces, particularly from Iranian expansionism (ECSSR, 2019b).

Some Saudi think tanks have indicated the need to re-examine existing security alliances in the region. They have also considered the possibility of establishing new alliances in the form of an "Arab NATO." A study published by Rasanah argued that there were many opportunities for such an alliance to succeed in light of the success of Gulf security cooperation and the Gulf's ability to deal with diverse security threats: the 2011 protests in Bahrain; foiling of many attempted terrorist and espionage operations in Bahrain, Kuwait, and Saudi Arabia; and the joint realisation of and cooperation among security agencies in GCC countries against the urgently escalating Iranian threat (Ghonaimy, 2019, pp. 1-23). However, the study also stressed the unlikelihood of bringing all countries in the region into this alliance, given the many disputes on various issues: stances on political Islamist groups; the conflicting relationships that different countries have with Iran; and disparate understandings about the nature of the alliance, its goals, and whether to deal with the Iranian threat or regional threats, in general.

The same view is adopted by the Gulf Center for Studies and Research in Kuwait that divisions among Gulf countries after the Arab Spring revolutions, as well as the good economic relations that some Gulf countries (such as Qatar and Oman) have with Iran, makes it problematic to think about forming an "Arab NATO." Additionally, although all Gulf countries are aware of the threat that Iran poses, they disagree over the appropriate mechanisms for dealing with Iran, whether by resorting to military action or pursuing diplomatic negotiations (Gulf Center for Studies and Research, 2019). Some Emirati think tanks want to include Israel in future regional security arrangements. Two years before the Israeli-UAE peace arrangement, Ketbi, president of the EPC, stated in her closing remarks at the fifth Abu Dhabi Strategic Debate (held in coordination with the Ministry of Foreign Affairs and International Cooperation) that the "deal of the century" marked the start of new security arrangements in the region, which would lead to the resolution of the Arab-Israeli conflict, stability in Iraq, and building of a new state in Syria (Emirates Policy Center, 2018a).

Conclusion

Although the Arab revolutions of 2011 were not originally a focus for think tanks, the regional conditions that emerged in the wake of 2011 prompted think tanks to search for solutions to restore regional stability and mitigate the consequences of the uprisings. The Gulf crisis marked a turning point that has reshaped perceptions of GCC think tanks regarding the sources of threats to regional security and mechanisms for dealing with these threats. In these cases, the think tanks' visions closely mirror the official policies later announced in these countries. This applies to both national and foreign think tanks in GCC countries.

The paper demonstrates that some policies executed by GCC countries were curiously similar to policy proposals of think tanks that were announced previously. One such case was that of the Emirates Policy Center's proposal for developing diplomatic and economic relations with Israel to preserve regional stability, released just before the official decision to normalise relations with Israel. Despite the disparities among GCC think-tank views, there are also some similarities in their geographical definitions of regional security. Most of them see the security sphere extending to Asian countries and the Horn of Africa; additionally, most focus on traditional security threats.

According to think tanks, the most significant threats to GCC countries are terrorist groups and Iran. However, Qatari and Kuwaiti think tanks have indicated that it might be possible to establish normal relations with Tehran and settle regional differences. By contrast, the positions of the Emirati and Saudi think tanks seemed to be stricter on Iran. Emirati and Saudi think tanks consider Turkey a threat, while Qatari think tanks support the Turkish role in the region and have drawn attention to its role in alleviating the blockade on Qatar and curbing Saudi and Emirati influence. At the same time, Israel is no longer seen as posing a regional threat.

Most think tanks in the GCC countries acknowledge the significance of the US role in regional arrangements in the Middle East. Although they note the growing involvement of certain other international players, such as the Asian powers, Russia, and the European Union, they do not consider any of these forces to be a suitable substitute for the US's role in regional security. The majority of GCC think tanks are focused on their own country's role in any potential regional security alliance, with corresponding differences depending on the country in question. Notably, think tanks in GCC countries have contributed to the rise of "securitization" of the discourse at both the regional and international levels. The think tanks' approach to regional developments places security at the forefront and indicates that confronting security threats and preserving national security has become the priority for these institutions.

References

Abdo, Geneive (2020). "Pandemic Politics: Fighting Extremist Groups during COVID-19," Brookings, 1 July at https://www.brookings.edu/opinions/pandemic-politics-fighting-extremist-groups-during-covid-19/.

Abdurabb, K.T. (2012), "UAE Offices of Foreign Agencies Shut Down," *Arab News*, 6 April at https://www.arabnews.com/node/410280.

Abo El-Kasem, Mahmoud Hamdy (2020), "The Mutual Escalation Regarding the Nuclear File the Predominant Balances in the Course of the Crisis between the United States and Iran," Rasanah: International Institute for Iranian Studies, 12 February at https://rasanah-iiis.org/english/centre-for-researches-and-studies/the-mutual-escalation-regarding-the-nuclear-file-the-predominant-balances-in-the-course-of-the-crisis-between-the-united-states-and-iran/

Al-Jazeera Center for Studies (2016a), "Increasing Gulf Influence in the Horn of Africa," 7 November at http://studies.aljazeera.net/ar/centernews/2016/11/161107093800378.html.

Al-Jazeera Center for Studies (2016b), "Seminar: The Arab World and Iran … Challenges in the Relationship," https://bit.ly/3tzKb5n. Accessed on 15 December 2020.

Al-Jazeera Center for Studies (2018a), "Seminar with Al-Jazeera Center for Studies and Georgetown Qatar: Washington is No Longer the Only Player in the Gulf," 22 March at https://studies.aljazeera.net/ar/events/2018/03/180322055416587.html.

Al-Jazeera Center for Studies (2018b), "The UAE-Saudi Alliance: Cracks in the Foundation and Diminishing Feasibility," 28 November at http://studies.aljazeera.net/ar/reports/2018/11/181128122208215.html.

Al-Jazeera Center for Studies (2019), "Iran Faces a New Strategic Environment," https://bit.ly/3r04R4H. Accessed on 5 January 2021.

Al-Jazeera Center for Studies (2020), "Researchers in the Al-Jazeera Center for Studies Seminar Expect Improvement on Some Middle East Issues if Biden Wins," 28 October at https://studies.aljazeera.net/en/node/4817.

Alaaldin, Ranj (2019), "A Welcome Delay: The US Withdrawal from Syria," *ISPI Commentary*, Italian Institute for International Political Studies, 8 March at https://www.ispionline.it/sites/default/files/pubblicazioni/ispi_dossier_syraq_alaaldin_08.03.2019.pdf.

Alsulami, Mohammed (2020), "To Get Iran Right, Joe Biden Must Consult U.S. Middle East Allies," Rasanah: International Institute for Iranian Studies, 5 January at https://rasanah-iiis.org/english/?p=8628.

Arab, Kamal al-Din Sheikh Muhammad (2017). "Effects of the Gulf Crisis on Africa: Analysis of the Stances of Different Countries," Al-Jazeera Center for Studies, 20 June at https://studies.aljazeera.net/ar/reports/2017/06/170620104910363.html.

Arab Center for Research and Policy Studies (2018). "One Year after the Gulf Crisis: How Qatar Beat the Blockade," 4 June at https://www.dohainstitute.org/ar/PoliticalStudies/Pages/One-Year-On-Qatar-Beat-the-Blockade.aspx?fbclid=IwAR2Lj9_M705320c7HqRj1CRlo7jRVSVAWDgmEZVilDOpAi%20QpwHgKU2shTBc.

Arab Center for Research and Policy Studies (2021), "The Gulf Reconciliation Summit: Circumstances and the Significance of its Timing," 7 January at https://www.dohainstitute.org/ar/PoliticalStudies/Pages/The-Gulf-Reconciliation-Summit-Circumstances-and-Significance-of-its-Timing.aspx.

Bahrain Center for Human Rights (n.d.), "About," https://www.hhri.org/organisation/bahrain-center-for-human-rights/

Bensahel, Nora, Byman, Daniel L. and Pegahi, Nageen (2004), "Conclusions," in Bensahel, Nora and Byman, Daniel L. (eds.), *The Future Security Environment in the Middle East: Conflict, Stability, and Political Change*. Santa Monica, CA: RAND Corporation, pp. 299-315.

Brookings Institution (2007), "Brookings to Open Doha Center," 30 October at https://www.brookings.edu/news-releases/brookings-to-open-doha-center.

Emirates Center for Strategic Studies and Research (2013), "Sino-Indian Maritime Cooperation in the Indian Ocean: Implications for the GCC," 3 March at https://www.ecssr.ae/en/reports_analysis/sino-indian-maritime-cooperation-in-the-indian-ocean-implications-for-the-gcc/.

Emirates Center for Strategic Studies and Research (2016), "Has Russia Started to Give Up on al-Assad?" https://bit.ly/3u8USwe. Accessed on 8 January 2021.

Emirates Center for Strategic Studies and Research (2019a), "Arab Options in Confronting Iran, and What is Required of Them," 19 June at https://www.ecssr.ae/reports_analysis/%D8%AE%D9%8A%D8%A7%D8%25 Accessed on 20 November 2020.

Emirates Center for Strategic Studies and Research (2019b), "A Key Step to Contain Security Threats to the Gulf and Arab World," https://bit.ly/3r07GCP. Accessed on 20 November 2020.

Emirates Center for Strategic Studies and Research (2019c), "Pompeo's Middle East Trip … Examining the Outcomes and Implications," https://bit.ly/2QIEPaa. Accessed on 13 December 2020.

Emirates Center for Strategic Studies and Research (2019d), "What Role will Turkey Play in the Libyan Conflict?" https://bit.ly/3h3Yv3d. Accessed on 4 February 2021.

Emirates Center for Strategic Studies and Research (2020), "Despite Coronavirus, Combatting Terrorism Remains a Priority," https://bit.ly/38VQ44R. Accessed on 2 February 2021.

Emirates Policy Center (n.d.), "About Us," https://epc.ae/about-us.

Emirates Policy Center (2013), "Geopolitical Rivalry in Afghanistan, and the Regional Interests of Arabian Gulf Countries," 1 December at https://epc.ae/research-unit/165/unit/geopolitical-competition-in-afghanistan-and-regional-interests-of-arabian-gulf-countries/details.

Emirates Policy Center (2015), "Killing in the Name of Allah: Terrorist Groups, Structures, Trajectories and Ends," 5 November at https://epc.ae/research-unit/40/unit/killing-in-the-name-of-allah-terrorist-groups-structures-trajectories-and-ends/details.

Emirates Policy Center (2017), "The 'Belt and Road' Initiative: Geopolitical Implications for Iran," 24 May at https://epc.ae/ar/research-unit/307/unit/epc/details.

Emirates Policy Center (2018a), "Fifth Abu Dhabi Strategic Debate," Live Broadcast on YouTube [Video, at 33:07], 10-12 November at https://epc.ae/event/fifth-abu-dhabi-strategic-debate.

Emirates Policy Center (2018b), "Can the Houthis Block International Navigation Lanes in the Red Sea?" 15 February at https://epc.ae/ar/publication/254.

Emirates Policy Center (2018c), "Monthly Report on Turkey," Issue 12.

Evans, Rob (2016), "British Thinktank Received £25m from Bahraini Royals, Documents Reveal," *The Guardian*, 6 December at https://www.theguardian.com/world/2016/dec/06/british-thinktank-iiss-received-25m-from-bahraini-royals-documents-reveal.

Ghonaimy, Abdul Rauf Mostafa (2019), "The Arab NATO: Contexts, Challenges, and Chances of Success," Riyadh: Rasanah: International Institute for Iranian Studies, 29 July at https://rasanah-iiis.org/english/centre-for-researches-and-studies/the-arab-nato-contexts-challenges-and-chances-of-success/

Government Communications Office (n.d.), "2022 FIFA World Cup," https://www.gco.gov.qa/en/focus/2022-fifa-world-cup-qatar.

Gulf Center for Studies and Research (2019), "A Potential US-Iranian War could Spark a Sectarian War in the Region," 22 May at https://bit.ly/3s1fp53.

Kuwait News Agency (2009), "IISS: The World's Leading Think Tank in its Field—Bahrain FM," 29 September at https://www.kuna.net.kw/ArticlePrintPage.aspx?id=2028115&language=en.

Emirates Policy Center (2018), "The US Presence in Iraq post-ISIS: Characteristics, Goals, and Prospects," 22 February at https://epc.ae/ar/publication/252.

Kasolowsky, Raissa (2012), "UAE Shuts Down Office of US Research Institute RAND," Reuters, 20 December at https://www.reuters.com/article/us-emirates-rand-idUSBRE8BJ0K320121220.

Khatri, Shabina S. (2013), "Rand and Qatar Foundation Officially Part Ways after 10 Years," *Doha News*, December 23, https://www.dohanews.co/rand-and-qatar-foundation-officially-part-ways-after-10-years/.

King Abdullah Petroleum Studies and Research Center (KAPSARC) (n.d.), "About," https://www.kapsarc.org/about/.

Koch, Christian (2014), "Gulf Research Center (GRC): Promoting Social Development in the Arab Gulf Region," in McGann, James G. Viden, Anna and Rafferty Jillian (eds.), *How Think Tanks Shape Social Development Policies*. Philadelphia, PA: University of Pennsylvania Press, pp. 162-172.

Maloney, Suzanne (2019), "There is an Off-ramp in the US-Iran Crisis: How Not to Miss It," Brookings, 10 June at https://www.brookings.edu/opinions/there-is-an-off-ramp-in-the-u-s-iran-crisis/.

Ma'oz, Zeev (1997). *Regional Security in the Middle East: Past, Present, and Future.* New York: Routledge.

Al-Maraghi, Fathi (2016), "After Iranian Threats, Maldives Announces that Ties will be Cut-off with Tehran," Rasanah: International Institute for Iranian Studies, 18 May at https://rasanah-iiis.org/?p=869.

McGann, James G. (2008-2021). Global Go to Think Tanks Index Reports. University of Pennsylvania, Think Tanks and Civil Societies Program.

The National (2012), "UAE in Final Bid to Host World Expo 2020," 5 December at https://www.thenationalnews.com/uae/uae-in-final-bid-to-host-world-expo-2020-1.367106.

Nicander, Lars (2015), "The Role of Think Tanks in the U.S. Security Policy Environment," *International Journal of Intelligence and Counterintelligence*, 28(3), pp. 480-501.

Emirates Policy Center (2017), "Russian Interference in Libya: Implications, Risks, and Future Scenarios," https://bit.ly/3eQmVvO. Accessed on 2 December 2020.

Orient Research Center (n.d.), "About Us," https://www.orientresearchcentre.com/en/about-us-en/.

Özkizilcik, Ömer and Yeşiltaş, Murat (2019), "Turkish Policy in Syria and its Prospects from a Turkish Perspective," Al-Jazeera Center for Studies, 12 March at https://studies.aljazeera.net/ar/reports/2019/03/190312095058935.html.

Pautz, Hartwig (2011), "Revisiting the Think-Tank Phenomenon," *Public Policy and Administration*, 26(4), pp. 419-435.

Pethiyagoda, Kadira (2018), "India's Pursuit of Strategic and Economic Interests in Iran," *Brookings Analysis*, September, Issue 23, Brookings Center, Doha https://www.brookings.edu/wp-content/uploads/2018/09/Indias-Pursuit-of-Strategic and-Economic-Interests-in-Iran-Arabic.pdf.

Raine, John (2017), "Iran, Russia and Turkey are Winners in Fractured Middle East," *IISS Analysis*, 1 December at The International Institute for Strategic Studies, Manama, https://www.iiss.org/blogs/analysis/2017/12/iran-russia-turkey.

Raine, John (2019), "Iran in the Gulf: Signaling, Skirmishing, or War?" *IISS Analysis*, 21 June at The International Institute for Strategic Studies, Manama, https://www.iiss.org/blogs/analysis/2019/06/iran-in-the-gulf.

Mohamed, Ola Rafiq (2020), "The Impact of the Coronavirus Crisis on Terrorism: Patterns and Expectations,"The Emirates Policy Center, 6 May at https://epc.ae/brief/the-impact-of-coronavirus-crisis-on-terrorism-patterns-and-expectations.

RAND International. RAND-Qatar Policy Institute (2003-2013). https://www.rand.org/international/qatar.html.

Rasanah: International Institute for Iranian Studies (2019a), *Iran in 2018: Annual Strategic Report,* No. 2, https://rasanah-iiis.org/english/wp-content/uploads/sites/2/2019/03/Iran-in-2018.pdf.

Rasanah: International Institute for Iranian Studies (2019b), "The US Designation of the IRGC as a Terror Group: Connotations and Iran's Reaction," 15 April at https://rasanah-iiis.org/english/?p=6446.

Scobell, Andrew (2018), "China's Search for Security in the Greater Middle East," in Reardon-Anderson, James (ed.), *The Red Star and the Crescent: China and the Middle East.* New York, NY: Oxford University Press, pp. 13-36.

Stone, Diane (2013), "The 'Policy Research' Knowledge Elite and Global Policy Processes," in Josselin, Daphné and Wallace, William (Eds.), *Non-State Actors in World Politics.* London: Palgrave Macmillan, pp. 113-132.

Tawasul (n.d. a), About Tawasul. https://tawasul.co.om/.

Tawasul (n.d. b), Know more about us. https://tawasul.co.om/abtus.html.

TRENDS Research and Advisory (n.d.), "About Us," https://trendsresearch.org/about-us/.

Urrutia, Olivier (2013), "The Role of Think Tanks in the Definition and Application of Defence Policies and Strategies," *Policy Papers,* No. 2, Madrid: Spanish Institute of Strategic Studies, https://revista.ieee.es/article/download/340/572.

Vertin, Zach (2019), "Turkey and the New Scramble for Africa: Ottoman Designs or Unfounded Dears?" Brookings, 19 May at https://www.brookings.edu/research/turkey-and-the-new-scramble-for-africa-ottoman-designs-or-unfounded-fears/.

Yadlin, Amos and Al-Ketbi, Ebtesam (2021), "The US Must Move Forward, Not Back, on Iran," Emirates Policy Center, 28 January at https://epc.ae/brief/the-united-states-must-move-forward-not-back-on-iran.

Youness, Mohamed Abdallah (2018), "The Continuity and Change of the Gulf States' Image in the Israeli Epistemic Community," in Khatib, Dania Koleilat and Maziad, Marwa (Eds.), *The Arab Gulf States and the West: Perceptions and Realities—Opportunities and Perils.* Oxon: Routledge.

6. The Jasmine Revolution in Tunisia

Nina Slama

On 17 December 2010, a desperate Tunisian merchant named Mohammed Bouazizi could not stand the mistreatment he experienced at the hands of the Tunisian police. He set himself on fire in front of a municipality office in Sidi Bouzid. His act led to nationwide protests against unemployment, poverty, and corruption, known as the "Jasmine Revolution," representing the Tunisian national flower's purity, tolerance, and sweetness. The protests were met with excessive force by the Tunisian police causing the death of dozens. This led the protesters to call for the resignation of President Zine al-Abidine Ben-Ali, who had ruled the country for more than two decades. Ben-Ali tried to appease the popular uprising by assuring he would promote political and economic reforms (Yıldırım, 2017). Nevertheless, the protesters continued to express their discontentment by confronting the police.

Ben-Ali and his family were compelled to flee Tunisia and find refuge in Saudi Arabia. The Tunisian people toppled Ben-Ali's government in 28 days. The Jasmine Revolution inspired people across the Middle East and North Africa (MENA) to call for political change in their respective countries. It was considered the spark that triggered the Arab Spring and this chapter focuses on the Jasmine Revolution and present the political, economic and societal changes it brought to Tunisia. It will also show how the government has dealt with the eruption of the Covid-19 crisis to maintain political and economic stability.

The Jasmine Revolution

During the 1980s and the 1990s, large protests erupted in the MENA region following the decreasing oil prices. Every time the leaders of Egypt, Morocco, Tunisia, Algeria and Jordan wanted to liberalise their economies and remove food subsidies, people protested in the streets. A majority of countries introduced economic and political reforms, nonetheless. On 7 November 1987, Zine al-Abidine Ben-Ali became the President of Tunisia after his predecessor President Habib Bourguiba was considered physically and mentally unfit to stay in office. Ben-Ali created a good educational system, a prospering middle class and an efficient public sector. He kept a stranglehold on the political system, not allowing any expression of dissent against his government. As a result, Islamists, who were at the forefront of opposing his policies, were oppressed and not allowed to prosper.

Nonetheless, Ben-Ali was seen as a reformist leader in the West for his efforts at bringing economic reforms and liberalisation that brought stability to Tunisia. The West perceived Ben-Ali as an important leader who fought terrorism, cooperated with the European Union (EU) on migration and welcomed Western investors. However, he did not manage to provide jobs for the educated Tunisian youth and could not fulfil economic promises (Hamid, 2011; Pevná, 2011; Maalej, 2012; Bishku, 2013; Günay and Sommavilla, 2020).

The Jasmine Revolution erupted in rural areas of Tunisia and later in the big cities. It started in the town of Sidi Bouzid, where the rate of unemployment was high, following the self-immolation of Bouazizi, a young Tunisian street vendor, mistreated by the Tunisian police and local officials, as they harassed him, humiliated him and confiscated his merchandise (Abdullatif, 2013; Bishku, 2013; El Meehy, 2013; Hess, 2013; Özekin and Akkaş, 2014). His tragic death sparked protests in different areas of Tunisia. The police used excessive violence, and the insurgent cities were put under siege. The revolt was expanded to the national level and was led by the middle class.

The international community named this uprising the Jasmine Revolution. However, the demonstrators preferred to name this as the Revolution of Dignity and Freedom since they called for civil liberties, the resignation of Ben-Ali and restoration of dignity in the country (Mabrouk, 2011; Aleya-Sghaier, 2012; El Meehy, 2013; Alvi, 2014; Kılavuz, 2020). Tunisia suffered from corruption, unemployment, and a lack of economic prospects and freedom. In addition, the country was considered to be a police state (Mabrouk, 2011; Alvi, 2014). The Tunisian police used excessive force against the demonstrators. Ben-Ali's party, the Democratic Constitutional Rally (RCD), deployed its militia forces to oppress the demonstrators and terrorise the opponents. These militia forces included lower classes and criminals. During the upheaval, 338 people were killed, and 2,147 were wounded (Aleya-Sghaier, 2012; Bishku, 2013; Hmed, 2015).

Role of General Rashid Ammar and the Tunisian Army in the Revolution

The Tunisian chief of staff General Rashid Ammar played an important role in ousting Ben-Ali to exile. The army was responsible for maintaining law and order in the country (Hilal, 2012). It was smaller than the police, marginalised, not well funded, and focused primarily on border defence (Barany, 2013). It was not bound to Ben-Ali by ethnic, tribal or sectarian ties (Mansfield and Snyder, 2012) and did not want to act against its own people during the upheaval (Kumaraswamy, 2011; Bellin, 2012; Barany, 2013; Özekin and Akkaş, 2014), as it came from the same ethnoreligious group of the demonstrators (Levinson, 2012). It was apolitical and did not have any incentive to keep Ben-Ali in power. Its main role during the Jasmine Revolution was to separate Ben-Ali's forces from the demonstrators to protect the latter.

Ben-Ali decided to fire General Ammar and put him under house arrest on 12 January 2011, as the latter did not follow his orders of using force against the protestors in the towns of Sidi Bouzid and Kasserine. On 14 January 2011, Ben-Ali and his family were compelled to leave Tunisia and find refuge in Saudi Arabia after 23 years in power. He was the first Arab leader to be ousted following a relatively peaceful uprising, which was not followed by civil war or foreign intervention (Hamid, 2011; Schraeder, 2012; Singh, 2012; Chakchouk et al., 2013; Koehler, 2017). The Ben-Ali family led an ostentatious life with funds from drug trafficking, corruption, money laundering, extortion, and preferential treatment of business friends (Levey, 2011; Maalej, 2012).

Ben-Ali and his wife were prosecuted in absentia by a Tunisian court and sentenced to 35 years in prison (Amara, 2011). However, Saudi Arabia refused to extradite them to Tunisia (Alvi, 2014). Prime Minister Mohamed Ghannouchi decided to reinstate General Ammar on 14

January 2011, and the popularity of the army increased since it ensured the safety of the citizens and fought the militia forces of Ben-Ali's regime (Aleya-Sghaier, 2012; Mühlberger, 2015). The Jasmine Revolution inspired many people across the MENA region to call for political change in their respective countries. It sparked popular uprisings in Egypt, Libya, Yemen, Bahrain, Syria and many other countries (Singh, 2012; Ma'oz, 2012; Hess, 2013; Alvi, 2014).

Role of Social Media and Online Activism in the Revolution

Social media platforms played a significant role in permitting Tunisian activists to criticise their government publicly and organise extended anti-regime demonstrations (Khondker, 2011; Graziano, 2012; Hess, 2013; Flynn, 2018). The security forces' violence was documented in cell phone cameras and published on social media networks, such as Twitter and Facebook, and satellite television, such as Al-Jazeera and Al-Arabiya. These platforms helped gather and mobilise thousands of people, organise mass demonstrations and gain global support (Khondker, 2011; Bellin, 2012; Rousselin, 2016; Smidi and Shahin, 2017; Letsa and Wilfahrt, 2018). The Tunisian diaspora was the main contributor to Tunisian activism on the Web. They had free access to the Internet and were not restricted or censored, like their fellow citizens living inside Tunisia (Lecompte, 2009; Graziano, 2012).

Anonymous activists carried out Operation Tunisia, in which they shut down several government servers and provided access to information that criticised the Tunisian government. They enabled the Tunisian people to access information and share it quickly, after years of media platforms being controlled and manipulated by Ben-Ali's regime and this enhanced the scope of the Jasmine Revolution (Howard and Hussain; 2011; Khondker, 2011; Alqudsi, 2012; Aman and Jayroe, 2013; Müller and Hübner, 2014; Jordan, 2015; Smidi and Shahin, 2017). Social media networks also enabled women to be politically involved in the revolution and mobilise people in the streets. Islamist movements and conservative people did not want to see the participation of women in the political and societal spheres. Women were also tortured and raped during the upheaval. However, they could promote gender justice and rights for women to a certain extent (Aleya-Sghaier, 2012; Radsch and Khamis, 2013; Donnalyn, 2014, Manea, 2014).

The Tunisian youth was at the forefront of the revolution, although they were not politically or civically engaged (Gabsi, 2017). A majority of them came from Kasserine, Sfax, Sousse and Tunis. Most of them were unemployed, students and civil servants. Before the eruption of the revolution, they established different networks based on their place of residence, support of sports teams and their regions of origin. These networks created a sense of solidarity. The police were never welcome in their neighbourhoods. This is one of the reasons that led the youth to confront police forces to express their dissatisfaction with the inequalities in the country. The youth who came from privileged backgrounds also took part in the revolution since they could not foresee any future under Ben-Ali's rule. Most of them came from Manzah, Manar, Ariana, La Marsa and Carthage and were active on the internet and social media platforms. These platforms enabled them to be informed, share information and organise different rallies. However, they did not confront police forces as the youth from unprivileged backgrounds did (Aleya-Sghaier, 2012).

Interim Government and Political Transition

Under Article 57 of the Tunisian constitution of 1959, the speaker of the Tunisian parliament Fouad Mebassa became the interim president after Ben-Ali fled the country. Prime Minister Mohamed Ghannouchi wanted to fulfil the demands of the Tunisian people by giving general amnesty for political prisoners, abrogating the ban Ben-Ali imposed on political parties, which were considered dangerous and dissolving the RCD party (Aleya-Sghaier, 2012; Hilal, 2012; Yıldırım, 2017). However, Ghannouchi did not want to resign and promised to do so after the elections. His unwillingness to leave the government consolidated a coalition of leftists, Islamists, human rights activists, communists and trade unionists. Nevertheless, he established the Higher Commission for Political Reform, which comprised 155 members and was responsible for the democratic transition in Tunisia. Mohamed Ghannouchi tried to form two governments, which the people rejected for being related to Ben-Ali's party. He eventually resigned on 27 February 2011, and Mohammed Beji

Caid Essebsi became the interim Prime Minister (Hamid, 2011, Hilal, 2012; Murphy, 2013).

As the election date for the National Constituent Assembly (NCA) was proclaimed, a new election law was presented, and an independent electoral authority was established. Its role was to organise elections within four months. It dissolved the Tunisian constitution of 1958, drafted a new constitution and acted as a transitional government. When the numbers of voter registration were low, the independent election commission postponed the elections twice to extend the registration period and promote greater participation (Hilal, 2012; Murphy, 2012). The appointment of the High Commission for Political Reform and the relatively stable administrative institutions ensured an efficient and relatively peaceful political transition (Anderson, 2011; Hilal, 2012). The United States (US), the EU and other Western non-state actors contributed to the political transition by funding institution-building efforts, political parties, police forces training and administration. They believed that the democratisation process in Tunisia would lead to the end of Islamist extremism in the country. The US President Barak Obama increased the military aid to Tunisia to fight the Islamic State (IS) in Libya and the Sahel. Obama changed the status of Tunisia to a major non-NATO ally. The EU also provided military support to ensure border security and prevent terrorist infiltration and immigration from Africa to Europe (Günay and Sommavilla, 2020).

The Return of the Islamists to the Political Arena

After two decades in exile, Rached Ghannouchi and other Islamist Ennahda (revival in Arabic) movement leaders returned to Tunisia on 30 January 2011. The Tunisian people welcomed them since they were oppressed by the Ben-Ali regime (Özcan, 2018). The Islamic Tendency Movement (MTI) in Tunisia was established in 1981 and was led by Rached Ghannouchi and Abd al-Fatah Muru. This movement was oppressed by the Tunisian government and did not have any political power. When Ben-Ali came to power in 1987, the relations with the Islamists improved. In 1989, the MTI changed its name to Hizb Ennahda (Revival Party) and decided to accommodate itself to the secular concept of the state. Nevertheless, Ennahda was not allowed to be part of the political system and remained an illegal movement during Ben-Ali's rule. The leaders of Ennahda were imprisoned or exiled since Ben-Ali perceived them to be a threat to his regime, as they were gaining popularity among the people (Allani, 2009; Pevná, 2011; Hilal, 2012; McCarthy, 2014).

On 23 October 2011, Tunisia conducted its first democratic elections. These elections were relatively free, fair and non-violent. For the first time, the Tunisian people were able to participate in an election under the control of an independent electoral body (Aboussi, 2020). The Ennahda party won 89 of the 217 seats in the NCA. It established a moderate Islamic government and wanted to address economic, political and societal issues through reconciliation and national unity. Ennahda supported the constitutional process and even opposed the implementation of shari'a, or Islamic law, in the Tunisian constitution, although some members of Ennahda wanted to do so. This government comprised of the Congress for the Republic Party (CPR), a centre-left secular party that secured 29 seats and the Democratic Forum for Labour and Liberties (FDTL) party, a centre-left secular party that had 20 seats. This national unity government, which included Islamist and secular parties, was known as the Troika. The Secretary-General of Ennahda, Hamadi Jebali, became Prime Minister, and Ben Jafer from the FDTL became the president of the NCA. Moncef Marzouki, the leader of the CPR and a human rights activist, became the President of Tunisia on 12 December 2011 (Mansfield and Snyder, 2012; Ma'oz, 2012; Bishku, 2013; Cavatorta and Merone, 2013; Zemni, 2015).

Ennahda wanted to show its willingness to reconcile with secular and leftist leaders and politicians who were part of the old regime. This is why Ennahda accepted Mohammed Beji Caid Essebsi, a minister under Bourguiba and Ben-Ali governments, as the head of the interim cabinet on 15 March 2011 (Boubekeur, 2016). In addition, the leaders of Ennahda encouraged women to join the party and appointed Mehrezia Labidi as the vice-president of the Constituent Assembly. Labidi was the first woman to serve in the highest government position in the Arab world (Wolf, 2013). However, despite its electoral triumph, the Ennahda-led government could not ensure economic and political stability. The increasing rates of unemployment and the surge of Salafi violence led to sharp criticism of the government (Haynes, 2013).

The Salafists were against the formation of a national unity government comprising of Ennahda and the secular parties. They also opposed the implementation of secular principles in the new constitution. The voices of criticism towards Ennahda rose with the assassination of leftist opposition leader Chokri Belaid on 6 February 2013, and secular opposition leader, Mohammed Brahmi on 25 July 2013. Interior Minister Lotfi Ben Jeddou believed that the local Salafist movement Ansar al-Sharia in Tunisia (AST), Partisans of the Islamic law in Arabic, which was established after Ben-Ali's fall in 2011, was behind both assassinations. These assassinations sparked nationwide protests in which the demonstrators blamed the Ennahda party for not taking strong measures against Salafists who incited against secular politicians. The opposition and civil society called for the dissolution of the government. Prime Minister Jebali and 42 members of the opposition resigned, and the main trade union in Tunisia called for a general strike.

Due to the increasing public pressure, the AST was banned on 27 August 2013. Many AST members were arrested while others fled the country to join Islamists in Libya or Syria. Ennahda left the government on 28 September 2013 to promote a political settlement (Ayari, 2015; Wolf, 2017; Neo, 2019). The National Dialogue Quartet, a group of civil society organisations, was established following the assassinations of Belaid and Brahmi. Its objective was to solve societal differences by creating a national dialogue between Islamist and secular parties. It comprised unions, lawyers, and human rights activists and was awarded the Nobel Peace Prize in 2015 for promoting social reconciliation in Tunisia (Amara, 2020). However, the interim government and political parties could not address youth's concerns about unemployment and the worsening of the economic situation (Gabsi, 2019). The government could not fight the spreading corruption (Mansouri, 2020) and did not include the youth in the decision-making or the political transition process, despite their prominent role in the revolution (Murphy, 2012).

A New Constitution and Fresh Elections

On 26 January 2014, the new constitution was adopted, and the Second Tunisian Republic was established. It determines Tunisia as a republican civil state which is sovereign and has an Arab-Islamic identity. It also embodies individual rights and freedom and brings decentralisation of power. The prime minister became the head of government, and the president became the head of state. It also ensures a multiparty system and balance of power (Quamar, 2015; Henneberg, 2019). The Tunisian constitution was approved by an overwhelming majority of 200 out of 216 members of the NCA and was considered to be the most liberal constitution in the Arab world (Quamar, 2015; Günay and Sommavilla, 2020). There was a great level of compromise between different Tunisian factions during the drafting of the constitution. These factions included Islamist and secular parties, the executive and military, judicial branch and the constituent assembly (Jamal and Kensicki, 2016). They were all able to form a large consensus without renouncing their fundamental beliefs (Lavie, 2019) while conducting a national dialogue (Sharqieh, 2013).

Parliamentary and presidential elections were held in the same year. The secular Nidaa Tounes Party (Call for Tunisia in Arabic), won 86 out of 217 seats in the parliament on 26 October 2014. Its leader, Mohammed Beji Caid Essebsi became the President of Tunisia on 21 December 2014. Some people were afraid Essebsi would go to the path of the old regime, as he was the interior minister under Bourguiba and the speaker of parliament under Ben-Ali. According to the new constitution, Essebsi became responsible for the country's defence, national security, and foreign affairs. A coalition government was formed. In the beginning, the Nidaa Tounes-led government did not want to include Ennahda in the coalition. However, it was impossible to form a stable government without the Islamists, as the Islamist party had secured 69 seats. Therefore, Prime Minister Habib Essid formed a new government, including Ennahda, on 2 February 2015. Because of some differences, 22 members of the Nidaa Tounes party resigned, and Ennahda became the largest party in the parliament. It promoted a national dialogue for addressing internal issues and protecting the achievements of the revolution. The state of emergency, which has been in place since the end of Ben-Ali's rule, was lifted in March 2014 (Esposito, Sonn and Voll, 2015; Yıldırım, 2017).

Islamist Extremism in Tunisia

The democratisation process in Tunisia was challenged by Islamist extremists who carried out terrorist attacks to lead the country towards a radical Islamist path (Neo, 2019; Günay and Sommavilla, 2020). On 18 March 2015, two gunmen in military uniforms carried out a terrorist attack at the Bardo museum in Tunis. The museum is situated next to the parliament, where legislators were discussing an anti-terror law when the attack was taking place. The attackers, Yassine Labidi and Saber Khachanoui were Tunisian citizens. They killed 22 people; most of them were tourists from Japan, Italy, Colombia, Australia, France, Poland and Spain. Two Tunisians were also killed in the attack. The IS claimed responsibility for the attack. Up to 5,500 Tunisians went abroad to join the ranks of IS in Iraq and Syria between 2011 and 2015, making Tunisia the largest provider of foreign fighters to the organisation. Hundreds of them returned to Tunisia and posed an imminent threat to the national security of the country. The Bardo museum attack led to extended anti-terror demonstrations, which included tens of thousands of Tunisians and condemnations from across the world (Benmelech and Klor, 2020; Crone, 2017; de Roy van Zuidewijn, 2014; Jawaid, 2017; Joffé, 2016; Quek and Alkaff, 2019).

On 26 June 2015, Seifeddine Rezgui carried out a terrorist attack by shooting at people in the Tunisian resort of Port El Kantaoui, near Sousse, killing 38 people. He was also a Tunisian citizen. Most of the victims were British. Rezgui was shot dead on site by the police. The British Prime Minister David Cameron said Britain's military involvement in the fight against IS in Iraq led the organisation to target its citizens worldwide. Following the attack, more than 3,000 British tourists decided to fly back to Britain (Gardner, 2018). According to a Tunisian judge, the attack could have been stopped if the security forces were operating properly. Therefore, Western countries helped Tunisia to improve its security capabilities by providing knowledge and resources, as it was considered to be an important interest to them (Gardener, 2017; 2018).

These terrorist attacks hurt the already fragmented Tunisian economy and the flow of foreign currency, which greatly depend on tourism. About half a million Tunisians were working in the tourism industry. Others, such as farmers who were selling their commodities to hotels, were indirectly benefiting from tourism. As countries worldwide had recommended their citizens not to travel to Tunisia, thousands of Tunisians lost their jobs, and hundreds of hotels were compelled to close doors (Kirkpatrick, 2015;

Neo, 2019). Instead of addressing socio-economic problems, which were the main drivers behind the eruption of the revolution, a great portion of the Tunisian budget had to be allocated to fighting Islamist extremism.

To maintain the country's national security, President Essebsi declared a state of emergency on 4 July 2015. The state of emergency extended the authority of the executive, reduced the power of parliament, and suspended civil rights and liberties (Günay and Sommavilla, 2020). The Tunisian parliament passed a new counterterrorism law on 24 July 2015, with 172 members of parliament (MPs) voting in favour. The new law replaced the anti-terrorist law of 2003, legislated under Ben-Ali, and posed a threat to fundamental freedoms and liberties of accused citizens during their investigations for alleged acts of terrorism. This measure reduced the scope of democracy in Tunisia (Sadiki, 2015) and negatively impacted the political, economic, and societal reforms introduced in the country in the aftermath of the revolution. Nevertheless, the Tunisian civil society welcomed these policies and perceived them to be the key to guarantee security and stability in the country (Günay and Sommavilla, 2020).

In January 2016, widespread demonstrations occurred in Tunisia because of the government's incapacity to address the unemployment crisis (BBC, 2016a). In July 2016, a motion of no-confidence was taking place in parliament, as Prime Minister Habib Essid was criticised for failing to promote economic reforms to reduce the rate of unemployment. An overwhelming majority of 188 MPs voted to dismiss Essid (BBC, 2016b) and the president designated Youssef Chahed to succeed him (Delmas, 2018). Chahed formed a unity government, which was approved by 167 MPs. He became the youngest prime minister since Tunisia gained its independence in 1956 (BBC, 2016c). Chahed, a member of the Nidaa Tounes party, tried to develop the Tunisian economy by convening a conference that gathered foreign investors who committed to invest €14 billion in the country. He also worked on integrating Tunisia into the Common Market for Eastern and Southern Africa (COMESA) Free Trade Agreement and wanted to promote reforms that would boost the Tunisian economy. However, economic recovery was proving difficult.

Chahed was also trying to act against corruption by promoting legislation to protect whistle-blowers before arresting businesspeople accused of corruption. Although politicians supported Chahed's initiative, they wanted to provide amnesty to the businessmen accused during the Ben-Ali's regime (Lefèvre, 2017; Yardımcı-Geyikçi and Tür, 2017). The relations between Essebsi and Chahed soured in 2018, as Essebsi asked Chahed to seek a confidence vote because he could not address the country's political and economic crisis. Essebsi explained that the legitimacy of Chahed to serve as prime minister came from his designation and that he has to gain the approval of the parliament to stay in office. Ghannouchi opposed toppling Chahed's government as he was afraid that it would lead to a political vacuum (Bouali, 2018). Chahed eventually remained in office.

The Rise of the Independents

President Essebsi died on 25 July 2019. He was the first freely elected president in Tunisia and the oldest sitting president in the world. He was able to maintain stability but was criticised for conducting authoritarian policies due to security challenges imposed by jihadists acting on the Tunisian soil. As a result, the speaker of the parliament Mohammed Ennaceur became the interim president (BBC, 2019).

Nabil Karoui formed the centrist party Qalb Tounes (Heart of Tunisia in Arabic) party a couple of months before the 2019 presidential election in Tunisia (Allahoun, 2019). On 23 August 2019, he was jailed because of money laundering and tax evasion. He denied all the charges and believed they were politically motivated to weaken him. He spent the entire campaign period in prison and was released days before the second-round run-off election. His detention and inability to campaign damaged the credibility of the election, as he could not communicate with voters (Barabarani, 2019). His political opponent and future president, Kais Saied, announced he would not campaign while Karoui was in prison (Jawad, 2019).

Kais Saied became the president of Tunisia on 13 October 2019 (Mansouri, 2020). Said is a retired law professor without any political experience who had kept a low profile throughout the political campaign and did not have the support of any political party (Allahoun, 2019). Many believed that his openness and his strong sense of equity led him to win the hearts of Tunisia's youth, as they perceived him to be a leader who would ensure their future. Said promised he would fight corruption, promote social justice and address the slowdown of the economy. He also said that education is the key to fighting extremism and promised to decentralise the government by empowering local governments and change the way representatives are elected to the parliament. However, he openly expressed a conservative stance about homosexuality, death penalty and equal inheritance for men and women (Wolf, 2019).

The Tunisian Parliament could not form a government because of political cleavages, which emerged after the parliamentary elections. On 6 October 2019, the Tunisian people were discontent about the previous government led by Essebsi's party Nidaa Tounes. Ennahda won 54 seats, Qalb Tounes won 38 seats, social-democrat parties won together 41 seats, and other parties won together 26 seats. Habib Jemli was designated to form the government but was ousted from the government, as 134 MPs voted against the formation of his government. It was the first time the Tunisian parliament democratically objected to a government formation (Delmas, 2020c). Said decided to give the task to the unpopular politician Elyes Fakhfakh who won only 0.3 per cent of the votes during the presidential elections. His party of the FDTL was not represented in the parliament. Ennahda decided not to be part of the government because it aspired to form a national unity government, while Fakhfakh formed a minority government to establish a constitutional court. Although Ennahda lost 15 seats in these elections, it remained the largest political party in Tunisia (al-Thabeti, 2020). Nevertheless, Fakhfakh was able to form a government with Ennahda's support since the latter wanted to avoid the dissolution of the parliament (Ounnes, 2020).

Coronavirus Pandemic

The eruption of the Covid-19 pandemic made it difficult for the Tunisian government to fulfil the promise of fast economic recovery. The pandemic was followed by a national lockdown, increased recession and unemployment. The Tunisian economy is based on agriculture, phosphate mines, textile and tourism. These sectors were heavily harmed by the health crisis (Delmas, 2020b). As a result, Ennahda proposed a no-confidence vote against Fakhfakh. On 15 July 2020, 105 MPs submitted a petition to the parliament and demanded to organise a no-confidence vote against

Fakhfakh's government over suspected corruption and conflict of interests (Arif, 2020). Fakhfakh dismissed six ministers who belonged to Ennahda and submitted his resignation to the president (Elthabti and Topcu, 2020a). The youth and sports minister, local affairs minister, information technologies minister, health minister and the higher education and scientific research minister were dismissed from their functions (al-Thabti, 2020).

Following Fakhfakh's resignation, President Said appointed Interior Minister Hichem Mechichi to form a government. Mechichi is an independent politician who is not affiliated with any political party (Arif, 2020). Mechichi said it was necessary to form an independent technocratic government because of the differences between the political parties (Hammoudi, 2020). On 25 August 2020, Mechichi formed a technocratic government approved by 134 MPs (Elthabti and Topcu, 2020b). Parliament Speaker Rashid Ghannouchi said it was necessary to assure social and political stability to deal with the country's challenges during the pandemic (Ounas, 2020).

In December 2020, Saied declared he would launch a national dialogue which would include political parties and youth in order "to correct the revolution that has deviated from its goals a decade after its outbreak" and promote economic, social and political reforms which will address unemployment, corruption and provision of public services (Amara, 2020). These same issues led to the eruption of the Jasmine revolution in 2011 (Delmas, 2020a). Tunisian politicians, including President Saied, tried to divert the public opinion by debating on France to apologise for crimes committed during and after the colonisation period of Tunisia and compensate victims who suffered from the colonial rule (Salmi, 2020), and blaming the Jews for being behind the economic hardships of the country (Cohen, 2021).

On 14 January 2021, a young shepherd from the Siliana region of Tunisia was assaulted by a policeman after his flock of sheep accidentally entered the seat of the governorate. This aggression was recorded and uploaded on social media networks and led to widespread demonstrations organised by the Tunisian youth. The demonstrations erupted a decade after the Jasmine Revolution. The demonstrators called for political, economic and societal changes which would allow them to live a dignified life. The grievances that led to the Jasmine revolution's eruption were not properly addressed by the successive Tunisian governments and threatened to destabilise the country (Yousfi, 2021). Politicians and activists exchanged accusations for inciting violence, riots and protests in several regions of the country (Al-Mannai, 2021). After a decade since the revolution, the Tunisian people are still marching in the streets to express their distress and call for living a better life.

Conclusion

The Jasmine revolution brought a regime change in Tunisia. The ability of the interim governments to promote a relatively peaceful political transfer was praised by many countries around the world. Tunisia was able to adopt a new constitution and assure political stability by striving to form national unity governments based on dialogue and compromise between different political factions. However, the Tunisian governments were not able to overcome economic hurdles since the eruption of the revolution a decade ago. The country is still trying to address the issues of poverty, unemployment and corruption. Socioeconomic distresses could destabilise the country, especially after the eruption of the Covid-19 pandemic, which was another blow to the already fragmented Tunisian economy. If politicians can put their interests aside and work together, they would be able to address these issues and bring economic and societal change to the country.

References

Abdullatif, Amna (2013), "Voices of women in the Arab Spring," *Journal of Social Science Education*, 12 (1), pp. 14-30.

Aboussi, Mourad (2020), "The emigrant political participation in Morocco and Tunisia: Diasporic civil society and the transnationalization of citizenship in the Arab Spring context," *The Journal of North African Studies*, 25 (2), pp. 228-250.

Aleya-Sghaier, Amira (2012), "The Tunisian Revolution: The Revolution of Dignity," *The Journal for the Middle East and Africa*, 3 (1), pp. 18-45.

Allahoun, Ramy (2019), "Kais Said: Who is Tunisia's new president?" *Al-Jazeera*, 23 October at https://www.aljazeera.com/news/2019/10/23/kais-saied-who-is-tunisias-new-president

Allani, Alaya (2009), "The Islamists in Tunisia between confrontation and participation: 1980-2008," *The Journal of North African Studies*, 14 (2), pp. 257-272.

Al-Mannai, Shaima (2021), "Protestors, security officials clash in Tunisia," Anadolu Agency, 19 January at https://www.aa.com.tr/en/africa/protesters-security-officials-clash-in-tunisia/2115715

Alqudsi, Taghreed (2012), "Creative use of social media in the revolutions of Tunisia, Egypt and Libya," *International Journal of Interdisciplinary Social Sciences*, 6(6), pp. 147-158.

al-Thabti, Adel (2020), "Tunisia Ennahda slams removing its ministers from gov't," Anadolu Agency, 16 July at https://www.aa.com.tr/en/africa/tunisia-ennahda-slams-removing-its-ministers-from-govt/1912552

Alvi, Hayat (2014), "The human rights and development impetuses for Tunisia's Jasmine Revolution," *Contemporary Review of the Middle East*, 1 (1), pp. 25-51.

Aman, Mohammed M. and Jayroe, Tina J. (2013), "ICT, social media, and the Arab transition to democracy. From venting to acting," *Digest of Middle East Studies*, 22 (2), pp. 147-347.

Amara, Tarek (2020), "Tunisia president to launch dialogue to 'correct the revolution' process," Reuters, 30 December at https://www.reuters.com/article/us-tunisia-politics-president-idUSKBN29425Z

Amara, Tarek (2011), "Tunisia's Ben-Ali sentenced in absentia to 35 years in jail," Reuters, 20 June at https://www.reuters.com/article/us-tunisia-benali-trial-idUSTRE75J2A020110620

Anderson, Lisa (2011), "Demystifying the Arab Spring," *Foreign Policy*, 90 (3), pp. 2-7.

Arif, Talal (2020), "Interior minister to form new government in Tunisia," Anadolu Agenc, 26 July at https://www.aa.com.tr/en/middle-east/interior-minister-to-form-new-government-in-tunisia/1922575

Ayari, Farida (2015), "Ennahda movement in power: A long path to democracy," *Contemporary Review of the Middle East*, 2 (1&2), pp. 135-142.

Barabarani, Sofia (2019), "Mistrust of elites rise of Tunisia's presidential hopefuls," *Al-Jazeera*, 12 October at https://www.aljazeera.com/features/2019/10/12/mistrust-of-elites-fuels-rise-of-tunisias-presidential-hopefuls

Barany, Zoltan (2013), "Reforming defense: Lessons from Arab republics," *Strategic Studies Quarterly*, 7 (4), pp. 46-69.

BBC (2019), "Beji Caid Essebsi: Tunisia's first freely elected president dies aged 92," 25 July at https://www.bbc.com/news/world-africa-49111905

BBC (2016c), "Tunisia parliament approves unity government of Youssef Chahed," 27 August at https://www.bbc.com/news/world-africa-37203025

BBC (2016b), "Tunisia parliament votes to sack PM Habib Essid," 30 July at https://www.bbc.com/news/world-africa-36934770

BBC (2016a), "Tunisia protests: President vows to end 'ordeal' of unemployment," 22 January at https://www.bbc.com/news/world-africa-35384181

Bellin, Eva (2012), "Reconsidering the robustness of authoritarianism in the Middle East: Lessons from the Arab Spring," *Comparative Politics*, 44 (2), pp. 127-149.

Benmelech, Efraim and Klor, Esteban F. (2020), "What explains the flow of foreign fighters to ISIS?" *Terrorism and Political Violence*, 32 (7), pp. 1458-1481.

Bishku, Michael B. (2013), "Is it an Arab Spring or business as usual? Recent changes in the Arab world in historical context," *Journal of the Third World Studies*, 30 (1), pp. 55-77.

Bouali, Karim (2018), "Tunisia's Ennahda opposes PM dismissal: Ghannouchi," Anadolu Agency, 28 July at https://www.aa.com.tr/en/africa/tunisia-s-ennahda-opposes-pm-dismissal-ghannouchi/1216546

Boubekeur, Amel (2016), "Islamists, secularists and old regime elites in Tunisia: Bargained competition," *Mediterranean Politics*, 21 (1), pp. 107-127.

Cavatorta, Francesco and Merone, Fabio (2013), "Moderation through exclusion? The journey of the Tunisian Ennahda from fundamentalist to conservative party," *Democratization*, 20 (5), pp. 857-875.

Chakchouk, Moez; Kehl, Danielle; Ben-Avie, Jochai and Coyer, Kate (2013), "From revolution to reform: Recommendations for spectrum policy in transitional Tunisia," *Journal of Information Policy*, 3, pp. 575-600.

Cohen, Edy (2021), "The president of Tunisia slanders the Jews," *Perspectives*, no. 1947, 3 March at The Begin-Sadat Center for Strategic Studies, Bar-Ilan University, Israel, https://besacenter.org/perspectives-papers/tunisia-kais-saied-jews/

Crone, Manni (2017), "Islamic State's Incursion into North Africa and Sahel: A threat to al-Qaeda?" *Connections*, 16 (1), pp. 63-76.

Delmas, Benoît (2020a), "Tunisie: Alarme sociale dans le Sud [Tunisia: Social alarm in the south]," *Le Point*, 25 June at https://www.lepoint.fr/afrique/tunisie-alarme-sociale-dans-le-sud-25-06-2020-2381710_3826.php

Delmas, Benoît (2020b), "Tunisie: "La pire récession depuis l'indépendance" [Tunisia: The worst recession since the independence]," *Le Point*, 6 May at https://www.lepoint.fr/afrique/tunisie-la-pire-recession-depuis-l-independance-06-05-2020-2374385_3826.php

Delmas, Benoît (2020c), "Coup de tonnerre politique en Tunisie [Political lightning strike in Tunisia]," *Le Point*, 11 January at https://www.lepoint.fr/afrique/coup-de-tonnerre-politique-en-tunisie-11-01-2020-2357227_3826.php

Delmas, Benoît (2018), "Tunisie: Divorce acté entre la Kasbah et le palais de Carthage [Tunisia: An acted divorce between the Kasbah and the Cathage palace],"

Le Point, 6 November at https://www.lepoint.fr/afrique/tunisie-divorce-acte-entre-la-kasbah-et-le-palais-de-carthage-06-11-2018-2269009_3826.php

Donnalyn, Pompper (2014), "Female Tunisian Revolutionaries: Leadership and social (dis)order in global news production," *Mass Communication and Society*, 17 (4), pp. 487-508.

El Meehy, Asya (2013), "'It's the economy, stupid?' The uprisings in Bahrain, Egypt and Tunisia," *Critique Internationale*, 61 (4), pp. 51-67.

Elthabti, Adel Bin Ibrahim Bin Elha and Topcu, Gulsen (2020b), "Tunisia: Government wins confidence vote," Anadolu Agency, 2 September at https://www.aa.com.tr/en/africa/tunisia-government-wins-confidence-vote/1960371

Elthabti, Adel Bin Ibrahim Bin Elha and Topcu, Gulsen (2020a), "Tunisia: 6 ministers dismissed from government," Anadolu Agency, 16 July at https://www.aa.com.tr/en/africa/tunisia-6-ministers-dismissed-from-government/1912079

Enahaili, Aziz (2010), "Tunisia," in Rubin, Barry (Ed.), *Guide to Islamist Movements*, New York: M. E. Sharpe, pp. 391-406.

Esposito, John L.; Sonn, Tamara and Voll, John O. (2015), *Islam and Democracy after the Arab Spring*, Oxford: Oxford University Press.

Flynn, Matthew J. (2018), "Cyber rebellions: The online struggle for openness," *Journal of International Affairs*, 71 (1.5), pp. 107-114.

Gabsi, Zouhir (2019), "Tunisia's youth: Awakened identity and challenges post-Arab Spring," *British Journal of Middle Eastern Studies*, 46 (1), pp. 68-87.

Gardner, Frank (2018), "Tunisia tourism: Is it safe for UK holidaymakers?" BBC, 12 February at https://www.bbc.com/news/uk-43030864

Graziano, Teresa (2012), "The Tunisian diaspora: Between 'digital riots' and Web activism," *Social Science Information*, 51 (4), pp. 534-550.

Günay, Cengiz and Sommavilla, Fabian (2020), "Tunisia's democratization at risk," *Mediterranean Politics*, 25 (5), pp. 673-681.

Hamid, Shadi (2011), "Tunisia: Birthplace of the Revolution," in Kenneth M. Pollack et al (Eds.), *The Arab Awakening: America and the Transformation of the Middle East,* Washington, DC: Brookings Institution Press, pp. 111-116.

Hammoudi, Alaa (2020), "Tunisia's PM-designate to form technocratic cabinet," Anadolu Agency, 11 August at https://www.aa.com.tr/en/africa/tunisia-s-pm-designate-to-form-technocratic-cabinet/1937763

Haynes, Jeffrey (2013), "The 'Arab Uprising', Islamists and democratization," *Mediterranean Politics*, 18 (2), pp. 170-188.

Henneberg, Sabina (2019), "Before and after Bin Ali: Comparing two attempts at political liberalization in Tunisia," *Review of Middle East Studies*, 53 (2), pp. 306-320.

Hess, Steve (2013), "From the Arab Spring to the Chinese Winter: The institutional sources of authoritarian vulnerability and resilience in Egypt, Tunisia and China," *International Political Science Review*, 34 (3), pp. 254-272.

Hilal, Leila (2012), "Charting transitions in the Middle East: Lessons learned from Tunisia and Egypt," *Insight Turkey*, 14 (2), pp. 1-12.

Hmed, Choukri (2015), "Répression d'Etat et situation révolutionnaire en Tunisie (2010-2011), [Repression of the state and the revolutionary situation in Tunisia (2010-2011)]," *Vingtième Siècle. Revue d'Histoire*, 128. pp. 77-90.

Howard, Philip N. and Hussain, Muzammil M. (2011), "The role of digital media," *Journal of Democracy*, 22 (3), pp. 35-48.

Jamal, Amal and Kensicki, Anna (2016), "A theory of critical junctures for democratization: A comparative examination of constitution-making in Egypt and Tunisia," *Law, and Ethics of Human Rights*, 10 (1), pp. 1-38.

Jawad, Rana (2019), "Tunisia election: The 'robot' and the pasta magnate freed from jail," BBC, 11 October at https://www.bbc.com/news/world-africa-49987047

Jawaid, Arsla (2017), "From foreign fighters to returnees: The challenges of rehabilitation and reintegration policies," *Journal of Peacebuilding & Development*, 12 (2), pp. 102-107.

Joffé, George (2016), "Global Jihad and foreign fighters," *Small Wars & Insurgencies*, 27 (5), pp. 800-816.

Jordan, Tim (2015), *Information Politics: Liberation and Exploitation in the Digital Society,* London: Pluto Press.

Khondker, Habibul H. (2011), "Role of the new media in the Arab Spring," *Globalizations*, 8 (5), pp. 675-679.

Kılavuz, Tahir M. (2020), "Determinants of participation in protests in the Arab Uprisings," *Uluslararası Ilişkıler*, 17 (67), pp. 81-96.

Kirkpatrick, David D. (2015), "Tunisia museum attack is blow to Nation's democratic shift," *The New York Times,* 18 March at https://www.nytimes.com/2015/03/19/world/africa/gunmen-attack-tunis-bardo-national-museum.html

Koehler, Kevin (2017), "Political militaries in popular uprisings: A comparative perspective on the Arab Spring," *International Political Science Review*, 38 (3), pp. 363-377.

Kumaraswamy, Polur R. (2011), "The Arab Spring," *India International Centre Quarterly*, 38 (1), pp. 52-62.

Quamar, Muddassir Md. (2015), "Tunisia: Presidential and parliamentary elections, 2014," *Contemporary Review of the Middle East*, 2(3), pp. 269-288.

Lavie, Limor (2019), "Consensus vs. Dissensus over the 'civil state' model: A key to understanding the diverse outcomes of the Arab Spring in Egypt and Tunisia," *British Journal of Middle Eastern Studies*, DOI: 10.1080/13530194.2019.1651631

Lecompte, Romain (2009), "Internet et la reconfiguration de l'espace public tunisien: Le rôle de la diaspora [Internet and the reconfiguration of the Tunisian public space: The role of the Diaposra]," *TIC & Société*, 3 (1-2), pp. 199-229.

Lefèvre, Raphaël (2017), "The roots of growing social unrest in Tunisia," *The Journal of North African Studies*, 22 (4), pp. 505-510.

Levey, Stuart (2011), "Fighting corruption after the Arab Spring," *Foreign Affairs*, 16 June at https://www.foreignaffairs.com/articles/middle-east/2011-06-16/fighting-corruption-after-arab-spring

Levinson, Micah N. (2012), "The rhythm of revolution," *Comparative Strategy*, 31 (2), pp. 162-170.

Maalej, Zouheir A. (2012), "The 'Jasmine Revolt' has made the 'Arab Spring': A critical discourse analysis of the last three political speeches of the ousted president of Tunisia," *Discourse and Society*, 23 (6), pp. 679-700.

Mabrouk, Mehdi (2011), "A revolution for dignity and freedom: Preliminary observations on the social and cultural background to the Tunisian revolution," *The Journal of North African Studies*, 16 (4), pp. 625-635.

Manea, Elham (2014), "The Arab popular uprisings from a gender perspective," *Zeitschrift für Politik*, 61(1), pp. 81-100.

Mansfield, Edward D. and Snyder, Jack (2012), "Democratization and the Arab Spring," *International Interactions*, 38 (5), pp. 722-733.

Mansouri, Fethi (2020), "Youth and political engagement in post-revolution Tunisia," *British Journal of Middle Eastern Studies*. DOI: 10.1080/13530194.2020.1765142

Ma'oz, Moshe (2012), "The 'Arab Spring' and the new geo-strategic environment in the Middle East," *Insight Turkey*, 14 (4), pp. 13-23.

McCarthy, Rory (2014), "Re-thinking secularism in post-independence Tunisia," *The Journal of North African Studies*, 19 (5), pp. 733-750.

Mühlberger, Wolfgang (2015), "Assessing the impact: North African militaries in the Arab Spring," *Security and Peace*, 33 (1), pp. 7-14.

Müller, Marion G. and Hübner, Celina (2014), "How Facebook facilitated the Jasmine Revolution. Conceptualizing the functions of online social network communication," *Journal Social Media Studies*, 1 (1), pp. 17-33.

Murphy, Emma C. (2013), "The Tunisian elections of October 2011: A democratic consensus," *The Journal of North African Studies*, 18 (2), pp. 231-247.

Murphy, Emma C. (2012), "Problematizing Arab youth: Generational narratives of systematic failure," *Mediterranean Politics*, 17 (1), pp. 5-22.

Neo, Ric (2019), "The Jihad post-Arab Spring: Contextualising Islamic radicalism in Egyp and Tunisia," *African Security Review*, 28 (2), pp. 95-109.

Ounas, Yusra (2020), "Tunisia needs stability to face challenges," Anadolu Agency, 3 September at https://www.aa.com.tr/en/middle-east/tunisia-needs-stability-to-face-challenges/1962226

Ounnes, Yousra (2020), "Ennahda says seeking to avoid early election in Tunisia," Anadolu Agency, 19 February at https://www.aa.com.tr/en/africa/ennahda-says-seeking-to-avoid-early-election-in-tunisia/1738737

Özcan, Sevinç A. (2018), "The role of political Islam in Tunisia's democratization process: Towards a new pattern of secularization?" *Insight Turkey*, 20 (1), pp. 209-226.

Özekin, Muhammed K. and Akkaş, Hasan H. (2014), "An empirical look to the Arab Spring: Causes and consequences," *Turkish Journal of International Relations*, 13 (1-2), pp. 75-87.

Pevná, Katarína (2011), "Revolutions in Tunisia and Egypt and political participation of Islamists," *International Issues & Slovak Foreign Policy Association*, 20 (2), pp. 35-53.

Quek, Natasha and Alkaff, Syed H. B. O. (2019), "Analysis of the Tunisian terrorist fighters phenomenon," *Counter Terrorist Trends and Analyses*, 11 (5), pp. 1-5.

Radsch, Courtney C. and Khamis, Sahar (2013), "In their own voice: Technologically mediated empowerment and transformation among young Arab women," *Feminist Media Studies*, 13 (5), pp. 881-890.

Rousselin, Mathieu (2016), "Modern communication technologies and the extension of the territory of struggle: Conceptualizing Tunisia's jasmine revolution," *New Media and Society*, 18 (7), pp. 1201-1218.

Sadiki, Larbi (2015), "Tunisia is sacrificing its democracy for safety," *Al-Jazeera*, 10 August at https://www.aljazeera.com/opinions/2015/8/10/tunisia-is-sacrificing-its-democracy-for-safety

Salmi, Yamna (2020), "Tunisia lawmakers reject motion on French colonial rule," Anadolu Agency, June 10, https://www.aa.com.tr/en/africa/tunisia-lawmakers-reject-motion-on-french-colonial-rule/1871602

Schraeder, Peter J. (2012), "Tunisia's Jasmine Revolution and the Arab Spring: Implications of international intervention," *Orbis*, 56 (4), pp. 662-675.

Sharqieh, Ibrahim (2013), "Tunisia's lessons for the Middle East," *Foreign Affairs*, 17 September at https://www.foreignaffairs.com/articles/tunisia/2013-09-17/tunisias-lessons-middle-east

Singh, Blamiki P. (2012), "The future of democracy," *World Affairs*, 16 (4), pp. 18-47.

Smidi, Adam and Shahin, Saif (2017), "Social media and social mobilization in the Middle East," *India Quarterly*, 73 (2), pp. 196-209.

Letsa, Natalie Wenzell and Wilfahrt, Martha (2018), "Popular support for democracy in autocratic regimes," *Comparative* Politics, 50 (2), pp. 231-250.

Wolf, Anne (2019), "In search of 'consensus': The crisis of party politics in Tunisia," *The Journal of North African Studies*, 24 (6), pp. 883-886.

Wolf, Anne (2017), *Political Islam in Tunisia: The History of Ennahda*, Oxford: Oxford University Press.

Wolf, Anne (2013), "An Islamist 'renaissance'? Religion and politics in post-revolutionary Tunisia," *The Journal of North African Studies*, 18 (4), pp. 560-573.

Yardımcı-Geyikçi and Tür, Özlem (2018), "Rethinking the Tunisian miracle: A party politics view," *Democratization*, 25 (5), pp. 787-803.

Yıldırım, Ramazan (2017), "Transformation of the Ennahda movement from Islam Jama'ah to political party," *Insight Turkey*, 19 (2), pp. 189-214.

Yousfi, Hèla (2021), En Tunisie, la révolution au quotidien [In Tunisia, a revolution on a daily basis]. *Le Point*, 27 January at https://www.lepoint.fr/afrique/en-tunisie-la-revolution-au-quotidien-27-01-2021-2411535_3826.php

Zemni, Sami (2015), "The extraordinary politics of the Tunisian revolution: The process of constitution making," *Mediterranean Politics*, 20 (1), pp. 1-17.

7. (Un)Development Effects of Real Estate Boom in Egypt after the Arab Uprising

Sameena Hameed

Introduction

There has been enormous euphoria following the 2011 Arab uprisings about the growth and resilience of the real estate sector, and its contribution to the growth of the Egyptian economy (Oxford Business Group, 2018; American Chamber of Commerce, 2016). The demand for real estate has been propped up by an annual increase of population by 2.5 million and about a million marriages with attended demand for housing. Besides, real estate was the principal beneficiary of the state investing massive resources in the national projects, including building three smart cities to boost growth, provide jobs, and attract private/foreign investors (Sayigh, 2020). Economic turbulence, weakening Egyptian Pound (EGP) and political instability in the neighbourhood added to the growth of the real estate sector.

In Egypt, about 95 per cent of the population live in 5 per cent of the territory along the Nile valley. Egyptian governments, since the 1950s, have invested in grandiose projects to build new desert cities to relocate 20 million or more people to 50 new towns and cities (Sayigh, 2019, p. 104). Since his ascendance to power in 2013, President Abdel Fattah El-Sisi has made land reclamation and real estate development the focal point of his economic recovery plan. As a result, the state became the principal player and stakeholder in the sector. Egypt has introduced several regulatory reforms in 2017 and 2018, including the New Investment Law (Law 72 of 2017) and amendments in the Company Law that aimed to provide a regulatory framework for the government to give more investment-related incentives and guarantees.

The government also aimed to attract foreign investors to several "mega projects," including a large-scale industrial and logistic zone around the Suez Canal, a new administrative capital, a 1.5-million-hectare land reclamation plan and the golden triangle economic zone between the Red Sea and River Nile.

At the same time, in 2016, in lieu of the US$ 12 billion International Monetary Fund (IMF) loan, Egypt had to roll out an economic reform programme that included a floating exchange rate, which devalued the EGP overnight from EGP8 for US$ 1 to EGP12 to US$ 1 (El Baradei, 2019). Reduction of subsidies, the introduction of value-added taxes and currency devaluation aggravated the inflationary pressure on goods and services. The impact on real estate was phenomenal, and with more relaxed payment terms of 5-7 years, many investors saw real estate investment as an attractive alternative to hedge against currency devaluation and inflation. The cascading effect of the real estate boom through the decade after the Arab uprising has produced and masked socio-economic regression and deprivation.

Methodology: The chapter uses census data between 2006 and 2017 and various statistical bulletins published by the Egyptian Central Agency for Public Mobilization and Statistics (CAPMAS) for 2010-19. An analysis of the socio-economic data of the governorates where the construction activity was predominant is done to examine the effects of the real estate boom on population. The data on construction has often been used to mirror the effect of the real estate sector. To eliminate the exogenous effect of the COVID-19 pandemic on economic activities, the data for 2020 has not been considered. Besides, the average exchange rate of the mentioned period has been used to convert figures obtained in the Egyptian Pound.

The Arab Spring and the Real Estate

Egypt has all the trappings of the rentier economy, with a sizable contribution of oil and gas receipts to the government revenues and Gross Domestic Product (GDP). Further, the strategic rent from Suez Canal was about 2 per cent of GDP in 2010-11 (Central Bank of Egypt 2012, p. 72). The state-led model of growth and development had also generated significant regulatory rents.

The economy was growing reasonably well in 2009-10 with a real GDP growth rate of 5 per cent (Central Agency for Public Mobilization and Statistics [CAPMAS] 2011a, p. 71). Due to the global slowdown in the aftermath of the 2008 financial crisis, the revenues from the Suez Canal had declined in 2009 against that of 2008; the aircraft movements in the Egyptian airports had also registered a decline of about 10.2 per cent. In 2010-11, the GDP at market price was about US$ 127.7 billion, and the real growth rate became dismal at 1.8 per cent. Agriculture and the allied sectors were the dominant sources of employment for about 28.2 per cent of the labour force.

The years 2008 and 2011 had seen spikes in international food prices (Abbott, Hurt and Turner, 2011). Egypt, which had been largely import-dependent for wheat, livestock and other essential edibles, became especially vulnerable to the rising food prices. The impact was visible in the fall in per capita annual consumption of vital edibles like cereal, legumes, fruits and meat (ibid., p. 38) while the country acquired self-sufficiency in rice, vegetables, poultry and milk and citrus fruits. Its self-sufficiency had improved for wheat from 53.4 per cent in 2006-07 to 74 per cent in 2008-09 (ibid., p. 39). However, as indicated by the Consumer Price Index (CPI) (urban), the inflation rate had remained consistently high since 2008, reducing the purchasing power of people.

The prospects of the vast majority of people to improve their living conditions were bleak. The private banks lent disproportionally to politically connected firms between 2003-11 (Diwan and Schiffbauer, 2018). Unemployment was phenomenally high among the educated. According to the 2006 census, only 9.5 per cent population had a university degree, while 28.5 per cent were intermediates and above, and 31.8 per cent had completed school education. About 30.1 per cent of the population were completely illiterate. The inability to meet basic needs of development was manifested in the sharp fall of nearly 50 per cent in enrolment in secondary education from 60 per cent in 2009-10 to 24 per cent in 2010-11 for boys and from 59 to 29 per cent for girls (CAPMAS, 2017a, p. 604).

Between 2011 and 2013, the political instability and mass protests that ousted first Hosni Mubarak in February 2011 and later Mohammed Morsi in July 2013 hit the traditional sources of growth and foreign exchange. As a result, the real GDP growth rate hovered around 2 per cent, and the growth rate (at constant prices) for most sectors was below 3 per cent, except for construction and communications (ibid.). On the other hand, real estate showed higher growth rates than that of the GDP and most other sectors during political and economic instability (Figure 1).

Figure 1: Real Growth Rates 2011-17 (in per cent)

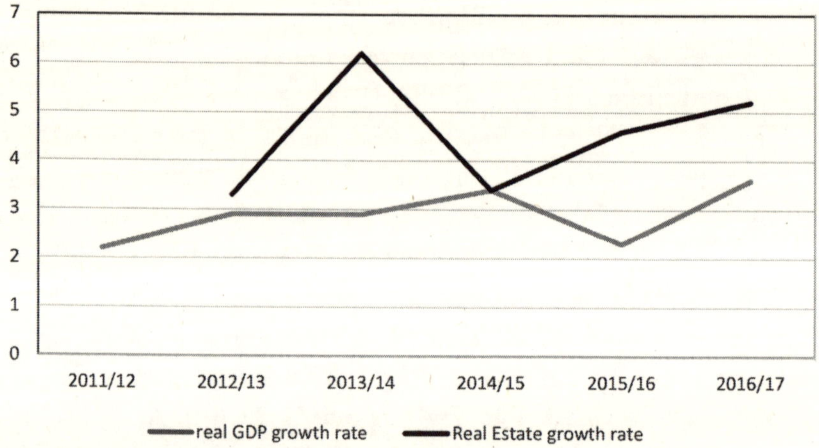

Sources: Compiled from CAPMAS Statistical Year Book 2016 and 2019.

The real estate market saw a tremendous boom after the uprisings as Egyptians rushed to invest in property to escape from the falling value of the Egyptian Pound (Laessing, 2013). Demand for real estate increased to hedge against the rising inflation (Figures 2 and 3). Besides, Egyptians, like in other Arab societies, are expected to live in an independent furnished apartment after marriage. According to the World Bank, about 12-20 million Egyptians (nearly a quarter) were living in informal housing in 2015. There has been an estimated demand of one million new flats per year as against the annual supply of about 350,000 flats (Megahid, 2017).

In November 2016, Egypt signed a US$ 12 billion loan agreement with the IMF conditioned with the structural adjustment of its economy. When the EGP was devalued significantly in November 2016, it affected the construction cost through higher prices of imported material. Within a week or two after devaluation, real estate prices shot up by 15-20 per cent and investors in speculation of a further increase in prices rushed to invest in the upcoming projects (Osman, 2017). The new project developers were quickly selling their bookings because the transaction in the resale market had dried up by the inflexible payment terms, where sellers demanded most of the money upfront (ibid.). With the currency devaluation of about 49 per cent between October 2016 and March 2019, the housing prices became lucrative also for the Egyptians living abroad (Global Property Guide, 2019). Through the decade, the demand for real estate had been robust (Figure 3).

Figure 2: Inflation Rate, Consumer Price Index for Urban Areas

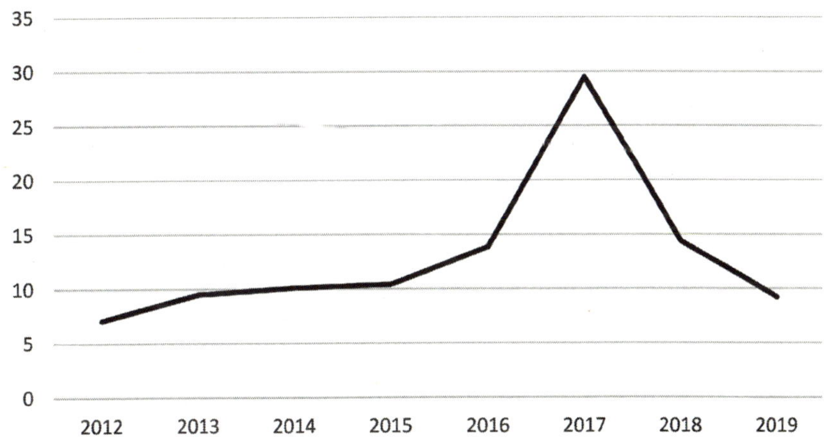

Source: Compiled from Central Bank of Egypt, Time Series, https://www.cbe.org.eg/en/EconomicResearch/Statistics/Pages/Inflationhistorical.aspx

Under President Sisi, the state became the principal player and stakeholder in real estate. For 20 years until October 2016, the public investment in housing did not exceed more than US$ 2.8 billion, the bulk of which was done after 2018 (Oxford Business Group, 2018). In December 2015, President Sisi issued a decree that privileged military to form companies or partnerships with local and foreign investors and giving the armed forces a share in the revenues where the companies are sold and enabled them to retain ownership of land (Momani, 2018). The Ministry of Defence had been deeply entrenched in the real estate dealings owing to its control over land licensing (Sayigh, 2019). Although they were involved in reclaiming lands and building several

Figure 3: Egypt Real Estate Demand Index

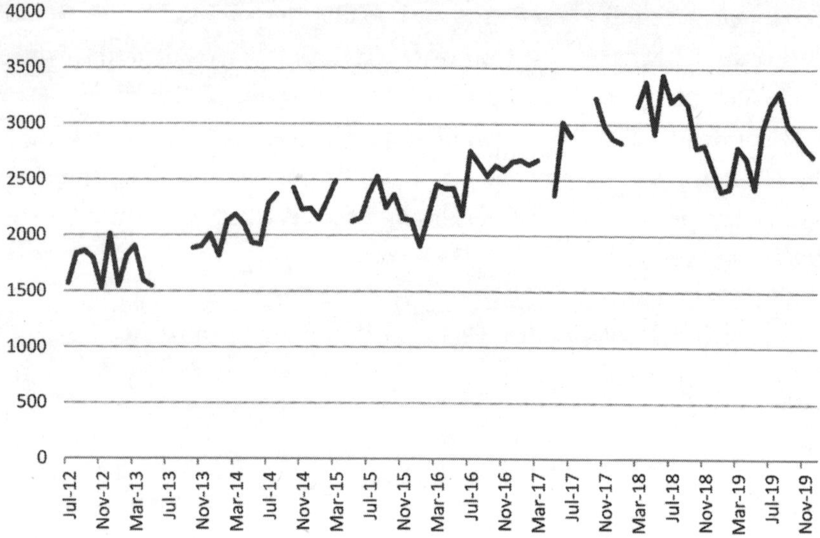

Source: Compiled from Aqarmap monthly real estate index https://aqarmap.com.eg/en

desert cities, most of them became white elephants with enormous cost to the exchequer. Unfazed by these failures and openly rebuking feasibility studies, President Sisi launched ambitions land reclamation and mega city projects. Between 2014 and 2019, an estimated EGP200 billion (about US$ 15 billion) worth of state funding went to national projects in real estate (Sayigh, 2020). According to CAPMAS, about EGP672 million (US$ 38 million) worth of construction was done in real estate and renting sectors by the government contractors in 2017-18 against about EGP252 million (US$ 14 million) by the private sector (CAPMAS, 2018a).

Crowding out Effect: Political Economy of Real Estate Finance

The financial sector plays an important role in sectoral growth both from the supply-side and demand side. Availability of finance to the real estate developer and the consumer is essential for project development and sale. The mortgage market is still underdeveloped though the mortgage law had been passed in 2001. The Egyptians have to make down-payments of about 15-20 per cent for a house with their savings and pay the remaining in the 4-5-year instalment plan (Oxford Business Group, 2017). Without mortgaging finance, the low- and middle-income families cannot afford formal housing. The Central Bank took a few initiatives to boost housing finance, comprising allocation of EGP10 billion for home finance by the banks, keeping below the market interest of 5 per cent for low-income buyers and reduced down payment requirements. However, the mortgage finance industry stood only at about EGP 1.1 billion (about US$ 6.25 million) in November 2017 (Wood, 2018). A range of regulatory requirements continues to hamper the growth of the mortgage market, like the requirement of completion of 40 per cent construction which hindered the developer and the buyer to avail finance at the early stage. A number of real estates developers are now tying up with the banks to finance the project development and extend home loans to potential consumers.

The robust growth expectations of the real estate sector had contributed to its active trading in the Egyptian stock markets. As a result, the real estate sector shares had the highest P/E ratios[1] on 29 December 2010 among the five most active sectors in the Egyptian stock exchange (Egyptian Stock Exchange [EGX], 2011, p. 13). It implied the shares of the real estate companies had been overvalued in anticipation of robust growth. The sector had the second largest trading volume of about 2.8 billion shares with a valuation of EGP13 billion (US$ 1.8 billion) in 2010. By 2017, the real estate shares were trading at the volume of 20 billion and a valuation of about EGP52 billion (US$ 2.9 billion) (EGX, 2017). As a result, its share in market capitalisation had increased from 5 per cent (sixth rank) in 2010 to peak at 12 per cent in 2015 and 10.2 per cent in 2019 (Table 1). In 2010, besides banking and financial services, three sectors—construction and material, telecommunications, travel and leisure—were ahead of the real estate market capitalisation (Table 1). However, by 2019, real estate crowded out of all other productive sectors and had the third-largest market capitalisation after banking and financial services.

The Gulf real estate company was listed in the EGX for the first time in 2015 (EGX, 2015, p. 8). There has been an increase in foreign investment in the real estate sector. The net foreigners' purchase of equities and bonds

Table 1: Per cent share of sectors in market capitalisation in the Egyptian Stock Exchange

2010	2015	2019
Construction and material (23%)	Banks (20%)	Banks (30.4%)
Telecommunications (16%)	Construction and material (19%)	Financial services (10.8%)
Banks (11%)	Real estate (12%)	Real estate (10.2%)
Financial services (8%)	Financial services (9%)	Industrial goods, services and automobiles (7.6%)
Travel and leisure (6%)	Telecommunications (8%)	Personal & household products (6%)
Real estate (5%)		Health & pharmaceutical (4.7%)

Source: EGX annual reports 2010, 2015, 2019.

between November 2016 and December 2019 increased by EGP64.2 billion (US$ 3.7 billion) compared to the increase of EGP9.2 billion (US$ 1.1 billion) between September 2013 and October 2016 (EGX, 2019, p. 24). The banking, financial services and real estate sectors registered the first, second and third largest foreigner's net purchase, respectively, with the share of the real estate at 13.5 per cent (ibid.).

The initial state-driven investment in real estate in 2015 later dovetailed into private investment from the Gulf real estate developers, especially from the UAE (Sinno, 2017). The Arab investment had boosted the real estate and construction sectors in Egypt, especially during the phase when the political risk was high after the Arab uprising (ibid.). The GCC banks, especially from UAE, Qatar and Kuwait, also have significant exposure to lending in real estate in Egypt. Table 2 shows the FDI into Egypt and the share of Arab countries which increased from nearly 14 per cent in 2012-13 to about 21 per cent in 2019-20. A lower share during 2016-17 was possibly due to increased portfolio investments in the government debt instruments as interest rates (and the rates on treasury bills and government securities) peaked in that period (Figure 4).

To curb the inflationary impact of the currency devaluation in 2016 and attract foreign investment in government debt instruments (Hafez 2019), the Central Bank of Egypt raised the interest rates significantly

Table 2: Foreign Direct Investment in Egypt (US$ million)

	2009-10	2012-13	2013-14	2014-15	2015-16	2016-17	2017-18	2018-19	2019-20
UAE	303.5	480.6	401.2	1 382.5	1 328.7	836.9	1075.4	1104.2	1617.5
Saudi Arabia	323.4	191.7	284.4	649.1	313	343.7	296.7	478.1	448.6
Qatar	70.4	375.6	109.1	94.4	194.8	169.4	165	382.2	679.4
Bahrain	64.1	262.7	193.7	136.5	164.7	113.0	88	192	324
Kuwait	188.7	46.4	129.6	236.8	132.5	149.8	111.5	684.2	347.5
Total Arab Countries (value, %)	1439.5 (13.1%)	1 456.4 (14.2%)	1 290 (11.8%)	2 277.7 (18.2%)	2 277.7 (18.2%)	1 800.0 (13.5%)	1925.5 (14.6%)	3258.4 (20%)	3258.5 (21%)
Total FDI inflows	11008.1	10 273.6	10 892.9	12 546.2	12 528.7	13 366.1	13163.1	16393.5	15 836.6

Source: CAPMAS, Statistical yearbook 2020; CAPMAS, Egypt in Figures 2021.

(Figure 4). In FY 2016-17, budgetary expenditure on housing increased by 276 per cent (Oxford Business Group, 2018) and in 2016 the government launched the new administrative capital project, Cairo Capital, to be built over 700 square kilometre area between Cairo and the Red Sea. The increase in interest rates was followed by the large inflows of foreign institutional investments in government debt instruments (Wagdi, Tarek and Edres, 2018). Nevertheless, it affected the cost of borrowing for the buyers along with reduced disposable income.

The paradox of real estate development is a glut of property vacant or under construction along with housing shortages. The estimated properties vacant and under construction were about 17 per cent (CAPMAS, 2017), and against the estimated shortage of about 3 million housing units, about 5.6 million units remained vacant as of June 2019 (Oxford Business Group, 2020). High inflation and high-interest rates made housing unaffordable for common Egyptians (Megahid, 2017). Many of the megaprojects, including the Arabtec social housing project, had been criticised for excluding 50 per cent of the Egyptians from benefiting from its terms and for failing to resolve the housing crisis (Sinno, 2017). The foreign investors and private developers have shifted the supply in favour of high-income housing (Rania Nasreldin, 2019). The five-year programme launched by the government in 2014 for providing one million subsidised housing to the low-income citizens could only benefit less than 25 per cent of the intended beneficiaries by July 2019 (Oxford Business Group, 2020).

The high returns on holding government debt instruments have crowded out funding to the private sector in other productive activities. Since 2011, banks had a high level of exposure to government debts, accounting for about 40 per cent of banking system assets (US Department of State, 2019). There had been crowding out of the private sector by the government financial instrument, which implies that the financing of the budgetary deficit was at the expense of the financing the process of economic development (Wagdi, Tarek, Edres, 2018, p. 168). Besides, high interest rates also depressed the demand for credit from the industry and other business enterprises. The share of the private sector in the total loan has declined from 80.5 per cent in 2014-15 to 61.5 per cent in 2018-19 (CAPMAS, 2020).

Figure 4: Interest Rates in Egypt, 2012-19

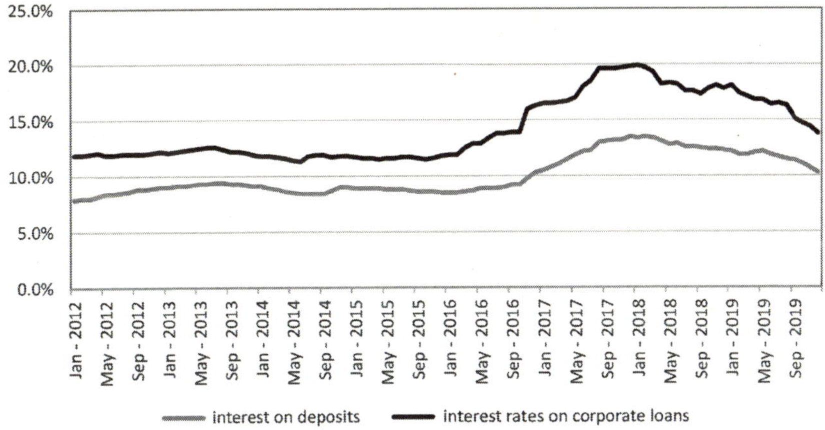

Source: Compiled from Central Bank of Egypt

Developmental Backsliding under the Real Estate Boom

The prospects of the job market also shaped people's attitudes towards education and participation in the labour force, especially that of females. The growth in real estate and the attended construction sectors has produced jobs that prefer males and are predominantly semi-skilled and temporary in nature. The impact is visible in many socio-economic indicators. The phenomenal growth of the real sector is reflected in the increase in its share of GDP from 2.6 per cent in 2009-10 to 11.2 per cent in 2019-20 (Table 3). The construction sector also gained about 2.1 per cent share in the same period.

Table 3: Sectoral Contribution to the GDP (per cent)

	2009-10	2019-20
GDP	100	100
Agriculture and allied sectors	14.0	12.1
Mining (oil and Gas & others)	14.4	7.5
Manufacturing	16.9	17.0
Whole sale &retail trade	11.6	14.5
Construction	4.6	6.7
Real estate activities	2.6	11.2
Financial intermediaries	3.9	3.8
Tourism	3.5	2.3

Source: CAPMAS, Egypt in figures 2011, 72; Egypt in figures 2021, 112.

As discussed, real estate had a crowding-out effect on the other private sector industries' access to finance in the capital and banking sectors. Consequently, the growth of most of the other sectors had been shunted. This is reflected in the drastic decline (by 50 per cent and more) in the number of new economic establishments in almost all the sectors by 2015 (383,444) from its levels in 2010 (1,214,901) rising marginally in 2016 only to fall in 2017 (CAPMAS, 2018b, p. 42).

The reduced opportunities for the growth of other sectors manifest in multiple ways. The poverty levels have phenomenally increased[2] in the urban governorates comprising Cairo, Alexandria, Suez and Port Said, from 9.6 per cent in 2010-11 to 26.7 per cent in 2017-18 (Table 4). The same was the situation in rural areas of Lower Egypt governorates.[3] The poverty levels in the Upper Egypt governorates were much higher in 2009 and did not witness any improvement by 2017-18. However, the relative increase in poverty levels in the different governorates has been caused by growing unemployment in the period (CAPMAS, 2018c).

Table 4: Poverty Level (in per cent) by Governorates in Egypt

	2010-11	2017-18
Urban Governorate	9.6	26.7
Lower Urban Governorate	10.3	14.3
Lower Rural Governorate	17.0	27.3
Upper Urban Governorate	29.5	30.0
Upper Rural Governorate	51.4	51.9
Total	25.2	32.5

Source: CAPMAS Egypt in Figures 2011; Egypt in Figures 2020.

The per cent of households in the lowest 20 per cent of the consumption slide had increased from 9.5 per cent in 2010-11 to 14.4 per cent (Table 5). Even the per cent of households in the highest 20 per cent consumption slide has decreased, implying an overall impoverishment of the Egyptian society. The average household income has increased by 2.5 to 3 times from the level in 2010-11. Nevertheless, with a 2.5 to 3 times increase in the cost of most household expenditure items between 2010 and 2019, as shown in Table 6, the real gains seem marginal.

Table 5: Average Annual Household Consumption and Percentage share in each percentile slide

Quantiles	Consumption Share (%), 2010-11	Annual Average Consumption of Household (LE), 2010-11	Consumption Share (%), 2017-18	Annual Average Consumption of Household (LE), 2017-18
Less than 20%	9.5	13,981.4	14.4	35,844.2
From 20% to less than 40%	13.3	17,427.8	16.5	43,250.3
From 40% to less than 60%	16.6	19,204.6	18.3	48,382.9
From 60% to less than 80%	21.3	21,553.0	22.0	52,100.6
From 80% to 100%	39.3	31,537.0	28.8	69,592.6

Source: CAPMAS, Egypt in Figures 2021; Egypt in Figures 2016.

Table 6: CPI by Groups, Base Year 2010=100

Groups	2019
Food and Non-alcoholic Beverages	382.9
Housing, Water, Electricity, Gas & other fuels	186.4
Transport	283.4
Communication	110.6
Education	364.0
Healthcare	243.6
Clothing and Footwear	217.0

Source: CAPMAS, Egypt in Figures, Price Indices 2020, p. 128.

Lack of employment opportunities had been a dominant concern of the Egyptians who took to the streets to overthrow the fossilised regime of President Mubarak. About 39.7 per cent of the total unemployed persons had a university education and above, while about 42.2 per cent had technical and intermediate education (CAPMAS, 2011a, p. 28).

The unemployment rates in urban governorates and most of the lower governorates had increased between 2010 and 2016 (CAPMAS, 2018c), and subsequently, there had been a general fall in the unemployment rates by 2019 (Table 7). However, the share of university graduates and above in the total unemployed persons had become the highest since 2016 (CAPMAS, 2017, p. 116) and was about 43.8 percent in 2019 (CAPMAS, 2020). It implies a subsequent reduction in unemployment rates after 2016 had been mostly among people with an intermediate level of education. Therefore, the growth process has produced lesser quality jobs for the youths with higher education.

Table 7: Annual Estimates of Labour Force Status, 2010-19 (million, per cent)

	2010	2011	2012	2013	2014	2015	2016	2017	2018	2019
Total Labour Force	26.1	26.5	27.0	27 6	27.9	28.4	28.9	29.5	28.7	28.4
Male	20.1	20.5	20.9	21.2	21.3	21.7	21.9	22.5	22.8	23.3
Female	6.0	6.0	6.2	6.5	6.6	6.7	7.0	7.0	6.0	5.1
Total Number of unemployed	2.4	3.2	3.4	3.7	3.7	3.6	3.6	3.5	2.9	2.2
Unemployment Rates %	9.0	12.0	12.7	13.2	13.0	12.8	12.5	11.8	9.9	7.9
Female Unemployment %	22.6	22.7	24.1	24.2	24.0	24.2	23.6	23.1	21.4	21.7

Source: CAPMAS, Statistical Yearbook Labour 2020, https://www.capmas.gov.eg/Pages/Publications.aspx?page_id=5104&Year=23563

There had been a significant fall in the share of agriculture and allied sector employment from 28.2 per cent in 2010 (CAPMAS, 2011a, p. 23) to 21.1 per cent in 2019 (CAPMAS, 2021). On the other hand, the construction sector has gained from 11.3 per cent to 14 per cent in the same period (ibid.). Table 8 shows the contribution of construction sector in the total employment in the different governorates. Construction has been the second most important activity after agriculture in seven (Luxor, Qena, Suhag, Asyout, Menia, Fayoum, Beni Suef) out of nine governorates of Upper Egypt providing 16-30 per cent of the employment in 2019. It

Table 8: Construction Activity and Education Level in Different Governorates, 2019

Region	Governorates	Share of construction in employment (%)	Never Enrolled (6-18 years) (%) Census 2017		Drop Out (Above 4 and more) (%) Census 2017		Share of University Graduates in total population (%)	Rate of Unemployment Among university graduates (%)
			Male	Female	Male	Female		
Urban Governorates	Cairo	13	17.1	21.6	5.3	5.7	24.8	50
	Alexandria	11	19.0	23.8	10.2	10.1	18	44.6
	Suez	13	16.0	20.4	5.5	5.9	19.8	41.9
Lower Egypt Governorates	Dakahlia	12	20.8	25.3	8.9	6.5	11.3	49.2
	Sharkia	11	22.8	29.6	7.1	5.0	11.8	42.8
	Kalyoubia	13	21.2	27.8	3.1	7.1	11.5	46.4
	Gharbia	11	19.1	25.9	9.1	6.6	0.3	62.0
Upper Egypt Governorates	Luxor	30	21.7	32.3	6.4	9.3	8.0	68.1
	Qena	23	23.6	37.4	6.1	10.0	8.0	36.2
	Suhag	22	28.2	40.9	8.6	8.4	11.1	40.9
	Asyout	22	29.7	40.5	7.6	6.9	6.7	36.7
	Menia	16	30.5	43.6	5.8	5.0	6.2	33.7
	Fayoum	17	29.4	38.5	6.9	6.7	7.5	39.0
	Beni Suef	18	29.0	41.1	7.6	6.2	14.3	58.5
Total Egypt		14.0	26.8		7.6	7.0	12.4	43.8

Source: Compiled from CAPAMS, Statistical Yearbook 2020.

had provided 11-13 per cent of employment in three (Cairo, Alexandria and Suez) of the four urban governorates and four (Dakahlia, Sharkia, Kalyoubia and Gharbia) out of nine governorates in Lower Egypt.

The predominance of construction activities in many governorates, especially in Upper Egypt, has led to some socially regressive effects. Employment in the construction sector is mostly male-dominated and semi-skilled. The CAPAMS data on the enrolment in primary education also revealed that the percentage of persons (between 6-18 years) who were never enrolled in primary school ranged from 26.5 to 36.8 per cent in the Upper Egypt governorates. The disparity between males and females primary enrollment ratio was higher in these governorates. The females were at least 10 per cent less likely than males to enrol in primary education (Table 8).

Nevertheless, among the enrolled persons, the drop-out per cent (of children four years and above) among the males was higher than that of females (Table 8) in most of the governorates in Upper and Lower Egypt. The national average of drop out per cent among males was also higher than females apparently because of compulsions of rising poverty and more availability of semi-skilled jobs, and therefore the males appeared less interested in continuing secondary education. Consequently, the near parity in the male and female enrolment per cent for secondary education in 2009-10 disappeared subsequently, and the gap increased significantly in favour of the females by 2018-19 (Table 9). The sharp fall in the enrolment per cent was registered in 2010-11, even before the onset of the Arab uprising in Egypt. However, after some improvement in the first half of the decade, the enrolment per cent has fallen more for males than females during 2014-18, reflective of their increasing disengagement from higher education (Table 9).

One of the most visible manifestations of social regression is the decline in female work participation during 2017-19. The female labour force increased from about 6 million in 2010 to about 7 million in 2017 and subsequently declined to about 5 million in 2019 (Table 7). Thus, the female labour force declined by almost 2 million in two years, apparently due to the pessimism generated by prevailing high female unemployment rates and disproportionate growth of the real estate and construction sectors that mostly provided male-preferred and often temporary jobs

Table 9: Percentage Enrolment by Stages of Education

Stage of education	2009-10		2010-11		2011-12		2012-13		2014-15		2018-19	
	Male	Female	Male	Female	Male	Female	Male	Female	Male	Female	Male	Female
Primary	96.0	95.0	103.0	100.0	101.5	98.5	92.6	97.2	95.5	96.7	92.1	101.1
Secondary	60.0	59.0	24.0	29.0	26.3	31.5	26.9	33.4	29.6	36.4	26.9	35.2

Sources: CAPMAS Statistical Yearbook 2017, p. 604; Statistical Yearbook 2020.

opportunities. About 457,458 persons were employed in the construction sector, of which about 189,657 (41.5 per cent) had temporary employment (CAPMAS, 2018a, p. 89).

The failure of economic growth to productively engage the Egyptian youth is manifested in a significant increase in decadal population growth registered in the census 2017. Population decadal growth rate at 2.56 per cent had been the highest since the 1980s and second highest in all the preceding 14 censuses (CAPMAS, 2021, p. 11). The census of 2017 recorded the highest percentage of the population below five years of age at 13.6 per cent (ibid., p. 25). The decade has been that of a baby boom in Egypt and had reversed the decline of the dependency ratio in the preceding decade. The dependency ratio had declined from 69.4 per cent in 2000 to 54.8 in 2010 but had increased significantly from 53.9 in 2016 to 61.6 in 2017 (ibid., pp. 11-12). The real estate-led growth in Egypt has led to the development backsliding in the society, in general, and among females, in particular.

Conclusion

The economic and political instability in the aftermath of the Arab uprising in Egypt led to the real estate boom as people rushed to invest to hedge against the rising inflation and falling value of the EGP. President Sisi made the real estate and construction sectors the driver of economic growth and employment. The state initially emerged as the lead player but later dovetailed to significant foreign investment, especially from the rich GCC countries. The devaluation of the Egyptian Pound significantly benefitted the real estate sector both from the demand and finance sides. Through the decade, the real estate sector outperformed the other sectors except banking and the financial services in the Egyptian Stock Exchange and, in the process, crowded them out from the finance in the capital market. High returns on government debt also crowded out the private sector from bank credit. Nevertheless, the currency devaluation and high interest rates simultaneously produced vacant and under-construction properties and housing shortages, as a vast proportion of the Egyptians could not afford to buy the houses.

The disproportionate growth of the real estate sector has stifled the growth of other sectors, and consequently, the job opportunities for the labour force with higher education were limited. There were some socially regressive effects of the increase in male-preferred, largely semi-skilled and often temporary opportunities in the construction and real estate sectors. There was a significant decline in the female labour force during 2017-19. Males were less likely to enrol in secondary education, and their drop-out rates were higher. However, in the Upper Egypt governorates, where construction was the second-largest source of employment after agriculture, females were at least 10 per cent less likely than males to get enrolled in primary education. The second highest decadal population growth rate in the decade of the Arab uprising marks the culmination of a socially-regressive model of real estate-led growth in Egypt.

Notes

1. P/E is Price-to-earnings ratio relates to companies' current share price to its earning per share. High value of P/E implies the share of the company is overvalued as investors expect high growth in future.
2. Devaluation of Egyptian Currency in November 2016 partly caused the general increase in poverty between 2010/11 and 2017/18 levels as the cost of living increased significantly.
3. Lowers Egypt and Upper Egypt governates refer to the lower and upper riparian regions of the River Nile.

References

Abbot, Philip C., Hurt, Christopher and Tyner, Wallace E. (2011, July). What's driving food prices in 2011? Farm Foundation, https://ageconsearch.umn.edu/record/112927/files/FoodPrices_web.pdf. Accessed on 1 June 2021.

American Chamber of Commerce (2016). Real Estate Big Picture, https://www.amcham.org.eg/publications/industry-insight/issue/1/Real-Estate's-Big-Picture . Accessed on 1 June 2021.

CAPMAS (2011a). Egypt in Figures, 2011, https://www.capmas.gov.eg/Pages/Publications.aspx?page_id=5104. Accessed on 1 June 2021.

CAPMAS (2017). Statistical Year Book, 2017. Retrieved from https://www.capmas.gov.eg/. Accessed on 1 June 2021.

CAPMAS (2018 c). Annual Bulletin of Statistics Employment and Wages 2018, Retrieved from https://www.capmas.gov.eg/. Accessed on 1 June 2021.

CAPMAS (2018a). Bulletin: Anthem and Construction - Public Sector and Business 2017-18, Retrieved from https://www.capmas.gov.eg/. Accessed on 1 June 2021.

CAPMAS (2018b). Final Results of the Economic Census 2017-18, https://www.capmas.gov.eg/Pages/Economicnew.aspx?page_id=2029._Accessed on 1 June 2021.

CAPMAS (2020). Statistical yearbook 2020, https://www.capmas.gov.eg/Pages/Publications.aspx?page_id=5104&Year=23561. Accessed on 1 June 2021.

CAPMAS (2021). Egypt in Figures, 2021. Retrieved from https://www.capmas.gov.eg/. Accessed on 1 June 2021.

Central Bank of Egypt (2012). Annual Report 2011-12. Retrieved from https://www.cbe.org.eg/en/EconomicResearch/Publications/Pages/AnnualReport.aspx. Accessed on 1 June 2021.

Delmendo, Lalaine C. (2019, June 2019). Egypt's house prices falling sharply: Outlook look positive, Global Property Guide, https://www.globalpropertyguide.com/Middle-East/Egypt/Price-History. Accessed on 29 May 2021.

Diwan, Ishac and Schiffbauer, Marc (2018). Private banking and crony capitalism in Egypt. *Business and Politics*, vol. 20, no. 3, pp. 390-409.

Egyptian Stock Exchange (2011). Annual Report 2011, Retrieved from https://www.egx.com.eg/en/Services_Reports.aspx._Accessed on 1 June 2021.

Egyptian Stock Exchange (2015). Annual Report 2015, Retrieved from https://www.egx.com.eg/en/Services_Reports.aspx._Accessed on 1 June 2021.

Egyptian Stock Exchange (2019). Annual Report 2019, Retrieved from https://www.egx.com.eg/en/Services_Reports.aspx._Accessed on 1 June 2021.

El Baradei, Laila (2019, July). "Egypt's currency devaluation & impact on the most vulnerable". *International Relations and Diplomacy*, 7 (7), pp. 303-316.

Hafez, Tamer (2019, August). Egypt at interest rates crossroads, America Chamber of Commerce in Egypt. https://www.amcham.org.eg/publications/business-Monthly/issues/284/august-2019/3879/egypt-at-interest-rate-crossroads. Accessed on 1 June 2021.

Laessing, Ulf (2013, 3 April), Mid east money-Egyptian buy into real estate to escape the currency dive, 3 April, Reuters, https://www.reuters.com/article/egypt-housing-idUSL5N0CO1KT20130403. Accessed on 1 June 2021.

Megahid, Ahmed (2017, 28 August). Owning a house becomes unthinkable for many Egyptians. *The Arab Weekly*, https://thearabweekly.com/owning-home-becoming-unthinkable-many-egyptians. Accessed on 3 June 2021.

Momani, Bessma (2018, 30 January). Egypt IMF programme: Assessing the political economy challenge. Brooking Doha Centre Publications, https://www.brookings.edu/research/egypts-imf-program-assessing-the-political-economy-challenges/. Accessed on 25 May 2021.

Osman, Abdel-Azim (2017, 4 January). How has the floating of Egyptian Pound impacted Egypt's real estate Market? *Egyptian Streets* https://egyptianstreets.

com/2017/01/04/how-has-the-floating-of-the-egyptian-pound-impacted-egypts-real-estate-market/. Accessed on 1 June 2021.

Oxford Business Group (2017). Egypt Report 2017, https://oxfordbusinessgroup.com/overview/place-call-your-own-residential-commercial-and-retail-space-sees-sustained-demand. Accessed on 26 May 2021.

Oxford Business Group (2018). Egypt Report 2018, https://oxfordbusinessgroup.com/overview/setting-sale-sector-remains-robust-amid-challenging-economic-climate. Accessed on 1 June 2021.

Oxford Business Group (2020). Egypt Report 2020, https://oxfordbusinessgroup.com/overview/room-grow-large-scale-infrastructure-and-urban-development-projects-should-drive-long-term-sector. Accessed on 10 June 2021.

Sayigh, Yazid (2019). Owners of the republic: Anatomy of Egypt's military economy. Carnegie Middle East Centre https://carnegie-mec.org/2019/11/18/owners-of-republic-anatomy-of-egypt-s-military-economy-pub-80325. Accessed on 1 June 2021.

Sayigh, Yazid (2020, 26 October). Egypt's military as the spearhead of State Capitalism. Carnegie Middle East Centre, https://carnegie-mec.org/2020/10/26/egypt-s-military-as-spearhead-of-state-capitalism-pub-83010. Accessed on 1 June 2021.

Sinno, Maïa (2017), The Gulf Takeover of Cairo's Megaprojects, *Égypte/Monde Arabe*, Troisième série, 16, pp. 125-141.

US Department of State (n.d.). 2019 Investment Climate Statements: Egypt, https://www.state.gov/reports/2019-investment-climate-statements/egypt/. Accessed on 26 May 2021.

Wagdi, Osama, Tarek, Yasmin and Edres, Nihad (2018). "Performance of stock and treasury bills under inflation and floating: Evidences from Egypt", *International Journal of Economics and Finance*, 10(6), pp. 160-173.

Wood, David (2018, June). Bringing mortgages to the middle class. American Chamber of Commerce in Egypt, https://www.amcham.org.eg/publications/business-Monthly/issues/270/june-2018/3734/bringing-mortgages-to-the-middle-class. Accessed on 26 May 2021.

8. Arab Spring and Arms Trade in MENA

Lakshmi Priya

Introduction

The Arab Spring protests that engulfed the Middle East and North Africa (MENA) in 2011-12 significantly influenced foreign policy, economy, demography, and security of regional countries. It also affected the regional geopolitics and political economy and forced a reset in the strategic calculations of the regional states. One of the outcomes of this reset manifested through the change in the region's existing dynamics of the arms trade. Being a hotbed of conflicts, the region is a recipient of a large number of arms even before 2011, but the outbreak of several civil wars, such as in Syria, Libya, and Yemen, proliferation of terrorist groups, such as the Islamic State (ISIS), and sharpening geopolitical competition among regional states gave impetus to arms trade in the region.

Among the leading regional importers of arms are the six Gulf Cooperation Council (GCC) states. Saudi Arabia, for example, is the world's largest buyer of arms between 2016 and 2020, while Qatar increased its arms procurement during the same period, compared to 2011-15, by 361 per cent (Wezeman et al., 2021). However, the rise in military expenditure is not confined to the Gulf Arab countries and others such as Egypt, Israel and Jordan, too increased their expenses by 7.3 per cent, 2.7 per cent and 2.5 per cent, respectively. The major beneficiaries of the rise in arms trade were the top international arms exporters, including the United States (US), Russia, United Kingdom (UK), France, Germany, China, and the upcoming regional arm exporter, Turkey. Israel, another Middle Eastern country that has emerged as an important arms exporter, has not found many buyers in MENA region due to the complex regional security situation.

This chapter discusses the geopolitics of global arms trade and analyses the factors that drive the arms industry. It situates the regional trends in MENA with the political economy of international arms transfers while analysing the factors that drive the regional countries to spend a considerable budget for the military. It further examines the impact of the Arab Spring on arms trade in the region. Finally, the chapter finds a parallel in the upward trajectory of the threat perception among regional countries and arms trade between 2011 and 2020.

The Geopolitics of Arms Trade

The urge to ensure security and minimise threat is ingrained among the individuals and states, and one of its manifestations is the flourishing arms industry. Trading in arms and military equipment goes back to historical times, with the beginning of organised arms trade going back to the 16th and 17th centuries when the European and North American merchants traded guns and gunpowder to Asia and Africa. Arms trade got an unprecedented impetus due to the technological developments and industrial revolution. Political dimension got associated with the arms trade during World War I when it acted as a tool for expression of foreign policy despite private ownership of the manufacturing companies. America traded arms to its allies even before Woodrow Wilson's formal declaration of war on Germany. After the World War II, the US and the Soviet Union emerged as the major arms exporters by selling weapons to their respective allies engaged in proxy wars and soon arms race became a defining feature for Cold War politics. Considering the heavy military burden and other associated vices, treaties to curb the arms race, including the Nuclear Test-Ban Treaty (1963), Strategic Arms Limitation Treaty (1972 and 1979), and Strategic Arms Reduction Treaty (1991), were signed between the two superpowers.

Global Arms Exporters

The US has dominated the global arms trade since the disintegration of the Soviet Union and remains the world's largest arms exporter catering to 96 countries and constituting 37 per cent of the total export during 2016-20 (da Silva et al. 2021). It is also the biggest spender with a military budget of US$778 billion, comprising 39 per cent of the global military spending. One of the factors that make the US the largest military spender is the diverse military responsibilities the global power undertakes around the world. As per its 2018 National Defence Strategy, the US military is responsible for deterring war, maintaining homeland security, maintaining a favourable regional balance of power in the Indo-Pacific, Europe, Middle East, and the Western Hemisphere, dissuading non-state actors from acquiring and using weapons of mass destruction and preventing terrorists from supporting external operations against the US and its partners overseas (US Department of Defence 2018). Further, with emphasis on reform, modernisation and technological innovations, the US is likely to remain the largest spender and exporter in the future (Vergun, 2021).

The second-largest exporter is Russia, contributing upto 20 per cent of the total global arms exports during 2016-20 and catering to the 45 countries (da Silva et al., 2021). After the disintegration of the Soviet Union in 1991, Russia's weapons production had decreased by more than 50 per cent. Owing to inflation and economic slowdown, Russian weapon acquisition too had witnessed a decline. The downward trajectory in the overall military expenditure continued for nearly a decade. Towards the end of the 1990s, the Russian government revived its military reforms and enhanced its military exports. After 2000, Russian military expenditure constantly grew, except for a brief lull in 2017-18 (Cooper, 2017). The proportion of the Russian defence industry to exports constantly increased since 2000, and between 1998 and 2013, Russian arms exports exceeded procurement expenditures every year; moreover, in 2013, exports ran to US$ 15.7 billion, 65 per cent more than the procurement (Crane et al., 2019).

France, Germany, UK, Spain and Italy are among the top ten exporters for 2016-20 and account for 22.2 per cent of the global arms exports (da Silva et al., 2021). Realising the significance of arms export in providing domestic armed forces with high-performing and innovative weapons, France worked on increasing its share in global arms export; it contributed more than 8 per cent for 2016-2020 as the third-largest contributor. France is further working towards diversifying exports as focusing only on the European market limits the French defence industry and it finds the Indo-Pacific region a lucrative venture

(Ministry of the Armed Forces, France, 2020). Arms export of Germany, the fourth-largest contributor, increased by 21 per cent during 2016-20 compared to 2011-15 as it contributed 5.5 per cent of the global arms export (da Silva et al., 2021). Despite having a strict licensing policy, Germany has faced domestic protests against arms exports impacting the arms industry; thus, in 2018, the collective export licenses came down to 15 from 2,546 in 2008 (SIPRI, 2018). According to the Social Democratic Party (SDP), one of the ruling parties, Germany should export fewer weapons and certainly not to parties that wage war among themselves (Nehra, 2020).

The UK (sixth), Spain (seventh) and Italy (tenth) contributed 3.3, 3.2 and 2.2 per cent to the global share during 2016-20, respectively. At the beginning of Arab Spring, the UK faced increased domestic criticism for exporting weapons to affected countries that might be one of the factors responsible for a decrease of 27 per cent in arms export during 2016-20 compared to 2011-15. Spain's export decreased by 8.4 per cent for the same period, and Italy reduced arms export by 22 per cent. However, the UK government described arms exports as essential for its national security and made exports a core task of the Ministry of Defence for the first time in 2015 (Brook-Holland, 2018).

China (fifth), Israel (eighth) and South Korea (ninth) are the three Asian countries to figure among the top ten exporters and contribute 5.2, 3.0 and 2.7 per cent to the global arms exports, respectively (da Silva et al., 2021). China's arms exports had increased over 77 per cent during 2011-15 but during 2016-20, its arms export decreased by 7.8 per cent. Some countries' reluctance to import Chinese arms due to political and security concerns and sanctions by the US and European Union (EU) drove China to steer towards the lucrative market in the Middle East. On the other hand, South Korea has come a long way in two decades as it climbed to the ninth position in 2020 from the 31st position in 2000.

Israel is the only country from the region that figures in the top ten exporters and exports arms to all corners of the world except the Middle East. Until now, its exports to the region has been miniscule due to strategic concerns; however, with the signing of the Abraham Accords, its share in the Middle East arms trade might increase in future.

Major Arms Importers

As far as arms imports are concerned, data compiled by Stockholm International Peace Research Institute (SIPRI) indicates that the largest importing region during 2016-20 was Asia and Oceania, constituting 42 per cent of the global arms imports, followed by the Middle East (33 per cent), Europe (12 per cent), Africa (7.3 per cent) and the Americas (5.4 per cent) (da Silva et al., 2021). The top ten arms importing countries globally in the order of ranking were Saudi Arabia, India, Egypt, Australia, China, Algeria, South Korea, Qatar, United Arab Emirates (UAE) and Pakistan.

It is important to understand the factors that compel a country to import arms and allocate a significant portion of its GDP. Several studies have been conducted on the subject. It is evident that majorly the quest for security leads a country to invest in arms procurement even if it means a huge diversion of funds from welfare measures (Luck, 1977; Pierre, 1982). Arms transfer influences a state's foreign policy and is also influenced by the same; for instance, interstate conflicts mandate heavy acquisition of arms by a concerned state, but the availability of arms also affects their propensity to initiate interstate conflicts (Dharia, 2019). Of the 24 countries which experienced at least one major armed conflict in 1997, the US sold arms or provided military training to 21 of them at some point during the 1990s (SIPRI, 1998).

Threat to internal security and domestic instability also propels states to import arms (Sanjian, 1999). Sometimes the uplift in regional and international status associated with possession of arms leads a country to import advanced weapons. Possession of arms nurtures hegemonic masculinity among individuals as well as states. Angela Stroud (2012) interviewed 20 men in the US to explore how they drew on discourses of masculinity to explain their use of concealed handguns and found that they used it to compensate for lost strength as they age. Similarly, states with less than adequate resources might resort to importing advanced weapons to thwart their insecurity and gain a sense of respect from competitors.

The exporter countries use arms sales to support their global allies against opponents, as evident during the Cold War and even provide subsidies (García-Alonso and Levine, 2005) or link it with aid (Howell and Lind, 2009). More importantly, the economic gains associated with arms sales provide a major push for arms exporters. Arms sale helps finance domestic defence and security industry and boosts indigenous arms capabilities, reducing dependence on outside powers (Liberman, 1996).

Arms Trade in MENA

The arms trade in MENA increased by 25 per cent between 2011 and 2020 (Figure 1). The region is home to five of the top ten and more than one-third of the top 30 arms importing countries. The top importers in the region are Saudi Arabia, Egypt, Algeria, Qatar, UAE, Iraq, Israel, Turkey, Oman, Jordan, and Morocco, while the top exporters are Israel, Turkey and UAE. In addition to conflicts and instability that fuel the demand for arms, strong ties with extra-regional powers, oil wealth and grants and aid from major exporters facilitate strong arms imports by the regional countries. The US is a major supplier while producers like Russia, France and China provide arms of lesser value like armed unmanned aerial vehicles and air defence systems and in a smaller volume.

Figure 1: Region-wise Arms Import Trend, 2011-2020

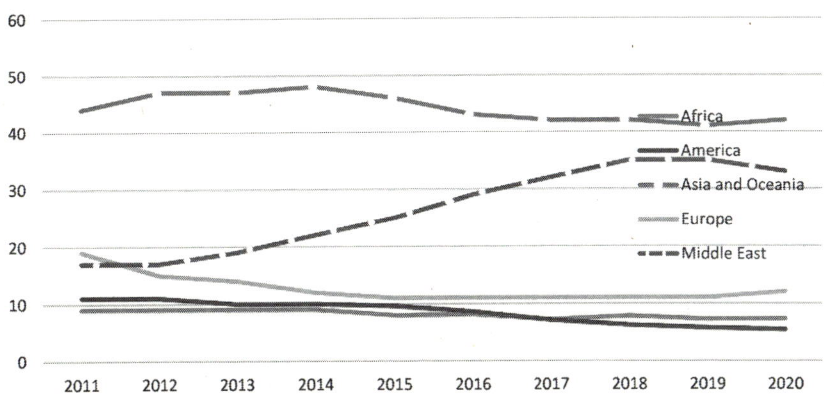

Source: The data has been taken from SIPRI Trends in International Arms Transfers 2011-2021. For each year, the data represents a percentage of total global arms import going to a region in the last five years; for instance, data for 2011 represents the arms transfer average of 2007-11.

Among the major regional actors, Israel insists on maintaining a large and technologically advanced military, keeping in mind the threats for its security, and other countries respond by enhancing their budget allocation for arms. Iran's rivalry with its neighbouring Gulf countries and Israel and conflicts in Iraq, Syria, Libya and Yemen create a hostile environment and contribute to the growing need for arms imports. In addition, transnational terrorist threats and fear of domestic rebellion encourage states to purchase arms. International credibility and national pride associated with a strong military also fuel arms procurement in large quantities. Moreover, for countries seeking to demonstrate influence and power, constant up-gradation of arms is needed as the existing arms become obsolete and advanced and more efficient ones are invented, constantly adding to the demand for arms.

Due to the technological superiority of the US and its quest for regional dominance, it is the single largest supplier to the region for over two decades. It intends to strengthen intra-regional cooperation to counter Iran, prevent Russia and China from making inroads in the region, and reinforcing Egypt and Jordan's peace treaties with Israel. During 2016-20, the US supplied around 45 per cent of the arms imported by the MENA countries (Wezeman et al., 2020). The US further intends to reduce its direct military involvement by supplying arms to Gulf Arab countries

Russia contributes 19.3 per cent of the arms import to the region and is perceived as an alternative supplier and leverage to bargain with the US. It provides cheaper weaponry and systems and does not impose preconditions related to human rights and secondary use. European arms exporting countries are important suppliers though they remain conflicted regarding the sale of weapons and protection of human rights. China is a new entrant in the Middle Eastern arms market and is probably testing waters before setting its own industrial and strategic goals. It aims to sell advanced technologies such as drones that other suppliers are reluctant to sell. As far as the impact of arms import on the internal dynamics of the Middle Eastern countries is concerned, Israel is a major beneficiary and Saudi Arabia and UAE have been able to project power beyond borders.

Israel is the only regional country to figure in the top ten exporters in the world. The US that limited its supplies over alienating the Arab states in the 1950s and 1960s became its major partner after the 1970s. Over the years, Israel imported arms mostly from the US (around 78 per cent) with minor contributions from Germany, Italy, Canada and France. Supplies from the US ensure Israel has an advantage over its neighbours. The two countries signed a Memorandum of Understanding (MoU) whereby the US Congress would provide US$ 38 billion in military aid over ten years, from 2019 to 2028. Since 1984, the US has specially allowed Israel to spend a portion of its military assistance on domestic arms production.

In addition to Israel, Turkey is another major exporter from the region and contributed 0.7 per cent of the global arms export in 2016-2020. It is the thirteenth-largest exporter globally and supplied armoured vehicles, ships, aircraft, artillery, engines, missiles and sensors to importers, including Oman, Turkmenistan and Malaysia (*The Daily Sabah,* 2021). Also, Turkey managed to reduce its arms imports by 59 per cent in 2016-20 compared to 2011-15.

Impact of the Arab Spring

Arab Spring protests, while raising hopes for a positive change early on, led to a serious escalation in violence and conflicts. This heightened fears of prolonged instability and led to a rise in the arms trade and military expenditure in most countries, including those not directly hit by massive protests. Tunisia, the birthplace of Arab Spring, increased its GDP allocation for military expenditure from 1.2 per cent in 2010 to 2.5 per cent in 2019 (The World Bank, 2021). Its arms import expenditure increased from US$ 7 million in 2010 to US$ 180 million in 2018. In 2019, it imported arms worth US$ 15 million. In addition to the heavy weaponry, the demand for small arms and light weapons was fuelled by the violent tribal and religious fighting along the Tunisia-Libya border (Kartas, 2013).

Egypt, which witnessed massive protests leading to the fall of Mubarak in February 2011, is among the largest importers of arms globally; it is the third-largest importer after Saudi Arabia and India for 2016-20 (da Silva et al., 2021). Egypt saw a sharp rise in its military expenditure and arms procurement since 2011. The major suppliers to Egypt are the US, Russia and France. In 2011-2015, 45 per cent of the Egyptian arms were imported from the US, but the figure dropped to 8.7 per cent in 2016-2020 as Russian arms formed 41 per cent and French arms formed 28 per cent of the imports (Wezeman et al., 2021). During 2016-20, procurements from Russia include 18 MiG-29s, 12 Ka-52S Rotary wing combat aircraft, S-300 VM, I Missile Corvette (Thomas et al. 2020). Further, Egypt purchased 24 Rafale fighter jets, two Mistral helicopter carriers, ships, fighter jets and military satellite communications systems from France in 2015-2016 (Nkala, 2016).

Other North African countries that witnessed Arab Spring protests include Algeria, Libya and Morocco, and along with Tunisia, they constituted nearly 75 per cent of the African arms imports. Their arms imports increased by 20 per cent between 2009–13 and 2014–18 (Wezeman et al., 2019). Algeria increased its military expenditure from 3.5 per cent in 2010 to 6.3 per cent of the GDP in 2016. In 2019 it spent 6.1 per cent of the GDP on military expenditure. Its arms import increased from US$ 835 million in 2010 to US$ 2.9 billion in 2016; however, in 2019, it imported arms worth US$ 165 million (The World Bank, 2021). Algeria is one of the top three arms importers of Russia, Germany, China, Sweden and UAE. Its arms imports increased by 64 per cent higher in 2016–20 as compared to 2011–15. Algeria and its regional rival Morocco accounted for 70 per cent of the total African imports of major arms in 2016–20. Algeria depends heavily on Russian arms as Moscow remained its largest arms supplier in 2016–20 and provided 16 combat aircraft, 42 combat helicopters and two submarines. Unlike Algeria, Morocco's arms import decreased by 60 per cent between 2011–15 and 2016–20 and is heavily depended on the US that supplied 90 per cent of its arms imports in 2016–20 (Wezeman et al., 2021).

Libya's GDP allocation for military expenditure increased from 1.49 per cent in 2008 to 15.48 in 2014 (The World Bank, 2021).[1] Its expenditure on arms import increased from US$ 8 million in 2011 to US$ 116 million in 2013. Its arms export expenditure decreased from 27 million in 2010 to nil in 2011 (ibid.). Before 2011, Libya was "one of the largest and most diverse owners of conventional weapons in Africa and had one of the world's highest rates of civilian gun ownership" (Alaraby and Müller, 2020, p. 4). During the fight between Gaddafi's forces and the rebels, countries like UAE and Qatar supplied weapons to the latter. After the fall of the Gaddafi regime, the stockpile of weapons fell in the hands of the militias. A large number of small arms and light weaponry were diverted to terrorist groups such as Ansar Al-Shari'a. Despite the arms embargo on Libya, regional and international players like UAE,

Qatar, Turkey, Egypt, Russia, and France provide heavy artillery, anti-tank missiles, drones, and other heavy weaponry to their allies and their affiliated groups (Robinson, 2020).

Iraq became a hotbed of ISIS activities after the Arab Spring protests and witnessed increased arms imports. It contributed 0.4 per cent to the global share and spent 4.3 per cent of its GDP on military expenditure in 2020 as compared to 2.3 per cent in 2011 (da Silva et al., 2021). At the height of the war against ISIS, Iraq's arms imports bill in 2016 touched US$1.5 billion. The country has also diversified its suppliers, reducing its dependence on the US as Russia, South Korea and China, emerged as major exporters of arms to Iraq (Thomas et al., 2020). Iraq received 18 F-16s, 175 Abrams tanks, F-16 munitions from the US; and Mi-28 Havoc "Night Hunter" attack helicopters from Russia. Notably, in 2019, Iraq's arms imports bill was reduced to US$ 250 million, and Russia was the only supplier, reflecting Moscow's inroads in the MENA arms market. The reduction of arms import from the US is a manifestation of Washington's commitment to the withdrawal of combat forces from Iraq and the failure of Baghdad in managing US-Iran tensions. In recent years, Iraq has expressed interest in Russian S-400s; purchased military unmanned aerial vehicles from China; and welcomed Iranian military assistance.

Syria, a country that came under the ambit of Arab Spring as early as 2011, is still reeling with civil war in mid-2021. In 2010, Damascus spent 4.0 per cent of its GDP on military and its arms imports increased from US$ 205 million in 2009 to US$ 506 million in 2013. Before the beginning of protests in 2011, the Assad regime had invested in modernisation of its military and sophisticated weaponry as reflected in increased arms import during 2007-2008. Hence, Syria's arms import increased from US$ 20 million in 2007 to US$ 294 million in 2008. Russia provided more than 70 per cent of Syria's import of conventional arms during 2008-2012 and facilitated arms transfer from Iran. It is a major military partner of Syria, while countries including the US, Qatar, Saudi Arabia, UAE, Jordan, Turkey, Israel, and Croatia militarily supported the opposition groups in Syria. Russian aircraft manufacturer MiG upgraded four Syrian Air Force MiG-29 fighter jets to the MiG-29SM specifications by adding new air-to-surface weapons, air-to-air missiles and an upgraded radar system.

Russia signed an agreement with Syria in 2017, allowing Russian forces to remain in Syria for the next 49 years with an automatic extension for 25 years while doubling the space for warships and securing the rights for an airbase. For Russia, the military intervention in Syria has provided the opportunity to revive its geopolitical influence (Hetou, 2019, pp. 67-92) and military inroads in the region, including as an alternative supplier of weapons to the US (Enders, 2018).

Yemen that witnessed protests as early as 2011, continues to suffer from civil war and a worsening humanitarian crisis. Before the beginning of the crisis, Yemen's arms imports had soared from US$ 5 million in 2009 to US$ 258 million in 2010. Protests that began with the demand for employment escalated into calls for the removal of President Ali Abdullah Saleh, who was eventually killed by the Houthi militias in 2017. The political failure of Saleh's successor, Abdrabbuh Mansur Hadi and the proxy war between Saudi Arabia and Iran has led to an unprecedented proliferation of arms in the country with 40-60 million weapons possessed by its inhabitants. American and European weapons, including army vehicles like Navistar multi-role armoured vehicles, anti-tank TOW missiles, MG3 machine guns, rocket launchers (RPG-32), reached Yemen through Saudi Arabia and UAE. On the other hand, Iran supplied arms, including anti-ship missiles, explosives, short-range surface-to-surface missiles and small arms to Yemen through the Omani borders (Bayoumi and Stewart, 2016). Despite the UNSC resolution 2216, unanimously adopted in 2015, requiring member-states to take the necessary actions to prevent the direct and indirect supply or sale of arms to the Yemeni combatants, including the Houthis and other militias, the arms transfer to Yemen has continued unabated (United Nations, 2015).

Among the top importers of arms in the region are the GCC countries. Bahrain witnessed series of protests and, during 2011-12, earmarked US$ 1.5 billion defence budget in 2020 (International Institute for Strategic Studies [IISS] 2020, p. 342). Bahrain is one of the five destinations for defence equipment manufactured in Turkey. Manama's arms import increased from US$ 23.8 billion in 2009 to US$ 29.9 billion in 2011, even though budget allocation for the same period decreased from 2.6 per cent to 2.4 per cent of the GDP.

Saudi Arabia is the largest arms importer globally, contributing 11 per cent of the global arms imports during 2016-20 (da Silva et al., 2021). Riyadh increased its share of imports in 2016-20 from 2011-15 by 61 per cent, and the US, UK and France are its major suppliers constituting 79, 9.3 and 4.0 per cent of its total imports, respectively. Spain, Germany, China and Russia are other exporters to the Kingdom. Contributing around 2.9 per cent of the global share, Saudi Arabia spent US$ 57 billion on military expenditure in 2020. The huge arms transfer reflects and reinforces the strong ties between Saudi Arabia and the US.

However, due to the differences between the two countries, Riyadh intends to diversify its arms imports, and Russia and China seem to be the beneficiaries. Saudi Arabia has also begun planning to reduce external military dependence by enhancing domestic defence production. In May 2017, Crown Prince Muhammad bin Salman announced a government-owned company called Saudi Arabian Military Industries (SAMI) to manage air and land systems, weapons and missiles, and defence electronics to achieve 50 per cent domestic military procurement by 2030 (al-Baqmi 2017). To that end, the arms sales announced during President Trump's May 2017 visit include arrangements for producing certain items within Saudi Arabia. For instance, a US$ 6 billion agreement between Lockheed Martin and TAQNIA planned for the assembly of 150 Blackhawk helicopters in Saudi Arabia (Arab News, 2017). Currently, Saudi Arabia has 150 F-15s, 47 C-130s, 47 AH-64 Apache, Patriot PAC-2, nine fast attack craft, four missile corvettes, 161 155 mm self-propelled howitzers and 833 battle tanks supplied by the US. However, Riyadh is in talks for the S-400 anti-aircraft missile system from Russia (Reuters, 2017) and has signed a deal with Beijing to establish a Chinese factory to manufacture military UAVs for Saudi Arabia's expanding drone fleet (*Middle East Eye*, 2017).

Qatar is the eighth largest arms importer in the world, contributing 3.8 per cent of the global arms imports during 2016-20. Doha increased its share of imports in 2016-20 from 2011-2015 by 361 per cent. The US, France and Germany are its major partners contributing 47, 38 and 7.5 per cent, respectively, to Doha's arms imports (da Silva et al., 2021). Italy, China and Russia are other arms import partners for Qatar.

The US is Qatar's major arms import partner, and it hosts 379th air expeditionary wing and several other US and coalition assets at Al-Udeid Air Base, including US Central Command's (CENTCOM) Combined Air Operations Center. It currently has eight C-17As, four C-130J-30s, seven AH-64s and ten Patriot PAC-3 batteries procured from the US.

The UAE is the ninth-largest arms importer globally, contributing 3 per cent of the global arms imports during 2016-20. The US, France and Russia are its major partners contributing 64, 10, 4.7 per cent, respectively to its imports. Italy, Spain and China are other arms suppliers to UAE. The US is UAE's major partner; however, like Saudi Arabia, it is also diversifying its arms basket and is looking forward to importing arms from Russia. The UAE signed an agreement with Russia in 2017 to develop a fifth-generation fighter jet, along with a separate purchase by the UAE of Russian Sukhoi Su-35 fighters (de Briganti, 2017).

Nonetheless, the UAE has been trying to buy F-35 fighter jets from the US, giving it an edge over its regional rivals and competitors. One of the concessions which the UAE received in lieu of normalizing relations with Israel and signing the Abraham Accords was the promise to get F-35 fighter jets. In January 2021, the US signed a deal to sell 50 F-35s and 18 MQ-9 Reaper drones to the UAE (Stone, 2021). Currently, UAE has 79 F-16s, 8 C-130s, eight C-17As, 19 AH-64 Apache, two THAAD batteries and 165 155 mm self-propelled howitzers. In addition, the UAE has reportedly procured Chinese surveillance drones, outfitted them with targeting systems and operated them in Libya and Yemen. The Emirates is also at the forefront of developing an indigenous arms industry, and in 2014 established the Emirates Defence Industries Company (EDIC) by consolidating many small state-owned firms to reduce its reliance on foreign suppliers and diversifying its hydrocarbon-based economy. EDIC has signed contracts with Algeria, Russia and Kuwait. Indigenous Emirati equipment, including locally made armoured vehicles, assault rifles, and personnel carriers, have been used prominently in the Saudi-led coalition's war in Yemen and Libya.

Oman is the 24th largest arms importer in the world and accounting for 1.2 per cent of the global share of arms imports in 2016-20, which is an increase of 12 per cent from 2011-15. Oman is among the top three importers for the UK, Turkey and Norway and receives 17, 19 and 47 per cent of their exports, respectively (da Silva et al., 2021). It spent 6.7 per cent of its GDP on military expenditure in 2020, and the US arms sale to Oman doubled from US$ 1.08 billion during 2000-09 to US$ 2.6 billion during 2010-2017. Kuwait's military expenditure decreased in 2020 for the first time since the oil price collapse in 2014, falling by 5.9 per cent. Despite this, Kuwait's military burden rose by 1 per cent point to 6.5 per cent of GDP. The fall in the price of oil because of declining demand due to the COVID-19 pandemic had a particularly negative impact on Kuwait's economy in 2020, affecting its arms imports (da Silva et al., 2021).

Jordan spent 5 per cent of its GDP on military expenditure in 2020, increasing 2.5 per cent over 2019. It is the 28th largest arms importer globally and imports arms from the US, Netherlands and UAE that contributed 36, 22 and 11 per cent, respectively to its total arms imports. It is the second-largest import partner of UAE and contributes 21 per cent of Emirates arms exports. Jordan's arms imports increased from US$ 90 million in 2010 to US$ 389 million in 2018 (The World Bank, 2021).It is a major importer of small arms, and in 2016 it was a tier-three importer with its small arms import hovering between US$ 50–99 million (Picard et al., 2019). Lebanon's military expenditure increased from 4.0 per cent in 2009 to 4.2 per cent of the GDP in 2019. As a result, its arms imports increased from US$ 1 million in 2011 to US$ 74 million in 2019.

As far as Iran is concerned, United Nations Security Council resolutions have restricted the transfer of major arms to Iran since 2010, and it remained in force until the end of 2020. Since 1994, Iran's arms import peaked in 2006 to decline again in 2012-13 due to the economic and financial sanctions imposed by the UN, US and EU. Iran's military expenditure increased by 25 per cent between 2015 and 2017 after the lifting of some of the US and EU sanctions. However, in 2018 military spending decreased again as the Iranian economy went into recession. As a result, the level of arms imports by Iran decreased significantly from 1994 to 2018 compared to its neighbours; however, its capacity to produce major arms, including ballistic missiles, cruise missiles and unmanned aerial vehicles, has kept it afloat.

Conclusion

Arms trade in MENA witnessed a significant increase between 2011 and 2020. The US is the dominant arms supplier to the regional countries, but increasingly, countries such as Russia, China, South Korea, UK, France, Italy and Turkey are finding opportunities to sell more arms, partly because of increased demands. Russia is among the most important beneficiaries of the increased demands of major regional players, including Egypt, Syria and GCC countries. China is still testing waters and can be contenders of a larger share over time. Regardless of whether they were directly affected by the Arab Spring protests or not, the regional countries increased arms imports due to the rise in conflicts and geopolitical competition, raising the threat perceptions. The conflicts have also been used by external powers as platforms to showcase their advanced weapons. Meanwhile, some Gulf countries intend to enhance their domestic arms production capacity and join Israel, Turkey and UAE as arms exporters, which can propel an arms race in the region.

Note

1. Current data for Libya is not available.

References

Alaraby, Muhammad and Müller, Alexander (2020), "Countering Illicit Arms Transfers in the MENA Region: The Case of Yemen and Libya," MENA Peace and Security Project, October, Friedrich-Ebert-Stiftung, Berlin, https://library.fes.de/pdf-files/iez/16657.pdf

al-Baqmi, Shuja (2017), "Saudi Arabia Launches 'SAMI' for Military Industries," *Asharq Al-Awsat*, May 18, https://eng-archive.aawsat.com/shuja-baqmi/news-middle-east/saudi-arabia/saudi-arabia-launches-sami-military-industries

Arab News (2017), "Saudi-US Arms Deal includes Plans for 150 Lockheed Martin Black Hawk Helicopters," May 20, https://www.arabnews.com/node/1102226/saudi-arabia

Bayoumi, Yara and Stewart, Phil (2016), "Exclusive: Iran Steps up Weapons Supply to Yemen's Houthis via Oman—Officials," Reuters, October 20, https://www.reuters.com/article/us-yemen-security-iran-idUSKCN12K0CX

Brook-Holland, Louisa (2018), "An Introduction to UK Arms Exports," *House of Commons Library Briefing Paper*, No. 8312, May 16, https://commonslibrary.parliament.uk/research-briefings/cbp-8312/

Cooper, Julian (2017), "Prospects for Military Spending in Russia in 2017 and Beyond," Working Paper, University of Birmingham, https://www.birmingham.ac.uk/Documents/college-social-sciences/government-society/crees/working-papers/prospects-for-military-spending-in-Russia-in-2017-and-beyond.pdf

Crane, Keith, Oliker, Olga and Nichiporuk, Brian (2019), "Trends in Russia's Armed Forces: An Overview of Budgets and Capabilities," Rand Corporation, https://www.rand.org/content/dam/rand/pubs/research_reports/RR2500/RR2573/RAND_RR2573.pdf

da Silva, Diego Lopes, Tian, Nan and Marksteiner, Alexandra (2021), "Trends in World Military Expenditure 2020," *SIPRI Factsheet*, April, https://sipri.org/sites/default/files/2021-04/fs_2104_milex_0.pdf

de Briganti, Giovanni (2017), "UAE Swings to Russia for Future Combat Aviation," *Defense-Aerosapce.com*, February 21, https://www.defense-aerospace.com/articles-view/feature/5/181311/uae-swings-to-russia-for-future-combat-aviation%2C-signs-3-agreements.html

Dharia, P. Saumil (2019), *Dangerous Weapons: Arms Transfer, Interstate Conflict, and Dependence*, Ph.D. Thesis, University of Missouri—Columbia, https://mospace.umsystem.edu/xmlui/handle/10355/72212

Enders, David (2018), "Syria becomes a Testing Ground as Russia Revives its Defence Industry," *The National*, March 13, https://www.thenationalnews.com/world/mena/syria-becomes-a-testing-ground-as-russia-revives-its-defence-industry-1.712786

García-Alonso, María del Carmen and Levine, Paul (2003), "Arms Export Controls, Subsidies and the WTO Exemption," Studies in Economics Discussion Paper, No. 0304, University of Kent, Department of Economics, Canterbury.

Hetou, Ghaidaa (2019), *The Syrian Conflict*, London: Routledge.

Howell, Jude and Lind, Jeremy (2009), *Counter-Terrorism, Aid and Civil Society: Before and After the War on Terror*. London: Palgrave Macmillan.

International Institute for Strategic Studies (IISS) (2020), *Military Balance 2020*, https://www.iiss.org/publications/the-military-balance/military-balance-2020-book

Kartas, Moncef (2013), "On the Edge? Trafficking and Insecurity at the Tunisian–Libyan Border," *Small Arms Survey*, Graduate Institute of International and Development Studies, Geneva.

Liberman, Peter (1996), "Trading with the Enemy: Security and Relative Economic Gains," *International Security*, vol. 21, no. 1, pp. 147-175.

Luck, Edward C. (1977), "The Arms Trade, *Proceedings of the Academy of Political Science*, vol. 32, no. 4, pp. 170-183.

Middle East Eye (2017), "China's Saudi Drone Factory Compensates for US Ban," March 29, https://www.middleeasteye.net/fr/news/china-build-factory-saudi-arabia-fill-drone-shortage-1200657135

Ministry of Armed Forces, France (2020), "Arms Export: Report to Parliament 2020," https://www.defense.gouv.fr/actualites/articles/exportations-d-armement-le-rapport-au-parlement-2020

Nehra, William (2020), "German Arms Export Hit a Record High in 2019," *I AM EXPAT*, January 9, https://www.iamexpat.de/expat-info/german-expat-news/germanys-arms-exports-hit-record-high-2019

Nkala, Oscar (2016), "Egypt, France to Sign Arms Deal Mid-April," *Defense News*, April 6, https://www.defensenews.com/industry/2016/04/06/egypt-france-to-sign-arms-deal-mid-april/

Picard, Michael, Holtom, Paul and Mangan, Fiona (2019), *Transfers, Transparency, and South-east Asia Spotlight*, Trade Update 2019 Report, December, Small Arms Survey, Graduate Institute of International and Development Studies, Geneva, http://www.smallarmssurvey.org/fileadmin/docs/S-Trade-Update/SAS-Trade-Update-2019.pdf

Pierre, Andrew (1982), *The Global Politics of Arms Sales*, Princeton: Princeton University Press.

Reuters (2017), "Kremlin Says S-400 Missile Talks with Saudi Arabia on Track," October 9, https://www.reuters.com/article/us-russia-saudi-missiles-idUSKBN1CE0ZY

Robinson, Kali (2020), "Who's is Who in Libya's War," Council on Foreign Relations, https://www.cfr.org/in-brief/whos-who-libyas-war

Sanjian, Gregory S. (1999), "Promoting Stability or Instability? Arms Transfer and Regional Rivalries, 1950-1991," *International Studies Quarterly*, vol. 43, no. 4, pp. 641-670.

Stockholm International Peace Research Institute (2018), "Report by the Government of the Federal Republic of Germany on its Policy on Exports of Conventional Military Equipment in 2018," https://www.sipri.org/sites/default/files/2021-04/germany_arms_exports_report_2018_english.pdf

Stone, Mike (2021), "UAE Signs Deal with US to Buy 50 F-35 Jets and up to 18 Drones: Sources," Reuters, January 20, https://www.reuters.com/article/usa-emirates-f35-int-idUSKBN29P2C0

Stroud, Angela (2012), "Good Guys with Guns: Hegemonic Masculinity and Concealed Handguns," *Gender and Society*, vol. 26, no. 2, pp. 216-238.

The Daily Sabah (2021), "Shift toward Local Production Slashes Turkey's Arms Imports: SIPRI," March 15, https://www.dailysabah.com/business/defense/shift-toward-local-production-slashes-turkeys-arms-imports-sipri_

The World Bank (2021), "Arms Imports: SIPRI Trend Indicator Values," https://data.worldbank.org/indicator/MS.MIL.MPRT.KD?end=2019&locations=DZ&start=1963&view=chart

Thomas, Clayton, Sharp, Jeremy M., Blanchard, Christopher M. and Arabia, Christina L. (2020), "Arms Sales in the Middle East: Trends and Analytical Perspectives for US Policy," *Congressional Research Service Report*, No. R44984, November 3, https://fas.org/sgp/crs/mideast/R44984.pdf

United Nations (2015), "Security Council Demands End to Yemen Violence, Adopting Resolution 2216, Security Council 7426th Meeting, April 14, https://www.un.org/press/en/2015/sc11859.doc.htm

US Department of Defense (2018), "Summary of the National Defense Strategy of the United States of America," 2018, https://dod.defense.gov/Portals/1/Documents/pubs/2018-National-Defense-Strategy-Summary.pdf

Vergun, David (2021), "Deputy Secretary of Defense Nominee Emphasizes Reform, Modernization," February 2, United States Department of Defence, https://www.defense.gov/Explore/News/Article/Article/2490642/deputy-secretary-of-defense-nominee-emphasizes-reform-modernization/

Wezeman, Pieter D., Fleurant, Aude, Kuimova, Alexandra, Tian, Nan and Wezeman, Siemon T. (2019), "Trends in International Arms Transfer 2018," Stockholm International Peace Research Institute, March, https://www.sipri.org/sites/default/files/2019-03/fs_1903_at_2018.pdf

Wezeman, Pieter D., Kuimova, Alexandra and Wezeman, Siemon T. (2021), "Trends in International Arms Transfer 2020," Stockholm International Peace Research Institute, March 15, https://www.sipri.org/sites/default/files/2021-03/fs_2103_at_2020_v2.pdf

9. Lebanon's 17 October Revolution, WhatsApp and Mass Mobilisation

Joseph Alagha

Introduction

In almost all countries, the status of the economy determines politics and policy but in Lebanon, it is the other way around. Lebanon is an anomaly where politics dictates and enforces economic, fiscal, and monetary policies. Since the early 1990s, successive governments lent, without collateral, huge amounts of money from the Central Bank (BDL), which they did not pay back. As the public fiscal debt skyrocketed, BDL used the citizens' bank accounts to fund the corrupt Lebanese state expenses, pay civil servants, and import consumer goods. Thus, the debt became unsustainable and is over US$ 100 billion, which is 176 times more than the GDP (National News Agency, Lebanon [NNA] 2020); something the economy of a small country of five million citizens cannot cope up with, especially since Lebanon hosts around two million refugees (Syrian, Palestinian and Iraqi), the highest refugee ratio per capita worldwide.

In short, even before the October 2019 WhatsApp revolution erupted in reaction to the government-imposed WhatsApp tax, the economic situation was on the verge of collapse, and the political system was in dire straits due to constant political bickering. A tug of war that put the country on hold or in a state of political paralysis resulted from decades of faulty governance and elitist-hegemonic political participation. The ruling elite is putting their bets on the potential non-harvested oil and gas maritime fields (blocs), but their serious disagreements have prevented the realisation of these natural treasures. However, these fields were discovered around the same time as neighbouring countries, such as Israel, which has been harvesting oil and gas for years and has signed deals worth billions of dollars with Egypt and Jordan.

The Lebanese consensual politics dictates the presence of no winners and no losers or a zero-sum game. To uphold the rule of law, the power-sharing formula in the Lebanese political system divided the spoils among the 18 constituents of the Lebanese mosaic, myriad, or simply, the major sects,[1] while upholding the 50-50 per cent power-sharing formula between Muslims and Christians in the Parliament, Council of Ministers (Cabinet), and Civil Servant's appointments, especially high-ranking public positions. The Lebanese political system is characterised by clientelism, or the infamous five 'isms': nepotism; favouritism; sectarianism; confessionalism; and most importantly, crony capitalism, in a deep state[2] or (*imperium in imperio*), typified by the erosion of the rule of law and is governed by the spoils system, as opposed to the merit system. However, a law founded the post of the Ombudsman in 2005, until today it has not been implemented; maybe because the Ombudsman is the cornerstone of the merit system and a guarantee of the rule of law.

In short, "vetocracy" (consensual democracy and coalition government), as well as "mafiocracy" (crony capitalism), are the salient features of the quasi-democratic political system in Lebanon. As such, political life is characterised by an omerta—a Mafia code of silence or a strong social bond and blind allegiance, homage and loyalty to the power elite, or the leader (*za'im*)—coupled with bonanza saving schemes in the Lebanese "Banana Republic", that is, a country that chronically suffers from political and economic instability. This is deplorable since, in 1955, Lebanon was among the ten best countries in the world, and its GDP per capita was higher than that of France and the then West Germany. In the 1950s and 1960s, Lebanon was known as the "Switzerland of the Middle East" (Hudson, 1976).

The WhatsApp Revolution

Why are the Lebanese youth agitated against their leadership? In Lebanon, the culture of corruption is rampant and deeply engrained epidemic. Since the civil war ended in 1990, the warlords became the political leaders and appropriated the wealth, embezzling tangible and intangible resources of the country. This means that the rich become richer and the poor poorer.

In November 2019, 1 per cent of the Lebanese owned 58 per cent of the means of production and distribution; 0.8 per cent owned 49 per cent of the deposits in bank accounts, and these are the politicians and their retinue. Over the past 40 years, the power elite has embezzled over US$ 800 billion in public funds and tax evasion. Out of this, 56 Lebanese politicians smuggled and transferred US$ 189 billion from their Swiss accounts to Luxembourg and other safe havens. It is worth noting that the Swiss authorities agreed to cooperate with the Lebanese government in its future investigation into the matter (Diab, 2019).

From 1984 to 2020, Lebanese public debt increased from US$ 1 billion to almost US$ 100 billion, 38 per cent of which were recurrent government subsidies for the National Electricity Company (EDL), which loses around US$ 2 billion annually, and there is hardly any electricity produced. Private generators make up for the electricity shortages. In other words, the average Lebanese citizen pays two bills for electricity. The same goes for water. Consumer products are becoming inaccessible to citizens due to skyrocketing prices in a country that exports US$ 2 billion and imports US$ 20 billion a year! Many factories and businesses became bankrupt and many employees lost their jobs.

The trigger: The WhatsApp tax

The direct trigger that made around a million take to the streets on 17 October 2019 was the government's WhatsApp tax of US$ 6 per month or 20 cents per day, as proposed in the 2020 budget plan. People of different sects, religious denominations, age groups and genders flooded the streets, and everyone was shouting "Revolution".

Scenes of national unity reminiscent of the March 2005 First Cedar Revolution, which forced the withdrawal of Syrian forces after 29 years, following the assassination of Prime Minister Rafik Hariri, demonstrated the strong social bond, social cohesion and community cohesion of the Lebanese across the sectarian divide. The demonstrators used the word, *waja'* (pain) to indicate their grievances. Although the demonstrators formed ad hoc committees, they were disorganised and lacked uniform voice and demands. They were scattered and had no unified leadership or ideology, and offered no feasible alternative to the government or cabinet. Thus, there seemed to be no horizon for the 'Uprising' to bear fruit, and this is what the political elite was aiming at, in order to sow discord between the demonstrators and stop their socio-political movement.

Although the government retracted the WhatsApp tax on the evening of 17 October, instead of appeasing the demonstrators, it emboldened them to demand more concessions from the cabinet, calling for the fall of the regime, and chanting the Arab Spring call of down with the regime: "The people want the downfall of the political system." In the Lebanese context, this does not mean only the Cabinet or the Council of Ministers headed by the Sunni Prime Minister, but also the Maronite President and the Shi'ite Speaker of the Parliament and the resignation of the parliament as a whole. In reference to the protestors' demands for the resignation of the three aforementioned leaders, the crowds chanted: "All of them must step down"; Other slogans read: "Down with the Oligarchy: Power to the People"; "Down with the rule of the Central Bank (BDL)"; "Lebanon's Uprising"; "Revolution"; "Civil State without a sectarian system"; "You (political elite and ruling class) are the civil war, and we (demonstrators) are the popular revolution" (personal recollection; Alaraby, 2019).

The Government's reaction

The Council of Ministers held a meeting on 21 October 2019, and a decision was taken to uphold accountability and transparency. This became known as the Hariri reform plan that had no chance of being implemented by the corrupt political elite and the failing private and public financial institutions. The basic points of the plan are the following: (1) approving and ratifying the state budget of 2020 with a 0.63 per cent deficit, which is unprecedented during the past 30 years; (2) an annual tax on the Central Bank (US$ 3 billion) and private banks (US$ 400 million) to reduce state debt by 50 per cent; (3) a promise of no new taxes on the citizens; (4) reducing 50 per cent of the salaries and benefits of the current and former politicians (presidents, ministers and members of parliament); (5) closing the Ministry of Information and reducing 70 per cent of the budgets of state councils [such as Council of the South; Council for Development and Reconstruction; Ministry of the Displaced, etc.]; (6) reducing the operational budget deficit of the National Electricity Company (EDL) to US$1 billion; (7) approving and ratifying a General Amnesty Law and Old Age Law before the end of the year, as well as programmes for poor families and increase housing loans for the youth, etc.; (8) putting the US$ 11.8 billion CEDRE Conference loan (De la Mure, 2018; Consultation and Research Institute, 2019) and the McKenzie plan (Chbeir and Mikhael, 2019) on track, as roadmaps for structural reform.

Echoing the demonstrators' demands, on 23 October 2019, the speaker of the parliament Nabih Berri said: "The time is ripe to establish a civil state" (NNA, 2019). President Michel Aoun delivered a National Address on 24 October, arguing that the protests have no horizon of changing the political system since this could only be done through institutional processes of the Lebanese state and not on the street. Aoun stressed that reform is a political process, clarifying that when he was an MP ten years ago, he proposed many draft legislations to stamp out corruption, including a special tribunal to look into the crimes of the theft of public money, retrieving stolen money, and lifting the immunity and the banking secrecy on civil service employees, that is former and current ministers, presidents, MPs, and government employees, but they have not been voted upon until now.

In his mid-tenure national address, on 31 October 2019, President Aoun gave a speech in which he proposed a uniform (civil) personal status law for the 18-sects that form the Lebanese myriad, which is unprecedented.[3] Aoun promised to clamp down on corruption and called for establishing a civil state where all citizens are on par in front of the law (rule of law; everyone is under the law). He called for appointing the ministers based on their merit and specialisation rather than due to their political allegiance (*Al-Jazeera*, 2019). Nevertheless, these measures did not appease the demonstrators. On the contrary, the demonstrations increased nationwide, and most of the key roads were blocked, thus paralyzing the whole country and its already ailing economy. The street was not impressed and reiterated: "All of them, means all of them"; "Leave, means leave; your tenure caused hunger, and people want the downfall of the regime".

On 3 November 2019, mass mobilisation continued via a demonstration that portrayed women's empowerment. The demonstrators roamed the streets of Beirut, demanding women's rights and gender equality. The women– who represented all walks of life, religious-political confessions, and age groups—raised feminist slogans. Some of the banners read: "Our Revolution is a feminist revolution"; "I'm going to cause the downfall of the regime, which is sectarian, hierarchal-patriarchal, racist, and capitalist"; "Women have the right to grant the nationality to their children;"[4] "No to violence against women"; "It's never too late for the future of our children"; "I want to see my children"[5]; "The revolution is a female"; "Power to women", etc. In short, the women demanded gender equality in four domains: social, economic, political, and, most importantly, legal, because many women do not have access to the justice system or justice (Ferzli, 2019; Barakat, 2019).

Hariri's resignation and ensuing events

On the 13th day of mass mobilisation, that is on 29 October 2019, violent confrontations erupted between the demonstrators (victims) and their opponents [thugs, infiltrators] who came armed with sticks and stormed the public squares of Riad el Solh and Martyr's Square in Beirut. The attackers destroyed and burned the protestors' tents, demolished the loudspeakers and other properties such as cars and TV crews' equipment (NNA, 2019). Although they came under fierce rock-throwing, security forces intervened by firing teargas and pushing the attackers away from the public squares of the demonstrations, thus gradually restoring law and order. Living up to his promise of not allowing anyone to crack down on the demonstrators, under street pressure, Prime Minister Hariri announced his resignation via a televised 1.22-minute short address (CNN, 2019).

Afterwards, Hariri went and submitted his resignation to the president (NNA, 2019). In an interview with *Al-Mayadeen TV*, the veteran politician, ex-MP Walid Jumblatt called for the formation of a technocrat government as soon as possible, hoping that: "In these critical times, I call for peaceful and calm dialogue to prevail among the various parties", warning that the fall of the regime or the political system cannot be accomplished in this way (*Al-Mayadeen* 2019). In turn, the Maronite Patriarch Beshara al-Ra'i condemned the attack on the demonstrators and hoped that the resignation of the cabinet would be seen as a positive step towards a speedy formation of a new reform Cabinet, which is tasked with finding a comprehensive solution to the political and economic crisis (NNA, 2019).

Diab's Rescue Cabinet (Jan-Aug 2020)

The demonstrators were asking for a revamp of the entire political system. They demanded the resignation of the entire political establishment, as a step towards changing the political system to make it more equalitarian and representative: "The people want the downfall of the political system"; "All of the politicians must go". After mandatory parliamentary consultations, on 19 December 2019, President Aoun named Hassan Diab—Engineering Professor and Vice-President of External Affairs at the American University of Beirut (AUB)—to head the new technocrat cabinet, thus giving in to popular demand to form a non-political, specialists' Cabinet.[6] On 21 January 2020, Diab formed his 20-member cabinet, twelve of whom holding US passports. For the first time in Lebanese history, the cabinet contained six women ministers, including the Deputy Prime Minister, who was also the Minister of Defence, unprecedented in the Arab world (NNA, 2020). The Ministers of Justice and the Youth and Sports are well-known political and social activists, campaigning for change and reform, thus supporting the WhatsApp Revolution. The remaining three women ministers, the Ministers of the Displaced, Labour, and Information (spokesperson of the cabinet), were also vocal in supporting the WhatsApp Revolution.

On 7 March 2020, Prime Minister Diab made the watershed announcement that Lebanon has defaulted on its debt (NNA, 2020). Six days after the 4 August 2020 Beirut Port mega-explosion, under street pressure and massive demonstrations, Diab and his Cabinet resigned. At the time of writing this chapter (May 2021), Diab was still heading a caretaker government, as political bickering and foreign influence prevented prime minister-designate Hariri from forming his technocrat cabinet. Lebanon lives in a political vacuum, economic malaise, social turmoil, and institutional paralysis, along with a fast-deteriorating fiscal and monetary situation.

The death of the social contract

There are deep-rooted problems facing the Lebanese political system, which is based on polyarchy (Dahl, 1971) or the philosophy of elite accommodation. The most salient feature of the system is its consensual politics, or consociational democracy, as Arend Lijphart (1969, p. 211) calls it. Lijphart proposes that a consociational democracy has to fit four main criteria. First, the elites representing the leading societal groups should participate in an overarching decision-making structure. Second, this structure should incorporate a veto mechanism for each of these groups. Third, proportionality should be the guiding principle in all forms of political representation. Finally, every group should be allowed to arrange their internal matters independently (1977).

How does the Lebanese Islamist resistance movement Hizballah situate itself within the political bickering on nation-building and institutional and constitutional reforms? Both parties—Hizballah and its allies and Hizballah's opposition parties—agree on Lijphart's first and fourth criteria but disagree on the second and third. Hizballah was able to obtain veto power in the 2008-2009 Cabinet, a short-lived experience that impeded the proper functioning of the cabinet and was severed in subsequent cabinets. Nevertheless, Hizballah and its allies still call for proportionality to give Lebanon's eighteen ethno-confessional communities more equitable representation. Noteworthy, based on this law, the parliamentary elections of 6 May 2018 were conducted. Therefore, in Lebanon, contrary to Lijphart's stipulations, veto power seemingly does not work, while the issue of proportional representation remains debated. Nevertheless, as Hizballah MP 'Ali Fayyad noted, the institutionalisation of structures fostering consensus between the societal elites remains the core of Lebanon's political system and its success—namely, political stability—depends on the extent to which elites manage to agree on structural political dilemmas, most notably reforms across the board and ending chronic corruption (2008).

More likely, each party has its own understanding and conception of what democracy means. It seems that the predicaments characterizing the Lebanese cabinet formation process have little to do with pro-and anti-democratic tendencies. For almost all political parties, the question was not whether democracy was desirable, but what kind of democracy would be preferred, and what sort of political system ought to be compatible with it? While the parties opposed to Hizballah promoted a majoritarian democracy (50 per cent plus), Hizballah and its allies preferred a consensual democracy, proportional representation, and lowering the voting age to eighteen, which, in practice, boils down to demographic majority rule since Muslims number around 75 per cent, while the Christians number around 25 per cent (United States Central Intelligence Agency, 1988).

Although Lebanon's 1990 Constitution, known as the Ta'if Agreement, stipulated bicameralism, only a Lower House of 128-member materialised, while the 100-seat Senate never saw the light due to political bickering and structural disagreement about running the political system. The Lebanese political pluriform system, its legal pluralism, the allotted parliamentary seats, etc., all point out to the salient role of coalition governments, which, unfortunately, are highly unstable, even in advanced Western democracies, because of their failure to continuously sustain the demands of their constituent members. Unlike Western democracies, where political parties seek to implement their election programmes and campaign promises, in Lebanon, as a form of psychological conditioning, people vote on the basis of personal religious loyalty to their political or feudal leader (*al-za'im*), who in turn showers them with spoils. This chronic system of reaping the rewards and benefits results in fragmentation and more sectarianism.

For instance, the previous Hariri Cabinet (December 2016-January 2020), which took more than nine months to be formed, was a coalition of nine political parties that were haphazardly assembled to perpetuate the same parliamentary composition in the Council of Ministers, thus preventing any tangible opposition from taking place and without tangible checks and balances. This process sets limitations on the proper functioning of the quasi-democratic system of consensual politics, which eventually leads to the paralysis and stagnation of the entire political system due to excessive negotiations, bargaining, and compromise required for decision making to take place. This polarisation and pillarisation resulted in crippling the entire democratic process, pluralism, and the rule of law. Thus, the Lebanese sectarian political system leads to corruption and concentration of power among the ruling elite at the expense of the average citizens classified among the 18 officially recognised sects or ethnoreligious denominations. This pillarisation led to polarisation and a fragmented political system and the public sphere. Hundred years after the founding of the Republic of Lebanon (*Le Grand Liban*) on 1 September 1920, the country is still struggling with nation-building, in the hope of founding a viable political system that could sustain the Lebanese mosaic together. Although as a measure of pluralism, almost every pillar group, or political party has its own TV, radio, and media outlets—the rule of thumb is not to antagonise or bully one another.

The only way to reform the political system is to treat it as a positive law, an artificial law, and not as a Gospel, as a divine law with the halo of being an untouchable; a law that cannot be reformed. For instance, since 1776 the US Constitution has been amended 27 times; the first ten amendments are known as the 'Bills of Rights. When do the Lebanese get their 'Bills of Rights? Why does the Lebanese political elite consider their constitution as a 'divine revelation' that is immune to reform? The situation is back to nought with Hariri failing to form a new cabinet after months of his appointment. Why does not the parliament, which represents the will of the people, enacts simple procedural reforms such as limiting the duration for the designated prime minister to form his cabinet to one month, and on a parallel track, stipulate that the office of the presidency cannot remain vacant for more than one month, after which it is incumbent upon the legislature to elect a new president? These simple procedural suggestions are capable of giving a push to a paralyzed, stagnant political system.

Almost all the politicians are avoiding the inevitable national congress required to draft a new, modern, and viable constitution. They are turning a blind eye and a deaf ear to the badly needed reforms the international community is repeatedly asking for to bail out Lebanon. Three Paris Conferences, the Mckinsey Plan, CEDRE, and other promises of reform delayed the crisis until it exploded as deadly cancer nibbling the Lebanese body politique. The Lebanese economy has been crippled to the extent that all sectors including banking, finance, retail, manufacturing, services and agriculture are functioning on borrowed time. The devalued Lebanese Pound and inflation have made the consumer and necessary commodities out of reach of the common people. The Minister of Interior has warned that the Security Forces cannot maintain law and order in case another 'WhatsApp revolution' erupts.

What could be the way forward?

Lebanese people's popular disenchantment with faulty governance, elitist political participation, and rampant-chronic corruption led to protests and mass mobilisation, thus ushering the WhatsApp Revolution. That said, without the required structural reforms, International Monetary Fund (IMF), the World Bank, NGOs and state-donors would be hesitant to pump fresh dollars in the arteries of the comatose Lebanese economy. Within these limitations, the average Lebanese citizen is anticipating whether street politics and mass mobilisation will win more concessions from the political establishment at a time when stringent COVID-19 lockdown measures and state repression have drastically limited massive street demonstrations. Furthermore, the fragmentation of the demonstrators into a myriad of more than 100 different groups—without effective leadership and sharp recovery plans—has compromised the uniformity of their demands. On mass mobilisation and *Revolution without revolutionaries*, Asef Bayat writes,

> But the street politics of revolutionary times exhibits its constraints when the exceptional episode comes to an end, when the ordinary people long for normalcy, expecting rewards for the hardship they have endured in the revolutionary battles, and when reforming or building institutions becomes necessary. This means that political engagement and mobilization cannot remain only in the main squares for long but have to be adjusted to the everyday of people's lives, in the backstreets, neighbourhoods, households, workplaces, schools, and villages. The ways in which the revolutionary movements come to fruition, and the ideas and strategies they carry, greatly influence the shape of mobilization beyond the streets. (Bayat, 2017, p. 134)

According to this scenario, the Lebanese WhatsApp Revolution adopted another modus vivendi and modus operandi. It did not wither away; rather, it began a new phase. In the process of time, routinisation of charisma requires revolutionary fervour to remain on low fire, and thus it might take another form and trajectory. Bayat argues that in the Arab world, public squares are a social construction and sometimes they degenerate into traffic circles. He highlights this quiet encroachment were the nerve centres, which form the heart of the revolutionary movement, are in constant need of creating new socio-political spaces that would either bloom or wither away as the circumstances dictate.

Would the WhatsApp Revolution would lead to chaos and further deterioration; or would it succeed in ironing out clientelism and keeping corruption at bay, thus delivering the much desired political, social and economic reforms? This belated phase of the Arab Spring, or the WhatsApp Revolution, did not cause Lebanon to shift from being the "Switzerland of the Middle East" in the twentieth century to being one of the most debt-ridden countries in the twenty-first century. Decades of neglect, corruption, political bickering, and crony capitalism led to this trend of downward-spiral collapse, to the extent of triggering some political analysts to postulate the death of the nation at its centennial, while others affirmed that the 1960s Lebanon of economic development and modernisation is already a bygone and is dead and buried.

Conclusion

Lebanon lives a precarious existential, foundational and normative moment in the wake of perplexing domestic, regional, and international circumstances, coupled with the lack of historic and charismatic leadership. The salient features of the Lebanese quasi-democratic political system are an omerta—or a strong social bond and blind allegiance, homage, and loyalty to the feudal lord (*za'im*)—coupled with bonanza saving schemes that characterise a "Banana Republic", a country that suffers from chronic political and economic instability. In the wake of the incessant flux that the MENA Region is experiencing, Lebanon is facing the existential threat of ceasing to be. This sharp meltdown provoked the French Foreign Minister Jean-Yves Le Drian to launch the dictum of 'help us to help you', warning of the death of Lebanon, if swift and drastic measures are not taken to form a new Cabinet that is capable of stamping out the rampant culture of corruption and clientelism. From this lens, Lebanon's 17 October WhatsApp Revolution and mass mobilisation was a reaction against faulty governance, elitist political participation, and a call for proper statesmanship.

Notes

1. The 18 officially recognised etho-religious groups are the following: 'Alawite; Armenian Catholic; Armenian Orthodox; Assyrian Church of the East; Chaldean Catholic; Copts; Druze; Greek Catholic; Greek Orthodox; Ismai'li; Jewish; Latin Catholic; Maronite; Evangelical (Protestant); Sunni; Shi'a; Syriac Catholic; and Syriac Orthodox.

2. Lebanon is a deep state in the sense of being controlled by elite politicians and entrenched, career civil servants (government employees) acting in a non-conspiratorial manner, to further their own interests and the interest of those who put them in power without due regard to the interest of the state, or public interest per se.
3. In 1998, the late ex-President Elias al-Harawi challenged religious personal status laws and proposed a draft legislation of civil marriage, which both Christian and Muslim religious and political leaders did not welcome and vehemently criticised.
4. It is worth noting that the Lebanese Law of Nationality is patriarchal in orientation, where the man can grant the Lebanese nationality to any women he marries; while the women cannot even grant the Lebanese nationality to her children if she is married to a non-Lebanese.
5. In reference to the unjust religious custody laws, which are patriarch in orientation, thus granting the man special prerogatives. Lebanon has no civil personal status laws, a reality that leads to non-uniformity of the law and discriminatory practices due to the presence of 15 different religious courts dealing with such cases.
6. Interestingly, AUB's President Dr. Fadlo Khoury has been vocal in his support of the WhatsApp Revolution, and he toured the public squares disseminating his message and guiding the protestors.

References

Ferzli, Elie (2019), "The Country is Overflowing with its People," *Al-Akhbar*, 4 November, pp. 6-7.

Barakat, Jana (2019), "'Our Revolution is Feminist': Women on Beirut Streets," *Al-Araby*, 3 November 2019, https://www.alaraby.co.uk/%22%D8%AB%D9%88%D8%B1%D8%AA%D9%86%D8%A7-%D9%86%D8%B3%D9%88%D9%8A%D8%A9%22-%D8%AA%D8%B8%D8%A7%D9%87%D8%B1%D8%A9-%D9%84%D9%84%D9%86%D8%B3%D8%A7%D8%A1-%D8%AA%D8%AC%D9%88%D8%A8-%D8%A8%D9%8A%D8%B1%D9%88%D8%AA, Accessed 14 October 2021.

Al-Jazeera (2019), "Lebanese President Aoun Calls for 'Non-Sectarian' System," 1 November, https://www.aljazeera.com/news/2019/11/1/lebanese-president-aoun-calls-for-non-sectarian-system, Accessed 14 October 2021.

Al-Mayadeen (2019), "The Lebanese president will call for parliamentary consultations to choose the prime minister-designate this week," 19 October 2019, https://www.almayadeen.net/news/politics/1355426/%d8%a7%d9%84%d8%ad%d8%b1%d9%8a%d8%b1%d9%8a-%d9%8a%d8%b6%d8%b9-%d8%a7%d8%b3%d8%aa%d9%82%d8%a7%d9%84%d8%aa%d9%87-%d8%a8%d8%aa%d8%b5%d8%b1%d9%81-%d8%b1%d8%a6%d9%8a%d8%b3-%d8%a7%d9%84%d8%ac%d9%85%d9%87%d9%88%d8%b1%d9%8a%d8%a9, Accessed 14 October 2021.

Bayat, Asef (2017), *Revolution without Revolutionaries: Making Sense of the Arab Spring*, Stanford: Stanford University Press

Chbeir, Rouba and Mikhael, Marwan (2019), "What the McKinsey Report says about Lebanon: Overview and infocus sections," Bloominvest Bank, 16 February, https://blog.blominvestbank.com/wp-content/uploads/2019/02/What-the-McKinsey-Report-says-about-Lebanon-Overview-and-in-focus-sections.pdf, Accessed 14 October 2021.

Consultation and Research Institute. (2019). *Summary of Lebanon Economic Vision*. https://www.fes-lebanon.org/fileadmin/user_upload/documents/Mckinsey_Plan/Summary__of_the_Economic_Vision.pdf

CNN. (2019). "Lebanese Prime Minister Saad Hariri announces resignation" https://edition.cnn.com/videos/world/2019/10/29/lebanon-saad-hariri-prime-minister-resignation-intl-ldn-vpx.cnn

Dahl, Robert A. (1971). *Polyarchy: Participation and Opposition*. New Haven: Yale University Press.

Diab, Youssef (2019), "Scandal of Lebanese Politicians' Transfer of Billions of Dollars abroad 'Confuses' Banks," *Asharq Al-Awsat*, 29 December, https://english.aawsat.com//home/article/2057301/scandal-lebanese-politicians%e2%80%99-transfer-billions-dollars-abroad-%e2%80%98confuses%e2%80%99-banks, Accessed 14 October 2021.

Fayyad, Ali (2008), *Fragile States: Dilemmas of Stability in Lebanon and the Arab World*, Oxford: International NGO Training and Research Centre (INTRAC).

Hudson, Michael C. (1976), "The Lebanese crisis: the limits of consociational democracy", *Journal of Palestine Studies*, 5 (3/4): 109–122.

Lebanese National News Agency (NNA). (2020, 6 May). http://nna-leb.gov.lb/ar/show-news/477434/

Lijphart, Arend (1969). "Consociational democracy". *World Politics*, 21(2): 207-225.

Lijphart, Arend (1977). *Democracies in plural societies: a comparative evaluation*. New Haven: Yale University Press.

De la Mure, F. (2018, 6 April). *Lebanon - CEDRE Conference « Conférence économique pour le développement, par les réformes et avec les entreprises »*. https://www.diplomatie.gouv.fr/en/country-files/lebanon/news/article/lebanon-cedre-conference-06-04-18

Saadeh, S. (2002). "Basic issues concerning the personal status laws in Lebanon". In Thomas Scheffler (Ed.), *Religion between violence and reconciliation* (pp. 449–456). Beirut: Ergon Verlag.

Salamey, I. (2014). *The Government and politics of Lebanon*. New York: Routledge.

Salibi, Kamal (1990). *A House of many mansions: the history of Lebanon reconsidered*. California: University of California Press.

Traboulsi, Fawwaz (2012). *A History of Modern Lebanon*. London: Pluto Press.

United States Central Intelligence Agency (1988), "Contemporary Distribution of Lebanon's Main Religious Groups," Washington, D.C.: Central Intelligence Agency, Retrieved from the Library of Congress, https://www.loc.gov/item/91684898/.

10. The Arab Spring and Extremism among Sunni Minorities in Iran

Maria Elizabeth Joseph

Sunni Muslims constitute about 6-8 million, comprising 8-10 per cent of the total 80 million population of Iran (Elling, 2013). They primarily belong to Kurdish, Achomi, Turkmen and Baluch ethnicities, besides a small Arab minority in Khuzestan. A majority of the Iranian Sunnis settled along the peripheral provinces follow Shafi'i or Hanafi Schools. In addition, there is an unaccounted rise in Zikri Muslims, a minority group exclusively present among the Baluch and a surge in Sunni Muslims adhering to Salafism (Elling, 2013).

Scholarly works underline that sections of the Sunni minorities, mainly the urban middle class and the educated elites supported the creation of the Islamic Republic (Harrison, 1980; McDowal, 1996; Taheri, 2009; Dudoignon, 2017). Following the establishment of the Islamic Republic of Iran in 1979, Sunni minorities demanded political and cultural autonomy within an institutional framework. However, rather than accommodating the Sunni minorities and recognizing them in the Constitution, the Islamic Republic followed the Pahlavi policy vis-à-vis the minorities (Harrison, 1980; Dudoignon, 2017).

Historiography on Sunni minorities refers to political, economic and cultural discrimination by the Islamic Republic (Halliday, 1983; Bruinessen, 1986; Ashraf, 1993; McDowall, 1996; Vali, 1998; Farhi, 2005; Sanassarian, 2000; Keddie, 1995, 2006; Saleh, 2012, 2013, 2015; Elling, 2013; Zambelis, 2013, 2014; Dashti, 2017; Dudoignon, 2017; Bengio, 2018). Nikki Keddie (1995) identifies a sustained political and economic centralisation to control Sunni-dominated regions causing resentment against the state.

Mohammad Khatami's win in the 1997 presidential elections backed by his commitment to upholding liberal values and tolerant ideals provided some hope for ethnic minorities. His campaign "Iran for all Iranians" led to a significant voter turnout in Sunni-dominated provinces (Dudoignon, 2017). However, by 1999, Khatami's promise for dignity and political inclusion failed, and in 2000, hardliners blocked the candidacy of Sunni parliamentarian Jalal Jalalizadeh to its presiding board. In response, Ayatollah Vahid Khorasani vowed to issue a *fatwa* delegitimizing the assembly and walk barefoot on the streets wrapped in a shroud "If a Sunni was installed above Shias" (Faramarzi, 2018, p. 3). Keddie (2006) further argues that Sunni Muslims in Iran "were not a recognized category… (were) disfavored in mosque buildings, representation, and other ways, partly owing to the economic underdevelopment of their regions and their cross-border ties" (p. 312).

The Sistan-Baluchestan province is one of the most deprived provinces in Iran that holds the record for absolute poverty in the country. An estimated 45 percent of the population lived below poverty line in 2016 (Ranjpour, 2020). Located at one of the world's busiest narcotics corridors adjacent to Pakistan's Baluchistan province, the locals, particularly the Baluch, are subject to widespread repression by Iranian security forces. This discrimination and repression led to the foundation of *Jundallah* (Soldiers of God) in 2002, which, in turn, brought the Baluch under spotlight. Keddie (2006) argues that the founding members of Jundallah organised the group to improve the lives of Baluch people. However, countless Baluch civilians have lost their lives throughout the group's terrorist attacks, proving it to be a liability for the Baluch cause (Elling, 2013).

Following the unrest in Kurdistan and Baluchestan[1] from 2005 through 2007, the situation deteriorated for Sunni minorities in Iran. Security forces attacked protesters and arrested dissenters in Sunni-dominated areas. Iranian security agencies and political elites underline the influence of Iraq's Al-Qaeda amid the surge in sectarian violence and radicalisation among Sunni Muslims (Elling, 2013). The suicide bombing in 2008 by Jundallah exposed the country's failure to curb Sunni extremism along its borders.

As religiosity permeates all aspects of the Baluch life, the Sunni clergy played a significant role in maintaining peace and stability along

Iran's south-eastern frontier through the 1980s and 1990s. According to Stéphane Dudoignon (2017), the Iranian state actively financed and encouraged Ashari, Deobandi and Muslim Brotherhood institutions since the 1970s and has since used the clergy's influence to advance its diplomacy in Arab word. However, in the aftermath of the Arab Spring, their power and influence have been curtailed. Dudoignon (2017) further argues that Tehran's control over the Sunni ulema increased after Muslim Brotherhood-backed groups briefly took power in Tunis and Cairo. Despite the Sunni ulema publicly censuring Sunni extremist groups and developing a new 'Islamic Diplomacy', the state's insecurity and paranoia towards its Sunni Muslim minority increased. The state suppressed any public expression of sympathy towards the Arab Spring, tightened censorship on publication, destroyed Sunni places of worship and higher religious schools, and imprisoned, executed and assassinated Sunni leaders (ibid.).

The suppressive tactics did not prevent a fresh outbreak of assaults by Sunni extremist forces in Iran. Chris Zambelis (2014) notes the use of social networks and a visible connection between Jundallah and the newly established extremist groups (Jaish al-adl, Harakat Ansar Iran, etc.) both in their operative tactics and philosophy. Jaish al-adl, among other cross–border anti–Shia groupings in Iran and Pakistan, began to identify with Al-Qaeda. This shift also came amid Iran's military intervention in Iraq, Syria and indirectly in Yemen. Apart from the resurgence in Sunni extremism within the state, evidence refers to the union of Iran's Baluch, Kurds and Arabs with the Jabhat al-Nusra, an Al-Qaeda affiliate in Syria.

While the Islamic State (ISIS) started losing territory in 2017 and 2018, it simultaneously gained global attention in its ability to radicalise Muslims and orchestrate transnational attacks. The Islamic State's brazen attempt to unite Iran's Sunni extremist groups and the alleged role of Iran's Kurds in the ISIS twin attack at Khomeini's mausoleum and inside Iran's parliament complex on 7 June 2017 fuelled fears of radicalisation and militancy among the Kurdish minority, who mostly adhere to Sunni Islam. Furthermore, in 2018, the state media reported the presence of a former Islamic State militia from Iraq along its north-western frontier region bordering Iranian Kurdistan.

As cross-border militancy continues to threaten Iran's porous borders with Iraq, Pakistan and Afghanistan, local Sunni militants continue to impede the stability of the state. Arguably, this has been exacerbated by the suppressive and discriminatory policies of the state vis-à-vis the Sunni minorities.

Pre-2011 Sunni extremist groups

Influential Sunni extremist groups since the Islamic Republic's formation in chronological order are Moneem Group (after Abdul Moneem, founder of the group), Hizb al-furqan (Party of the Two), Sepah-e Rasulullah (Army of the Prophet), Jundallah (The Popular Resistance Movement of Iran), Sepah-e-Sahaba-Iran (Army of Prophet's Companion-Iran), Jaish ul-Husain (Army of Husain), Jaish ul-Adl (Army of Justice), Harakat Ansar Iran (The Movement of Iran's Supporters) and Jaish-e Nasr (Army of Victory).

The Abdul Moneem group, also Abu Salman or Yusuf group, is the earliest known militant group founded by Abdul Moneem (Hoshang, 2015). The group took responsibility for the 1994 explosion at Imam Reza's shrine in Mashhad that killed 26 and injured over 200. The state responded by arresting Baluch activists for their involvement. However, it is difficult to corroborate the group's impact and current status with the absence of reliable information.

In the mid-1990s, Hizb al-furqan, also Al-Forqan or Salzman-e Hezb-e Ahl-e Sonnat-e Iran, founded by Moulvi Abdoljalil Qanbarzahi, operated from the Nimroz province in Afghanistan. The group supported the Taliban and engaged in cross-border skirmishes with Iranian security forces. Although the group did not recover from its losses after the US-NATO airstrikes in Afghanistan, Qanbarzahi influenced Baluch militants and Abdolmalek Rigi, the founder of Jundallah. Moulabakhsh Derakhshan established Sepah-e Rasulullah in the 1990s. The group operated closely with Sepah-e Sahabah-e Pakistan and Lashkar-e Jhangvi in Pakistan. Some evidence points to the group's inner workings with Al-Qaeda members (Hoshang, 2015). There is a dearth of written evidence on the group's influence, but its group members either split or merged with Jundallah under Rigi's leadership in 2002 (Hoshang, 2015).

Jundallah emerged in 2002 and focused its activities within Baluchestan to highlight ethnic suppression and discrimination towards Sunni minorities in Iran. Along with minor skirmishes and a jihadi-style beheading of a captured Iranian officer, Jundallah carried out five suicide attacks against Iran's security forces (three attacks targeted Shia places of worship). Their suicide attacks and violence attracted global attention and raised fear among Iran's security forces. On 15 December 2010, two days before the street vendor in Tunisia set himself ablaze and triggered what is now known as the Arab Spring, a suicide bombing rocked the southwestern province of Iran, killing forty and wounding more than ninety near a Shi'ite mosque in Chabahar. This incident is the last known attack by Jundallah in response to Abdolmalek Rigi's execution on 20 June 2010. In August 2012, the group denied any affiliation towards Jaish ul-Husain and Harakat Ansar Iran.

Post-2011 Sunni extremist activities

With the Arab Spring, radical anti–Shia, militant groups such as Sepah-e Sahaba-e Iran, Jaish ul-Husain, Jaish ul-Adl and Harakat Ansar Iran emerged. Sepah-e Sahabah-e-Iran was founded on 14 March 2011 and is ideologically affiliated with Sepah-e Sahabah-e Pakistan (Hoshang, 2015). The group identifies and punishes any ethnic Baluch who collaborates with Iranian intelligence agencies. While there is no reliable information on Jaish ul-Husain, soon after Rigi's execution, Jundallah split into three groups, Jaish ul-Adl, Jaish ul-Nasr and Lashkar e-Khorasan. Of the three that operate from Pakistan, Jaish ul-Adl continues to challenge the Iranian state. Iran's state media publicised Abdul Rauf Rigi's execution, the founder and leader of Jaish ul-Nasr, on 28 August 2014 in Quetta for his alleged ISIS links. Lashkar-e-Khorasan, considered an offshoot of ISIS, remains influential in Pakistan and coerces Zikri Muslims to convert to Sunni Islam. Harakat Ansar Iran, operating since 2011, demanded a Baluch state and a return to Sunni Persia (Koch, 2018). Sunni extremist groups within Iran successfully exploited internet-based communication technologies to attract recruits and propagate their agenda. Harakat Ansar Iran, for example, used multilingual blog posts and social media tools to disseminate its propaganda. Hashim Azizi, one of the group's founding members and head of communications, previously held close links with anti-Shia groups in Pakistan and assisted Jundallah in its clandestine activities (Koch, 2018). The group claimed responsibility for a suicide attack outside the Imam Hussein Mosque in Chabahar in Sistan

Baluchestan on 19 October 2012 (Zambelis, 2014). Two Basij officers were killed in the attack, and many others were wounded (Reuters, 2012).

The attack on the shrine was the second such attack after Jundallah had attacked it in December 2010. By November 2013, the group began to identify with Al-Qaeda (Koch, 2018). The organisation replaced its Baluch flag with a Black flag inscribed with the Shahada within a white circle at the centre (ibid). The group further omitted the word Iran from its name to steer clear of territorial constraints, typical of Salafi-Jihadist organisations. Also, having previously worked with Baluch extremist groups, Ansar Iran announced its merger with Hizb al-Furqan (Party of the Two) and established the Harakat Ansar al-Furkan fi Bilad al-Fares (The Movement of Supporters of the Koran in Persia) in December 2013. The group endeavoured to expand its operations beyond Iranian Baluchestan and reinstall the Islamic Caliphate. The penetration of Salafist ideology through Persian-language Sunni religious websites has created "a new generation of Salafi-inspired religious and political activists within Iran who are questioning the authority of the Ashari, Deobandi and the Muslim brotherhood leadership" (Farmarzi, 2018, 10).

Sunni leaders in Iran additionally feared that Iran's military intervention in Iraq, Syria and Yemen and its behaviour towards Sunni Muslims abroad could play into the hands of Salafist recruits (ibid). So, although the role of Iranian Sunnis in Syria is understudied, there is evidence that Iranian Sunni groups, particularly the Baluch guerrillas, arrived in Syria as early as November 2011 (Dudoignon, 2017). Kurdish media also provides stories and videos of Iranian Kurds and their association with Jabat al-Nusra (Hawramy, 2017). Ethnic Baluch, Kurds and Arabs formed a substantial part of Harakat al-Muhajirin Ahl-Sunat Iran (The Sunni Immigrant Movement of Iran) that joined the Al-Qaeda affiliate Jabhat al-Nusra, which became Hay'at Tahrir al-Sham (HTS or the Organization for the Liberation of the Levant). An interview with a member of Harakat al-Muhajirin Ahl-Sunat Iran detailed how Iranian Sunnis travelled by air and road to reach Syria. Although the group distanced itself from ISIS, its primary purpose was to establish a Caliphate (Hauch, 2018). After its public breakup with Al-Qaeda in 2017, HTS, under the leadership of Abu Mohammad al-Jolani, is locally focused on establishing the Islamic Rule in Syria (Newlee, 2018).

In 2018, Ansar al-Furqan attacked police headquarter in Chabahar, killing two officers and injuring 41 (Hafezi, 2018). While the IRGC blamed regional powers, Baluch locals claimed that the attack was in response to the state's incentive-based discriminatory and demographically designed policy to target Sunni-dominated regions (*Asharq Al-Awsat*, 2018). Ansar Al-Furqan also took responsibility for bombing an oil pipeline in Arab-dominated Ahvaz in December 2017 (Koch, 2018). In the aftermath of the Arab Spring, evidence refers to a rise in Arab militancy in Khuzestan Province driven by socio-economic, cultural and environmental grievances (Zambelis, 2017). Although Sunni Arabs are a minority, some members of the Shia community are converting to Sunni Islam (ibid). The radical group, Arab Struggle Movement for the Liberation of Ahwaz, claimed responsibility for an attack in the Khuzestan province in January 2017 that killed two IRGC soldiers. The group also took responsibility for blowing up several oil pipelines. On 22 September 2018, members belonging to the group masked as military personnel attacked a military parade in Ahvaz, killing twenty-nine. The ISIS later disputed the claims and took responsibility for the shooting (Reuters, 2018).

On 30 March 2017, ISIS released a veiled threat against the Supreme Leader and IRGC. The thirty-six-minute Persian feature production titled "Persia, Between Yesterday and Today" appealed to Iran's Sunni minorities to unite against Iran (Zambelis, 2017). This incident was immediately followed by the assassination of a senior IRGC personnel on 10 April and two IRGC officers at a military operation in Zahedan on 12 April by unidentified Sunni militants (Majidyar, 2017). The ISIS further took responsibility for the twin attack on the Majles-e Shoraye Eslami (Islamic Consultative Assembly), also referred to as Iran's parliament and Ayatollah Khomeini's mausoleum that killed twelve and wounded 46. Amaq, the mouthpiece of ISIS, released a twenty-four-second video shortly after the attack that captured the carnage inside the parliament.

On 8 June, the news agency released another footage by a Kurdish-speaking militant calling on Iranian Sunnis to take up arms against the state (Zambelis, 2017). It is alleged that four out of the five assailants belonged to the Kurdish province of Kermanshah and had fought in Mosul and Raqqa before returning to Iran in 2016 (Hawramy, 2017). The ISIS-affiliated Kurdish channels have circulated videos of Iranian

Kurds in Mosul and Raqqa (ibid.). In the aftermath of the attack, Kurdish representatives of the parliament and the Friday prayer leader at Kermanshah denounced the attack and reiterated Kurdish loyalty towards the Islamic Republic (IRNA, 2017). Also, the Writers Association of Iran defended the ethnic minority and requested the state not to use this attack as an excuse to stifle socio-political freedoms in the country (Majidyar, 2017).

The threat of radicalised Kurdish minorities and the resumption of Kurdish insurgency against the state in 2016 by banned Kurdish militia refers to the state's failure in providing socio-economic and cultural incentives towards this ethnic minority. Iranian Kurdish groups led by the Kurdistan Democratic Party of Iran (KDPI) and Kurdistan Freedom Party (PAK), largely based in the Kurdistan Region of Iraq (KRI), cited the repression of Iranian Kurds and the consistent denial of political rights and economic opportunities as one among many factors for their collective resistance against the state (Milburn, 2017). Also, Kurdish groups referred to the rise in arbitrary arrests and the execution of a hundred Iranian Kurdish activists and Iranian Kurdish opposition party members in 2015.[2]

While the ISIS threat loomed, Jundallah's successor, Jaish ul-Adl, continued its attacks. Jaish ul-Adl launched its first attack in October 2013 with the abduction and killing of 14 Iranian border guards in Saravan, Sistan Baluchestan, in response to Iran's involvement in the Syrian war. The group also referred to the atrocities and discriminatory policies towards Iran's Sunni minorities (Notezai, 2016). In February 2014, the extremist group abducted thirteen border guards. However, they were released soon after mediation by Sunni ulema (Aman, 2016). On 6 April 2015, the state news agency, IRNA, reported a clash with militants at the town of Negour along Iran-Pakistan's border killing eight border guards (Zambelis, 2015). Jaish ul-Adl claimed responsibility announcing it on its social media accounts via blog posts, Twitter and its Facebook account (Notezai, 2016). In April 2017, it mounted an attack in Mirjaveh, a border town, killing nine Iranian guards and injuring two (Zahid, 2017). In June 2018, another border skirmish in Mirjaveh killed three militants and two IRGC officers. Contradicting the IRGC, the militant group announced that it did not sustain causalities but killed 11 guards (Majidyar, 2018).

In October 2018, the group kidnapped 11 border guards; five were released on 15 November 2018, and four were rescued by the Pakistani army on 21 March 2019 (Mohan, 2021). On 4 February 2021, an intelligence operation in Pakistan led by IRGC rescued the remaining two (Mohan, 2021). This operation came almost a year after a deadly suicide attack killed 27 border guards and wounded 13 on 13 February 2019 (Dehghanpisheh and Sharafedin, 2019). The latest in a series of attacks against Iran's security forces took place in Saravan, where militants assaulted IRGC's engineering unit on 3 March 2021, wounding one while another went missing. The attack came right after protests and violent clashes erupted in Baluchestan over the fatal shooting of fuel smugglers.

State's response

While the world watched the MENA region engulf in protests in 2011, Tehran quietly promoted Jama'at-i Da'wat was Islah-i Iran (The Appeal and Reform Society of Iran) (JDII) as a political party to stall a 'Sunni Spring' within Iran (Dudoignon, 2017). With the waning influence of the Sunni ulema, the Kurdish-born JDII took over as the official spokesperson of the Sunni Muslims in Iran from 2009. The political echelons in Tehran simultaneously acknowledged the political and diplomatic role of JDII in the Arab world. In the aftermath of the Arab Spring, Khamenei dispatched a Muslim Brotherhood leader as his envoy to Tunisia following the election victory of Ennahda, a party inspired by Egypt's Muslim Brotherhood (Dudoignon, 2017). However, the state kept the Sunni ulema on a tight leash post-2011 despite the clergy's consistent statements against the Sunni extremist groups operating in Iran. The assassination of a Sunni cleric, Mawlawi Mustafa Jangizayi, by unknown assailants in 2012 led to a wave of protests within Baluchestan. In the weeks leading up to his assassination, Jangiyazi tried to mobilise the Sunni youth to participate in the upcoming presidential elections. Iran responded to the protests with state militarisation and detained several Sunni religious scholars (Dudoignon, 2017).

Iran executed sixteen Baluch civilians in response to the Jaish ul-Adl attack in 2013 (Aman, 2016). Sunni religious leader Moulavi Abdol Hamid condemned the attack on Iran's forces and voiced the group's destructive impact on the ethnic Baluch. Mounting cross-border terrorism in 2014 led to an increase in military and border guards patrolling the 300-kilometre stretch in the Saravan region in Baluchestan that borders Pakistan (Dudoignon, 2017). In April 2015, Iranian security forces killed Ansar Iran's leader Hashim Azizi, but a spate of attacks continued to hurt the security forces stationed in Baluchestan. Around the same time, Ayatollah Khamenei remarked on the severity of the ISIS threat and a possible spillover within Iran which shares a 900-kilometre border with Iraq (Akbarzadeh et al., 2019). However, at a public event in September 2015, Ahmad Reza Pourdastan, the Commander of Ground Forces, noted a consolidated effort by both the public and security forces to stall ISIS infiltrators (IRNA, 2015).

Meanwhile, Iran cracked down on critics from Sunni-dominated regions for their views on role in Syria, Iraq and Yemen by detaining and arresting for their views on from Khuzestan and Sistan Baluchestan, including Mawlawi Faz-ul-Rahman Kouhi, a prominent Sunni leader in the Peshamag region (Majidyar, 2017). Also, with mounting economic challenges, public opinion showed a decline in support of the state's involvement in Syria (Zogby, 2016). Iran simultaneously increased its intelligence and surveillance activities in the Kurdistan Region of Iraq (KRI) with the revival of Kurdish insurgency and targeted and blamed Iraq for failing to protect its north-eastern border and accused Saudi Arabia and others of funding and arming Iranian Kurdish groups (Milburn, 2017).

While criticism brewed domestically against the state's activities abroad, state media revealed that the IRGC forces managed to stall 1,500 Iranians from joining ISIS (IRNA, 2016). This rising threat from ISIS emergence in Iraq forced the IRGC to request the Sunni clergy to ensure stability in south-east Sistan Baluchestan and simultaneously referred to the ongoing projects in the Sunni dominated province. According to IRGC, 5,000 new projects to alleviate poverty and 3,000 additional projects in construction, rural development, electricity, Sunni prayer homes and housing and jobs, with 79 per cent of the projects were already implemented in Sunni regions (Majidyar, 2017). However, these economic concessions did not stall the return of Jaish ul-Adl in 2017. Iran responded by accusing Pakistan of consistently failing to take action against terrorist outfits operating on their soil. Pakistani policy of allowing the Iranian militant groups is a response to Iran's role in the Baluch separatist activities within Pakistan's Baluchistan province (Dudoignon, 2017). Nonetheless, it also has the geopolitical component of the Iran-Pakistan-Saudi Arabia triangle.

While Iran's intelligence unit terminated thirty terrorist cells during the Iranian calendar year ending March 2017 (Majidyar, 2017), the June 2017 ISIS attack was a turning point in Iran's internal struggle with militancy. Iran launched a counterterrorism operation in response to the attack, suppressing protests movements and arresting civilians from Kermanshah, Kurdistan, West Azerbaijan and Hormozgan (Majidyar, 2017). The emergence of ISIS in Afghanistan and Pakistan put Iran on alert. By August 2017, Iranian security forces claimed to have neutralised at least a hundred terrorist groups. With the cooperation of a regional country, Iran's intelligence unit detained 27 terrorists linked to ISIS, 10 in a training base across the border and 17 within Iran (Majidyar, 2017). However, the Intelligence Ministry refused to reveal the name of the country and the location of the operation (ibid.). The state dismantled a terrorist unit in Qasr-e Qand province in Sistan Baluchestan, killing Jalil Qanbarzehi, the head of Ansar al-Furqan and militants linked to the group. The state foiled another attack by the group at Chabahar and arrested suspects from the north-western province of Kermanshah, Kurdistan and West Azerbaijan (Majidyar, 2017). While incidents in 2017 undermined Iran's national security, 2018 showed no respite as state media reported discovering consignments containing explosives along the border. The security forces foiled attacks around its peripheral provinces and killed militants in Sistan Baluchestan in skirmishes that also killed IRGC officers.

The year was also filled with violent protests in Khuzestan, forcing the state to consider further militarisation in the province (Majidyar, 2018). The February 2019 attack that killed 27 IRGC soldiers in Baluchestan came a day before the Pulwama attack targeted Indian military forces. The attack followed an impromptu meeting between Foreign Ministers from India and Iran on 17 February to cooperate and combat terrorism within the region. Due to mounting international pressure, the Pakistani foreign ministry announced its willingness to cooperate with any investigation. On 17 November 2020, Pakistan killed a key member of Jaish ul-Adl,

Omar Shahoozi, and his two sons (Aman, 2020). The timing is significant as it happened a day before Javad Zarif, Iran's Foreign Minister visited Islamabad. Ironically the top leader of Jaish ul-Adl met a similar end as his predecessor, Abdolmalek Rigi, in 2010.

Along its eastern frontier, Iran has made significant strides in reaching out to the Taliban to secure peace in the neighbourhood. The visit by a Taliban delegation to Tehran in February 2021 signals a public acknowledgement of the Sunni radical group's political influence in the region (Aman, 2021). However, Iran is likely to wait until the completion of the US withdrawal from Afghanistan to test the impact of this outreach. Meanwhile, cross-border Sunni terrorist groups continue to threaten Iranian security from outside.

Conclusion

The rise in Sunni extremism in Iran in the aftermath of the Arab Spring is linked to several domestic and regional factors. Sunni dissent against the state is rooted in Iran's policies of economic discrimination, denial of political and cultural rights and continued arbitrary arrests and human rights violations under the guise of security threat. Post-2011, the state clamped down on protest movements by Sunni groups demanding better rights. The rise of ISIS, its success in wooing a section of the alienated minorities and Iranian military interventions in Syria, Yemen and Iraq aggravated the already complex relationship between Sunnis and the Islamic Republic.

Notes

1. Baluchestan refers to the Baluch dominated Sistan—Baluchestan province in Iran. In Pakistan, the province is referred to as *Baluchistan,* while the ethnic group is referred to as *the Baloch.* In Oman and UAE, the ethnic group is referred to as the Al-Balushi, indicating Baluch ancestry.
2. See "Amnesty International Report 2016/2017, Iran 2016/2017," Amnesty International, and "Joint Letter: To Permanent Representatives of Member States of the Human Rights Council, Council Cross-regional Civil Society Organizations in Support of United Nations Human Rights Council Resolution to Renew Mandate of Special Rapporteur in Iran," Human Rights Watch, March 16, 2017.

References

Akbarzadeh, Sharam, Ahmed, Zahid Shahab, Laoutides, Costas and Gourlay, William (2019). The Kurds in Iran: balancing national and ethnic identity in a securitised environment. *Third World Quarterly*, 40:6, pp. 1145-1162.

Aman, Fatemeh. (2016). Iran's uneasy relationship with its Sunni minority, Middle East Institute. Retrieved from https://mei.edu/publications/irans-uneasy-relationship-its-sunni-minority

Aman, Fatemeh. (2021). Iran—Taliban growing ties. What's Different This Time?. Atlantic Council. Retrieved from https://www.atlanticcouncil.org/blogs/iransource/iran-taliban-growing-ties-whats-different-this-time/

Asharq Al-Awsat (2018). Iran Protests Widen as Rouhani Calls for Calm. Retrieved from https://english.aawsat.com/home/article/1129696/iran-protests-widen-rouhani-calls-calm

Ashraf, Ahmad. (Winter-Spring, 1993). "The Crisis of Ethnic Identities in Contemporary Iran". *Iranian Studies*, Vol. 26, No. 1/2.

Bengio, Ofra. (2018). "Kurdistan's Moments in the Middle East". Moshe Dayan Center for Middle Eastern and African Studies, Tel Aviv University.

Bruinessen, Martin Van. (1986). "The Kurds between Iran and Iraq." *MERIP Middle East Report*, No. 141, 14-27.

Dashti, Naseer. (2017). *The Baloch conflict with Iran and Pakistan: Aspects of a National Liberation*. United States: Trafford Publishing.

Dehghanpisheh, Babak and Sharafedin, Bozorgmehr. (2019). "Suicide bomber kills 27 members of Iran's elite Revolutionary Guards", Reuters. Retrieved from https://www.reuters.com/article/us-iran-guards-attacks-idUSKCN1Q2230

Dudoignon, Stéphane A. (2017) *The Baluch, Sunnism and the State in Iran : From Tribal to Global.* New York: Oxford University Press.

Elling, Rasmus Christian. (2013). *Minorities in Iran: Nationalism and Ethnicity after Khomeini*. New York: Palgrave Macmillan.

Faramarzi, Scheherezade. (2018). "Iran's Sunnis Resist Extremism, but for how long?" Atlantic Council.

Farhi, Fairdeh. (2005). "Crafting a national identity amidst contentious politics in contemporary Iran". *Iranian Studies*, 38:1, 7-22.

Hafezi, Parisa. (2018), "Suicide bomber kills at least two in attack on south-east Iran police HQ", Reuters. Retrieved from https://www.reuters.com/article/us-iran-blast-idUSKBN1O50MH

Halliday, Fred. (1983). "A dictatorship under the name of Islam". *MERIP Middle East Report*, Vol. 1, No 3.

Halliday, Fred. (1982/1983). "The Iranian Revolution: Uneven development and religious populism". *Journal of International Affairs*, Vol. 36, No. 2, 187-207.

Harrison, Selig. (1981). *In Afghanistan's Shadow: Baluch Nationalism and Soviet Temptations*. Washington, DC: Carnegie Endowment for International Peace.

Hawramy, Fazel. (2017). "Iran Wakes Up to Salafist Recruitment in Kurdish Regions", *Al-Monitor*. Retrieved from https://www.al-monitor.com/pulse/originals/2017/06/iran-tehran-isis-attacks-kurdistan-salafist-recruitment.html

Hoshang, Noraee. (2015). "Sunni Militants in Iran: Activities, Ideological Sources and Political Strategies". *International Research Journal of Social Sciences*, Vol. 4(3), 79-87.

Islamic Republic News Agency (2015). "Iranian Sunni Ulema condemn Saudi Attacks on Yemen". Retrieved from https://en.irna.ir/news/81575910/Iranian-Sunni-Ulima-condemn-Saudi-attacks-on-Yemen

Islamic Republic News Agency (2015), "No need for concern over ISIL threats anywhere in Iran". Retrieved from https://en.irna.ir/news/81764301/No-need-for-concern-over-ISIL-threats-anywhere-in-Iran-Commander

Islamic Republic News Agency (2016), "President Rouhani warns against enemies efforts to disunity Muslims". Retrieved from https://en.irna.ir/news/82165467/President-Rouhani-warns-against-enemies-efforts-to-disunite

Islamic Republic News Agency (2017), "Kurdish people loyal to Islamic Republic". Retrieved from https://en.irna.ir/news/82567831/Kurdish-people-loyal-to-Islamic-Republic

Keddie, Nikki R. (1995). *Iran and the Muslim World: Resistance and Revolution*. New York: NYU Press.

Keddie, Nikki R. (2006). *Modern Iran : Roots and Results of Revolution*. Yale University Press.

Koch, Ariel. (2018). "Al Qaeda in Baluchistan and its connection to the war in Syria". *BeeHive*, Vol. 6, Issue 9, 9-14.

Lars Hauch, "Interview with an Iranian Fighter in Hayat Tahrir al-Sham", *Long War Journal*, 18 September 2018. Retrieved from https://www.longwarjournal.org/archives/2018/09/interview-with-an-iranian-fighter-in-hayat-tahrir-al-sham.php

Majidyar, Ahmad (2018). "Islamic State making inroads into Iran". Middle East Institute. Retrieved from https://www.mei.edu/publications/islamic-state-making inroads-iran

Majidyar, Ahmad. (2017). "Enduring Security Problems in Southeast Iran Compels IRGC Leadership to seek Sunnis help", Middle East Institute. Retrieved from https://www.mei.edu/publications/enduring-security-problems-southeast-iran-compels-irgc-leadership-seek-sunnis-help

Majidyar, Ahmad. (2017). "Iran Helped by Foreign Spy Agency Arrests 27 'Islamic State-linked Terrorists.'" Middle East Institute. Retrieved from https://www.mei.edu/publications/iran-helped-foreign-spy-agency-arrests-27-islamic-state-linked-terrorists

Majidyar, Ahmad. (2017). "Authorities in Iran Kill Four Individually Allegedly Linked to the Islamic State". Middle East Institute. Retrieved from https://www.mei.edu/profile/ahmad-majidyar?page=4

Majidyar, Ahmad. (2017). "Militants Kill Eight Iranian Border Guards near Turkish Border". Middle East Institute. Retrieved from https://www.mei.edu/publications/militants-kill-eight-iranian-border-guards-near-turkish-bȯrder

Majidyar, Ahmad. (2018). "IRGC forces killed in armed clash with Pakistan-based Jaish ul-Adl militants", Middle East Institute. Retrieved from https://mei.edu/publications/irgc-forces-killed-armed-clash-pakistan-based-jaish-ul-adl-militants

McDowall, David. (1996). *A Modern History of the Kurds*. London: I. B. Tauris.

Milburn, Franc. (2017). "Iranian Kurdish Militias: Terrorist-Insurgents, Ethno Freedom Fighters, or Knights on the Regional Chessboard?". *CTC Sentinel*, Vol. 10, Issue 5, 29-35.

Mohan, Geeta. (2021). "Iran conducts surgical strike in Pakistan, frees border guards held by Baloch terrorists", *India Today*. Retrieved from https://www.indiatoday.in/world/story/iran-frees-frees-border-guards-held-by-baloch-terrorists-pakistan-1765981-2021-02-04

Newlee, Danika. (2018). "Hay'at Tahrir al-Sham (HTS)", Center for Strategic and International Studies. Retrieved from https://www.csis.org/programs/transnational-threats-project/terrorism-backgrounders/hayat-tahrir-al-sham-hts

Notezai, Muhammad Akbar. (2016). "Can ISIS gain a foothold in Baluchistan", *The Diplomat*. Retrieved from https://thediplomat.com/2016/01/can-isis-gain-a-foothold-in-balochistan/

Ranjipour, Ali. (2020). "Poverty in Iran: Sistan and Baluchistan". *Iran Wire*. Retrieved from https://iranwire.com/en/features/5841

Reuters (2018). "Islamic State says Iran attack will not be the last: Al-Fuqan". Retrieved from https://www.reuters.com/article/us-iran-military-attack-islamicstate-idUSKCN1M62FS

Reuters (2021). "Iran hangs Baluch militant for killing of two Revolutionary Guards", judiciary says. Retrieved from https://www.reuters.com/article/us-iran-execution-idUSKBN29Z0AR

Saleh, Alam and James Worrall. (2015). "Between Darius and Khomeini: Exploring Iran's National Identity Problematique". *National Identities* 17, No. 1, 1-25.

Saleh, Alam. (2012). "Iran's National Identity Problematic". *Sfera Politicii* 20, No. 4.

Saleh, Alam. (2013). *Ethnic Identity and the State in Iran*. London: Palgrave Macmillan.

Sanassarian, Eliz. (2000). *Religious Minorities in Iran*. UK: Cambridge University Press.

Spycer, Jonathan and Weinthal, Benjamin. (2016). "Iranian Kurds join the Fight", *American Interest*. Retrieved from https://www.the-american-interest.com/2016/12/15/iranian-kurds-join-the-fight/

Suicide Bomber Kills Two Guards at South Iran Mosque (2012), Reuters. Retrieved from https://www.reuters.com/article/uk-iran-bombing/suicide-bomber-kills-two-guards-at-south-iran-mosque-idUKBRE89I0M220121019

Taheri, Ahmad Reza. (2009). "The Baluch in Post Islamic Revolution Iran: A Political Study". Ph.D. Dissertation, University of Pune, India.

Vali, Abbas. (1998). "The Kurds and Their Fragmented 'Others': Fragmented Identity and Fragmented Politics". *Comparative Studies of South Asia, Africa, and the Middle East*, Vol. XVIII No. 2, 83-94.

Zambelis, Chris. (2014). "The evolution of Baluch insurgency in Iran". *CTC Sentinel*, Vol. 7, Issue 3, 17-20.

Zambelis, Chris. (2015). "Iran Confronts Intensifying Insurgent Offensive in Sistan-Balochistan Province". *Terrorism Monitor*, Vol. XIII, Issue 8, 6-8.

Zambelis, Chris. (2017). "Terror in Tehran: The Islamic State Goes to War with the Islamic Republic". *CTC Sentinel*. Vol. 10, Issue 6, 16–21.

Zogby Research Services. (2016). "Middle East 2016: Current Conditions and the Road Ahead". Retrieved from https://static1.squarespace.com/static/52750dd3e4b08c252c723404/t/58509580ff7c5039b9505e67/1481676164948/SBY2016+FINAL.pdf

11. Digitalisation of Conflict and Cooperation in the Middle East

Robit Sharma

It has been a decade since the world witnessed the Arab populace pouring onto the streets to protest against their despotic rulers in what was initially termed the onset of a new phase of democratic transition in the Arab world or an Arab Spring. The spark that originated in Tunisia swept the Middle East and inspired a wave of uprisings. The grievances over authoritarianism, corruption, and poverty that were the immediate trigger for the protests gradually transformed into a relentless conflict, which has yet to offer a constructive future to the people in the region. Notwithstanding the limited reach, the internet undeniably enabled the Arab uprisings, where social media platforms such as *Facebook* and *Twitter* were instrumental in galvanizing the popular protests. Through such platforms, people anonymously shared their opinions, disseminated information while sitting at some remote locations. The youthful protestors saw social media platforms as a tool to bring about positive change. Little did they know that the state will later use the same tool that caught the governments unprepared and enabled free speech to quell dissent and suppress opinions.

The ill-prepared governments soon realised the potential of digital space and have become adept at using these channels to spread misinformation via numerous fake accounts. Domestic laws are being tailored to regulate speech on the internet, arrest bloggers, and induce self-censorship in connivance with social media companies. Internet that offered optimism as it enabled information sharing with an international audience is now under the grip of authoritarian governments in the region. Nonetheless, the spread of the internet is commendable in the

Middle East as it gained considerable social and political application and influence.

The International Telecommunication Union (ITU) estimates that by the end of 2019, "... a bit more than 51 per cent of the global population, or 4 billion people were using the internet" (ITU, 2021). The rise is significant since the number of worldwide internet users was 3.7 billion in 2018. The Arab world has its fair share of internet users, accounting for 56 per cent of its population (ibid.). The internet accessibility in the Gulf Cooperation Council (GCC) countries is above 90 per cent, which has placed them better positioned to take advantage of digitalisation than others. The upwards trend in internet accessibility varies by country and is largely driven by the declining cost of smartphones and other appliances (Langendorf, 2020).

Countries like Saudi Arabia, Qatar, and the UAE have claimed to deploy the first 5G network in the region, which is a critical step for digital transformation (Grace, 2020). The 5G technology offers unparalleled internet speed, much better than the 4G, which would enhance emerging technologies like the Internet of Things (IoT) and Artificial Intelligence (AI) (Jouaid, 2020). Such technologies, if appropriately channelised, will transform the urban hubs in the Arab world into digitally-equipped smart cities (Malek, 2020).

Digitalisation appears promising; however, like earlier advancements in ICT, it is a double-edged sword with vulnerabilities, susceptible to misuse by threat actors (individuals, groups, and even states). Since most critical infrastructures, such as power grids, nuclear power plants, etc., are connected to the network, the likelihood of some adversary breaching the safety systems of these setups presents an ominous future. Cyberattacks can cripple the economy and security apparatus of nations (Kausch, 2017). States have recognised the potential of cyberspace (domain in which humans operate via the internet) as a tool in statecraft and diplomacy and undermining their adversaries. Cyberattacks are recurrent across the Middle East, and many of them are reportedly orchestrated by state actors (CFR, 2021).

To prevent or mitigate the intensity of cyberattacks, states, business organisations, and individuals are expected to work in tandem, formulating and effectively implement cybersecurity measures. Countries in the Middle

East have been cooperating to secure and enhance their several ambitious projects, which rest on the resilience of cybersecurity measures. Securing cyberspace is a challenging task, which requires innovation, expertise, and knowledge sharing. In terms of cybersecurity, Israel is the most advanced country in the Middle East and has reportedly collaborated with other countries in the region, with which it does not even have diplomatic engagement (Alexander, 2020). After the Abraham Accords, some of the cybersecurity collaboration between Israel and Bahrain and UAE are out of the closet, with shared optimism and enthusiasm (Reuters, 2020).

Digitalisation in the Middle East

For centuries, advancements in ICTs, ranging from telegraph to space technology, have invariably caused major socio-political and economic shifts (Whyte & Mazanec, 2019, p. 37). Digital technologies are no different except in their scope and ability to supplement the globalisation process. Digital technologies that are dependent on hardware, software and networks, have ushered in what Klaus Schwab (2016) dubbed as "The Fourth Industrial Revolution" (p. 8), which is more sophisticated and integrated than any other technology before. Individuals can now work remotely, a practice spurred after the COVID-19 outbreak. Restrictions to fight the pandemic have made people more reliant on the digital sphere, which has "...broadened and accelerated the Fourth Industrial Revolution" with the rapid expansion of e-commerce, online education, and digital health (WEF, 2021, p. 30). Evidently, amid the economic chaos, technology giants have had an economic leap, given the world's five "biggest tech companies represented 23 per cent of the S&P 500 by market capitalisation" in 2020, a significant rise from the previous year (ibid, p. 66). Undoubtedly, countries with a comprehensive digitalisation strategy along with cybersecurity measures have a promising future.

Many Arab countries depend on hydrocarbons, but increasing internet access provides a foundation for a new economic future (Langendorf, 2020). According to the Arab Youth Survey of 2020, "young Arabs are increasingly embracing the digital revolution", social media consumption is on the rise, which has also become a popular source of news (ASDA'A BCW, 2020, p. 67). This is reminiscent of the Arab Spring, where social media was used to mobilise the youth across the region, underlining the power and influence of digital space. However, social media's popularity is not limited to the youth and covers the whole gamut of the population, as evident in Table 1. Only a few selected countries are considered since they have exhibited a large appetite for digitalisation. Barring Iran, internet access across these countries is almost 95 per cent of their population. However, Iran stands out (along with Israel) for its ability to exploit cyberspace to undermine its adversaries.

Table 1: The digital landscape of the digitally advanced countries in the region

Countries	Total population (million)	Internet users (per cent of the population)	Active social media users (million)	Mobile subscriptions (million)
Bahrain	1.7	97	1.4	2.19
Kuwait	4.27	99	4.2	7.38
Iran**	82.9*	70	-	117.7
Israel**	8.5*	81.6	-	10.79
Oman	5.11	91	1.4	6.24
Saudi Arabia	34.8	93	25	40.2
United Arab Emirates	9.89	99	9.73	18.38
Qatar**	2.8*	99.7	-	3.8

Source: Arab Youth Survey, 12th Annual Edition (2020)[1]; UNDP Human Development Report (2020); The World Bank (2021)

* Total population of 1 July 2019 (UNDP).

** Countries not covered under Arab Youth Survey.

Many of these countries have transformed their quotidian affairs with a solid digital foundation by shifting to digital applications. Take, for instance, education. With the onslaught of the pandemic, countries such as Saudi Arabia and the UAE have swiftly revised their way to deliver online education or e-learning (Draycott, 2020). In the UAE, the online school approved by the Knowledge and Human Development Authority (KHDA) witnessed a 200 per cent surge in enrolment for online courses (Sircar, 2021). Key international players in the education-tech sector have observed a "five-fold jump in the number of subscribers to their platform"

(Mathew, 2021). Over the next few years, the regional e-learning market is estimated to grow by 15.2 per cent (Sharma, 2020).

The future of e-commerce and financial technology (fintech) in the Middle East looks promising. The Middle East e-commerce site, Souq, bought by Amazon for US$ 580 million in 2017, has put the regional technology industry on the map of global investors (Amaro & Acton, 2017). In the region that has historically been dependent on cash payments, where most of the population has jostled for financial inclusion, fintech offers an opportunity for online transactions (Harrlson, 2020). The Gulf States, along with Israel, have taken the lead in emerging technologies investments to integrate them with individuals, enterprises, and government machinery. The UAE has emerged as a fintech hub, with Abu Dhabi as the site of a large annual fintech festival (Treeck, 2020). Bahrain has come up with a dedicated Bahrain FinTech Bay to develop the fintech industries in the region. The digital boom in the region has enabled the digital-based start-up culture, which will undisputedly contribute to the regional economy. The Middle East's top 10 most funded start-ups are digital-based, which could not have been possible without any incubation that the regional governments provide, particularly the Gulf States (Mabrouk, 2020).

The Gulf States are also leading in envisioning and developing smart cities in the region by including them in their long-term economic strategies. The success of these developments to transform the urban centres are evident in the Smart City Index 2020, which illustrates a significant jump in the ranking of Abu Dhabi (42 as compared to 56 in 2019), Dubai (43 as against 45 in 2019) and Riyadh (53 as against 71 in 2019) (IMD, 2020). Other cities from the region that have made it to the list include Tel Aviv (50), Rabat (105), and Cairo (106).

The UAE has been outshining others, in pursuit of achieving the goals of the *Vision 2021*. The construction of a high-speed Hyperloop transportation between the Emirate of Dubai and Abu Dhabi, touted as environmentally friendly, with its ability to cover a distance of 150 kilometres in 12 minutes, will transform travelling (Mansoori, 2020). Futuristic projects like NEOM in Saudi Arabia (NEOM, 2021) and the South Saad Al Abdullah Smart City Project in Kuwait are some of the most promising infrastructure projects in the region, enabled by the collaboration between government and private sectors as well as civil society (*Gulf Business*, 2020). Such collaborations are also facilitating the transformation of healthcare. The Dubai Health Authority (DHA) has employed AI, while the tele-cardiology network established in Saudi Arabia provides a virtual care network across several hospitals (Fidanci, 2019).

Amid these encouraging developments fostered by digitalisation across the region, particularly the Gulf, too much dependency on cyberspace also entails some drawbacks. In the last decade, numerous cyberattacks have been reported across the region, especially in digitally advanced states like the Gulf. Such unauthorised intrusions in cyberspace have emanated from both the state and non-state actors in the form of cyber-espionage, subversions, cyber-crime, sabotages, etc.

Conflict and Challenges in the Cyberspace

The Middle East has been engulfed with wide-ranging conflicts, some perennial while some over a decade old. Most of these conflicts are unconventional, wherein not all the parties embroiled in conflicts are states. The rise of non-state actors has transformed the nature of warfare in the region. Given the advancement of ICTs, conflicts have moved into cyberspace, with both state and non-state actors exploiting the medium for political and economic gains. In this era of the fourth industrial revolution, the more technologically advanced and tech-dependent a state is, the larger it's vulnerability to cyberattacks.

Regional countries have become increasingly adept at conducting cyberattacks at home and abroad by themselves or by their proxies. Israel and Iran are at the forefront of exploiting cyberspace for statecraft, while other countries are slowly catching up. The victims of such attacks range from governments to the military, private sector to civil society (CFR, 2007). The Cyber Operations Tracker, a database prepared by the Digital and Cyberspace Policy programme at the Washington-based Council for Foreign Relations, which tracks publicly known cyberattacks by states or their affiliates, unveils a disturbing trend. So does the "significant cyber incidents" which focuses on "cyber attacks on government agencies, defense, and high tech companies, or economic crimes with losses of more than a million dollars" (CSIS, 2021). The incessant cyberattacks that regional countries are facing leave a significant mark on these databases.

Israel reportedly undertook the first known major inter-state cyberattack in the Middle East in 2007 against the Syrian Air Force, where Syrian radar and air defence systems were rendered ineffective (Cyber Operations Tracker, n.d.). Three years later, in July 2010, the "Stuxnet" worm was reported to have destroyed numerous centrifuges in Iran's Natanz uranium enrichment facility (McAfee, 2021). The attack was reportedly undertaken by the US and Israel, although neither country has openly admitted their role in the operation (Nakashima & Warrick, 2012). The destructive nature of the attack on its critical infrastructure spurred Iran to invest in cyber capabilities to enable deterrence (Hodgson et al. 2019). In 2012, Iran deployed the "Shamoon" malware to attack Saudi and Qatari oil and gas companies and on its success, renewed "Shamoon 2" in 2017, against Saudi Arabia's petrochemical and other sectors (Anderson & Sadjadpour, 2018). Under the spell of success, Iran has illustrated how militarily weaker countries can use cyberattacks to contend with more advanced adversaries.

Lately, in February 2021, suspected Iranian hackers targeted government agencies in the UAE and conducted espionage campaigns against Iranian dissidents across the Middle East (CSIS, 2021). In December 2020, Iranian hackers had undertaken a cyber theft wherein data was stolen from numerous Israeli companies (ibid.). In early May 2020, the network supporting shipping and cargo handling operations within the Iranian port of Shahid Rajaei was compromised by a cyberattack (*Al-Jazeera*, 2020). Israel presumably undertook the attack in retaliation for an Iranian cyberattack on its water infrastructure (*Times of Israel*, 2020). Both the attacks were not admitted by the respective governments, although the intentions behind them were muscle-flexing in cyberspace, an extension of the conflict in the digital medium. According to observers, through such posturing, each side attempting to establish "credible deterrent red lines to persuade the other side to cease" or face repercussions (Work & Harknett, 2020).

Generally, cyberattacks are alluring to threat actors as it is comparatively inexpensive, difficult to trace, could be launched across vast distances and could also be operated by a less powerful country, undermining the asymmetry in a conventional medium (Green, 2015, p. 2). Given these potential rewards of exploiting cyberspace without any potential setback, many other countries have weaponised the digital medium. For example, Lebanon, Morocco and Syria are militarily inferior but have used cyberattacks against their targets, both local and abroad. Lebanon and Morocco are suspected of using malware to target human rights activists, journalists, and military personnel for espionage purposes (Cyber Operations Tracker, 2021).

Saudi Arabia and the UAE have reportedly used Pegasus spyware developed by the NSO (Niv, Shalev, Omri) group to compromise the phones of 36 employees of the Doha-based Al-Jazeera news agency (Kirchgaessner & Safi, 2020). In addition, Syrian Electronic Army (SEA), a group of hackers and activists in support of Bashar al-Assad (suspected to have the Syrian government's backing), has reportedly targeted *Al-Jazeera* and Qatar Foundation (Fowler, 2013). Whether SEA is a government-backed group or just a group of individuals that operate out of "support" for their president, the Federal Bureau of Investigation (FBI) of the US has added one of its members to Cyber's Most Wanted list (FBI, 2021).

The cyberattacks unleashed by non-state actors are far greater in numbers and scale, although they lack vigour compared to state-sponsored attacks. The non-state actors have undertaken operations that range from cyber-terrorism to hacktivism and cybercrime. This does not imply that the states do not intend to commit such acts; given the nature of cyberspace, state and non-state actors, in the past, have assumed operations that include sabotage, subversions, and disruptions. However, since the non-state actors (proxies) have a limited pool of resources to undertake large, complex operations, they adopt emerging technologies in operations to afflict maximum damage on their adversaries.

The objectives of purported cyberattacks are also significant as it varies across actors. For example, the objective of a cyber-criminal would likely be online fraud. Similarly, an espionage operation for states, activism for hacktivists, and recruitment purposes for terrorists have political underpinnings. Notwithstanding the intention and type of actors, cyber-crimes incur a hefty cost on domestic and global economies. According to Costin Raiu, an anti-virus expert at the Russian security company

Kaspersky Lab, cyber-crime is a "...three-headed hydra...The first is that it's profitable. The second is that it's low-risk. The third and most important is that it's anonymous" (Grauman, 2012, p. 8).

Cybercrime, as estimated in a report by CSIS and McAfee, "may cost the world almost [US]$600 billion, or 0.8 per cent of global GDP" (Lewis, 2018, p. 4). Phishing remains the most popular way to commit cybercrime, while massive Distributed Denial-of-Service (DDoS)[2] attacks have imposed hefty costs on companies and individuals. The GDP of the Middle East and North Africa (MENA) region is assessed to be US$ 3.1 trillion, while the cyber-crime cost is estimated to be US$ 2-5 billion for the year 2017 (ibid.: 7). Furthermore, cybercrimes that entail intellectual property theft could potentially be a risk to national security as it might mean the exfiltration of military technology (ibid.: 15). Such incidents would likely compel the states and business enterprises to allocate a major chunk of resources to counter such threats. In addition, it will most likely tarnish the reputation of business enterprises for its lack of cybersecurity measures, along with damage to stock values (ibid.: 6).

Advancement in ICTs has also been quite convenient for terrorists' networks to operate unabashedly. Cyberspace allows terrorist organisations to "undertake specialised recruitment, to distribute information both widely and secretly, to publicise terror activities, and—though few such incidents have yet taken place- to terrorise via the prosecution of disruptive cyber-attacks" (Whyte & Mazanec, 2019, p. 182). Long before the Islamic State (ISIS) used cyberspace for its recruitment and propaganda drive, groups like Al-Qaeda had mapped out cyberspace as a battlefront to exploit it to broadcast beheadings of captives to the world (Nance & Sampson, 2017, p. 25). Later, ISIS improvised the methods of their predecessors, built on their tools and techniques while formalizing a structure of their operations in cyberspace (ibid: 33). ISIS had dedicated media centres for specific purposes that include (ibid: 34)

1. Al-Furqan: The main publishing centre for video, audio, and print;
2. Al-Hayat Media Centre: Meant for outreach to the Western, non-Arabic speaking audience via video, audio, and print;
3. Al-Bayan Radio: FM headlines from Mosul;

4. Ajnad: Nasheed and sermons via audio;
5. Maktabat al- Himmah: Pamphlet propaganda via pdf and billboards; and
6. An-Naba: Weekly newspaper distributed in pdf.

This was just the surface of the group's *modus operandi* but sufficient to illustrate engagement in cyberspace. ISIS also used end-to-end messaging apps like Telegram, Signal, WhatsApp, and Wickr to be a key tool for its planning and recruiting (ibid: 62-64). ISIS is also the first terror group that seriously developed a "modest" cyberattack capability and "sophisticated computing and communications technologies" (Bronk & Anderson, 2017). Other major terror groups like Hamas and Hezbollah have also reportedly used cyberattacks against their adversaries' particularly Israel and associates (Wagenheim, 2020; Gross, 2020).

Curbing freedom

The progress in digital advancement served the states in the Middle East to bolster their control and surveillance over its population, dubbed as "digital authoritarianism" (Woodhams, 2019). The usual targets of such eavesdropping are journalists, activists, opposition figures, and other public figures considered a threat to the authorities. However, tech-savvy individuals have circumvented the authorities by shifting to more secured applications, such as Clubhouse, particularly in the Middle East, which provides them with the space for political discussions, a rarity in the region (Alhussein, 2021).

The unfettered and flagrant control of the state in the physical world has now moved to cyberspace. Middle Eastern countries lag far behind on internet freedom, largely due to their domestic laws that limit freedom of expression, access to information, and privacy of individuals (Shahbaz and Funk, 2021). Almost a decade back, during the Arab Spring, common people used the internet and social media to communicate, mobilise and stir the political debate that challenged the authoritarianism in the region. Although it ushered in limited political transformation, people and the states realised the potential of the digital medium to unravel the status quo.

Cooperation and Opportunities

The cyber landscape offers opportunities to the stakeholders, encourages cooperation between the states and business enterprises while emboldening knowledge sharing globally. Drawing digital borders are contrary to the characteristics of cyberspace, and cooperation is inevitable. Unlike physical space, enforcing cyber-sovereignty is not easy; the private sector's role is indispensable while individuals' participation is unavoidable. To ensure the seamless functioning of cyberspace, knowledge sharing between all the stakeholders is critical. Securing cyberspace and ensuring robustness is a precondition for a massive economic transformation that the Gulf States have envisaged for years to come.

Table 2: Country-wise, ICT goods exports

Countries	ICT goods exports (percent of total goods exports)*
Bahrain	0.4 (2018)
Egypt	2.9 (2019)
Israel	10 (2019)
Kuwait	0.1 (2019)
Qatar	Nil (2018)
Saudi Arabia	Nil (2019)
United Arab Emirates	7.8 (2019)

Source: The World Bank (2021)

* ICT goods exports include computers and peripheral equipment, communication equipment, consumer electronic equipment, electronic components and other information and technology goods.

Table 2 indicates the divide between the states in terms of their ability to innovate and produce ICT goods. In Israel and the UAE, ICT goods exports make a substantial part of their foreign trade. This illustrates the willingness of these states to invest in the future that lies in the digital medium. The table does not represent the overall robustness of the entire cyberspace in the region; however, it provides opportunities to the states that are lagging to collaborate with states leading in digital innovation. There have been instances where countries like Saudi Arabia and the UAE have had secret collaborations with Israel while having no diplomatic relations (that is, before the Abraham Accords).

Israeli-owned companies received contracts to secure critical infrastructures like oil and gas installations in the UAE and to set up mass civil surveillance systems of Abu Dhabi (Donaghy, 2015). In 2012, Israeli cybersecurity firms helped Saudi Arabia "assess and salvage" the cyberattack on its oil and gas installations. These firms are reportedly in talks to establish a presence in Neom (Fakhro, 2020). The UAE-based intelligence firm, DarkMatter, has reportedly been recruiting IDF veterans from elite cyber units, exhibiting covert cooperation between the countries (*Times of Israel*, 2019). In 2015, Israeli firm IntuView assisted Saudi Arabia in tracking jihadists on social media, which later expanded to include monitoring public opinions about the royal family (Zilber, 2019).

There is a vast potential for cooperation in cyberspace, even while states are engaged in scaling up their cyber capabilities, both offensive and defensive, because contrary to conventional wisdom, such posturing in cyberspace achieves de-escalatory effects (Handler, 2019). Israel, which was a pariah to the region, has leveraged its technological excellence to strengthen ties with the Gulf States (ibid.). According to observers, from the day of its establishment, Israel "grasped the diplomatic clout of weapons as a means to forge alliances" (Shejaf & Jacobson, 2018).

Driven by strategic considerations, the UAE has ensured that it avails itself to a large pool of knowledge and skills that will come along with its strong ties with Israel, and rightly so. Israel's cyber exports for 2020 are worth an estimated US$ 6.5 billion; 31 per cent of the world's cyber investments are in Israel; and 33 per cent of the cyber unicorns (private companies worth over US$ 1 billion) in the world are Israeli (INCD, 2021). Israel has also apparently eased its rules on cyber weapons or spyware exports (Cohen & Rabinovitch, 2019). Such exports to foreign governments and law enforcement agencies are approved by the Defence Exports Control Agency (Shejaf & Jacobson, 2018), despite the fear of these tools being used for cracking down on opposition figures, activists, etc.

The Gulf and Israel, given their excessive reliance on technology, are looking for an alliance to counter cyber threats, as evident from UAE's

Cyber Chief Mohamed al-Kuwaiti's statement advocating for joint exercises in cyber defence (Reuters, 2020). The Mohamed Bin Zayed University of Artificial Intelligence (MBZUAI) and the Weizmann Institute of Science have established a joint AI programme encompassing joint research projects, mutual visits, and student exchange programmes (*Saudi Gazette*, 2021). Israeli companies are being invited for the Gulf Information and Security Expo and Conference (GISEC), 2021, a promising sign of a long and robust tie between the Arab world and Israel (Frantzman, 2021). Countries have also mooted for more tech collaboration among Arab allies to harness the potential in the region (Kamel, 2021).

Even though the overt cyber cooperation between the erstwhile enemies is at a nascent phase, the developments are encouraging and could potentially percolate to the broader Middle East. Digitalisation will play a critical role in strategizing, pursuing, and achieving strategic goals; therefore, leaving it unsecured would be a strategic mistake. Inter-state cooperation and knowledge sharing are the keys to a robust cybersecurity framework, supplemented by a multi-stakeholder approach to include both state and non-state actors. The Middle East can further its cybersecurity interest by acting in unison on global cybersecurity platforms, inter-governmental and non-governmental. Since a large part of cyberspace depends on private players, the tech-focused companies in the region can contemplate entering into cybersecurity alliances like Global Cyber Alliance (GCA) and Cyber Threat Alliance (CTA) for both operational and normative alliances (Handler, 2019).

As discussed, cyberspace in the region is connected to several issues that could have a destructive impact across socio-economic layers of societies if left unguarded. The collaborative efforts can be used for capacity-building. A technologically advanced country can share its strategies, skills, and, at times, technology to identify, educate and nurture young minds digitally (Aboul-Enein, 2017). The states must undertake competence building at universities; update cybersecurity capabilities, and promote a culture of cybersecurity to the level of individuals (ibid.). Cyberspace may have made states and organisations vulnerable; however, the vast scope for cooperation is undeniable and must be taken advantage of, which the Middle East is fortunately pursuing.

Conclusion

A decade since the eruption of Arab Spring protests, peace continues to evade the Middle East. Countries such as Iraq, Syria, Libya, and Yemen are in disarray, more or less without any credible governing authority. Since 2011, digital media that played a critical role in mobilizing people against authoritarian regimes has been firmly implanted amongst the populace, albeit not uniformly. Much of the infrastructure to enable digitalisation is limited to rich Gulf States, Iran, and Israel. Digitalisation has also transformed the nature of conflicts while simultaneously exemplifying a promising future.

On the one hand, state and non-state actors have weaponised cyberspace, and on the other hand, digitalisation has unleashed some remarkable developments within society. The overarching nature of digitalisation has left nothing untouched that includes areas like education, financial institutions, and e-commerce. Conversely, it has also unleashed formidable challenges like a cyberattack, cybercrime, and cyber-espionage while amplifying the vulnerability of critical infrastructures. Cyberspace has also proven convenient for terrorists in advertising and successfully recruiting susceptible young minds falling prey to their messages.

States have used it to quell dissent, authorise surveillance, and restrict the free flow of information by shutting down major websites. Given the nature of cyberspace, people have found ways to circumvent surveillance, severely undermining the reach of the state. Digitalisation has also provided a medium for states and non-state actors alike to exchange knowledge and information. Israel, an erstwhile foe to the Gulf, has used its technological prowess to reach out to the Gulf, which embraces peaceful coexistence with the Jewish state for strategic reasons. Such developments manifest the potential of cyberspace both as an adverse and a promising tool to set off a transformation in the Middle East that was not fathomable a decade back.

Notes

1. Almost 4,000 face-to-face interviews of Arab youth (age group of 18-24) were conducted across 17 Arab states. The sample split is 50 : 50 male/female.
2. The intentional paralyzing of a computer network by flooding it with data sent simultaneously from many individual computers (See: Cyber Operations Tracker)

References

Aboul-Enein, Sameh (2017), "Cybersecurity Challenges in the Middle East," *Geneva Papers Research Series*, No. 22/17, Geneva Centre for Security Policy.

Alexander, Kristian (2020), "Israeli-Gulf Cyber Cooperation," *Modern diplomacy*, December 23, https://moderndiplomacy.eu/2020/12/23/israeli-gulf-cyber-cooperation/

Alhussein, Eman (2021), "Joining the Club: New Trends in Gulf Social Media," The Arab Gulf States Institute in Washington, February 19, https://agsiw.org/joining-the-club-new-trends-in-gulf-social-media/

Al-Jazeera (2020), "Israel cyberattack caused 'total disarray' at Iran port: Report," May 19, https://www.aljazeera.com/news/2020/5/19/israel-cyberattack-caused-total-disarray-at-iran-port-report

Al Mansoori, Hamad (2020), "From dream to reality: Developing sustainable smart cities in the United Arab Emirates," International Telecommunication Union, August 24, https://www.itu.int/en/myitu/News/2020/08/24/06/46/Smart-sustainable-city-development-UAE

Amaro, Silvia and Acton, Gemma (2017), "Amazon reaches deal to acquire Middle East e-commerce site Souq.com," *CNBC*, March 28, https://www.cnbc.com/2017/03/28/amazon-to-acquire-souqcom-a-large-e-commerce-site-in-the-middle-east.html

Anderson, Collin and Sadjadpour, Karim (2018), *Iran's Cyber Threat: Espionage, Sabotage, and Revenge*, Washington, DC: Carnegie Endowment for International Peace.

ASDA'A BCW (2020). *Arab Youth Survey: A Voice for Change.* 12th Annual Edition, https://www.arabyouthsurvey.com/

Bronk, Chris and Anderson, Gregory S. (2017), "Encounter Battle: Engaging ISIL in Cyberspace," *The Cyber Defense Review*, 2 (1), pp. 93-108.

Center for Strategic Studies (2021), "Significant Cyber Incidents," https://www.csis.org/programs/strategic-technologies-program/significant-cyber-incidents

Chaiban, Ted (2021), "COVID-19, an opportunity to bridge the digital gap and reform education systems in the region," UNICEF MENA, January 3, https://www.unicef.org/mena/stories/covid-19-opportunity-bridge-digital-gap-and-reform-education-systems-region

Cohen, Tova and Rabinovitch, Ari (2019), "Israel eases rules on cyber weapons exports despite criticism," Reuters, August 22, https://www.reuters.com/article/us-israel-hackers-idUSKCN1VC0XQ

Council on Foreign Relations (2020), "Cyber Operations Tracker," https://www.cfr.org/cyber-operations/

Council on Foreign Relations (2007), "Attack on the Syrian Air Force," https://www.cfr.org/cyber-operations/attack-syrian-air-force

Donaghy, Rori (2015), "Falcon Eye: The Israeli-installed mass civil surveillance system of Abu Dhabi," *Middle East Eye*, July 15, https://www.middleeasteye.net/news/falcon-eye-israeli-installed-mass-civil-surveillance-system-abu-dhabi

Draycott, Alexandra (2020), "Coronavirus drives remote learning's acceptance in the Middle East and beyond," *Arab News*, March 22, https://www.arabnews.com/node/1645091/middle-east

Fakhro, Elham (2020), "An Open Affair: As the UAE and Israel Normalize Ties, Gulf Actors Respond," *Jadaliyya*, August 20, https://www.jadaliyya.com/Details/41608

Federal Bureau of Investigation (FBI), United States (2021), "Cyber's Most Wanted," https://www.fbi.gov/wanted/cyber

Fidanci, Özlem (2019), "How technology can revolutionise healthcare across the MENA region," World Economic Forum, April 4, https://www.weforum.org/agenda/2019/04/how-ai-can-revolutionise-healthcare-across-the-mena-region/

Fowler, Sarah (2013), "Who is the Syrian Electronic Army?" BBC News, April 25, https://www.bbc.com/news/world-middle-east-22287326

Frantzman, Seth J. (2021), "GISEC cybersecurity confab in Dubai could be big for Israel," *The Jerusalem Post*, February 10, https://www.jpost.com/jpost-tech/gisec-cybersecurity-confab-in-dubai-could-be-big-for-israel-658454

Grace, Ryan (2020), "5G adoption and its implications in the Gulf states," Middle East Institute, Washington, DC, August 11, https://www.mei.edu/publications/5g-adoption-and-its-implications-gulf-states

Grauman, Brigid (2012), *Cyber-Security: The Vexed Question of Global Rules,* An independent report on cyber-preparedness around the world, Security and Defence Agenda, Brussels, Belgium, https://www.files.ethz.ch/isn/139895/SDA_Cyber_report_FINAL.pdf

Green, James A. (2015), "Introduction," in James A. Green (Ed.), *Cyber Warfare: A Multidisciplinary Analysis*, New York: Routledge, pp. 1-6.

Gross, Judah Ari (2020), "IDF: Hamas again tries to 'catfish' soldiers with fake women on social media," *The Times of Israel*, February 16, https://www.timesofisrael.com/idf-hamas-again-tries-to-catfish-soldiers-with-fake-women-on-social-media/

Gulf Business (2020), "Why partnerships are key to achieving the GCC's smart city ambitions," December 26, https://gulfbusiness.com/why-partnerships-are-key-to-achieving-the-gccs-smart-city-ambitions/

Handler, Simon (2019), "The Zero-Day War? How Cyber is Reshaping the Future of the Most Combustible Conflicts," *NextGov*, November 4, https://www.nextgov.com/ideas/2019/11/zero-day-war-how-cyber-reshaping-future-most-combustible-conflicts/161055/

Harrlson, Polly Jean (2020), "Report Finds E-Commerce and Digital Payments to Boom in MENAP in 2021," *The Fintech Times*, November 10, https://thefintechtimes.com/report-finds-e-commerce-and-digital-payments-to-boom-in-menap-in-2021/

Hodgson, Quentin E.; Ma, Logan; Marcinek, Krystyna; and Schwindt, Karen (2019). *Fighting Shadows in the Dark: Understanding and Countering Coercion in Cyberspace*, Santa Monica: Rand Corporation.

IMD (2020), "Smart City Index 2020," https://www.imd.org/smart-city-observatory/smart-city-index/

International Telecommunication Union (ITU) (2021), "Statistics," https://www.itu.int/en/ITU-D/Statistics/Pages/stat/default.aspx

Israel National Cyber Directorate (2021), "The Israeli cyber industry continues to grow: record fundraising in 2020," January 21, https://bit.ly/3yRcbnx

Jouaid, Abdallah (2020), "How 5G Technology Is Set To Change The World?" *Forbes*, October 8, https://www.forbesmiddleeast.com/innovation/5g/5g-healthy-fears-and-extraordinary-returns

Kamel, Deena (2021), "UAE calls for more tech collaboration among Arab allies," *The National*, February 20, https://www.thenationalnews.com/business/technology/uae-calls-for-more-tech-collaboration-among-arab-allies-1.1169478

Kausch, Kristina (2017), "Cheap Havoc: How Cyber-Geopolitics Will Destabilize the Middle East," *Policy Brief*, No. 35, November, German Marshall Fund of the United States, Washington, DC, https://www.gmfus.org/publications/cheap-havoc-how-cyber-geopolitics-will-destabilize-middle-east

Kirchgaessner, Stephanie and Safi, Michael (2020), "Dozens of Al Jazeera journalists allegedly hacked using Israeli firm's spyware," *The Guardian*, December 20, https://www.theguardian.com/media/2020/dec/20/citizen-lab-nso-dozens-of-aljazeera-journalists-allegedly-hacked-using-israeli-firm-spyware

Langendorf, Manuel (2020), "Digital Stability: How Technology Can Empower Future Generations in The Middle East," *Policy Brief*, March 24, European Council on Foreign Relations, London, https://ecfr.eu/publication/digital_stability_how_technology_can_empower_future_generations_middle_east/

Lewis, James (2018), "Economic Impact of Cybercrime- No Slowing Down," *CSIS Report*, February 21, https://www.csis.org/analysis/economic-impact-cybercrime

Mabrouk, Ahmed (2020), "These are the Middle East's Top 10 Most-Funded Startups 2020," *Forbes*, October 3, https://www.forbesmiddleeast.com/innovation/startups/these-are-the-middle-easts-top-10-most-funded-startups-2020

Malek, Caline (2020), "How GCC's smart cities will tackle urbanization challenges," *Arab News*, January 19, https://www.arabnews.com/node/1614996/middle-east

Mathew, James (2021), "Positive fallout of coronavirus: The Middle East comes to forefront of online education," *Arab News*, March 3, https://www.arabianbusiness.com/education/459448-positive-fallout-of-coronavirus-the-middle-east-at-forefront-of-online-education-sector

McAfee (2021), "What is Stuxnet?" https://www.mcafee.com/enterprise/en-in/security-awareness/ransomware/what-is-stuxnet.html

Nakashima, Ellen and Warrick, Joby (2012), "Stuxnet was work of US and Israeli experts, officials say," *The Washington Post*, June 2, https://www.washingtonpost.com/world/national-security/stuxnet-was-work-of-us-and-israeli-experts-officials-say/2012/06/01/gJQAlnEy6U_story.html

Nance, Malcolm and Sampson, Christopher (2017), *Hacking ISIS: How to Destroy The Cyber Jihad*, New York: Skyhorse.

NEOM (2021), "A Vision of the New Future," https://www.neom.com/index.html

Reuters (2020), "UAE, Israeli cyber chiefs discuss joining forces to combat common threats," September 24, https://www.reuters.com/article/israel-gulf-emirates-cyber/uae-israeli-cyber-chiefs-discuss-joining-forces-to-combat-common-threats-idUKL5N2GL4TR

Saudi Gazette (2021), "MBZUAI, Weizmann Institute of Science establish joint AI program," February 24, https://saudigazette.com.sa/article/603820/World/Mena/MBZUAI-Weizmann-Institute-of-Science-establish-joint-AI-program

Schwab, Klaus (2016), *The Fourth Industrial Revolution*, Geneva: World Economic Forum.

Shahbaz, Adrian and Funk, Allie (2021), *Freedom on the Net 2020: The Pandemic's Digital Shadow*, Freedom House, Washington, DC, https://freedomhouse.org/report/freedom-net

Sharma, Alkesh (2020), "Coronavirus: How tech is enabling the Middle East's students to cope with pandemic," *The National*, May 4, https://www.thenationalnews.com/business/technology/coronavirus-how-tech-is-enabling-the-middle-east-s-students-to-cope-with-pandemic-1.1014370

Shejaf, Hager and Jacobson, Jonathan (2018), "Revealed: Israel's Cyber-spy Industry Helps World Dictators Hunt Dissidents and Gays," *Haaretz*, October 20, https://www.haaretz.com/israel-news/.premium.MAGAZINE-israel-s-cyber-spy-industry-aids-dictators-hunt-dissidents-and-gays-1.6573027

Sircar, Nandini (2021), "Coronavirus UAE: Demand for online schooling on the rise," *Khaleej Times*, January 31, https://www.khaleejtimes.com/coronavirus-pandemic/coronavirus-uae-demand-for-online-schooling-on-the-rise

Times of Israel (2019), "UAE-based intelligence firm said recruiting IDF veterans from elite cyber unit," October 18, https://www.timesofisrael.com/uae-based-intelligence-firm-said-recruiting-idf-veterans-from-elite-cyber-unit/

Times of Israel (2020), "Israel aghast at Iran cyberattack on civilian water infrastructure—TV report," May 9, https://www.timesofisrael.com/israel-aghast-at-iran-cyberattack-on-civilian-water-infrastructure-tv-report/

The World Bank (2021), "ICT goods exports (% of total goods exports)", https://data.worldbank.org/indicator/TX.VAL.ICTG.ZS.UN

Treeck, Dominik (2020), "The GCC's digital economy is growing, but risks must be managed," *MENA Source*, December 9, Atlantic Council, https://www.atlanticcouncil.org/blogs/menasource/the-gccs-digital-economy-is-growing-but-risks-must-be-managed/

Wagenheim, Mike (2020), "Hezbollah hones expertise in training cyber-warfare agents," *The Jerusalem Post,* August 16, https://www.jpost.com/middle-east/hezbollah-hones-expertise-in-training-cyber-warfare-agents-638800

World Economic Forum (2021), *The Global Risk Report 2021*, January 19, https://www.weforum.org/reports/the-global-risks-report-2021

Whyte, Christopher and Mazanec, Brian (2019), *Understanding Cyber Warfare: Politics, Policy and Strategy*, New York: Routledge.

Woodhams, Samuel (2019), "Digital Authoritarianism is Rising in the Middle East," *Foreign Policy in Focus*, August 20, https://fpif.org/digital-authoritarianism-is-rising-in-the-middle-east/

Work, J. D. and Harknett, Richard (2020), "Troubled Vision: Understanding recent Israeli-Iranian Offensive Cyber Exchanges," *Issue Brief*, July 22, Atlantic Council, https://www.atlanticcouncil.org/in-depth-research-reports/issue-brief/troubled-vision-understanding-israeli-iranian-offensive-cyber-exchanges/

Zilber, Neri (2019), "Gulf Cyber Cooperation with Israel: Balancing Threats and Rights," *Brief Analysis,* The Washington Institute for Near East Policy, January 17, https://www.washingtoninstitute.org/policy-analysis/gulf-cyber-cooperation-israel-balancing-threats-and-rights

12. The Shadow Line: Turkey and the Arab Spring

Krzysztof Strachota

The Arab Spring can be understood in two ways. The first, a strict definition, calls it a series of socio-political protests that swept through the Arab world since December 2010, leading to a series of political changes but also counter-revolutionary actions. From this perspective, by the end of 2012, at the latest, the Arab Spring came to an end. The armed conflicts in Libya, Yemen and Syria rooted in the Arab Spring are treated as qualitatively different processes.

In the second, much broader sense, the Arab Spring is a sign of revolutionary changes related to politics, society, identity and other matters. The expression of these in early 2011 morphed into an exuberant wave, a nationwide Arab protest movement, resulting in a serious crisis for the old order; and in a few places, it collapsed. From this perspective, the Arab Spring is a process that is still unfinished—the deep causes of the protests have not been resolved. As a result, if restored, the order has a weak foundation and is at risk of being destabilised by internal and external factors (for example, the unfinished wars in Syria, Libya, and Yemen). In parallel, a ferment continues around fundamental identity questions concerning the role, nature and shape of the state, modernisation and development, relations with the world, especially the West.

Another fundamental question concerns the inclusion of Turkey in the discussion on the Arab Spring. Turkey is not an Arab state, it was not the arena of the 2011 wave of protests. A narrower definition of the Arab Spring excludes Turkey from the analysis. But when viewing the Arab Spring as an unfinished revolution, as a process of revising the old order and seeking a new one, alongside a desire to understand its nature, mechanisms and the potential of this process, Turkey becomes natural and even indispensable. Therefore, the co-constitutive aspect of the Arab Spring on Turkish domestic and foreign policy is a process that has so far evaded academic scrutiny and requires deeper examination. As this paper will set out to outline, viewing this kaleidoscopic process in the limelight of the aforementioned claim lays bare the need to frame Turkish policy and the revolutionary Middle East as a conjoined political process—one that cannot be studied separately.

Turkey as a non-Arab actor of the Arab Spring

Turkey's relations with Arab states are often neglected. Arab states were formed in open opposition to the Ottoman Empire and the domination of the Turks. A strong, sovereign, nationalist, but also Western-linked Turkey was different and hostile. On the other hand, though, it cannot be denied that they share several hundred years of history (common political, cultural, intellectual, in the social space and patterns) that radiated to the Arab world both by the power of the caliphate and by the imposition of pro-Western reforms. Even after the collapse of the Ottoman Empire, all the succession states (generally all new states in the Middle East) faced the same dilemmas regarding the construction of modern states and nations, systemic and identity solutions, institutional solutions (the role of the army), and relations with the outside world (the West, the Eastern bloc). In these processes, Turkey has usually been regarded as an important reference point (even in political tensions).

What is crucial, however, is the fact that, at the outbreak of the Arab Spring, Turkey embodied all the hopes raised by the protesters: the democratisation of political life (the democratic takeover of power by the AKP and civilian control of the army), economic and social development involving all the inhabitants of the country, effective mediation between social modernisation and cultural and religious tradition and close cooperation with the West (the adaptation of positive solutions) without falling into subordination. Thus, the Turkish experience crystallised into the so-called Turkish model, which is tempting for many Arab societies.

Turkey's involvement in the Arab Spring was also tangible. In various ways, Turkey was a mediator, supporter of revolutionary forces and a refuge for refugees. Furthermore, from the outset, Turkey expressed its ambitions to decide or co-decide on the future of the regional order, not only in its immediate neighbourhood (Syria and Iraq) but more broadly in the Persian Gulf (Qatar) or North Africa (Egypt and Libya). Finally, Turkey was ready to politically and militarily confront the countries (or their proxies) involved in the conflict, including Syria, Russia, Saudi Arabia and even the United States (US). Although the forms of activity and dynamism have changed, this policy is still being implemented by Ankara.

Finally, albeit in a specific and limited way, the Arab Spring has found an extension and development in Turkey itself. The fundamental processes of the last decade for Turkey are a direct consequence of the Arab Spring or the result of the lessons which the Turkish government learned from this process. This concerns the flourishing and twilight of neo-Ottoman politics, the concept of the nation realised by Turkey, attitudes towards Islam, national minorities and relations with the world and others.

The Turkish perspective on the Arab Spring helps to understand its phenomenon, its universal phenomenon in the broader region, the mechanisms that propelled it and, finally, the processes it has launched and which are still far from being completed. Therefore, it can be said even more strongly that without taking Turkey into account, it may be almost impossible to understand the Arab Spring. Certainly, it is impossible to understand today's Turkey in isolation from the Arab Spring.

Turkish Dream

In 2002, Turkey faced a serious systemic political, social and economic crisis. The traditional political forces were not equipped for the effective rule of the country. There was a clear threat from radical (in the Turkish sense) Islamic forces or a return to direct army rule (a warning sign was the extortion of the resignation of Necmettin Erbakan's government in 1997), and a lack of vision in foreign policy. In addition, there was growing public frustration caused by economic problems, demographic pressures, generational change, and tensions between nationalist elites, conservative provinces and the pro-Western liberals. The answer was the 2002 elections, which resulted in all the parties then represented in parliament finding themselves outside parliament, and the AKP coming to power. The AKP at the time was a new party with a character that was very difficult to define: it was headed by a man convicted for religious extremism namely, Recep Tayyip Erdogan.

At the same time, the AKP represented pro-Western, metropolitan liberals (in the political and economic sense) and conservatives from the provinces. It joined movements calling for religious renewal and the revitalisation of Ottoman traditions and forces interested in close cooperation—and integration—with the West (the EU and IMF). Since the AKP took power (which it still retains), it has consistently pursued an agenda representing a revolution in Turkish conditions. The first decade of AKP rule was a success (Matusiak, 2015). There was dynamic economic development (crucially, this was felt beyond the traditional economic centres) which effectively modernised the country and society (infrastructure, opening the way to social advancement, the formation of new elites). Tangible results were achieved in the democratisation of the proven political system, for example, by the weakening of the political role of the army (E-memorandum 2007, Balyoz and Ergenekon trials) and, on the other hand, by the opening of the EU membership process (2005).

The revolutionary consequences were seen in the revision of the exclusive Turkish nationalism concept and openness to religious (for example, the Alevi community) and national minorities (a process starting from broad cultural autonomy for Kurds to a peace process with the existential enemy of the republic, that is the Kurdistan Worker's Party (PKK)). Similar developments took place in Turkish foreign policy: openness to the world, a shift away from a policy of force in cross-border disputes (for example, Syria, Armenia and Iraqi Kurds) to in favour of intense (economic, social, cultural and political) soft power and the slogan "zero problems with neighbours." The Turkish politics of that time effectively combined contradictions: Islamic conservatism and modernisation; integration with the EU and the neo-Ottoman concept; East and West; deepening links with the world in strengthening its subjectivity (Reynolds, 2012; Ananicz, 2015). Turkey was in the vanguard of pointing to the same challenges and finding solutions that a few years later sounded almost identical in cafes and in streets and squares of Arab cities and remote Bedouin, Berber, and Kurdish villages.

A time of hope

The outbreak of the Arab Spring was read in Ankara as confirmation of the validity of Turkey's policy and confirmation of diagnoses regarding the future of the region, that is, the lack of alternatives to its own model. Western countries have unsuccessfully reconciled support for democratic change with concerns about the destabilisation and Islamisation of Arab partners (Egypt, for example), a policy of threats (Syria), direct military intervention (Libya) and restraint (most cases). In doing so, they cited the example of Turkey but did not coordinate with it. Meanwhile, Turkey has adopted a somewhat paternalistic but moderate stance between the leadership and the opposition (in Syria). Over time, support for the opposition (a safe haven for Syrian political and military opposition) or forces that took power due to the protests (Egypt and Tunisia) became clear.

In parallel, Turkey has developed cooperation with non-state and local actors; for example, the Muslim Brotherhood (Merley, 2011), the Turkmen minorities of Syria and Iraq, along with political and paramilitary wings, and above all, the Kurdistan Regional Government in Iraq (KRG), the formally autonomous entity de facto independent of Baghdad, where Turkey's economic, political and social influence was of strategic importance. The peak, from Turkey's point of view, the first phase of the Arab Spring, was 2012-13 when Turkey's authority was greatest, the Muslim Brotherhood ruled Egypt, and Assad's power in Syria was kept to a minimum and could continue based solely on Hezbollah and Iranian forces. One very important factor was the almost complete absence of external actors: the US withdrew its forces from Iraq and adopted a restrained attitude towards Syria, Egypt, and Libya. At that time, Iran was pursuing a restrained and defensive policy, and Russia was almost entirely absent.

It seemed to be a viable response to the demands of the Arab spring that Turkey would respond to the regional crisis with the ability to reconcile opposites and tolerate pluralism that Turkey was a magnetic pole and that stability could be based on soft instruments and an open concept of neo-Ottomanism.

Crisis

Meanwhile, since 2013, processes have grown that have revealed either the weaknesses of the Arab Spring or its alternative options regarding Ankara's assumptions (Kuru, 2015). The first group of phenomena were signs of the return of the old order. They were mainly expressed by the coup in Egypt, the ousting from power of the Muslim Brotherhood and the harsh repression policy (2013). The second group was the more active involvement in the conflicts of external states: Iran and Russia on the side of the regime in Syria (the Russian intervention since 2015); Saudi Arabia and its allies in the conflict in Yemen, finally, the US and its allies in the conflict in Syria and Iraq (Operation Inherent Resolve, 2014). The direct involvement of the powers firstly foreshadowed the re-establishment of the status quo ante (the foundations of the international order, including borders), and secondly, it thwarted Turkey's hopes of achieving its objectives by soft methods.

A separate group of phenomena—parallel or opposing to those mentioned above—was a radical attempt by local forces to rebuild the political and social order. Its peak personification was the establishment of the so-called Islamic State (al-Dawlah al-Islāmīyah, often referred to by one of its acronyms ISIS) in 2014—a total rejection of literally all aspects of the political, social and administrative order (Strachota, 2015). Instead, it called for the establishment of a cross-border, universalist and aggressive order based on Islam (a caliphate). Importantly, it was a project based on Islam, but extremely different from (and in competition with) the Turkish model and the Muslim Brotherhood and Iranian/Shia concepts. It is worth noting that it has been a unique step in the history of radical Muslim organisations, a step made in reality—based on real control of a territory and the creation of a comprehensive administration.

Turkey initially ignored the danger posed by ISIS—it was seen rather as a force that would clear the area of conflict from the pro-regime, pro-Iranian and, finally, Kurdish forces (in Syria) and open up space for Ankara's actions (Chudziak, 2016a). The second alternative and revolutionary political project alongside ISIS was the self-proclaimed autonomy and de facto para-state of the Syrian Kurds in 2014 (Autonomous Administration of North and East Syria, abbreviated as Rojava). This project undermined the far-left (de facto Western) assumptions of the nation-state form. For

Turkey, the critical challenge was that it established the PYD (Democratic Union Party) closely linked to the PKK, largely led by Kurds from Turkey and providing a viable alternative to how the AKP views the Turkish state and the solution of the Kurdish issue there (Acun & Keskin, 2017).

The problem had become increasingly important with the war against ISIS, in which the PYD grew into a major ally of the US and the coalition in Syria, gained powerful political and military support and an informal security umbrella. Over time it became an extension of a new version of the Turkish-Kurdish conflict in Turkey. In Ankara, this was read as an imminent threat to the republic's integrity and sovereignty in the country's southeast.

Between democracy and conspiracy

Developments in the neighbourhood have, in surprising ways, found a continuation (directly or indirectly) in the development of the internal situation in Turkey itself. The first group of phenomena (indirectly linked to the Arab Spring) were mass protests in the country caused by the controversy surrounding the development of Gezi Park in Istanbul (May 2013). Quickly, from local slogans, the protesters switched to political slogans (de facto against the AKP), and the protests became violent. They lasted for three months, involving between 3.5 and 7.5 million people, and 11 people were killed. They have shown that objective successes in Turkey's transformation have not kept up with the awakened hopes of society, especially its younger and urban members. Paradoxically, they have shown that Turkey, like the Arab states, is exposed to revolutionary sentiment in parts of society.

For Ankara, these events took on a particular burden with the simultaneous overthrow in Egypt of the Muslim Brotherhood government aligned with AKP, which was seen as the result of an army-inspired and implicitly Western-backed coup. According to similar logic—disturbingly close to the experience of the Arab Spring—there was soon an attempt to delegitimise the central authorities through the actions of the public prosecutor's office (December 2013). This crisis illustrated the scale of tensions within the ruling camp and the strength of the structures of the Gulen Movement, which was thought to be inspiring the actions of the prosecutor's office, and also to have extensive influence throughout the judiciary, police, special services, media, and broad influence in Turkish society (and in the world) associated with an extensive and active network of educational institutions.

On an ideological level, the Gulen Movement combined fervent (but specific) religiosity, modernist aspirations supported by a pro-American and pro-Israeli attitude, extreme hostility to the army (the main processes against the army's political position were led by the Gulen Movement) with suspicions that the organisation had an agency-related (deep state) pedigree and nature. However, a key event for Turkey was primarily the failed military coup on 15 July 2016, which the Gulen Movement—alongside representatives of the army—was accused of organizing, with US acceptance. The attempt to retake power through a military coup is a mechanism that links Turkey with the same political tradition that is common with Arab states and was refreshed during the Arab Spring. In this case, the Change Camp (AKP) won (Chudziak, 2017). The failed coup fundamentally influenced the functioning of the Turkish state. Firstly, the centralisation of power was put firmly on the front foot, widespread repression policy against real and alleged political opponents started, risking even the effective functioning of the state (the army, judiciary and education, where the purge was at its greatest) (Chudziak, 2016b, 2018).

Secondly, there has been a significant reduction in political ambitions, both internally and externally, to consolidate power and social support and strengthen the foothold gained. While the protests around Gezi, the AKP conflicts with the Gulen Movement and the failed coup in 2016 had an indirect and contextual link with the Arab Spring and in parallel with them, there were violent processes in Turkey directly arising from the situation in the Middle East.

Alternatives to neo-Ottomanism?

The first direct impact on Turkey has been Islamic State's expansion since 2014. The massive influx of refugees from Syria and Iraq (in 2014) has been an unprecedented challenge for Turkey. Millions more joined the already numerous group of refugees from the first phase of the war in a few months. Turkey became a major channel for the influx of refugees and migrants into Europe (which has significantly affected the nature of the Turkey-EU relationship), but even more importantly, it has increased the number of refugees in Turkey to nearly 4 million people (Jarosiewicz and Strachota, 2015). Turkey's open and hospitable policy towards them (from facilitating access to the labour market and public services to advanced mass citizenship projects) was a living illustration of the New Turkey, ready to bear the costs of regional responsibility. However, with the influx of refugees, the social situation has been exacerbated (especially in the south of the country) tensions with the local population and led to a consistent increase in nationalist tendencies—this has significantly reduced public support for the government's policy.

To make matters worse, due to the influx of refugees, the security situation has tightened—internal Syrian conflicts have moved to Turkey. This process has coincided with the reverse direction of the movement of people—Turkey has become a de facto channel for the metastasis of volunteers going to Syria for jihad. The organisational and human background and the sense of impunity of ISIS in Turkey, the West's pressure on Ankara to curb ISIS's activities on its territory and, finally, the growing conflicts between ISIS and its Turkish protégés in Syria and Iraq, have all led to a series of terrorist attacks and the Turkish state undertaking pacification activities against ISIS. At a high cost, ISIS's activity was curbed, but the central authorities once again (that is, alongside the conflict with the Gulen Movement) found that they do not have a monopoly on religious rhetoric and, worse still, they are in natural conflict with radical and completely unstable forces.

The second—far more crucial—challenge in domestic politics was the Kurdish issue. Kurds in Turkey make up 15-25 per cent of the country's population. From the perspective of the nationalistic Republic, Kurds were a population at least politically precarious, overly conservative and poorly modernised. Since the 1980s, the conflict between the PKK (a far-left and de facto separatist organisation) and the Turkish state (as well as conservative Kurdish elites) led to the radicalisation of both sides and has been treated as a fundamental threat to the territorial integrity of the state. The end of the Cold War (weakening the PKK's ideological assumptions and cutting off external support), Ankara's fierce pressure on Syria for harbouring the PKK, and finally, the arrest of its leader Abdullah Ocalan dramatically reduced tensions in the late 1990s. In turn, the rise to power of the AKP, the democratisation and blunting of the ethnic state concept in favour of political and cultural identity (Islam, Ottoman, civic), and finally, the broad provincial development agenda have dragged many of the Kurds over to the government's side (Strachota, 2013).

A more self-confident Ankara could afford to introduce elements of cultural autonomy for the Kurds (Kurdish media, language courses, etc.) to develop local parties appealing to the Kurdish electorate, effectively using Kurdish and pro-PKK sentiments. It culminated in the peace process with the PKK's military structures, which included elements of amnesty and the reintegration of fighters. A weakened PKK found itself in a deeply defensive position and accepted the new situation. The Arab Spring and the Syrian civil war have created new opportunities for the PKK. First of all, since 2011, the PYD has taken effective control of Kurdish-populated areas, but without entering into an open conflict with the regime—facilities free of Turkish influence have been established (International Crisis Group, 2017).

The breakthrough, however, was the expansion of ISIS in 2014 and the dramatic siege of Kobane, a Kurdish stronghold, which survives due to the PYD's determination, US support, but also Turkey's benevolent neutrality (including the transit of troops to the town). Kobane revived the Kurds' self-confidence in their own strength and support from the US—a process that would only grow in the years that followed, along with the PYD/SDF's key participation in the eradication of the Islamic State. Kobane's defence has also become a catalyst for the collapse of the normalisation process in Turkey—an ideological alternative to the AKP has emerged in Turkey, as has a political platform (HDP, Peoples' Democratic Party). Both Kurdish society and the party have come under strong pressure, whether reacting to developments in northern Syria as an effect of direct actions of the PKK or by the "normal" radicalisation of young people.

In parallel, the Turkish authorities and much of Turkish society have become much more entrenched in their instinctive negative aim at emerging Kurdish aspirations (the HDP has, in turn, been supported by Turkish left-wing groups). In June 2015, the HDP—unprecedentedly—won the parliamentary elections in southeast Turkey and scuppered the AKP's chances for a one-party government. The result of a snap election

(November 2015), in which the AKP increased its support and the HDP was weakened, gave back full power to the AKP. However, the new elections have already taken place in an atmosphere of renewed conflict. Kurdish radicals (most likely linked to the PKK as a whole or one of its factions, supported from Rojava) started urban guerrilla warfare in southern Turkey (September 2015, Cizre and other towns), and the HDP has also been forced to radicalise, leading to attempts to take control of administration structures in the region. The result was more than half a year of brutal pacification in the south-eastern provinces (International Crisis Group, 2016), the arrest of the HDP leaders and the radicalisation of policies towards Kurdish-controlled Syrian provinces, seen as a major source of problems.

The period of the Turkish experiment with openness to the Kurds, which was de facto a prerequisite for blunting the blade of republican nationalism and pursuing a universalist and post-nationalist project beyond Turkey's borders, has now been closed. Soon, as a side effect of this situation, relations between Turkey and the KRG cooled. Although cooperation between the KRG and Turkey have worked perfectly (for both sides) over the past decade, Turkey's renewed fear of the power of Kurdish nationalism has revived, as well as frustration on the relative weakness of the KRG itself (its authorities were unable to dismantle the PKK structures on its territory). These factors, together with international pressure, were the reason that Turkey was critical of the KRG's independence referendum proposal, did not recognise its results, and did not react when Tehran-backed Iraq buried any dreams of independence by occupying disputed Kirkuk and taking control of the entire (including the Turkish) KRG border (2017).

The Real New Turkey

Radical changes in the international dimension since about 2013 have been a major catalyst for Turkish policy. This factor thwarted hopes of gradual control of Syria by opposition forces, including Turkish protégés. This process gained particular momentum with the launch of a large-scale Russian operation in Syria (2015), which gradually allowed the regime to regain control of most of the country. In its current paradigm, Turkey was forced to observe the destruction of its Turkmen protégés by Russian intervention. Nevertheless, it did attempt to unilaterally halt Russian expansion by the downing of a Russian aircraft violating Turkish airspace (2015) (Rodkiewicz, 2015). This put Ankara on the brink of an open conflict with Russia, economic sanctions and exposed a series of terrorist attacks (it could be argued that the latter was not coincidental).

The situation for Ankara has become so dramatic that its relations with the West have been strained (including criticism for its authoritarian course and pacification of the Kurds), the difficult-to-mobilise resources allocated to the fight against ISIS (which Turkey has been accused of supporting), and the Kurds of the SDF (Turkey's arch-enemies) have become the main US allies. Russia and Iran have now become desirable partners for Turkey. Shortly thereafter, Turkish-American relations were further exacerbated with the coup—Washington refused to release Fethullah Gulen and sharply criticised the scale of the purges, especially in the army. Turkey faced a host of internal challenges: the problem with ISIS, the Kurdish issue, and above all, the coup, a feeling of being isolated by its allies, the prospect of a unilateral confrontation with Russia.

These accumulated in 2016 into a series of radical changes in Turkish policy: the resignation of Ahmet Davutoglu (prime minister, architect of Turkey's foreign policy), a de-escalation with Russia, increased assertiveness towards Western countries and, finally, a profound correction in policy towards the Middle East. Turkey moved away from a soft power policy, focused on local actors and how to use them as a tool of its politics, and moved onto hard realpolitik and hard power policy, both internally and externally.

As a result, Turkey dramatically reduced the role of non-state actors in its foreign policy. The role of opposition groups (militias, parties, local forces) has declined—they are still an important (but no longer the most important) instrument (and not a partner) in Ankara's politics. Instead of indirect action, Turkey has begun regular military operations in strategically important areas. Operations against Syrian Kurds became the norm; they include Operation Euphrates Shield (2016) (Yeşiltaş, Seren and Özçelik, 2017), Operation Olive Branch (2018) (Chudziak and Marszewski, 2018), Operation Spring Shield (2019); regular military operations in Iraqi Kurdistan against the PKK; and finally anti-regime operations in Idlib (Operation Spring Shield, 2020) (Strachota and Marszewski,

2020). A specific case has been Turkey's involvement in Libya—military intervention on the basis of an agreement with the official authorities (in practice irregular forces remaining in the deep defensive), in 2020. Another one was the transfer of Turkish troops to Qatar in the face of the boycott by Saudi Arabia and its allies (2017) (Lang and Strachota, 2017).

In parallel, relations with external forces (countries) involved in conflicts important to Turkey have increased significantly. Turkey has developed strong channels of political dialogue with competitors to regulate tensions and conflicts in the war zone. This is particularly clear in Russia's case (to a lesser extent Iran) and the foundation of the so-called Astana Process (2017) on the conflict in Syria, and a similar mechanism concerning Libya (2020) (Chudziak, 2020). Consultations with the US before anti-Kurdish operations in Syria (2019) played a similar role. It is characteristic that in practice, their aim has been to mitigate friction, not avoid it or to solve problems permanently. The change in approach to local problems is an extension of the broader revision of Turkish policy.

As a result of the experience of Turkey's Middle East policy, Ankara prioritises the national interest by opening up to strategic cooperation with rivals. This includes Russia, with whom it developed military cooperation (purchase of S-400 missile systems) and energy cooperation (nuclear and natural gas). But, on the other hand, it is ready for confrontational action against allies (worsening conflicts with Greece and Cyprus), tensions with France, the crisis in relations with the US, including on the S-400 and the F-35 aircraft programme (Strachota and Wilk, 2019), tensions with Israel and Saudi Arabia, tensions in relations with the EU.

Internally, the emphasis of the ruling party on consolidating power and society is crucial. On the one hand, the consolidation of power has taken place at the legal level (constitutional amendment in 2017; strengthening the power of the president) and, on the other hand, by pacifying the opposition (the purge after the failed coup and the repression of the HDP) and control of the media. This is undoubtedly a move towards a centralised and authoritarian model of the state. It was also done by expanding the ruling camp to include the nationalist MHP (Nationalist Movement Party, in the coalition from 2017), that is, a strong appeal to ethnocentric Turkish nationalism as a pillar of the republic. The symbolic fulfilment of Turkey's redefining process is expected for

2023—the centenary of the republic, an election year, and the expected entry into force of the new constitution.

The Arab Spring in the light of the Turkish experience

From Ankara's perspective, the Arab Spring confirms the scale and universality of the crisis felt throughout the region, including Turkey. This crisis concerns the international order (mechanisms for stabilizing the region, sustainability of borders, etc.), the internal order (political system and functioning of basic state institutions), the social order (aspirations of different social groups, new dynamics caused by demographics, etc.), and fundamental identity challenges. In some cases, there was a restoration of the old order, but without guarantees of the durability of solutions. In other cases, there has been a profound and irreversible erosion of the system (for example, Syria and Yemen).

The Arab Spring has shown the strength of alternative and revolutionary projects of the new order—one example of this is the rise of Islamic State or Kurdish para-states. It must be assumed that the current state of affairs does not exhaust the potential contained in them; neither the revival of universalist projects (based on Islam) nor of and revisionist national movements can be ruled out. In the case of Syria and Iraq, these projects have been blocked as a result of external circumstances and interventions, but without guaranteeing the sustainability of the results.

The crisis of the international system, as seen in the example of the Arab Spring, has brought irreversible changes in the functioning of the region. The West (the US and the EU) has ceased to be a guarantor and enforcer of stability and directions of development; nor is it the UN system. Western interventions (also Russia's) are target-oriented (for example, the eradication of the Islamic State) and do not aspire to (re)build order (as in Iraq after 2003). On the other hand, the interventions of local players (and Russia) are able to influence the local situation, guarantee the elementary sustainability of the state and its borders (Syria and Iraq), regulate relations with rivals (proxy war), but provide no opportunity of lasting stability or the basis of sustainable development. Moreover, it seems that these countries do not have the political will to set themselves such a goal. This means the perpetuation of peripheral areas exposed to chaos (with analogies to 1990s Afghanistan, with all the consequences).

The Arab Spring has strengthened the importance of an unpredictable social factor. The frustration and crisis of state structures reinforce the risk of social protests with an unpredictable ideological overtone. Concerning areas affected by deep crisis and war, this is compounded by various factors. These include the breakdown of state structures, for example, the erosion of the education system or public order. Another one is the crisis of traditional family and tribal structures. Demographic pressure also contributes to challenges; for example, the over-representation of children and young people, that is, a 'threat' to the transmission of traditional values. An additional factor is increasing (forced) social mobility, especially mass refugee migration, which in Syria irreversibly affected half of its pre-war population.

Turkey in the light of the Arab Spring

The Arab Spring has become a catalyst for Turkey putting down fresh roots in the Middle East. The region provided the main impulses that shaped the process of internal change and the revision of Turkey's foreign policy initiated by the AKP in 2002. Turkey is not a full member of the region but has reinvented itself in response to the challenges that have flowed from the Middle East. This is a hard process for Turkey and is still unfinished but irreversible.

Internally, Turkey was forced to give up ambitious projects to reduce Kemalism and authoritarian practices (in favour of liberal democracy), ethnocentrism (in favour of neo-Ottoman identity with a strong Islamic component), to diversify its economy with Middle Eastern markets and capital (right now the region generates costs, not profits), and other matters. Today Turkey is a country with a renewed mandate, with relatively effective institutions (the "reintegration" of the army into the state system is crucial), with a dynamic society and shuffled and renewed elites (for example, in the case of the army, this was directly as a result of purges and operations in Syria). Of course, the Republic faces several challenges. Its stability and success are not guaranteed, but this is a different Turkey than in 2002 and different from the one in plans related to the EU accession negotiations started in 2005.

Externally, the Arab Spring was the catalyst, first for enormous idealism and optimism in politics, then for near-catastrophe and isolation. Turkey has experienced a deep crisis of confidence with its Western allies—but this seems reversible, as long as neither side has an alternative for the current strategic relations. Similarly, Turkey has ridden a rollercoaster in its relations with Russia, avoiding irreparable re-evaluations while opening up intense proactive and pragmatic relations. Successes—and the no less numerous failures—in relations with Middle Eastern countries—both in soft power politics and in hard military action have created Turkey's new regional policy. Contrary to the Kemalist tradition, it is ambitious and proactive, while on the other hand being self-limiting, cautious, defensive and distrustful.

For ten hard years of the Arab Spring, Turkey has passed the elusive shadow line, losing its idealism, losing the charm and part of the hope it has offered around. Instead, today's Turkey is a country mature, experienced by hard realities, ready for a long, inevitable and brutal struggle for the fruits of the Arab Spring.

References

Acun, Can and Keskin, Bünyamin (2017), *The PKK's Branch in Northern Syria PYD-YPG*, SETA, Istanbul. April 14, https://www.setav.org/en/the-pkks-branch-in-northern-syria-pyd-ypg/

Ananicz, Szymon (2015), "Alone in Virtue: The "New Turkish" Ideology in Turkey's Foreign Policy," *OSW Point of View*, No. 49, April, Centre for Eastern Studies (OSW), Warsaw, https://www.osw.waw.pl/sites/default/files/pw_49_ang_alone-in-virtue_net.pdf

Chudziak, Mateusz (2016), "My Enemy's Enemy—Turkey's Stance on Islamic State," *OSW Commentary* No. 198. February 24, Centre for Eastern Studies (OSW), Warsaw, https://www.osw.waw.pl/sites/default/files/commentary_198.pdf

Chudziak, Mateusz (2016), "From Purges to a 'New Turkey'—the Final Stage of the State's Reconstruction," *OSW Commentary*, No. 228. December 12, Centre for Eastern Studies (OSW), Warsaw, https://www.osw.waw.pl/sites/default/files/commentary_228.pdf

Chudziak, Mateusz (2017), "The Coup as a Founding Myth: The Ideological Pillars of the New Turkey," *OSW Point of View*, No. 66, October, Centre for Eastern Studies (OSW), Warsaw, https://www.osw.waw.pl/sites/default/files/pw_66_the_coup_as_myth_net_0.pdf

Chudziak, Mateusz (2018), "Cadres Decide Everything—Turkey's Reform of its Military," *OSW Commentary*, No. 274. December 12, Centre for Eastern Studies (OSW), Warsaw, https://www.osw.waw.pl/sites/default/files/commentary_274.pdf

Marszewski, Mariusz and Chudziak, Mateusz (2018), "The Turkish Military Operation in Afrin, Northern Syria," *OSW Analyses,* January 24, https://www.osw.waw.pl/en/publikacje/analyses/2018-01-24/turkish-military-operation-afrin-northern-syria

Chudziak, Mateusz (2020), "Turkey's Military Mission in Libya," *OSW Analyses,* January 8, https://www.osw.waw.pl/en/publikacje/analyses/2020-01-08/turkeys-military-mission-libya

International Crisis Group (2016), "The Human Cost of the PKK Conflict in Turkey: The Case of Sur," *Crisis Group Europe Briefing* No. 80, March 17, https://d2071andvip0wj.cloudfront.net/b80-the-human-cost-of-the-pkk-conflict-in-turkey-the-case-of-sur.pdf

International Crisis Group (2017), "The PKK's Fateful Choice in Northern Syria," *Crisis Group Middle East Report* No. 176, May 4, https://d2071andvip0wj.cloudfront.net/176-the-pkks-fateful-choice-in-northern-syria.pdf

Jarosiewicz, Aleksandra and Strachota, Krzysztof (2015), "Turkey and the Syrian Refugee Problem," *OSW Commentary* No. 186. September 30, Centre for Eastern Studies (OSW), Warsaw, https://www.osw.waw.pl/sites/default/files/commentary_186.pdf

Kuru, Ahmet T. (2015), "Turkey's Failed Policy toward the Arab Spring: Three Levels of Analysis," *Mediterranean Quarterly,* vol. 26, no. 3, pp 94-116.

Lang, Józef and Strachota, Krzysztof (2017), "Turkey on the Qatar Crisis," *OSW Analyses,* June 21, https://www.osw.waw.pl/en/publikacje/analyses/2017-06-21/turkey-qatar-crisis

Matusiak, Marek (2015), "The Great Leap: Turkey under Erdogan," *OSW Point of View,* No. 51, May, Centre for Eastern Studies (OSW), Warsaw, https://www.osw.waw.pl/sites/default/files/pw_51_ang_great_leap_net.pdf

Merley, Steven G. (2011), *Turkey, the Global Muslim Brotherhood, and the Gaza Flotilla,* Jerusalem Center for Public Affairs, Israel, https://jcpa.org/text/Turkey_Muslim_Brotherhood.pdf

Reynolds, Michael A. (2012), "Echoes of Empire: Turkey's Crisis of Kemalism and the Search for an Alternative Foreign Policy," *Analysis Paper* No. 26, June. The Saban Center for Middle East Policy at Brookings, Washington, D.C., https://www.brookings.edu/wp-content/uploads/2016/06/25-turkey-reynolds.pdf

Rodkiewicz, Witold (2015), "Russian-Turkish Confrontation over Syria," *OSW Analyses,* December 12, https://www.osw.waw.pl/en/publikacje/analyses/2015-12-02/russian-turkish-confrontation-over-syria

Strachota, Krzysztof (2013), "Turkey and the Kurdish Problem," *OSW Point of View* No. 30, February, Centre for Eastern Studies (OSW), Warsaw, https://www.osw.waw.pl/sites/default/files/pw_30_en.pdf

Strachota, Krzysztof (2015), "The Middle East in the Shadow of Islamic State," *OSW Point of View* No. 52, July, Centre for Eastern Studies (OSW), Warsaw, https://www.osw.waw.pl/sites/default/files/pw_52_middle-east-in-shadow_net.pdf

Strachota, Krzysztof and Marszewski, Mariusz (2020), "Turkey on the Brink of War with Syria," *OSW Analyses*, February 13, https://www.osw.waw.pl/en/publikacje/analyses/2020-02-13/turkey-brink-war-syria

Strachota, Krzysztof and Wilk, Andrzej (2019), "The S-400 for Turkey: The Crisis in Turkish-American Relations Escalates," *OSW Commentary* No. 305, June 12, Centre for Eastern Studies (OSW), Warsaw, https://www.osw.waw.pl/sites/default/files/commentary_305.pdf

Yeşiltaş, Murat, Seren, Merve and Özçelik, Necdet (2017), "Operation Euphrates Shield: Implementation and Lessons Learned," SETA, Istanbul, November 14, https://setav.org/en/assets/uploads/2017/11/R97_Euphrates.pdf

13. Narratives on Arab World in Turkish Academic Discourse: Publications of State-Centric Institutions

Sinem Cengiz

Introduction

Turks and Arabs lived together under the rule of the Ottoman Empire for nearly four centuries. As a result of the centuries of coexistence, they developed "certain images and perceptions, misconceptions, and stereotypes about each other" (Mughisuddin, 1993, p. 151). Historical experiences played a significant role in forming the images about the self, and the other and these images were often reinforced by literature, school textbooks, media, cultural tools, and the rhetoric of the politicians. Studies on Turkish-Arab relations require examining the images formed towards the Arabs by Turks or vice versa. Although Arabs occupy a special place in the Turkish national imagination, a few studies address the subject. Most of the studies conducted are limited to the analysis of school textbooks and media outlets in which Arabs were framed around religion, prejudices, and regional backwardness. Other spaces, such as academia, where these framings are reflected have remained neglected.

Since the establishment of the Republic in 1923, Turkey's relations with the Arab world were neither hostile nor particularly warm but was cautiously distanced mainly due to the socio-political circumstances of the time and historical legacy. Thus, it is significant to explore Turkish framing of the Arab world in the past to reveal the dynamics that may still be at work in shaping the Arab image today. Through examining selected publications of the three state-centric institutions in Turkey, this chapter sheds light on the images used by the scholars in their depictions of Arabs and the Arab world, whether historically-rooted or reinforced by certain events throughout time, geostrategic conditions have shaped these images during the late 1980s and 1990s, two decades of serious tumult in Turkish-Arab relations (Dalacoura, 1990; Bölükbaşı, 1991; Olson, 1995; Sayari, 1997; Kirişçi, 1997; Naaz, 1999). These institutions, which enjoy the support of the state to some degree, are Foundation for Studies on Turkish-Arab Relations (TAIV), Foreign Policy Institute (FPI), and Center for Strategic Research (SAM) of the Turkish Ministry of Foreign Affairs.

The FPI, a think-tank founded in 1974 and located in Ankara, publishes works on Turkish foreign policy and international affairs. It is the oldest surviving think-tank in Turkey. It was established as a private organisation but enjoys significant support and engagement with the Ministry of Foreign Affairs. For example, the ministry supports the events organised by the think-tank and provides funding as well, and some of the diplomats who had served at the ministry are part of the editorial board of the journal. In addition, the institute publishes a biannual journal in English named *Foreign Policy.* The TAIV was established in 1984 by the Ministry of Foreign Affairs, and its chairman was former Foreign Minister Vahit Melih Halefoğlu. However, since the tenure of Foreign Minister Ahmet Davutoğlu in 2009, the institution is no longer affiliated with the ministry and serves as an independent organisation. In addition, it had an annual English language journal called *Studies on Turkish-Arab Relations,* published annually between 1985 and 1991. The SAM is a research centre at the Ministry of Foreign Affairs of Turkey established in 1995. It was founded to provide academic and scholarly studies on several issues to Turkish decision-makers. In addition, it has a quarterly English journal named *Perceptions* that includes articles by international and Turkish scholars. While *Perceptions* is accessible via the internet, *Studies on Turkish-Arab Relations* and *Foreign Policy* were accessed through Marmara University's and FPI's libraries, respectively.

The chapter explores three main research questions: (a) What is the historical context that shapes Turkish representation of Arabs and the Arab world?; (b) From a discourse analysis perspective, how are Arabs and issues related to the Arab world have been represented and under what socio-political circumstances those narratives were used in these journals during the late 1980s and 1990s?; and (c) What are the similar narratives used in Turkish framing of the region during the Arab Spring uprisings?

The chapter follows the discourse analysis methodology drawing upon the concepts of narratives, images, and framing as understood in social sciences. It provides a brief examination of the Arab image in Turkey from a historical perspective before discussing the findings divided into three thematic sections on historical legacy and Ottomanism, Kemalism and secularism, and finally, the question of security, including water security. This study on narratives on the Arabs and Arab world does not claim to be representative of Turkish academic discourse on Arabs and the Arab world rather reflects on certain prevalent stereotypical attitudes towards Arabs.

The study's findings reveal that the narratives on Arabs and the Arab world have generally emphasised politico-historical memory and a security perspective. In addition, the narratives frame the Arab world as inferior and belonging to a different civilisation, while underlining a self-confident and secular Turkish national identity. Though not new in terms of what the narratives are, the novelty is that the issues that occurred during the period under study underline additional aspects related to security; such as water security, the Kurdistan Workers' Party (PKK), and the Cyprus question.

Discourse Analysis

Discourse analysis is a textual analysis method that is much-favoured among constructivists and critical international relations (IR) scholars interested in the impact of identity, meaning, and discourse on world politics (Aydın-Düzgit & Rumelili, 2019, p.285). However, neither discourse nor discourse analysis has a universally acknowledged definition. In general terms, discourse analysis is defined as a qualitative methodology wherein one examines the meanings of texts in relation to the systems of power that shape and form them. It is a method of study that could be applied to several disciplines, including area studies, to understand the role of discourse in identity-building. It can be used as a framework of analysis of national identity (Phillips & Jørgensen, 2002, p. 2). It helps discover the ideological and power-related characteristics of discourse to examine how it relates to the socio-political environment.

Discourse analysis enables the expression of sets of values and mindsets. It not only serves as a useful method in analysing the power relations in a given circumstance and formulating perspectives, but it also makes it possible to examine how identities are represented by state or statist discourses. David Campbell (1992) underlines those discourses constitute the state and its identity through constructing 'others' and representing these others as antithetical, different and threatening to the 'self.' According to Edward Said (1995, p.332), the construction of identity in every age and society involves establishing 'us' and 'others.' The role of discourse as a tool to construct 'us' and the 'other' has been recognised by the discourse analysts such as Ruth Wodak and Michael Meyer (2001) in their theoretical writings.

Discourse does not take place in a vacuum and is rooted in a specific context and cannot be examined without considering the context. In the case of national identity, understanding the historical contexts is necessary because the history of each nation is marked by the presence of 'others.' According to Anna Triandafyllidou (1998), "national identity becomes meaningful only through the contrast with others" (p.593). Therefore, it is significant to explore the Turkish imagination of Arab to reveal the dynamics that shape the discourse towards Arabs. Since its establishment in 1923, the state pursued a policy to reinforce the modern and secular Turkish identity. This policy was reflected in media and education, imaging Arabs as 'others.'

Arab Image in Turkey: Historical Context

Following the First World War (WWI), the collapse of the Ottoman Empire ended the centuries of Turkish rule over Arabs. Since the establishment of the Republic, Turkey's general perception towards the Arab world was mostly shaped within the context of the Arabs' stance during WWI. One of the legacies of WWI was the strong antipathy towards the East in general and the Arabs in particular. The Arab revolts against Ottoman rule during WWI, causing the death of thousands of Ottoman soldiers, played a significant role in creating a negative image of the Arabs. According to Manfred Beller (2007), stereotypes or images are more pernicious than wars because wars end and are forgotten, but stereotypes or images constructed over time are remembered. The images of the 'others' have a significant impact on the passing down of the perceptions to future generations, and in times of political tensions, those images come to the surface, as happened with the Turkish reference to Arabs in the 1980s and 1990s. For many years, Turkey's perception towards the Arab world was constructed by the thought that "Arabs stabbed the Turks in the back" during WWI by aligning with the British forces and that this act made them traitors (Küçükcan, 2010, p.11). The legacy of 'betrayal' by Arabs against the Ottomans during the war left a bitter taste in Turkish consciousness. Soner Çağaptay (2020) notes that the best-known cultural icon of Turks commemorating the WWI is "Yemen Türküsü" (*Ballad of Yemen*), which tells the story of an Anatolian soldier who perished in Yemen—fighting Arabs (p. 170).

Based on the proposal of Benedict Anderson (2006) that the nations are "imagined communities," it is significant to examine the images of the members of the nation and the images of the 'other'. Images can be defined as "a subject's cognitive construction or mental representation of another actor [or oneself) in the political world" (Herrmann & Fischerkeller, 1995, p.415). Arabs considered Turks as those abandoning Islam for secularisation. Turks, on the other hand, considered the Arabs as "undisciplined and unreliable," recalling "their poor military performance in service with the Ottoman army" and "looked down upon the backwardness of the Arabs" (Vali, 2019, pp.273-274). The dominant view among Turks was "untrustworthy Arab and the uncivilised, backward Arab states governed by Shariat law" (Aykan, 1993, p. 92).

This imagination considerably impacted Turkey's foreign policy towards the Middle East (Bengio & Özcan, 2001; Martin, 2004; Bein, 2017). Despite having common historical, cultural and religious links, Turkey, in the republican era, preferred to distance itself from the region, particularly from the Arab world. In the republican era, Turkish elites "decided to cut the country's traditional ties with the Arab world, and [thereafter] republican Turkey distanced itself from Middle Eastern politics" (Karaosmanoğlu, 2000, p. 208).

In Turkey, Turkish-Arab relations were defined within negative historical memories reflecting in school textbooks, newspapers, literature and popular culture. One of the well-known anti-Arab expressions is a proverb, '*Ne Arab'ın Yüzü, Ne Şam'ın Şekeri*' (Neither face of Arab, nor candy of Damascus) serves as a good example to understand the anger against Arabs. Another negative expression widely circulated in contemporary Turkish popular culture is the metaphor '*Arap Saçı*' (like Arab's hair) which means a messy situation from which there is no exit. These imageries are rooted in the historical prejudices and traumatic experiences of the past, as Bülent Aras and Hasan Köni (2002) put it, "the Turkish establishment considered itself as the main successor state [of Ottoman Empire] with negative memories of Arabs; in contrast, the Arab states interpreted the demise of the Ottoman Empire as their emancipation from exploitation by an imperial power" (p. 50).

Turkish historiography too has been susceptible to conflicting depictions of Arab and Islam perpetuating the negative imagery (İhsanoğlu & Al-Din, 1991; Kayalı, 1997, Akturk, 2010, p. 635). History textbooks, elite discourse, films and the press have contributed to advancing the prejudices and stereotypes towards the Arabs (Küçükcan, 2010; Karpat, 1987, p. 17; Bozdaglioglu, 2003, pp. 112-115). Dietrich Jung (2005) refers to entrenched Turkish and Arabs stereotypes as 'historical burden' that have been reinforced in the course of the political history of the twentieth century (p. 1).

Narratives on Arabs: Journals of TAIV, FPI, SAM

Ofra Bengio and Gencer Özcan (2001) outline four major eras in Turkish-Arab relations: (1) 1923-45 (the years of alienation); (2) 1945-65 (the years estrangement and clash); (3) 1965-75 (the years of minor improvement); and (4) 1975-85 (the years of dramatic change for better relations) (p. 54). However, the period after 1985 and until the end of the 1990s has seen a serious deterioration of relations due to several issues.

Turkey underwent important changes in its economy and politics during the 1980s and 1990s (Müftüler, 1995, p. 86). During this period, the developments, such as economic liberalisation, paved the way for important transformations in Turkish foreign policy. In the 1980s, Prime Minister and President Turgut Özal played a crucial role in Turkey's opening to the Middle East, enhancing the country's relations with the Arab world and attracting Arab business interest (Rubin & Kirişçi 2001, p. 99). With the economic liberalisation policies, Turkey's economic relations with the Middle Eastern countries developed significantly (Yıldırım, Sezgin & Öcal, 2006, p. 198).

As Turkey was undergoing significant changes in its political and economic sphere, the world was also experiencing unprecedented events. With the end of the Cold War, Turkish academia's attention and interest focused on post-Cold War geopolitics and security impacting the global order. From the mid-1980s, with Turkey's applying for EU membership, more articles were written on Turkish-EU relations. During that time, Turkey was looking at the Arab world from a security-oriented perspective as a supplement to the West-oriented foreign policy due to the influence of military institutions on politics and the threats emanating from neighbouring Arab states.

As identified earlier, in the content analysis of the publications of TAIV, FPI and SAM during the 1980s and 1990s, three themes emerged: (1) historical legacy and Ottomanism; (2) Kemalism and secularism; and (3) security, both water security and those emanating from the PKK. The analysis of the writings of academics presents two interrelated points. First, Kemalism was not only representative of the state ideology but also as a path towards Turkey's western identity and as a way for the reproduction of discourse on Turkey's western identity. Second, rather than referring to the common history between Turks and Arabs, the Ottoman legacy was used as a reference to show that the Ottoman Empire is the centre and the Arab world is the related periphery to the former.

Historical legacy and Ottomanism

In Turkey, studies on the Arab world focused on politico-historical dimensions, particularly on Ottoman legacy and of Turkey's relations with the Arab countries. In the late 1980s, in journals of both FJI and TAIV, there is a considerable reference to the Ottoman legacy. However, the perception of Ottoman legacy differs widely in Turkey and the Arab world. Arabs were one of the most significant nations that lived within Ottoman rule, and their interaction with Turks throughout that period is crucial to understand the perceptions of both Arabs and Turks towards each other.

In "Arab and Turkish Public Opinion Attitudes Towards Questions of the Two Nations" published in *Foreign Policy*'s 1985 edition, Ömer

Kürkçüoğlu (1985) argues that "despite the fact that both nations have a lot in common, it is quite natural that they should have stereotypes against each other" (pp. 22-43). He makes a revision to what other Turkish scholars wrote about Turkish-Arab relations and analyses the image construction in both nations challenging the stereotypes developed by both sides. For example, he criticises the stereotype that "Arabs cannot govern themselves," arguing that "Arabs did establish their empires in the past and governed not only themselves but other nations, too. In today's world, too, most Arabs have won their independence ... and they are their own masters, no matter what difficulties they are faced with" (p. 24).

Kürkçüoğlu further adds that Arabs misinterpreted Turkey's modernisation as the preference of the West over the Arab world, arguing: "Ataturk believed that Turkey had to modernise itself as quickly as possible to make up for the lost time of centuries. After all, Turkey's history and geography, too, necessitated a more Europeanised (westernised) outlook" (p. 31). Also, indicating a stance that is both constructed by ideologies, and in turn, constructed the identities, he argues that the "Arab Revolt of 1916 indirectly contributed to the developments that led up to the establishment of the Turkish national identity and the modern state itself" (p. 27). Here, the author interprets a historical event as a reason for Turkish identity building; thus, the role of discourse in the reconstruction of Turkish identity is important in this example.

In the 1986 annual issue of *Studies on Turkish-Arab Relations*, another scholar Ali Karaosmanoğlu (1986), criticises Arabs for misunderstanding Turkeys' adoption of a secular state and supports Turkey's distanced policy towards the Middle East, adding that "... the comprehensive Middle Eastern subsystem in which everything is related to everything else and boundaries dividing local, national, regional and international are blurred. This, in turn, has strengthened Turkish people's conviction that the present circumspect policies of Turkey are the most appropriate in the Middle East context" (p. 163). The scholar underlines the necessity of maintaining a 'secular state' in the face of the situation of Arabs. From the author's point of view, it is clear that reference to 'secularism and Kemalism' is highly used to perpetuate the status quo of the state discourse.

In the 1987 annual issue of *Studies on Turkish-Arab Relations,* Metin Heper criticises Arab misperception of Turkey's Islam since the establishment of the Republic. Adopting a 'centre-periphery' narrative, Heper (1987) states that "approach towards Islam in Turkey rests upon a particular configuration of centre-periphery relationship—a phenomenon which has a close resemblance to that in Europe and a few other places but which has been alien to the rest of the Middle East" (p. 159). The Kemalist reforms, argues Heper, laid the foundation for the development of a viable and stable political system in Turkey in contrast to the Middle East (p. 160). In *Foreign Policy*'s 1976 annual issue, Selçuk Korkud (1976) refers to the misinterpretation of Turkey's secularism, saying, "secularism never meant denial of the values and the ties acquired through centuries by belonging to the same religion" (p. 20).

While referring to Turkey's principles in approaching the Middle East, Karaosmanoğlu (1983), in *Foreign Policy*'s 1983 annual issue, identifies five points related to Turkish and Arab understanding of secularism and nationalism. He underlines that "in contrast with the Arab nationalism, the Turkish nationalism has no religious component. It is a secular nationalism. The Turkish state system has a secular character" (p. 9). Similarly, in the 1991 annual issue of *Studies on Turkish-Arab Relations*, Heper (1991) asks whether democracy could be a panacea for the lingering instability in the Middle East. He argues that democracy cannot bring stability when the Middle Eastern rulers remain as traditional elites rather than real bureaucrats, comparing the success of non-Arab provinces of the Ottoman Empire to the Arab ones.

Heper (1991) further underlines that

> Ottoman (Turkish) polity too had a 'state tradition.' In fact, as compared to its brethren in western Europe, the state in the Ottoman polity had greater autonomy from civil society. This particular pattern of the ottoman political system, however, was not institutionalised in the Arab provinces of the empire. While in the non-Arab provinces of the empire (the Balkans and Anatolia), one came across 'bureaucratic politics', the Arab provinces were characterised by the 'politics of notables'. (pp. 107-108)

Some scholars based the reconciliation of Turks and Arabs after alienation from common heritage and common destiny shared in the Ottoman era.

For example, Caesar A. Farah (1986) argues that Istanbul has been the premier Islamic city and once the seat of the empire shared by Arabs and Turks for five hundred years and uses themes such as 'Ottoman umbrella' to emphasise that the Turkish-Arab relations are characterised with the narrative of 'Ottoman legacy' (p. 70). This places Ottoman at the centre and the Arab as the related periphery. Touching upon the period after the end of the Ottoman rule, Farah states that both sides got alienated to their inherited values that had bound them, adding "the triumph of Europe and her secular ideology was complete: Turks opted for European values, Arabs fell victims to them, and to a variety of political domination and implantations in their midst" (p. 62). From the author's writing, one traces the meaning that political practices of states, in return, reproduce identities, creating the 'us' and the 'others' with the political process of exclusion and inclusion.

In the same journal's 1986 edition, Karaosmanoğlu (1986) argues that Turkish people wish to improve their fraternal bonds with Arabs but are wary of prejudicing the internal and external security posture of Turkey given its geostrategic area. He further states, "what we need in Turkey and the Arab world is to make more intellectual effort to find out ways how to conceptualise Turkey's role in the region without overlooking its vital security concerns" (p. 163). In the late 1980s, with the deterioration of relations with its neighbours, namely Iraq and Syria, Turkish scholars emphasised the narratives of 'security', 'threat', and 'national interests' in their writings.

In the 1987 annual issue of *Studies on Turkish-Arab Relations*, Kemal Karpat (1987) argues that it is the Turkish and Arab school textbooks that shape images of the future generations, adding that a close and critical look at the textbooks is required to correct the faulty images (pp. 18-19). According to him,

> Many Turks would dismiss the Arabs as being unreliable or without sustained determination and the like, even though many of them did not encounter or talk to an Arab any time in their life. Yet, despite the obvious fallacies about each other's defects and qualities, Turks and Arabs continue to view each other in the light of their acquired images (Ibid., p. 18).

About the roots of the problematic relations between Turkey and some of its Arab neighbours, Karpat emphasises that a positive image about a given nationality is likely to produce positive reactions towards an individual of that nationality, while, in turn, a prior negative image can produce a chain of undesirable results.

In the 1993 annual issue of the *Foreign Policy*, a chapter "New Turkish-Arab Relations" has been devoted to analysing the historical misconceptions by focusing on the political disputes between Turks and Arabs and how the historical burden had caused an impact of exogenous influences on Turks and Arabs. It criticises the role of the foreign powers in creating misconceptions of the two nations towards each other, mainly focusing on the colonial era in the Arab world. It states:

> Turks and Arabs, have developed certain images and perceptions, misconceptions, and stereotypes about each other. Through time and events, misconceptions, either expressed in the literature or by rumours, anchored in the minds of the people on both sides... Often both sides perceived themselves at juxtaposition with each other, because of these persistent images. Turkish and Arab decision-makers are as affected as are the masses by the mutually created negative images about each other. (Foreign Policy Institute Journal, 1993, p. 63)

The journal maintains that many scholars and writers on Turkish-Arab relations have tended to concentrate on their interactions during the past hundred years or so while de-emphasizing their earlier relationships. "Although there is nothing inherently wrong with selecting a limited time-frame for analysis, in the case of Turkish-Arab relations, this approach often has produced a badly distorted picture that accentuates only the negative aspects of their relationship" (ibid., p. 65). The chapter identifies the main issues between Turkey and the Arab world as secularism, the Kurdish issue of the 1990s and the historical legacy based on nationalist revolts.

Kemalism and Secularism

Both history and geography play important roles in creating perceptions and images about one's own nation and that of others. Through narratives, a country's relations with others and an identity discourse are produced (Banchoff, 1999, p. 270). The narrative defines "who we are" and "who and what we stand for" by way of articulating "where we have been" (ibid.). Kemalism as a narrative was widely employed, and Turkey was defined as part of Europe; therefore, constructing the image of Arab as 'other', which opened the door for discussion of the 'otherness' of Arabs. Turkish scholars tend to refer to the Turkish ruling elite's approach as a policy to keep the legacy of the Mustafa Kemal Atatürk (Atatürk means Father of the Turks) and identify the country more with the West than the Middle East and the Islamic world (Sayarı, 1997, p. 51). As to how Kemalism was used as a reference in Turkish academia and how academic discourse was structured by this narrative, this chapter does not examine Kemalism as a regime type; but focuses on the studies that have used Kemalism as a set of ideas.

The role of Kemalism and its importance in foreign policymaking are widely studied. For some scholars, Kemalism, or in other words Ataturkism, is the founding ideology of Turkey (Zurcher, 1993, p. 181) and serves as the foundation of the modern Turkish state. It is defined as an ideology designed by reforms to separate the new Turkish state from its Ottoman past and adopt a western way of living, including embracing secularism as a principle (Cleveland & Bunton, 2013, p. 327). Others mention modernisation and westernisation as the main tenets of Kemalism (Gasiorowski, Long & Reich, 2013). Yet others argue that "Kemalism is a national ideology of modernisation and as such, it continues to be the most favoured ideology of Turkish political elite and intelligentsia" (Kılı, 1980).

Turkey's western orientation and aim of being a part of the European world were the key themes of Kemalism, and Turkey's path to the EU was considered as the protection of Ataturk's principles. Kemalism as a political project played an important role in building national identity. The key foreign policy doctrine of Kemalism is identified as "Peace at home, peace in the world" (Martin, 2014, p. 392) and served as an important policy in Turkey's relations with the world and the Middle East. Hence, "Turkish foreign policy stands on well-established principles driven from the Kemalist legacy" (Criss and Bilgin, 1997, p. 2). Kemalism promoted secularism and the adoption of European values (Naaz, 1999, p. 1549).

Thus, "secularism at the elite and state level has a long tradition in Turkey. Turkish elite considers themselves Europeans and desires their country to be European too" (Dalacoura, 1990, p. 220).

In the 1987 annual issue of *Studies on Turkish-Arab Relations*, Seyfi Taşhan (1987), in his article "Turkey between Europe and the Arab World," speaks about the implications of Turkey's growing relations with the European community on its relations with the Arab world. According to him, despite the existence of "the cultural, religious and historical bonds between Turkey and the Arab world, Turkish legal system, way of life, democracy, human right concepts, structures of bureaucracy, secularism and in general terms, Turkish *weltanschauung* [worldview] are similar to those of Western Europe" (p. 59). In *Foreign Policy*'s 1995 annual issue, while analysing Turkey's policy towards the Middle East, it was stated that "to those who claim that Turkey is not a European country because it is a Middle East country, the answer is no, it cannot be a Middle East country because it is a European one" (Ergüvenç, 1993, p. 1). Further, explaining that Turkey's lack of interest towards the Middle East is because of "the fact that history and religion, the two should be common denominators, are in fact the ones that distance Turkey from that part of the world. They are simply not the members of the same club" (ibid., p. 4).

Security (Water and PKK)

In the late 1980s, Turkey's relations with Iraq and Syria entered a difficult phase as Ankara increasingly started to have problems with its immediate neighbours (Altunışık & Tür, 2005). Hence, Turkey formulated its policy according to the threats it perceived by the Arab countries, which supported anti-Turkish causes such as the PKK, Cyprus and disputes over the distribution of water of the Euphrates and Tigris.[1] Additionally, Turkey's close relations with the West and its distanced stance to the region were interpreted by Arab countries as an 'unfriendly' attitude and as alienation from Islam (Karaosmanoğlu, 1983, p. 163). Turkey's good relation with Israel was already a reason for the indifferences between Turkey and the Arab world. To pressure Ankara due to its ties with Tel Aviv, Arab countries used several issues against Turkey, such as oil as a weapon, the Cyprus issue, the Palestinian problem, and secularisation in Turkey (Bengio, 2004, p. 3). Arab world's support for the Greek side led the Turks to come to terms with their cultural and historical bond (Criss and Bilgin 1997).

The publications by SAM (*Perceptions*) could be seen as representative of the main ideology and the discursive struggles of Turkey's elite in referring to these problematic issues. While examining *Perceptions* volumes from 1996-2000, which consisted of 180 articles, it is seen that only twelve or 6.6 per cent are about the Arab world and the Middle East. It indicates the limited interest of the Turkish academia and decision-makers on Turkish-Arab relations during that period. Due to the security-oriented foreign policy of the country, those articles were written around the narratives on water, the PKK and Cyprus when interpreting the Arab world, characterizing the region as the centre of problems that Turkey should not interfere with.

This has been explained in relation to the "already cool tendencies between Turks and Arabs towards each other due to the bad memories of the First World War and before. With the open support of some Arab countries, such as Syria, for the PKK, this cool leaning risked to worsen the relations and turn into hostilities" (Bal, 2004, p. 664). Thomas Diez (2005) identifies four main forms of 'Othering' in international politics as follows; representation of the other as a threat in terms of securitisation, representation of the other as inferior and self as superior, representation of the other as violating universal principles, and representation of the other as simply different. As to how the Arabs and the Arab world were represented in selected Turkish publications, Arabs were both represented as inferior, and in some context as different, as well as referred within the question of security.

In the early 2000s, a new wave of discourse was constructed, with the Turkish academia revising their studies on Arabs. There was again a particular emphasis on the importance of the Ottoman legacy through the "neo-Ottomanism" approach, which was one of the conceptual tools used by the country in its relations with the Middle East. Rather than adopting a security-oriented foreign policy based on a cautious and suspicious approach towards the Middle East, Turkey wanted to reassess its position in the region by embracing its former geopolitical space. This policy was named 'neo-Ottomanism', which became the main driver of Turkey's activism in the Middle East. Scholars mainly wrote articles on Turkey's historical, cultural and political attachment to the region. However, the "Ottoman legacy" is not a term that invokes a positive image in the countries that remained under the rule of the Ottoman Empire in the Middle East (Yılmaz & Yosmaoğlu, 2008, p. 677).

With the geopolitical developments since the so-called Arab Spring uprisings, Turkey's neo-Ottoman project failed as Arab countries did not perceive the Turkish involvement in the regional politics positively. The Arab understanding of Turkey that is shaped by the Ottoman legacy arose the fear that Turkey might once again increase its influence in the former Ottoman geopolitical space. Moreover, in the post-Arab Spring era, Turkey's relations with its Arab neighbours once again deteriorated due to the historical perceptions of the 'other.' The changing socio-political circumstances due to the uprisings in the region brought the security narrative to the agenda in Turkish scholars' reading of uprisings in the Arab countries. Nevertheless, the developments in the region have indicated that the power of historically constructed stereotypes do not disappear and come to the surface once again when history repeats itself at some point.

Conclusion

Despite some studies on the discourses used in Turkish media and school textbooks towards the Arabs, there is a huge gap in Turkish academia's understanding of the Arabs. This chapter examined some of the publications in which Turkish scholars penned articles on Turkish-Arab relations. How they perceive the 'others', the kinds of narratives used to define the others, indicate one's view of the status of 'others' within the context in which one lives. The content analysis of the publications of three state-centric think tanks in the 1980s and the 1990s reveals that the representations of the Arabs and the Arab world were dominated by the themes such as historical legacy and Ottomanism, Kemalism and secularism, and security issues, such as the water security and the PKK.

Given the socio-political juncture at which they were published, these writings somehow reflected the general stance of the Turkish state towards the Arab world. During that period, Turkey was looking at the Arab world from a security-oriented perspective due to both the influence of military institutions on political life in the country and the threats emanating from neighbouring states. The publications emphasised the security issues in the Middle East throughout the 1990s. The discourses and the political projects of the Turkish state at the time were focused on being part of Europe, westernisation, and maintaining distance from the Middle East. Much of the articles constituted attempts to hold a particular narrative to create Arabs as the 'others', which was in parallel with the state discourse.

It is reasonable to explore Turkish perception of Arabs and the Arab world in the past to reveal the dynamics that may still be at work in shaping the region's image in Turkey today. Stereotypes, prejudices and narratives towards Arabs and the Arab world have existed since the establishment of the Republic and seem to remain strong even today. The study argues that the discourse and narratives constructed towards Arabs and the Arab world in the late 1980s and the 1990s were not different from the previous eras. Moreover, similar narratives were even used in the early 2000s and after Arab uprisings that partly explain the change in the Turkish attitude towards the Middle East since the 1990s and the aggressive posturing during the Arab Spring uprisings.

Note

1. For the views of Turkish observers and analysts on the linkage between security and the water dispute, see Sabahattin Sen (1993), Güner (1998), Bölükbaşı (1993), Oktav (2003) and Erdem (2003).

References

Akturk, Ahmet S. (2010) "Arabs in Kemalist Turkish Historiography", *Middle Eastern Studies*, 46(5), 633-653.

Altunışık, Meliha & Tür, Özlem (2005). *Turkey: Challenges of Continuity and Change.* London: Routledge Curzon.

Anderson, Benedict (2006). *Imagined Communities: Reflections on the Origin and Spread of Nationalism.* London, UK: Verso.

Aras, Bülent and Köni, Hasan (2002). "Turkish-Syrian Relations Revisited", *Arab Studies Quarterly*, 24(4), 47-60.

Aydın-Duzgit, Senem & Rumelili, Bahar (2019). "Discourse Analysis: Strengths and Shortcomings". *All Azimuth*, 8 (2), 285-305.

Aykan, Mahmut B. (1993). "The Palestinian Question in Turkish Foreign Policy from the 1950s to the 1990s", *International Journal of Middle Eastern Studies*, 25(1), 91-110.

Bal, İdris (2004). *Ortadoğu'da İstikrarsızlığa yol açan faktörler ve PKK'nın katkısı. 21. Yüzyılda Türk Dış Politikası* (Factors leading to instability in the Middle East and the contribution of the PKK: Turkish Foreign Policy in the 21st Century). İstanbul: Nobel Yayın Dağıtım.

Banchoff, Thomas (1999). "German Identity and European Integration". *European Journal of International Relations*, 5(3), 259-289.

Bein, Amit (2017). *Kemalist Turkey and the Middle East, International Relations in the Interwar Period*, Cambridge University Press.

Beller, Manfred (2007). "Perception, Image, Imagology", in Leerssen, Joep & Beller, Manfred (eds.), *Imagology: The Cultural Construction and Literary Representation of National Characters*. Amsterdam, NL: Rodopi, 3-16.

Bengio, Ofra (2004). *The Turkish-Israeli Relationship: Changing ties of Middle Eastern outsiders*. New York: Palgrave Macmillan.

Bengio, Ofra, & Özcan, Gencer (2001). "Old Grievances, New Fears: Arab Perceptions of Turkey and its Alignment with Israel". *Middle Eastern Studies*, 37(2), 50–92.

Bozdaglioglu, Yücel (2003). *Turkish Foreign Policy and Turkish Identity: A Constructivist Approach*. London, UK: Routledge.

Bölükbaşı, Suha (1991). "Ankara, Damascus, Baghdad and the Regionalization of Turkcy's Kuıdislı Secessionism," *Journal of South Asian and Middle Eastern Studies* 14(4), 15-36.

Bülükbasi, Suha (1993) "Turkey Challenges Iraq and Syria: the Euphrates Dispute", *Journal of South Asian and Middle Eastern Studies*, 16(4): pp. 9–32.

Çağaptay, Soner (2020). *Erdogan's Turkey: Turkey and the Politics of the Middle East*. London, UK: IB Tauris.

Campbell, David (1992). *Writing Security: United States Foreign Policy and the Politics of Identity*. Minneapolis: University of Minnesota Press.

Cleveland, William L. & Bunton, Martin (2013). *A History of the Modern Middle East*. Boulder, CO: Westview Press.

Criss, Bilge & Bilgin, Pinar (1997). Turkish Foreign Policy towards Middle East. *Middle East Review of International Affairs*, 1(1), 14-32.

Dalacoura, Katerina (1990). "Turkey and the Middle East in the 1980s". *Millennium*, 19(2), 207-228.

Diez, Thomas (2005). "Constructing the self and changing others: Reconsidering normative power Europe", *Millennium-Journal of International Studies*, 33(3), 613-636.

Erdem, Mete (2003) "The Tigris-Euphrates Rivers Controversy and the Role of International Law", *Perceptions: Journal of International Affairs* 8: 1-14.

Ergüvenç, Şadi (1993). "Turkish Security and the Middle East", *Quarterly Review of the Foreign Policy Institute*, Ankara, 19(3-4), 1-12.

Farah, Caesar A. (1986). "Arabs and Turks: Common Heritage, Common Destiny". *Foundation for Studies on Turkish-Arab relations (TAIV)*, İstanbul, 61-75.

Foreign Policy Institute Journal, Chapter 1V: New Turkish—Arab Relations, *Quarterly Review of the Foreign Policy Institute* 1 (1993): 63-83.

Gasiorowski, Mark, Long, David E. & Reich, Bernard (2013). *The Government and Politics of the Middle East and North Africa*. Boulder, CO: Westview Press.

Göyünç, Nejat (1986). "Ottoman Central Administration and Arab Countries", *Foundation for Studies on Turkish-Arab relations (TAIV)*, Istanbul, 76-84.

Güner, Serdar (1998) "Signalling in the Turkish-Syrian Water Conflict". *Conflict Management and Peace Science*. 16(2): 185-206.

Heper, Metin (1987). "Some notes on State, Society and Islam in Turkey", *Foundation for Studies on Turkish-Arab Relations (TAIV)*, Istanbul, 157-163.

Heper, Metin (1991). "Democracy: A panacea for the lingering instability in the Middle East", *Foundation for Studies on Turkish-Arab Relations (TAIV)*, Istanbul, 105-108.

Herrmann, Richard K. & Fischerkeller, Michael P. (1995). "Beyond the Enemy Image and Spiral Model: Cognitive-Strategic Research after the Cold War", *International Organization*, 49(3), 415-450.

İhsanoğlu, Ekmeleddin & Al-Din, Muhammad S. (1991). *Al-Alaqat al-arabiyya al-turkiyya (Arap-türk Münasebetleri)*, (Arab-Turkish Relations) İstanbul: Research Center for Islamic History, Art, and Culture (IRCICA).

Jung, Dietrich (2005). "Turkey and the Arab World: Historical Narratives and New Political Realities", *Mediterranean Politics*, 10(1), 1-17.

Karaosmanoğlu, Ali L. (1983). "Turkey's Security and the Middle East". *Foreign Affairs*, 62(1), 157-175.

Karaosmanoğlu, Ali L. (1986). "Turkey's policy in the Middle East". *Foundation for Studies on Turkish-Arab relations (TAIV)*, Istanbul, 159-164.

Karaosmanoğlu, Ali L. (2000),"The Evolution of the National Security Culture and the Military in Turkey," *Journal of International Affairs*, 54(1), pp. 199-216.

Karpat, Kemal H. (1987). "Images of Turks and Arabs in School Textbooks". *Foundation for Studies on Turkish-Arab Relations (TAIV)*, İstanbul, 17-19.

Kayali, Hasan (1997). *Arabs and Young Turks: Ottomanism, Arabism, and Islamism in the Ottoman Empire, 1908-1918*. Berkeley, CA: University of California Press.

Kılı, Suna (1980). "Kemalism in Contemporary Turkey". *International Political Science Review*, 1 (3), 380–404.

Kirişçi, Kemal (1997). "Post-Cold-War Turkish Security and the Middle East", *MERIA Journal*, 1(2).

Korkut, Şenol (1976). "Istanbul Islamic Conference of Foreign Ministers", *Quarterly Review of the Foreign Policy Institute*, Ankara, 5(4), 18-22.

Küçükcan, Talip (2010). "Arab Image in Turkey". *SETA Research Report*, No. 1, 1-39.

Kürkçüoğlu, Ömer (1985). "Arab and Turkish Public Opinion Attitudes Towards Questions of the Two Nations". *Foreign Policy*, Ankara, 12(1-2), 22-43.

Martin, Lenore G. (2004). "Turkey's Middle East Foreign Policy," in Lenore G. Martin and Dimitris Keridis, eds., *The Future of Turkish Foreign Policy*. Cambridge, MA: MIT Press.

Martin, Natalie (2014). *Security and the Turkey-EU Accession Process Norms, Reforms and the Cyprus Issue*. Basingstoke: Palgrave Macmillan.

Müftüler, Meltem (1995). "Turkish Economic Liberalization and European Integration". *Middle Eastern Studies*, 31(1), 85-98.

Mughisuddin, Oya Akgonenc (1993). "Perceptions and Misconceptions in the Making of Foreign Diplomacy: A Study of Turkish-Arab Attitudes until the End of the 1970s". *Turkish Review of Middle East Studies*, No. 7, 147-169.

Naaz, Farah (1999). "Turkey and the Middle East in the 1990s", *Strategic Analysis*, 23(9), 1549-1560.

Oktav, Özden Z. (2003) "Water Dispute and Kurdish Separatism in Turkish-Syrian Relations", *The Turkish Yearbook of International Relations*: 91-117.

Phillips, Louise and Jørgensen, Marianne (2002). *Discourse Analysis as Theory and Method*. London: Sage Publications.

Olson, Robert (1995). "The Kurdish Question and Turkey's Foreign Policy 1991-1995, From the Gulf War to the Incursion into Iraq," *Journal of South Asian and Middle Eastern Studies* 29(1), 1-30.

Rubin, Barry and Kirişci, Kemal (2001). *Turkey in World Politics: An Emerging Multiregional Power*. Boulder and London: Lynne Rienner Publishers.

Sabahattin Sen, ed., Su Sorunu, Turkiye,ve Ortadogu (Istanbul: Baglam Yayinları, 1993)

Sahillioğlu, Halil (1986). "Administrative Division of Iraq during the Ottoman Period". *Foundation for Studies on Turkish-Arab relations (TAIV)*, Istanbul, 224-248.

Said, Edward (1995). *Orientalism: Western Concept of the Orient*. Harmondsworth: Penguin.

Sayarı, Sabri (1997). "Turkey and the Middle East in the 1990s". *Journal of Palestine Studies*, 26(3), 44-55.

Taşhan, Seyfi (1987). "Turkey between Europe and the Arab World", *Foundation for Studies on Turkish-Arab Relations (TAIV)*, Istanbul, 57-61.

Triandafyllidou, Anna (1998). "National identity and the other". *Ethnic and Racial Studies*, 21(4), 593-612.

Vali, Ferenc A. (2019). *Bridge Across the Bosporus: The Foreign Policy of Turkey*. Baltimore, MD: The Johns Hopkins Press, 2019.

Wodak, Ruth & Meyer, Michael (2001). *Methods of critical discourse analysis*. London: SAGE.

Yıldırım, Jülide & Sezgin, Expenditure Selami & Öcal, Nadir (2006). "The demand for military spending in Middle Eastern countries and Turkey", in Ott, Attiat F. & Cebula, Richard J. *Elgar Companion to Public Economics: Empirical Public Economics*. Edward Elgar Publishing.

Yılmaz, Şuhnaz & Yosmaoğlu, İpek K. (2008). "Fighting the Spectres of the Past: Dilemmas of Ottoman Legacy in the Balkans and the Middle East", *Middle Eastern Studies*, 44(5), 677-693.

Zurcher, Erik-Jan (2004). *Turkey: A Modern History*. London: I. B. Tauris.

14. China's Foreign Policy in the Middle East and North Africa after the Arab Spring

Mordechai Chaziza

Introduction

In the post-Arab Spring era, the most significant Chinese diplomatic and economic activity in the Middle East and North Africa (MENA) is the Belt and Road Initiative (BRI). It is a sprawling framework of trade and commercial ties between China and various regions that have become Xi Jinping's and the Chinese Communist Party's flagship foreign policy. The BRI primarily seeks to open up new markets and secure global supply chains for sustained Chinese economic growth and contribute to social stability at home (Watanabe, 2019).

The BRI has a maritime and land-based component. The maritime element is the Maritime Silk Road Initiative (MSRI), and the land-based equivalent is the Silk Road Economic Belt (SREB). The various sub-branches of the SREB (a series of land-based infrastructure projects including roads, railways, and pipelines) and the MSRI (made up of ports and coastal development) would create a transnational network connecting China to Europe and Africa via the Middle East (Xinhua, 2017).

China has emerged as the world's top trading nation; hence it needs to ensure that it has timely, efficient, and secure access to markets and resources, and therefore facilitation of trade and investment is a key focus. It should not be surprising that securing conventional and renewable energy and resources is another focus for China. Once completed, the BRI will provide land-based and sea-based alternatives for PRC to access the continents and access other countries to China. Transport link is a critical consideration, as China is vulnerable to choke points along its sea route. Such threats would be mitigated once land-based alternatives, including railroads, highways, and communication links, are in place (Lokhande, 2017).

The MENA region has become a crucial hub in realizing the BRI due to its geostrategic location (bringing together the land and maritime Silk Road) that links China to Middle Eastern, African, and European markets. Simultaneously, its vast hydrocarbon reserves are essential in driving the development projects that comprise the Silk Road. As an energy-rich zone, it plays a decisive role in the process of building the BRI. Sino-MENA cooperation can, therefore, be expected to expand as China's footprint expands across the Indian Ocean. This region also plays a prominent role in security coordination, economic cooperation and cultural exchanges under the BRI framework (Wu, 2015).

Popular protests in Libya, Egypt, Yemen, and Tunisia overthrew authoritarian governments and launched a period of difficult transitions. In Yemen, Libya and Syria, the rebellions turned into prolonged civil wars with devastating civilian casualties. Moreover, the spillover effects of the Arab Spring uprisings has been felt in the region and beyond. This chapter analyses China's policy in response to the ongoing civil wars in Yemen, Libya and Syria and the growing threats to the BRI framework by examining how the post-Arab Spring era affected Beijing's policy behaviour in MENA.

China's foreign policy in MENA: Objectives and Priorities

China's policy towards the MENA must be defined in a complex regional context involving plenty of local rivalries and severe great-power competition (Scobell, 2018). The Chinese policy intends to balance several objectives that may sometimes be in conflict or tension. First, Beijing strives to maintain mutual respect between China and each regional state, territorial integrity and sovereignty, and mutual non-interference in each other's internal affairs. Second, it wants a peaceful and stable international environment to advance China's modernisation drive, promoting development, and improving livelihood (Ministry of Foreign Affairs, the People's Republic of China, 2011).

Third, China wishes for a peaceful environment in MENA to protect its regional interests. Fourth, it aims to preserve good relations with all countries in the MENA, and finally, avoid a major confrontation with the US while limiting its regional hegemony and promoting regional and global multi-polarity (Cheng, 2016). Based on this policy, China seeks to strengthen the mutual interdependency with the MENA countries in various sectors such as energy and investments in construction and infrastructure projects and leverage its economic capabilities to realise the BRI framework.

The MENA region represents four significant priorities for China's foreign policy. Foremost among them is the region's criticality as a source of imported energy and an essential region for Chinese trade and investment. As the world's largest consumer of energy overall and the second-largest importer of crude oil, safeguarding a stable flow of crude oil from the MENA is a paramount concern (Zambelis, 2015). In 2019, almost half of Chinese imported crude oil originated from nine MENA countries (Workman, 2020). Second, the region is also a crucial part of China's BRI, especially its MSRI component. While the current BRI map does not officially include the MENA region (by design, the BRI is more a loose brand than a program with strict criteria), BRI Memorandums of Understanding (MoUs) have been signed with a majority of MENA countries, demonstrating China's expanding foothold in the region (Chaziza, 2020). In the past, the MENA was considered by Beijing a peripheral and relatively insignificant region. In contrast, with the post-2013 launch of the BRI, the region is considered a vital geostrategic global crossroads and China's most famous region beyond Asia-Pacific.

Third, Beijing views the MENA as an arena of great-power competition in which China, as a rising power, must be seen as a player (Scobell & Nader, 2016). Finally, China has vital security interests in the region: concerns regarding the spread of terrorism and extremist ideology from the MENA and its impact on Uighur separatism (Tiezzi, 2014). China fears that Uighurs fighting alongside Al-Qaeda and ISIS in the region may leave the fighting and attempt to return home. As they return, they may bring a newly Islamised narrative and motivation, which will challenge Xinjiang's social stability and economic development (Chaziza, 2018).

The chapter examines three conflict cases in the region since 2011 and China's engagement with them in Libya, Syria, and Yemen. Since 2011, PRC's policy in the MENA derives from its broader security and economic interests. Accordingly, China's two primary policy aims are to maintain a constructive relationship with all the stable, friendly governments, and capable of preventing the spread of transnational jihadist activity from its territory; and to develop an economic partnership that is compatible with and in furtherance of the BRI. PRC has pursued these aims during the post-Arab Spring era: first, its capacity as an emerging international conflict management actor has employed a flexible, non-directive, and non-coercive approach that utilises bilateral and multilateral channels, mediation diplomacy, and humanitarian assistance. Second, the fact that PRC has had minimal impact on the conflicts reflects its limited capacity and function of a purposefully modest investment in an instance where Chinese core interests are not directly engaged. Finally, China does not appear to be rushing to make a large financial commitment to post-war reconstruction.

Libya

Under the Gaddafi regime, PRC engaged in various infrastructure activities, and Libya sent considerable capital to China in return. Although the Libyan market was not a significant target for Chinese exports, it was important for Beijing to protect and promote its investments. As a result, about 75 Chinese enterprises operated in Libya before the outbreak of the First Libyan Civil War in 2011, with the volume of their contracts estimated at US$20 billion, and more than 36,000 Chinese employees are working on about 50 projects in sectors including housing construction, telecommunications, railways, and hydroelectric (Evron, 2013).

Most notably, the oil industry has long been at the core of the two countries' relationship. The North African country provided 3 per cent of China's crude oil supply, constituting roughly 150,000 barrels per day, or one-tenth of Libya's crude exports. Moreover, all of China's top state oil companies—China National Petroleum Corporation (CNPC), Sinopec Group, and CNOOC—operated Libya's infrastructure projects (Alkoutami & Wehrey, 2020).

At the beginning of the civil war in Libya, many Chinese companies were raided and robbed, and dozens of Chinese employees were seriously injured (Hook & Dyer, 2011). The Chinese leadership quickly moved to evacuate 35,860 Chinese citizens' workers from Libya (*Global Times*,

2011). This meant that all signed contract projects had to be stopped or postponed. Undoubtedly, Chinese enterprises were seriously damaged by the conflict and the business's suspension, but above all, losing fixed assets (Sohu Finance, 2011). After the end of the first civil war, it was not clear that Chinese enterprises could successfully return to Libya, resume their contract projects, and start new investments.

In the post-Gaddafi era, China's policy supports the status quo and maintaining a balanced vagueness in dealing with the evolving Libyan crisis. This undermined its ability to forge good relations with the National Transitional Council (NTC) as the legitimate authority in Libya (Sotloff, 2012). Decades of economic cooperation with the Gaddafi regime were seen as negative by NTC, which officially stated that nations that supported the dictator would be disadvantaged in the 'new' Libya and give preferential treatment to countries that opposed Gaddafi during the civil war (Arduino, 2020).

Since 2015, there have been many political developments. Throughout the passage of power from the NTC to the General National Congress (GNC) and finally to the Government of National Accord (GNA), Libya has sunk further into turmoil and is now divided between two rival administrations based in the country's east and west, with an array of fighters and militias backed by various foreign powers allied with each side. Libya entered a second civil war, as the GNA government headed by Prime Minister Fayez al-Sarraj has been locked in conflict with east-Libyan-based forces led by General Khalifa Haftar's self-styled Libyan National Army (LNA). Once again, a disrupted and destabilised Libya complicate China's economic engagement with the country (Alkoutami & Wehrey, 2020). In December 2017, the LNA seized Benghazi after three years of fighting. In February 2019, the LNA achieved victory in the Battle of Derna. The LNA then launched a major offensive in April 2019 in an attempt to seize Tripoli (Reuters, 2020a). In June 2020, the GNA captured all of western Libya, including the capital Tripoli. The next day the GNA launched offensive to capture Sirte. On 21 August, the GNA and the LNA both agreed to a ceasefire which was later cancelled (Reuters, 2020b).

Beijing's policy on Libya's post-conflict reconstruction is part of its overall policy to the MENA region, which is part of its foreign policy globally. From the beginning of the civil war in Libya, the Chinese government took a neutral stance, adhering to its fundamental principle of non-interference while undertaking responsibility for humanitarian aid (Junbo & Méndez, 2015). During the crisis, PRC's involvement in Libya has focused on economic penetration and behind-the-scenes diplomacy. Nonetheless, the Chinese policy of taking a neutral stance and providing humanitarian aid failed to get an economic foothold in Libya during the First Libyan War between the 2011 and civil war eruptions in May 2014 (Cafiero, 2020).

With the outbreak of the Second Libyan Civil War in 2014, Libya's complicated conflict posed new challenges to Chinese interests. Nonetheless, throughout this civil war, Beijing has maintained a balanced and cautious approach, focusing on long-term interests. Accordingly, China has pursued a foreign policy of cautious and diplomatic and economic diversification. Officially, PRC backs the GNA, and Chinese diplomats have met with GNA officials while having already begun eyeing deals, keeping economic channels open, and being careful not to burn any bridges with LNA.

When balancing competing interests, the path of least resistance is most appealing and fruitful, and, often, this is the path of neutrality. Beijing has denounced foreign interference and repeatedly called for a political solution to the conflict, endorsing a ceasefire and settlement among warring parties under the UN's auspices (Alkoutami & Wehrey, 2020). China's Libya policy made adjustments from its non-interference into a new "non-aligned" approach where Beijing is not staying out of the conflict and taking sides between the two warring parties. PRC's hesitation in taking sides points instead to a desire to maximise its diplomatic and economic gains irrespective of the conflict's outcome. Hence, China has placed bets on both sides of the conflict in an attempt to handicap the outcome and secure its interests (Arduino, 2020).

Moreover, PRC's adherence to strict multilateralism in the Libya conflict by supporting the multilateral peace initiatives instead of country-led initiatives (for example UAE, Italy, and France) aligns closely with its views on the international order and strategic priorities. This reflects China's sceptical view of external stakeholders' ability to influence Libya constructively. Within a UN framework, Beijing is likely to take a back seat and allow other great powers to dominate the Libyan conflict resolution. As a result, China supports multilateral peace initiatives from the side lines without acting as a central player. This demonstrates the limits of PRC's willingness to resolve Libya's conflict directly (Ramani, 2019).

These efforts reflect Beijing's long-term interest in integrating Libya into the BRI. Beijing views Libya—an oil-rich country connecting the Mediterranean Sea to sub-Saharan Africa—as a potentially valuable BRI partner (Hong Kong Trade Development Council, 2020). Beijing's desire to develop this partnership has been reciprocated by the GNA, whose diplomatic outreach to China has intensified (Xinhua, 2018). In July 2018, on the occasion of the 8th ministerial meeting of the Forum on China-Africa Cooperation, GNA Minister for Foreign Affairs Mohamed Taha Siala and Chinese State Councilor and Foreign Minister Wang Yi signed an MoU, paving the way for Libya to join the BRI and for the return of Chinese businesses to the country (*The Libya Observer*, 2018). China's partiality towards the GNA can be explained by maximizing its commercial opportunities to account for the conflict's unknown outcome.

In September 2018, the GNA's prime minister openly called for expanding Chinese investment in Libya. Furthermore, at the February 2019 Munich Security Conference, GNA representatives lauded Libya as a potential gateway for Chinese economic influence in central Africa (Ramani, 2019). In response to these statements, the Chinese Ambassador to Libya Li Zhiguo praised the GNA for improving Tripoli's security situation and stated that China had plans for a swift expansion of its economic presence in Libya (*Asharq Alwasat*, 2019).

In addition to carefully aligning its position with that of the UN in support of the GNA and courting Prime Minister Fayez al-Sarraj, China has kept its options open in the event Field Marshal Khalifa Haftar's LNA prevails. CNPC and its subsidiaries, for example, are poised to engage with an increasingly autonomous east, which comprises a large portion of Libya's oil infrastructure. A senior delegation from Libya's National Oil Corporation (NOC) visited China in July of 2019 to hold talks with CNPC officials regarding crude oil purchases and possible collaboration on exploring and developing Libya's oilfields and services (Zaptia, 2019). However, Chinese Libyan policy is based on cautious and limited engagement with Libya's complex conflict. PRC's assessment that the

Libyan crisis will end in ways that are unknown in the current period is wisest to hedge while pragmatically avoiding excessive entanglement in it.

In the MENA, PRC's approach to securing energy supply is based on bilateral contracts and large-scale investments in oil and gas producing countries' energy assets. China's search for energy security has led to deepening political and economic relationships with MENA energy producers and countries along the BRI, which have transit potential. Although energy was not initially identified as one of BRI's main areas, it has become an essential component in implementing China's energy security strategy. In addition, the BRI serves as a new platform for the development of China's overseas energy investment. For example, Libya is a major oil and gas supplier and one of the fifteen crude oil suppliers to China and in 2019 it provided 2 per cent (US$ 4.8 billion) of China's crude oil supply (Workman, 2020).

In the end, among the major international players in Libya, China is moving from a neutral position to increasing prominence, poised to advance its BRI framework regardless of which Libyan faction triumphs on the ground. Beijing has been careful to avoid conduct in Libya crises that could leave the BRI framework on bad terms with whichever side ultimately wins the civil war. The hope is that the Libyan civil war's victors will establish Libya as a China-friendly country for the BRI framework. The fact that the conflict has become a proxy war fuelled by rival foreign powers has made Beijing's task of crafting a principled and practical Libya policy even more challenging. Beijing has responded to this challenge by steadfastly supporting multilateral, as opposed to country-led peace initiatives - a position that aligns closely with its views on the international order and strategic priorities. This position also reflects China's sceptical view of individual external stakeholders' ability to influence Libya constructively. Though strongly favouring multilateral peace initiatives ideally operating with a UN framework, Beijing is unlikely to seek or play a central, direct role in resolving the conflict (Ramani, 2019).

Nevertheless, whereas countries such as the UAE, Russia, France, or Turkey can provide the powerful military hardware to win battles, China is one of the few nations that can provide financial and technical support to rebuild the country. As a result, China can play a significant role in Libya's reconstruction and redevelopment, regardless of which faction prevails in the ongoing civil war (Cafiero, 2020). Moreover, once the Libyan conflict reaches an equilibrium point, China will undoubtedly seek to exploit the BRI framework's synergy and Libya's post-conflict reconstruction. When that moment arrives, the cautious and limited engagement approach that Beijing has followed will likely provide China with a broader scope for intervention, not only into Libya's economic affairs but also its political sphere.

Yemen

Yemen has a significant and strategically important state in the southern Arabian Peninsula bordering Saudi Arabia, Oman, the Red Sea, and the Gulf of Aden within the Arabian Sea. Moreover, Yemen's geographical location makes it an essential state for the BRI framework because it enables an observation point over three regional trouble spots: the Arabian Gulf, Red Sea, and the Horn of Africa. In this regard, Yemen can be considered a geographical belt encompassing the southern part of the Gulf and the Arabian Peninsula, which controls the Bab al-Mandab Strait and the Red Sea navigational routes in the Arabian Sea (Al Awd, Bin Othman & Ismail, 2017).

Yemen enjoys a unique geographical strategic position at the BRI intersection between the SREB and the MSRI. The Strait of Bab al-Mandab is a strategic waterway and critical junction for world trade, located between Yemen, Djibouti, and Eritrea, where the Red Sea joins the Indian Ocean. Yemen can become the bridge between Asia and Africa, between the Indian Ocean and the Mediterranean, and is a vital component of China's infrastructure-based development strategy (Energy Information Administration, 2017). Thus, the BRI scheme gives China and Yemen extra incentive to boost cooperation, as this will help reduce risks and project costs and, in the long term, fully capture the mutual benefits of increased trade, investment, and connectivity in the MENA.

The Yemen civil war, which began in 2014, is one of the more complex events to have emerged since the Arab Spring. The current conflict has deep historical roots and reflects long-standing societal and political grievances within Yemen. As the Arab Spring swept through Egypt and Tunisia, Yemen's deep political divisions were further exacerbated by the involvement of competing for regional powers: Saudi Arabia and the United Arab Emirates backed Yemen's government while, to a lesser extent, Iran assisted the Houthis (Chang, 2018). Nearly a quarter of a million people have been killed directly by fighting and indirectly through a lack of access to food, health services, and infrastructure (Moyer, Bohl, Hanna, Mapes & Rafa, 2019).

The immediate interest at stake for Beijing in the Yemen civil war was protecting its economic investments and Chinese personnel's safety. According to the Chinese Ministry of Commerce, Beijing has 14 enterprises and 460 personnel in Yemen. China's trade projects concentrate on oil extraction, telecommunication, construction, roads and bridges, and fishery (Chaziza, 2015). In response to the Yemen crisis, China has completed personnel evacuation and temporarily closed its embassy in Sana'a and the Consulate General in Aden (Angela & Li, 2017).

Generally, China's policy towards the Yemeni conflict has been clear and consistent, driven primarily by its interest in maintaining close strategic relations with Saudi Arabia. In bilateral and multilateral initiatives, China has steadily supported the internationally recognised Yemen government, always stressing the importance of Yemen's national independence, sovereignty, and territorial integrity. Beijing has also regularly urged all parties to the conflict to reject violence and resolve the conflict by political means through intra-Yemeni dialogue (Burton, 2019).

Moreover, Beijing encouraged and supported regional countries to take the lead in addressing the crisis. It suggested that the international community supports the Yemeni political dialogue and provides development and humanitarian assistance (Xinhua, 2019). China also welcomed the Riyadh agreement signed between the Yemeni government and the Southern Transitional Council (STC) to form a new government and integrate the armed forces (*Global Times*, 2019).

China's growing economic ties in the MENA give it a large stake and influence to be more active in mediating conflicts. Unlike other major powers, Beijing has stayed out of regional rivalries and has forged ties with all sides. China also carries little of the historical or cultural baggage associated with other players in the region. As such, it is well-placed to serve as an honest broker in making dialogue possible (Chaziza, 2015). Following unsuccessful rounds of UN negotiations, Beijing tried to bridge the trust deficit between the Houthis, the Yemeni government, and the UN. In December 2016, a high-level delegation of Yemen's Houthi rebel movement held a three-day visit to China and met with the Foreign Ministry's Director-General Deng Li to discuss the ongoing conflict in Yemen (Cusack, 2016). Although Beijing's attempt to mediate was unsuccessful, Houthi leaders and representatives of the Yemeni government thanked China for its mediation efforts (Chang, 2018).

In the end, Yemen could emerge as a crucial component of China's MSRI projects due to its unique geographical strategic position and natural resources (Chaziza, 2019). However, Yemen's complex characteristics (mostly the political instability and the security situation) could raise challenges for Beijing's economic interests and BRI development. The maintenance of security at the Arabian Peninsula's southernmost pinch point (Bab al-Mandab Strait) is a genuine concern for the BRI framework that relies on the region's maritime trade (Chang, 2020).

Syria

The widespread destruction in Syria since March 2011 has been disastrous for the economy, human life (over half a million lives lost, 5.6 million Syrians became refugees, and more than 6.1 million people were displaced internally), and the country's critical infrastructure (UNHCR, 2019). The costs of repairing this damage are daunting to the international community. In August 2018, the UN Economic and Social Commission for Western Asia estimated the cost of damage at more than US$ 388 billion and lost productivity to GDP at around US$ 268 billion (UN Economic and Social Commission for Western Asia, 2018).

Throughout the nine-year Syrian civil war, Beijing's Syria policy has derived from its broader security and economic interests in the Middle East. China's two primary policy objectives are: first, the conviction that Chinese economic and security interests are best served by a stable and friendly regime in Damascus capable of preventing the country from becoming a sanctuary or training ground for radical jihadists, and second, developing economic interests that are compatible with the BRI framework (Calabrese, 2019). Since Chinese companies have experience in war-torn Middle Eastern nations, they are reportedly queuing up to win contracts for rebuilding entire towns and villages, roads, bridges, schools, hospitals, and communication networks in Syria's reconstruction process (O'connor, 2018).

From the beginning, China has held an absolute position in favour of the Assad regime and took concrete measures to support it. The collapse of Assad's regime will have a powerful effect over the entire Middle East-and a grave threat to China's interests, too; Assad's fall is expected to strengthen radical Islamic movements that Beijing regards as a direct threat to its national security (Evron, 2017). In many ways, Beijing is also in a far better position than the US or Russia to play the honest broker, precisely because of its lack of past involvement in the Syrian conflict. As a mediator, China offers a new setting and hope for fruitful peace negotiations because it enjoys a trusted relationship with the Syrian government and its opposition, the Syrian National Coalition (Chaziza, 2016).

Chinese mediation activities have manifested themselves in a range of diplomatic endeavours: it hosted representatives of both the Syrian government and opposition forces; appointed its Special Envoy to help mediate in the conflict in Syria; and Chinese special envoys for Middle East affairs have dedicated much of their mandate to shuttle diplomacy on Syria, exchanging views with regional stakeholders and seeking to promote political conciliation; it supported the mediation efforts of the Special Envoy of the UN Secretary-General for Syria; and provided multiple rounds of humanitarian assistance to relieve the suffering of the Syrian people (Chaziza, 2020).

In the UN Security Council, the Chinese delegation has consistently opposed coercive measures by blocking censures, demands for ceasefires, use of sanctions, and the International Criminal Court referral (Calabrese, 2019). On the other hand, Beijing supported the passing of UN Security Council Resolution 2254, which laid the framework for a possible end to the Syrian crisis (United Nations, 2015). China also took part in all international meetings in Vienna on the Syrian issue (Rudolf, 2016) and the convening of the International Syria Support Group. Besides, China participated in Geneva Conferences I and II (Xinhua, 2016) and welcomed the Astana Peace Process-launched by Russia, Iran, and Turkey (Ministry of Foreign Affairs of the People's Republic of China, 2017).

To avoid too sharp a break with its non-interference stance, China has not yet reached the point where it is willing or able to deepen its involvement. As a result, China's conflict mediation in the Syrian case, as in others, has consisted mainly of top-level, high-visibility activities. Though having grown more self-confident and assertive on peace and security matters, Beijing's continuing preference for playing a supportive rather than a leading mediation role has been borne out by the actions it has taken regarding Syria (Calabrese, 2019).

China has shown a willingness to mediate in the framework of its conflict management approach in the Syrian peace process, mainly because it realises that Syria's fragile situation is not favourable to its economic and strategic interests. However, it has never before played the role of lead mediator in the Middle East conflicts, perhaps because the region has always been within the US sphere of influence. Thus, China's mediation efforts in Syria remain limited due to both economic and strategic constraints and adherence to its long-standing non-interference principle, preferring multilateral peace mediation through the UN or other multilateral organisations (Chaziza, 2018).

Moreover, for many years, Syrian officials have consistently sought to present Syria as a key player in the BRI framework. At the crossroads of East and West, Syria's geographical location has a particular value for the Chinese MSRI. Possible development of its transport and ports (Latakia and Tartus) infrastructures, adequately connected and with the BRI, would allow China a further maritime outlet for its land trade and a formidable trade post in the Mediterranean. Nevertheless, the aim to increase the PRC's access and connect its economy with those of the Middle East, Central Asia, and Europe through massive infrastructure building could be seriously affected by the region's hotspots' instability. Syrian instability presents a formidable obstacle to the BRI's strategic design, as it undermines connectivity, threatens infrastructure projects, and makes an economic corridor through the volatile Middle East to the markets of developed Europe less viable (Chaziza, 2020).

Conclusion

Ten years after the Arab Spring uprisings, China has gradually consolidated its engagement and presence in the MENA in trade, energy, investment, ports, shipping, financial cooperation, tourism, manufacturing, cultural exchanges, and infrastructure projects. This involvement, primarily through the BRI framework, is part and parcel of Beijing's increasing share in trade and investment worldwide. This reflects both the re-centring of global manufacturing to coastal China and the need for energy and mineral resources from the MENA vital to support this process. However, China's role in the region is still in a nascent phase and rooted chiefly in economic interests.

In the post-Arab Spring era, mediation diplomacy has emerged as one of the central pillars of China's foreign policy objectives and practice in the MENA. Beijing's approach to the civil wars in Yemen and Syria has been shaped by its long-standing declaratory policy of respect for state sovereignty and non-interference in other nations' internal affairs. China certainly can intervene but lacks the will to get heavily involved in the military conflict in the region, as everywhere else in the world, limiting itself to multilateral peace mediations. Hence, China's mediation role in the MENA is part of a carefully devised strategy that suits its non-interference policy framework and is mostly aimed at constructive conflict management rather than conflict resolution. As a result, for the time being, the US, Russia, and the EU continue to be the most significant extra-regional actors in the MENA conflicts, while China is still a marginal and deliberately cautious player or mediator.

The MENA has been in a state of chaos for many decades, with each passing year bringing a new wave of instability and the US and other prominent power players failing so far to bring peace. China aims to increase access and connect its economy with the MENA through trade, and massive infrastructure building could be seriously affected by the instability generated in the region's hotspots. The civil wars present a formidable obstacle to the BRI's strategic design, as it undermines connectivity, threatens infrastructure projects, and makes an economic corridor through the volatile MENA to the markets of developed Europe less viable.

References

Al Awd, Yahya Yahya, Bin Othman, Muhammad Fuad, and Binti Ismail, Norafidah (2017), "Yemen-China Relations: History and Development in Bilateral Relations," *The Social Sciences, 12* (10), 1775-1794.

Alkoutami, Sandy and Wehrey, Frederic (2020), "China's Balancing Act in Libya," *Lawfare*, May 10, https://www.lawfareblog.com/chinas-balancing-act-libya

Asharq Alwasat (2019), "GNA Interior Minister Bashagha affirms Libya's desire for security cooperation with China," January 9, http://en.alwasat.ly/news/libya/232190

Arduino, Alessandro (2020), "Here's the real reason China isn't taking sides in Libya," *South China Morning Post*, January 28, https://www.scmp.com/week-asia/opinion/article/3047944/heres-real-reason-china-isnt-taking-sides-libya

Calabrese, John (2019), "China and Syria: In War and Reconstruction," Middle East Institute, Washington, DC, July 9, https://www.mei.edu/publications/china-and-syria-war-and-reconstruction

Cafiero, Giorgio (2020), "The Geopolitics of China's Libya Foreign Policy," *China MED iterranean*, August 4, https://www.chinamed.it/publications/the-geopolitics-of-chinas-libya-foreign-policy

Chang, I-wei Jennifer (2018), "China and Yemen's Forgotten War," *Peace Brief*, United States Institute of Peace, January 16, https://www.usip.org/publications/2018/01/china-and-yemens-forgotten-war

Chang, I-wei Jennifer (2020), "The Chinese Perspective on the Yemen Crisis," in Day, Stephen W. and Brehony, Noel (Eds.), *Global, Regional, and Local Dynamics in the Yemen Crisis*, Singapore: Palgrave Macmillan, pp. 97-111.

Chaziza, Mordechai (2015), "China's Middle East foreign policy and the Yemen Crisis: Challenges and Implications," *Middle East Review of International Affairs, 19* (2), 1-9.

Chaziza, Mordechai (2016), "Syria's Civil War: Stage for Greater Chinese Involvement in the Middle East?" *Middle East Review of International Affairs, 20* (2), 1-9.

Chaziza, Mordechai (2018), "China's Counter-Terrorism Policy in the Middle East," in Michael Clarke (Ed.). *Terrorism and Counter-Terrorism in China: Domestic and Foreign Policy Dimensions*, New York: Oxford University Press, pp. 141-156.

Chaziza, Mordechai (2018), "China's Mediation Efforts in the Middle East and North Africa: Constructive Conflict Management," *Strategic Analysis*, *42* (1), 29-41.

Chaziza, Mordechai (2019), "*China and the Persian Gulf: The New Silk Road Strategy and Emerging Partnerships*," London: Sussex Academic Press.

Chaziza, Mordechai (2020), *China Middle East Diplomacy: The Belt and Road Strategic Partnership*, London: Sussex Academic Press.

Cheng, Joseph Y. S. (2016), "China's Relations with the Gulf Cooperation Council States: Multilevel Diplomacy in a Divided Arab World," *The China Review, 16* (1), 35-64.

Cusack, Robert (2016), "Houthis go to China: Yemen's rebel delegation discuss peace-deal," *The New Arab*, December 1, https://www.alaraby.co.uk/english/

news/2016/12/1/houthis-go-to-china-yemens-rebel-delegation-discuss-peace-deal

U.S. Energy Information Administration (2017), "World Oil Transit Chokepoints," July 25, https://www.eia.gov/beta/international/regions-topics.php?RegionTopicID=WOTC

Evron, Yoram (2017), "China's Diplomatic Initiatives in the Middle East: The Quest for a Great-Power Role in the Region," *International Relations, 31* (2), 125-144.

Evron, Yoram (2013), "Chinese Involvement in the Middle East: The Libyan and Syrian Crises," *Strategic Assessment, 16* (3), 79-91.

Global Times (2011), "35,860 Chinese nationals in Libya evacuated: FM," March 3, https://www.globaltimes.cn/content/629380.shtml

Global Times (2019), "China hails Riyadh Agreement, hopes for Yemen peace, independence," November 7, http://www.globaltimes.cn/content/1169348.shtml

Hong Kong Trade Development Council (2020), "Libya: Economic Profile," https://beltandroad.hktdc.com/en/country-profiles/libya

Hook, Leslie and Dyer, Geoff (2011), "Chinese Oil Interests attacked in Libya," *Financial Times,* February 24, https://www.ft.com/content/eef58d52-3fe2-11e0-811f-00144feabdc0

Junbo, Jian and Méndez, Álvaro (2015), "*Change and Continuity in Chinese Foreign Policy: China's Engagement in the Libyan Civil War as a Case Study," Working Paper No. 5, London School of Economics and Political Science, Global South Unit*, http://eprints.lse.ac.uk/64375/1/LSE_Working_Paper_05_15%20%28Junbo%20%20Mendez%29.pdf

Lokhande, Sumedh Anil (2017), "China's One Belt One Road Initiative and the Gulf Pearl Chain," *China Daily*, June 5, http://www.chinadaily.com.cn/opinion/2017beltandroad/2017-06/05/content_29618549.htm

Ministry of Foreign Affairs, People's Republic of China (2011), "China's Peaceful Development," Information Office of the State Council, September 2011, Beijing, http://www.fmprc.gov.cn/mfa_eng/topics_665678/whitepaper_665742/t856325.shtml

Ministry of Foreign Affairs, People's Republic of China (2017), "Foreign Ministry Spokesperson Hua Chunying's Regular Press Conference," January 20, http://www.fmprc.gov.cn/mfa_eng/xwfw_665399/s2510_665401/t1432311.shtml

Moyer, Jonathan D., Bohl, David, Hanna, Taylor, Mapes, Brendan R. and Rafa, Mickey (2019), *Assessing the Impact of Conflict on Development in Yemen*, Sana'a: United Nations Development Programme, https://yemen.un.org/sites/default/files/2019-09/Assessing%20the%20Impact%20of%20War%20on%20Development%20in%20Yemen.pdf

O'connor, Tom (2018), "China may be the Biggest Winner of all if Assad takes over Syria," *Newsweek*, January 19, https://www.newsweek.com/china-did-not-fight-syria-won-war-754644

Poh, Angela & Li, Mingjiang (2017), A China in Transition: The Rhetoric and Substance of Chinese Foreign Policy under Xi Jinping. *Asian Security, 13* (2), 84-97.

Ramani, Samuel (2019), "Where does China Stand on the Libya Conflict?" *The Diplomat*, June 18, https://thediplomat.com/2019/06/where-does-china-stand-on-the-libya-conflict/

Reuters (2020a), "Libya's Haftar pulls back east as Tripoli offensive crumbles," June 5, https://www.reuters.com/article/uk-libya-security-idUKKBN23C11Q?edition-redirect=uk

Reuters (2020b), "Libya's Tripoli-based government and rival parliament take steps to end hostilities," August 5, https://www.reuters.com/article/us-libya-security/libyas-tripoli-based-government-declares-ceasefire-idUSKBN25H1BG

Rudolf, Moritz (2016), "China's New Era of Diplomacy: Engaging in Syria," *The Diplomat*, January 25, https://thediplomat.com/2016/01/chinas-new-era-of-diplomacy-engaging-in-syria/

Scobell, Andrew and Nader, Alireza (2016), *China in the Middle East: The Wary Dragon*, Santa Monica, California: RAND Corporation.

Scobell, Andrew (2018), "Why the Middle East matters to China," in Anoushiravan Ehteshami and Niv Horesh (Eds.), *China's Presence in the Middle East: The Implications of the One Belt, One Road Initiative*, Abingdon: Routledge, pp. 9-23.

Sohu Finance (2011), "Overview of Chinese companies' investment in Libya," August 23, http://business.sohu.com/20110823/n317112596.shtml

Sotloff, Steven (2012), "China's Libya Problem," *The Diplomat*, March 14, https://thediplomat.com/2012/03/chinas-libya-problem/

The Libya Observer (2018), "Libya joins China's Belt and Road Initiative," July 13, https://www.libyaobserver.ly/economy/libya-joins-china%E2%80%99s-belt-and-road-initiative

Tiezzi, Shannon (2014), "Why China Won't Lead in the Middle East, *The Diplomat*, July 28, https://thediplomat.com/2014/07/why-china-wont-lead-in-the-middle-east/

United Nations (2015), "Security Council Unanimously Adopts Resolution 2254 (2015), Endorsing Road Map for Peace Process in Syria, Setting Timetable for Talks," *Meetings Coverage and Press Release*, December 18, http://www.un.org/press/en/2015/sc12171.doc.htm

UN Economic and Social Commission for Western Asia (2018), "Experts discuss post-conflict reconstruction policies after political agreement in Syria,"

August 7, https://www.unescwa.org/news/syrian-experts-discuss-post-conflict-reconstruction-policies-after-political-agreement-syria

UN High Commissioner for Refugees (2019), "Operational Data Portal: Refugee Situations," September 26, https://data2.unhcr.org/en/situations/syria

Watanabe, Lisa (2019), "The Middle East and China's Belt and Road Initiative," *CSS Analyses in Security Policy* No. 254, December, https://css.ethz.ch/content/dam/ethz/special-interest/gess/cis/center-for-securities-studies/pdfs/CSSAnalyse254-EN.pdf

Workman, Daniel (2020), "Top 15 Crude Oil Suppliers to China," *World's Top Exports*, August 31, http://www.worldstopexports.com/top-15-crude-oil-suppliers-to-china/

Wu, Sike (2015), "The Strategic Docking between China and Middle East Countries under the 'Belt and Road' Framework," *Journal of Middle Eastern and Islamic Studies (in Asia)*, 9 (4), 1-13.

Xinhua (2016), "China calls for continuing intra-Syrian talks on time," March 25, http://news.xinhuanet.com/english/2016-03/25/c_135224317.htm

Xinhua (2017), "Full text: Vision for Maritime Cooperation under the Belt and Road Initiative," June 20, http://www.xinhuanet.com/english/2017-06/20/c_136380414.htm

Xinhua (2018), "Libya expresses willingness to join Belt and Road Initiative," April 17, http://www.xinhuanet.com/english/2018-04/17/c_137116652.htm

Xinhua (2019), "China urges regional countries to create conditions for Yemen to ease tensions: envoy," October 18, http://www.xinhuanet.com/english/2019-10/18/c_138480322.htm

Zaptia, Sami (2019), "Libya and China discuss oil cooperation in Libya," *Libya Herald*, July 26, https://www.libyaherald.com/2019/07/26/libya-and-china-discuss-oil-cooperation-in-libya/

Zambelis, Chris (2015), "China and the Quiet Kingdom: An Assessment of China-Oman Relations," *China Brief*, 15 (22), 11-15.

15. Bear Hug: Russia's Return to the Middle East

Uma Purushothaman

Russia's return to the Middle East through its intervention in Syria after the Arab Spring has made it a critical player in regional politics. But its influence spreads beyond Syria. It has strong relations not only with Syria, Iran, Egypt and Israel, but also with Turkey, Saudi Arabia, and other members of the Gulf Cooperation Council (GCC). Moreover, its foray into the Middle East has allowed it to project power abroad, in keeping with Putin's aspirations for Russia's re-emergence as a great power. This chapter examines Russia's return to the Middle within the context of Russia's foreign policy goals under Putin.

Russia's Foreign Policy under Putin

A cursory reading of Russia's foreign policy over the ages would bring out three themes and drivers, namely, (a) "…its quest for strategic depth and secure buffers against external threats, which…has guided its geographic expansion"; (b) "along with physical insecurity and expansion, the second key driver of Russian foreign policy has been its ambition for recognition as a great power" which the Kremlin deems is "necessary for legitimizing its geographic conquests and geopolitical ambitions"; (c) "the third driver, related to the first two, is Russia's complicated relationship with the West, which combines rivalry with the need for cooperation" (Gurganus and Rumer, 2019, p. 3).

Thus, safeguarding its vast and expansive territory, quest for power and identity, have defined the Russian foreign policy. These elements are naturally seen in Putin's foreign policy, particularly after rising oil prices gave Russia the flexibility to adopt an active and assertive foreign policy.

Examples of this are abound; "annexation of Crimea, the war in eastern Ukraine, the military deployment in Syria, the tense military standoff with the West in the Baltic and Black Seas," and the alleged "interference in US and European domestic politics" which "have all enhanced Russia's image as a major power with significant power projection capabilities, as well as Putin's reputation as a bold and skilled leader" (ibid., p. 2). Thus, restoring Russia's global status has been an explicit goal of Putin. These interventions are considered proof of Moscow standing up to the West and help to shore up Putin's domestic popularity.

Russia's activist foreign policy has been facilitated by some other factors as well. Long-term conflicts like Afghanistan, Iraq, Syria, and Libya have given Russia opportunities to introduce itself and establish "new facts on the ground" (ibid.). Moreover, growing political polarisation in the United States (US) and Europe, "the proliferation of information providers", and "widespread unhappiness with the ruling elites" after the 2008 global financial crisis have facilitated Russian interference (ibid., pp. 2-3). An additional element that is obvious from the way post-Cold War Russia has conducted its foreign policy is the "stability-over-democracy principle," which explains why Russia views Bashar al-Assad as being better than a "radical and split opposition" (Casula, 2017, p. 36).

The foundations of this principle can be traced to the colour revolutions of the 1990s in its neighbourhood, which left a deep impact on the Kremlin, making Russia a status quoist power except in situations that can be manipulated to its advantage like Ukraine and Georgia (ibid.). The colour revolutions and NATO interventions in Iraq, Libya, etc. were seen by Russia as a threat to "its notion of 'sovereign self-assertion' (*derzhavnoe samoutverzhdenie*)—its right, as Moscow would see it, to be a constant and influential player in world affairs" (Miron and Thornton 2021, p. 5). Thus, at the ideological level, Russia's Syrian intervention allowed it to challenge the liberal ideals of the West like globalisation which protects all kinds of freedom (individual, financial and political) and "promotes internationalised civil society as the main vehicle for political and social transformation" (Dannreuther 2015, p. 79). Thus, "Russia's perception of sovereign democracy focuses on the protection of the state's sovereignty and, subsequently, on domestic and regional stability, given that the state is the pivot for all necessary political and social changes" (ibid.).

Russia in the Middle East: Past as Prologue

The foreign policy concept of 2013 (MFA, Russia 2013) and 2016 (MFA, Russia 2016), reflect the Russian view on the changes in Middle Eastern societies and its opposition to the imposition of Western values and external interference. It views external interventions as having exacerbated tensions in these societies and promoting extremist ideas. The explicit references to the Middle East in these documents point to Russia's renewed focus on the region or its return to a region where it has long had interests.

For long, Russia has played an important role in the Middle East. From its rivalry with the Ottoman Empire to dividing up Iran with Britain during World War I War to supporting some allies in the Middle East, its roles have varied over time. Since the time of Catherine II, who brought the Russian Empire "its 'window on the Mediterranean' by founding Sebastopol in 1783, to the buildings of the 5th Soviet Operational Squadron, which crisscross Mediterranean waters since the 1970s, the Kremlin has continually sought to perpetuate its presence in the Mediterranean basin" (Berthelot, 2017, p. 170). The Middle East remained important to Tsarist Russia and later to the Soviet Union. It must be remembered that Russia and the Middle East are not geographically distant: "Grozny, Chechnya's capital, is only about 600 miles away from Mosul in Iraq" (Trenin, 2010, p. 3). The region naturally became an arena for power play between the two superpowers during the Cold War. The USSR had close ties with countries like Yemen, Syria, Egypt, and Iraq.

After the collapse of the Soviet Union, caught up in its own economic and political turmoil, Russia's role and influence in the region became rather limited. As a result, the region was marginal to Russia's national security in the 1990s as it was preoccupied with its economic crises and debating and evolving its own identity. As a result, the region received little attention from Russia during this period, falling victim to the overall retreat in Russian foreign policy.

Meanwhile, the deteriorating ties with the US and the West's refusal to accept Russia as an equal partner added to hostility within the Kremlin to the Western order led by the US. In the post-Gorbachev period, having abandoned official atheism and the separation of other countries into "reactionary and progressive", Russia sought to find economic partners among the rich monarchies of the Gulf (Vasiliev, 2018, p. 373). By the 2000s, Russia began to gradually change its foreign policy to focus on "the regions and countries/societal groups it once supported in its struggle against American imperialism" (Nalbandov, 2016, p. 406). This idea of reaching out to regions peripheral to Russia became stronger under Putin, who in 2007 declared Russia's unwillingness to accept the unipolar order led by the US (Nalbandov, 2016, p. 406).

The sharp increase in oil prices after the Global Financial Crisis in 2008 enabled Russia to pay off its foreign debts, accumulate large reserves of currency and break out of its inward-looking policies to supporting regimes deemed to be hostile to the US. One of the key areas which Russia focused on to regain its influence was the Middle East. The first indication of Russia's return was the entry of Russia as a member of the Quartet for the Middle East in 2002 following the second Intifada. Then, when the US launched the Iraq war in 2003, Russia, sensing an opportunity to revive its influence, began increasing its inroads into the region and started establishing "positive relationships with all the players", even those opposed to each other like Iran and Israel (Magen, 2013, p. 31). As Dmitri Trenin says, the Russian engagement in the Middle East is due to several factors like "commercial interests, concerns about the support ... from the region for insurgents and terrorists in Russia's North Caucasus, and the newly discovered spiritual attractions of the Holy Land and the ... beaches of the Mediterranean, the Red Sea, and the Gulf" (quoted in Nalbandov, 2016, p. 424).

Thus, the trinity of "security, business and spirituality", together with Moscow's desire to limit US influence in the region, enhance its political influence, and its keenness to portray itself as a reliable source of arms drove the Russian policy in the Middle East (Nalbandov, 2016, p. 425). Russia's demographic situation also contributes to its interest in the Middle East. "Russia's population is declining overall, but its Muslim population is growing; and the demographic balance between Muslims and Slavs will shift significantly over the next 30 years" (Stent 2020). Thus, the presence of "the largest Muslim minority in Europe" (Berthelot 2017, p. 178), most of whom are indigenous, comprising between 10 and 15 per cent of the population (14 to 20 million), inform Russia's need to revive its connections in the Middle East. There are also concerns regarding the radicalisation of Muslims, particularly due to the Chechen problem, as the Chechens had received support from some countries in the Middle East like Saudi Arabia in the past (ibid., pp. 178-179). Moreover, the second-biggest group of Islamic State (ISIS) foreign fighters in Syria came from the Russian Federation (Stent, 2020).

There are geo-economic reasons as well for Russia's return to the region. Russia and the Middle Eastern countries have similar economies, dependent acutely on revenues on sales of hydrocarbons. Therefore, there is a common interest in keeping oil and gas prices at the levels required for their economies to function properly. Moreover, Russian companies have interests in oil and gas projects in Iraq, Iran, Saudi Arabia, Libya, Algeria, etc. (Trenin, 2010, p. 6). Thus, Russia also seeks investments from these countries.

Many Middle Eastern countries buy Russian high-technology exports, and Russia has been exporting arms to countries such as Iran, Syria, and Algeria (Trenin, 2010, p. 6). With its numerous conflicts, the Middle East is naturally a ripe ground for Russia's arms exports. Between 2000 and 2019, for example, Russia supplied 19.3 per cent of the Middle East's arms (Thomas et al. 2020, p. 5). On their part, the Middle Eastern countries see several advantages in buying Russian weapons instead of American weapons; Russian weaponry and systems are often cheaper than US alternatives, and unlike the West, Russia does not impose preconditions related to human rights or secondary use on arms sales (ibid.). Moreover, for Russia, the arms industry "is one of only a few technology-intensive economic sectors in which Russia can be considered a world leader" (Connolly and Sendstad, 2017, p. 3).

Moreover, the defence industry is also socially significant since it accounts for a substantial share of employment in Russia. "With around 2.5 million workers, it is responsible for over 3 per cent of total employment, and around one-third of employment in manufacturing, with defence-industrial research and development (R&D) and production occupying a dominant place in many cities and regions" (Connolly and Sendstad 2017, p. 3). Thus, Moscow "wants to promote exports of arms, nuclear reactors, and other goods" as they are produced by enterprises necessary for "sustaining its current political and economic order" (Katz, 2015, p. 2).

For Putin, who considered the dissolution of the Soviet Union "the biggest geopolitical tragedy of the 20th century," a return to the Middle East would mark, in a way, the revival of the tarnished "Soviet glory" (Nalbandov, 2016, p. 425). This return was manifested spectacularly in Russia's intervention in the Syrian crisis, following a series of setbacks to the Assad regime and when the West had underestimated Russia. This is evident from the testimony of General Lloyd J. Austin III, the top US commander in the Middle East, before the US Senate Armed Services Committee, in September 2015, where he said that he and his colleagues in the Pentagon were "completely flummoxed" by the reasons for the Russian intervention in Syria (Garfinkle, 2016, p. 30).

Though Russia initially saw the Arab Spring as something which would weaken American imperialism, it did not anticipate that the protests would soon hit its ally, the Assad regime in Syria. In fact, it abstained from UNSC Resolution 1973 in 2011 on Libya to give the West a chance to resolve the crisis. However, soon, a sense of betrayal set in as the letter and spirit of the resolution was violated, and the West used the resolution to send troops and overthrow the Gaddafi regime. Moscow feared that this precedent would be used to "weaken it on its backyard" and enable "military-humanitarian interventions" that could weaken its allies or "re-ignite burnt embers, like in Georgia" (Berthelot, 2017, p. 174).

Other than the need to protect its ally, Moscow's decision to intervene was also pushed by the fear that Syria's collapse could weaken Iran's Shiite axis with which Moscow has strong ties. Moreover, in intervening in Syria, Moscow wanted to send a message to its partners that "we support our friends until the end" (Berthelot, 2017, p. 174). Other reasons were: to send a message to the West that Russia would react if its interests were threatened, its need to preserve its base at Tartus and finally because Putin had to present a more nationalistic posture in the Russian elections to cater to his base (Berthelot, 2017, pp. 174-75). The nature of the opposition to the Syrian regime, including the threat posed by ISIS, also caused concern in Moscow, as Russia itself has suffered from jihadist terrorism. As Trenin (2016, p. 4) says, Russia used military force due to fears that the Assad regime would be overthrown and replaced by the Islamic State. "Such a triumph for Islamic extremists would have encouraged their sympathizers across the Muslim world, including Central Asia and Muslim communities in Russia" (ibid.).

Russia also sensed that while the US is objectively strong in the region, it has become politically weak and acted accordingly (Garfinkle, 2016, p. 28). For Russia, Syria is a test case for its desire for a "post-West" world, a multipolar world where Russia is a global player (Yacoubian, 2021, p. 7). Taking all of this into account, Russia in 2015 intervened more decisively in the Syrian crisis, moving beyond just sending military advisors to sending warplanes and other weapons, thus preventing the creation of a No-Fly Zone in the North by Turkey (Berthelot, 2017, p. 177). Russia's Black Sea fleet was also sent to the eastern Mediterranean. Russian intervention proved decisive in securing the Assad regime and defeating the ISIS and other armed opposition groups. Moscow justified its intervention claiming Syria had formally requested Russian assistance (Phillips, 2016, p. 2 18).

What Russia's intervention also did was to underline Russia's ability to project power far beyond its traditional spheres of influence, posing a test to the so-far unchallenged US preponderance in the Middle East. This intervention had other benefits and "allowed Russia to show a certain know-how, test its weapons and strengthen its status as a leading exporter without too much damage" as most of the troops on the ground were either "Syrians loyal to the regime or foreign Shiites, framed by Tehran" (Berthelot, 2017, p. 177). It further helped its troops gain combat experience and helped advertise its "state-of-the-art weapons" to the rest of the world for future sales, as well as acting as a "warning and thus as a deterrent to NATO" (Miron and Thornton, 2021, p. 10). Moscow's actions in Syria forced the US to shelve the diplomatic isolation it had imposed on Putin since the Ukraine crisis, and in September 2015, Obama and Putin held their first direct dialogue since the crisis over Ukraine broken out (Phillips, 2016, p. 220).

Soon, the US was forced to consult Moscow closely as the Syrian peace process was revived. The military deployment gave valuable experience to Russia's recently reorganized air force (Phillips 2016, p. 220). Domestically, it boosted Putin's popularity by evoking a sense of pride in Russia's, return as a great power and distracting them from the economic hardships caused by the post-Ukraine sanctions. Pro-

Putin Russian Orthodox church leaders in Moscow tried to increase this "domestic support by offering the campaign religious legitimacy when a spokesman described it as a 'holy war' that would protect Syria's persecuted Christians, who were threatened by ISIS" (Phillips, 2016, p. 221).

Syria was in considerable debt to Moscow since 2011, including at least US$ 4 billion for unpaid arms contracts that would have been lost had Assad was defeated (Phillips, 2016, p. 221). The intervention further sent a message to the rest of the Middle East that Russia was serious about protecting its interests and could be counted on to protect its allies, unlike the West, which had washed its hands off its ally, Hosni Mubarak of Egypt in the wake of the Arab Spring protests. Russia's aura in the region was also strengthened because of its investments in building relations with several key Middle Eastern countries even before the Arab Spring.

Major Bilateral Relationships

Syria

Syria and Russia have been allies since Syria's independence from the French in 1946. This friendship was formalized by the Treaty of Friendship and Cooperation in 1980, which strengthened the relationship and Syria was one of the few countries which supported the Soviet Union's intervention in Afghanistan (Nalbandov, 2016, p. 428). With the Baath Party, which talked of Socialism, taking over power in Syria in 1963, the USSR's influence only increased by establishing its only naval base in the Middle East at Tartus in 1971. Syria was the second Arab country after Egypt to station regular Soviet troops and about "two air-defence regiments", as well as "military advisers" were deployed in Syria in the 1980s (Vasiliev, 2018, p. 384).

The collapse of the Soviet Union certainly led to an initial neglect of Syria, but Russia continued to be Syria's main supplier of arms, including surface-to-air missiles (Nalbandov, 2016, p. 429). The outbreak of the Arab Spring and the subsequent civil war proved to be an opportunity for Russia to consolidate its influence with the Assad regime. Russia, along with China, blocked several resolutions against Syria at the UN Security

Council. The use of chemical weapons near Aleppo in 2013 gave Russia a major diplomatic victory as it was able to block multilateral military action against the Syrian regime and assist in the handover and disposal of Syria's chemical weapons in 2013-14 (Nalbandov, 2016, p. 430).

Moscow later intervened on behalf of the Syrian regime. The steadfast support for its ally, Syria, did not go unnoticed by the other Middle East countries, which started contrasting this with how the West had behaved towards its allies during the Arab Spring. Putin built into these misgivings about the West by claiming that some countries were trying to "impose progressive development models" on Syria and other Near Eastern and North African countries leading to "great bloodshed" and asserting that in contrast, Russia's foreign policy was based on "international law, common sense, and the logic of peace" (Nalbandov, 2016, p. 430). Moreover, Russia's intervention in Syria helped it "to turn Syria into its geopolitical foothold in the region," as noted by Dmitri Trenin in 2016 (p. 3). Elaborating on this, Trenin says that "geographically, Syria is positioned between Moscow's other allies: Iran, Iraq, and the Kurds to the north and east, and Egypt to the southwest" (Ibid). He adds that "all these countries together stretching from the Caspian Sea and the Persian Gulf to the Mediterranean and Red Seas, would form a new axis of Russia's friends in the region"(ibid.).

This should theoretically allow Russia to play a long game in the Middle East. However, the Syrian regime is still not fully in control of all its territory; in addition to Russian forces, Syria is also host to Iranian forces and its proxies, American and Turkish forces; and Israel regularly violates its airspace posing serious challenges to Russia and Assad.

Israel

The Soviet Union helped in the establishment of the state of Israel and was the second country to accord it diplomatic recognition after the US. However, as Israel became more allied to the West over the years, the two countries drifted apart, with the Soviet Union adapting a more pro-Arab and pro-Palestinian position. As a member of the Quartet on the Middle East, Russia has spelled out its desire to establish a Palestinian state and recognized it as an independent state in 2011. However, relations with Israel remain strong because of economic and cultural ties, thanks to over a million Jews of Russian origin in Israel, comprising about one-fifth of Israel's population (Trenin, 2016). In 2009, the two countries lifted mutual visa requirements. In addition, the 9/11 attacks and the fear of radical Islam brought Moscow and Tel Aviv closer. Israel also provided technical assistance to Russia during the Chechen war.

Though Israel and Russia disagree on several issues like Iran, Hamas and Hezbollah, both believe that Islamist terrorism is their chief enemy (Trenin 2016, p. 4). Russia is also seen as a restraining influence on Iran by Israel (Stent 2020). Russia's leading strategic thinker, Dmitri Trenin (2016), avers that the transformation in Russia's relations with Israel constitutes "one of the most fundamental reversals" in Moscow's foreign policy (p. 4) in comparison to the earlier USSR regime.

Turkey

Russia-Turkey relations defy an easy definition and description; sometimes they work as friends, and sometimes like enemies, particularly in the post-Arab Spring period. In social media parlance, the relationship could best be described as 'complicated.' "Rivalry mixed with hostility has defined their relations since the 17th century, and this still informs their current views of each other with historical stereotypes" (Aydin, 2020, p. 1). Ottoman and later republican Turkey saw the forays towards the south by Tsarist Russia and later, the USSR as "existential" threats, inexorably connected to the reduction of their own territories (ibid.). During the Cold War, they were on opposite sides, with Turkey becoming a member of NATO. Though the two states no longer shared a land border after the Cold War, they began competing for influence in Eurasia (ibid., p. 2). This rivalry spilled over to the Chechen conflict, and Russia claimed that the Chechens were obtaining assistance from Turkey; in response, it extended support to Turkey's separatist Kurdish group, the Kurdistan Workers' Party (PKK) (ibid.). Russia's attempts to regain influence in its "near abroad" brought the two countries against each other in the South Caucasus. As for Turkey, the countries' independence was a strategic priority because this eliminated a land border with Russia (ibid.).

After 9/11 and the entry of the West in the Black Sea and the Caucasus through EU expansion and US military advisors, Ankara decided to build stronger relations with Moscow (ibid.). Therefore, in the 2000s,

Moscow and Ankara strengthened their relations through cooperation in energy, construction, and tourism and kept their security issues separate from economic relations. Russia became one of Turkey's top trading partners, exporting oil, gas, and metals. The two countries have signed several agreements on nuclear energy. The wedge between the West and Turkey around this time drove the latter closer to Russia. There has been a considerable strengthening of military and security cooperation with both undertaking naval exercises in the Black Sea and supply of Russian weaponry to Turkey because of the latter's interests in the latest Russian technology which its "NATO allies could not or would not provide" (Vasiliev, 2018, p. 356). They also agree that non-regional powers should not interfere in the affairs of the Caucasus and that the Iranian nuclear issue should be resolved only by political means (ibid., pp. 356-57).

The civil war in Syria had a substantial effect on Russia-Tukey relations. Turkey was unhappy with Russia's intervention and complained of frequent violations of its frontier by Russian planes and even downed a Russian plane in November 2015. Despite bitterness over this, the two countries did not break off, showing the resilience of their ties. Soon after, President Erdogan flew to Moscow, where he admitted that "without Russia's participation it's impossible to find an answer to the Syrian problem" (Hale 2019, p. 31). Defying the US and despite being a NATO ally, Turkey also bought the S-400 air defence system from Russia. While their mutual estrangement from the West drives Russia and Turkey towards each other, it is unclear if their relationship would stand strong if either of them were to substantially improve its relations with the West (Aydin, 2020, p. 4).

Iran

Historically, one of the two contacts of Russia in the Middle East, along with Turkey, Iran was divided into Soviet and British spheres of influence during the World War II. At the same time, its history predisposes Iran towards anti-Russian hostility (Brzezinski, 2006, p. 196). Moreover, Iran shares with Turkey an interest in opening up Central Asia to international economic access, which clashes with Moscow's "interest in monopoly control over the flow of Central Asian energy to global markets" (Brzezinski, 2006, p. 196).

Russia's attitude toward Iran's nuclear programme has been mixed. While recognizing Iran's right to develop peaceful nuclear energy and participating, despite Western pressure, in the construction of the nuclear power plant in Bushehr, Russia is against Iran developing nuclear weapons as it feels it would set off a domino effect in the region, destabilize the region and would be an unacceptable threat to Russia's own security (Vasiliev, 2018, pp. 359-60). Therefore, Moscow was part of the Joint Comprehensive Plan of Action (JCPOA) signed between P5+1 and Iran in July 2015. Otherwise, Moscow and Tehran have been on the same page on many issues, and several times Moscow has refused to support unilateral sanctions against Tehran. Furthermore, Russia and Iran supported the coalition headed by the US against the Taliban in Afghanistan in 2001, and during the Russian-Georgian conflict in August 2008, Iran declined to condemn either side (ibid., p. 365). Russia has also been supplying military equipment to Iran.

Moscow has been relatively unconcerned about Iran's activities elsewhere in the Middle East and sees the Tehran-Hezbollah connection as a way for Iran to get within striking distance of its regional adversary, Israel, which it views as a proxy for the US (Trenin, 2011, p. 124). Moscow also views Hamas, another of Iran's friends, as a political group with an unconventional military arm rather than a terrorist organisation (Trenin, 2011, p. 124). It supplies weapons to Iran. Their de facto alliance supporting the Assad regime in the Syrian civil war has strengthened their relations, as has their isolation by the West.

Saudi Arabia

Russia's relations with the Saudis are "testy" (Trenin, 2016, p. 3). The USSR was the "first country to recognize the independence of the Saudi state created by King Abd al-Aziz in 1926," though diplomatic ties were broken off in 1938 (Issaev and Kozhanov, 2021). The two countries did not "even have diplomatic contacts during the Cold War" and "during the Soviet Union's intervention in Afghanistan, the Saudis were among the main donors to the Afghan mujahideen" (Trenin, 2016). Ties were revived only in 1990 (Issaev and Kozhanov, 2021). Saudi Arabia's "financial support for re-Islamisation of the former Soviet space" and the spread of radicalism caused concern in Moscow, particularly because of its problems in Chechnya (ibid.). Between 1997 and 1999, according to the US State Department, charitable organisations from the Gulf countries allocated more than US$ 100 million to support the Chechen separatists (Vasiliev, 2018, p.374). Moreover, the two countries are competitors in the oil market, and Russia often competed with the Saudi-led Organization of Petroleum Exporting Countries (OPEC) over markets and prices.

Some factors which brought the two countries closer were the strain in US-Saudi relations after 9/11, Russia's desire to build ties with the Muslim world through Saudi Arabia and the US invasion of Iraq with Russia opposing the war and Saudi Arabia refusing to join the US-led coalition (Vasiliev, 2018, p. 374). Saudi Arabia is diluting its criticism of Russian policy in the North Caucasus and Chechnya and Russia becoming an observer state in the Organization of Islamic Conference (later renamed Organization of Islamic Cooperation; OIC) in 2005. For the first time, a Russian head of State (Putin) visited Saudi Arabia in 2007. During the visit, Putin received the state's highest award—the Order of King Abdul Aziz. King Abdullah had visited Moscow in 2003 when he was the Crown Prince (Berthelot, 2017, p. 178). Riyadh, meanwhile, was unhappy with the US policy towards Iran during the Obama administration though Trump attempted to mollify it. King Salman visited Russia in 2017, and Putin visited Saudi Arabia in 2019, leading to the conclusion of deals worth over US$ 2 billion comprising 20 bilateral agreements. For the Saudis, ties with Russia are "part of a general diversification of their foreign policy away from overreliance on the US" (Trenin, 2016, p. 3).

Though in 2021, the two countries have better relations than during the Cold War and have a common objective in stabilizing oil prices and supporting the Sisi regime in Egypt, their respective ties to the US and Iran remain an obstacle in consolidating the relations. They have signed several agreements of cooperation in the oil and gas sectors and space and science and technology. However, they are on opposite sides in the Syrian civil war. Saudi Arabia, however, believes that Russia can be a restraining factor on Iran (Stent, 2020). With the Biden administration's focus on human rights, its temporary freeze on weapons transfers to Saudi Arabia, and its ending of support to the war in Yemen, Saudi Arabia might be tempted to move closer to a Russia which ignores human rights issues.

With each of these key countries that have been examined, Russia's geostrategic and economic ties have visibly improved and have deepened. The Middle Eastern regimes, on their part, have both strategic and economic reasons to reach out to Russia. The fact that Russia's policy towards the region is "free of messianism, and Russia cannot be viewed as part of any kind of alliance" has been of great advantage to Moscow (Issaev and Kozhanov, 2021). Russia clearly wants to diversify its relations in the Middle East and strengthen bonds with the regional countries, indicating that it intends to play a "long game" there (Unnikrishnan and Purushothaman, 2017, p. 255).

Conclusion

Russia's return to the Middle East has been flaunted at home as one of the most important successes of Putin's foreign policy. After spending several years out in the cold, Russia has returned to the Middle East and has proved for now that it is an indispensable power broker, who the region can turn to on issues as varied as stabilizing global oil prices to the Israel-Palestine conflict. Its trade with the region is also rising. At the same time, in returning as a key player, it has exposed the West's weaknesses and broken partly free of the isolation imposed on it by the West after the Crimean crisis. It has also managed to sustain productive relations with all the key players in the region, including those who are/were against each other as well as non-state actors. As Angela Stent (2020) says, it is the "only major power which talks to all sides in all conflicts in the region". Russia's policy of engaging with all the region's powers has paid off, giving it the reputation of being a pragmatic, non-ideological, flexible, and credible partner.

Russia's return to the Middle East has been enabled by the divisions within the West, and the attempt by the US to return to isolationism, first under Obama, Trump and now Biden. Russia's re-insertion into the cauldron of Middle East politics brings with it a set of challenges. For instance, Russia will have to continue playing the delicate balancing game between Tehran and Riyadh, and Ankara and Damascus. Second, it might find itself pulled into other conflict situations that might emerge in the future. Third, its dabbling in Middle East politics could create more enemies for it, particularly jihadi terrorists who see it as a foreign power just as they see/saw the US as a foreign power. This could again make Russia the target of terrorist attacks. Fourth, it will have to invest money in the long term to sustain and justify its presence in the region. This might be hard in the face of sanctions imposed by the West and the slowing down of its economy, particularly in the post-COVID scenario.

Russia has certainly made several foreign policy gains through its re-entry into the Middle East, as outlined above. However, it remains to be seen if it can consolidate its gains. If it can, it would prove to the world that Russia is an irreplaceable power in the Middle East. Some of the regimes in the region might welcome Russia's return as it gives them more manoeuvrability in foreign policy in terms of choices, particularly since Russia is also a permanent member of the UNSC. However, if Syria again slips into chaos, Russia would have invested much financial and diplomatic capital for no gain. It also needs to be seen how the COVID-19 pandemic will affect the economies of the Middle East and Russia. For now, Moscow has used the pandemic to boost its soft power in the region through vaccine diplomacy. Finally, Russia will only sustain its presence in the region if it can diversify its economy away from the export of hydrocarbons and ensure that its economy grows at a reasonable pace. Only if it builds a strong manufacturing base will its economy strengthen, and can it credibly project power abroad. There is also the question of "who after Putin?" If the pro-democracy movement in Russia gains strength and a democratic leader comes to power, there is no guarantee that he or she will want to project power in the Middle East like Putin. Russia may then focus internally like it did in the 1990s. But these are big questions for the future for which there are no easy answers.

References

Aydın, Mustafa (2020), "The Long View on Turkish-Russian Rivalry and Cooperation," Research Report, *On Turkey*, No. 5, June, German Marshall Fund of the United States, Washington, DC, https://www.jstor.org/stable/resrep25035

Berthelot, Pierre (2017), "Russia in the Middle East: A New Dominant Actor?" *Rising Powers Quarterly*, 2 (1), pp. 169-181.

Brzezinski, Zbigniew (2006), "Putin's Choice" in Lennon, Alexander T. J. and Kozlowski, Amanda (Eds.), *Global Powers in the 21st Century Strategies and Relations*, Cambridge, MA: MIT Press, pp. 175-200.

Casula, Philipp (2017), "Russia's Foreign Policy from the Crimean Crisis to the Middle East: Great Power Gamble or Biopolitics?" *Rising Powers Quarterly*, 2(1), pp. 27-51.

Clayton, Thomas, Jeremy M. Sharp, Christopher M. Blanchard, Christina L. Arabia (2020), "Arms Sales in the Middle East: Trends and Analytical Perspectives for US" *Congressional Research Service Report*, No. R44984, November 23, https://fas.org/sgp/crs/mideast/R44984.pdf

Connolly Richard and Sendstad, Cecilie (2017), "Russia's Role as an Arms Exporter: The Strategic and Economic Importance of Arms Exports for Russia," Research Paper, March, Russia and Eurasia Programme, Chatham House, The Royal Institute for International Affairs, London, https://www.chathamhouse.org/sites/default/files/publications/research/2017-03-20-russia-arms-exporter-connolly-sendstad.pdf

Dannreuther, Roland (2015), "Russia and the Arab Spring: Supporting the Counter-Revolution," *Journal of European Integration*, 37 (1), pp. 77-94.

Garfinkle, Adam (2016), "Russian Motives in Syria and the Implications for US Policy," in Hof, Frederic C., Inozemtsev, Vladislav, Garfinkle, Adam and Ross, Dennis, *The Kremlin's Actions in Syria: Origins, Timing, and Prospects,* Washington, DC Atlantic Council, pp. 28-37.

Gurganus, Julia and Rumer, Eugene (2019), "Russia's Global Ambitions in Perspective," *Working Paper*, February, Carnegie Endowment for International Peace, Washington, DC, https://carnegieendowment.org/files/RumerGurganus_Perspective_final.pdf

Hale, William (2019), "Turkey, the US, Russia, and the Syrian Civil War," *Insight Turkey*, 21 (4), pp. 25-40.

Issaev, Leonid and Kozhanov, Nikolay (2021), "Diversifying Relationships: Russian Policy toward GCC," *International Politics*, DOI: https://doi.org/10.1057/s41311-021-00286-4

Katz, Mark N. (2015), "Conflicting Aims, Limited Means: Russia in the Middle East," *Policy Brief* No. 201, May, Fundación para las Relaciones Internacionales y el Diálogo Exterior (FRIDE), Madrid and Brussels, https://www.files.ethz.ch/isn/191176/PB201_Russia_in_the_Middle_East.pdf

Miron, Marina and Thornton, Rod (2021), "Emerging as the 'Victor'(?): Syria and Russia's Grand and Military Strategies," *The Journal of Slavic Military Studies*, 34 (10), pp. 1-23.

Phillips, Christopher (2016), *The Battle for Syria: International Rivalry in the New Middle East*, New Haven, CT: Yale University Press.

Stent, Angela (2020), "Russia's Return to the Middle East," *The Foreign Service Journal*, July/August, https://afsa.org/russias-return-middle-east

The Ministry of Foreign Affairs of the Russian Federation [MFA, Russia] (2016), "Foreign Policy Concept of the Russian Federation...," December 1, https://www.mid.ru/en/foreign_policy/official_documents/-/asset_publisher/CptICkB6BZ29/content/id/2542248

The Ministry of Foreign Affairs of the Russian Federation [MFA, Russia] (2013), "Foreign Policy Concept of the Russian Federation," February 18, https://www.mid.ru/en/foreign_policy/official_documents/-/asset_publisher/CptICkB6BZ29/content/id/122186

Trenin, Dmitry (2010), *Russia's policy in the Middle East: Prospects for Consensus and Conflict with the United States*, New York: The Century Foundation.

Trenin, Dmitry (2011), *Post-Imperium: A Eurasian Story*, Washington, DC: Carnegie Endowment for International Peace.

Trenin, Dmitry (2016), "Russia in the Middle East: Moscow's Objectives, Priorities, and Policy Drivers," Carnegie Endowment for International Peace, Washington, DC, https://carnegieendowment.org/files/03-25-16_Trenin_Middle_East_Moscow_clean.pdf

Unnikrishnan, Nandan and Purushothaman, Uma (2017), "Russia in Middle East: Playing the Long Game?" *India Quarterly*, 73 (2), pp. 251-258.

Vasiliev, Alexey (2018), *Russia's Middle East Policy: From Lenin to Putin*, London: Routledge.

Yacoubian, Mona (2021), "Understanding Russia's Endgame in Syria: A View from the United States," The Geneva Centre for Security Policy, https://dam.gcsp.ch/files/doc/understanding-russias-endgame

16. Arab Spring and India

P. R. Kumaraswamy

The decade-long political turmoil and instability in several Arab countries since December 2010 posed severe challenges to India as the region, often seen as an extended neighbourhood, is of considerable importance. How did India respond and handle the Arab Spring protests? Was there a common Indian approach towards popular protests in different Arab countries, or was it country/situation-specific? What were the strategies adopted by New Delhi, and how effective were they? Since the demands of the protesting population, mainly youth, were universal good governance and accountability, did the Indian positions convey any moral and ethical considerations?

The importance of the Middle East[1] for India is too widely articulated to be repeated here. While the immediate Gulf region attracts wider attention, the broader Middle East is critical for India's economic growth and progress. Historical ties, religious influences, geographic proximity, trade relations, energy security considerations, labour migration and substantial annual remittances add a strategic dimension to India-Middle East relations. One could argue that the Gulf region is far more important to India than the immediate South Asian neighbourhood; while the latter poses security challenges, the former offers immense opportunities. Unfortunately, the relative advantage of the Middle Eastern region has not been reflected in official circles; policymakers and academics have not woken up to the full potential of the Middle East, especially the Persian Gulf region, in shaping India's destiny and hence, do not go beyond customary pleasantries and lip service.

Despite the Covid-19 pandemic and its cascading effects, the Persian Gulf region continues to be India's largest trading partner and home to nearly nine million Indian workforces who remitted over US$ 40 billion in 2020. Moreover, the region continues to meet about two-thirds of India's hydrocarbon demands. There are considerable interests among the Gulf Arab countries, especially Saudi Arabia and UAE, to partake in India's economic growth through investments and partnership. Hence, political uncertainty, instability and violence in the Arab world should be worrying for India.

A decade after Mohamed Bouazizi unintentionally sparked off and let loose the latent Arab discontent against insensitive and often oppressive rulers, the Arab Spring could only achieve modest success. Tunisia, a small country with 11 million people, made some progress towards democratically choosing its government despite the upsurge of violence from militant Islamist forces. It was possible primarily due to the foresight and accommodation shown by Ennahda, the leading Islamist forces in the country committed to democracy and political inclusion. However, the progress card for the rest of the countries is negative; unable to capitalise on the much-heralded Tahrir Square moment, Egypt witnessed backsliding into military rule; Libya and Yemen plunged into civil war following regime change; the political survival of President Bashar al-Assad is accompanied by internal strife, large-scale population displacement and violence that resulted in the deaths of over 200,000 Syrians; promises of reforms did not materialise in Bahrain; the ripple effects in other parts of the Arab world did not bring about any meaningful progress towards democracy. While local and national elections were held in several countries, democracy remains elusive to the Arab world.

While a country-wise narrative would be informative, the commonality of popular Arab demands requires a broader regional understanding of the Indian response. Though the entire Middle Eastern region is important, the Gulf Arab region can be prioritised over the Levant and North Africa, and this is reflected in India's response to popular protests. This duality is also reflected in the approach of the Indian foreign policy community and their approach. For example, the vital importance of the Gulf region resulted in lesser focus and response than to Egypt; likewise, ideological preferences resulted in foreign policy elites siding with the Syrian regime than with the protesting public.

Indian Responses

One could broadly divide the Indian reaction to the Arab Spring protest into the following categories.

Absence of political visits: The most visible but rarely noticed response has been the absence of any political visits to the Arab world until the arrival of Prime Minister Narendra Modi. President Pratibha Patil visited UAE and Syria in November and December 2010, just days before the outbreak of the Arab Spring, and once the popular protests broke out, Indian leaders kept away from the Arab world, and their visits were confined to the three non-Arab countries, namely, Iran, Israel and Turkey. While some Arab leaders visited India, especially on the eve of the 16th Lok Sabha elections, no Indian president, vice-president, prime minister or foreign minister visited the Arab world between November 2010 and September 2014, when External Affairs Minister Sushma Swaraj visited Bahrain. The only exceptions were the visit of External Affairs Minister S M Krishna to Palestine (along with Israel) in January 2012 and to the UAE in April that year. MoS E Ahamed visited Egypt, Palestine and Jordan in 2011 and Bahrain in 2013. Either caution or neglect, the absence of political visits to the region was glaring.

Evacuation: Bringing home its citizens stranded in the conflict zones was the most visible Indian response to the Arab Spring. When popular unrest broke out, there was a sizeable Indian population in the Middle East and the presence of its nationals in Egypt and Yemen considerably shaped and even determined the official position. The evacuation required some cooperation and coordination with host governments and resulted in India not making any public statements about developments in Egypt, for example, until the mission was accomplished.

In the wake of the Arab Spring protests, India brought home 3,600 of its nationals from Egypt, close to 18,000 from Libya in 2011 and 2,793 in 2014; and over 4,500 from Yemen in 2015. These numbers were much smaller than the 150,000 evacuated from Kuwait in 1990 following the Iraqi invasion but required considerable local coordination with the growingly unpopular Arab regimes. As a result, India did not make any formal statement concerning protests against Mubarak and moved its mission in Libya to D'Jerba in neighbouring Tunisia and later to Malta (Indian Embassy in Libya, 2018). Moreover, the evacuation from

Yemen, which happened between 1 and 11 April 2015, required logistical arrangements with Saudi Arabia, and Prime Minister Modi spoke to King Salman on 30 March 2015, seeking Saudi support and coordination.

Travel Advisory: To ensure its citizens' welfare and prevent the logistical nightmare of mass evacuation, the Indian government has been issuing travel advisories. The civil war situation resulted in India cautioning its citizens from undertaking non-essential travel to Iraq; similar moves vis-à-vis the Arab Spring protests had an interesting pattern. However, these advisories were belated, selective and appeared to have been less effective. While the Tahrir Square protests began on 25 January 2011, a travel advisory for journalists was issued on 3 February. On 20 February, it advised its nationals to 'avoid non-essential travel' to Libya and was repeated long after the evacuation of its citizens; for example, the September 2015 one warned citizens "to avoid travelling to Libya and NOT to take any employment" in that country, and the May 2016 advisory imposed a travel ban to Libya "irrespective of the purpose." The first travel advisory for Yemen was issued on 11 March 2011 and was repeated subsequently. Like other countries, India was surprised by the events in Tunisia and did not respond to the Jasmine Revolution. Syria is an interesting case. Its first advisory "to avoid all non-essential" travel to Syria had to wait until 7 January 2012 and was repeated in May and July that year.

However, its position on Bahrain was nuanced. On 17 August 2011, the MoS E Ahamed informed the Lok Sabha that the ministry "had issued travel advisories for our nationals in Bahrain to avoid non-essential travel" but no further details are available and the MEA website does not carry any separate travel advisory for Bahrain (India, Lok Sabha, 2011). However, responding to media query MoS Ahamed remarked that the embassy has asked the Indian community in Bahrain, "to keep a low profile, stay indoors and to avoid all non-essential travel within the country" (India, MEA, 2011b). This was reiterated and expanded following a meeting between the Indian ambassador and Bahraini Prime Minister on 17 March, and the embassy observed that it "will issue suitable travel advisories should it become necessary. Until then, the present advisory which asks Indians in Bahrain to keep a low profile, stay indoors and to avoid all non-essential travel within the country stands.

The Indian Embassy has also advised the Indian associations that those family members and others whose presence in Bahrain is not necessary should consider leaving the country, if so inclined" (India, MEA, 2011c). Otherwise, India did not restrict travel to Bahrain, which witnessed severe social unrest since February 2011, requiring a military intervention in the form of Peninsula Shield Force the following month. In short, more than the situation on the ground, the political calculations influenced the travel advisory route.

Both evacuation and travel advisory did not impede the flow of Indian migrant workers to war-torn countries. On the contrary, for want of better opportunities at home, migrant workers tended to ignore the official warning and continue to travel to war-torn countries like Iraq. One could notice a similar trend in the wake of the Arab Spring protests, and for example, in July 2016, the government informed the Lok Sabha that there were 'around 1,750 Indian nationals in Libya' long after the evacuation from that country (India, Lok Sabha, 2016). On 24 November 2016, External Affairs Minister Swaraj said that 'there were over' 9,000 Indians in Iraq and about 100 in Syria despite the civil wars in both the countries (India, Rajya Sabha, 2016) and in 2020, the number of Indians in Yemen was estimated at 10,500. In May 2011, Foreign Secretary Nirupama Rao told her audience in Paris that despite the evacuation of close to 18,000 persons, "2000 Indians (have) elected to stay back" in Libya (India, MEA, 2011e). This necessitated another round of evacuation in 2014.

Interestingly, the evacuation was not a considered option vis-à-vis the GCC countries, which have a sizeable Indian expatriate population. Violent clashes between protesters and security personal were reported in Manama since February 2011. At that time, there were about 350,000-450,000 Indians in the island kingdom. On 18 February 2011, assuring the welfare of the citizens in the Kingdom, the Indian government observed: "We hope calm soon returns and prevails in Bahrain" (India, MEA, 2011a) and the following month hosted the Bahraini Foreign Minister who promised to ensure "the safety and security of the Indian community numbering well over 350,000" (India, MEA, 2011d). The Bahraini minister's visit was preceded by the visit of Bandar bin Sultan, Secretary-General of the Saudi National Security Council. With Saudi-led military forces coming to the rescue of the beleaguered Al-Khalifa rule in Bahrain, these two visits in quick succession were closely linked. Otherwise, India never made any public statement concerning events in Bahrain.

Studied Silence: The most significant hallmark of the Indian response to the Arab Spring has been 'studied silence' (Kumaraswamy, 2012). Though actively following the events, especially their ramification upon the large Indian community in the Gulf Arab countries, India avoided any public statement or stand concerning the events. In the words of Professor Gulshan Dietl, if its response to Tunisian events "was a total silence," its response to Tahrir Square protests "was muted as well" (Dietl, 2013, p. 140). Underscoring the vital importance of the Gulf Arab countries for India's economic growth and welfare, former diplomat Ranjit Gupta advised "a low-key non-intrusive" (Gupta, 2013, p. 150) policy approach to the region and warned against "ideologically motivated domestic criticism about supposedly abandoning the so-called arbitrarily defined 'independent' foreign policy or criticism by foreign countries on this account" (Gupta, 2013, p. 148).

There were suggestions that "India's policies must be country, region and issue-specific" (Gupta, 2013, p. 148). However, if one examines the overall approach to the uprising, India has been cautious and restrained towards the Arab Spring. Since the Tunisian protests had a cascading effect upon the larger Arab world, India could not adopt a country or region-specific approach. Indeed, despite the absence of strategic interests or diaspora concerns, India did not react to popular protests in Jordan, which undermined the stability of the Hashemites in the early stages. Moreover, open criticisms of President Mubarak would have jeopardised India's evacuation plans from Egypt and would have placed at odds with King Abdullah of Saudi Arabia, who was rallying behind Cairo until Mubarak's resignation.

At times the Indian silence goes to absurd levels. As observed elsewhere,

> Reading the *Annual Report for 2010-11* ... [Ministry of External Affairs], one would remain ignorant of the Arab Spring. *The Report*, which chronicles official positions on global affairs up to March 31, 2011, does not make any reference to the events happening in the Middle East. Two presidents had been overthrown by then, but the entries dealing

> with India's ties with Tunisia and Egypt are silent on this. Nor does the *Report* mention India's endorsement of the UNSC Resolution 1970, which referred [Muammar Qadhafi] to the International Criminal Court (ICC) for a war crimes trial. Some have called these omissions a "deafening silence". (Kumaraswamy, 2012, p. 5)

Principles of Arab Spring: The protesting Arab population demanded good governance, political reforms, an end to authoritarianism, youth employment and empowerment. These are the natural yearning for any modern society. Most of the protests were peaceful and non-violent, and this was the case even in Libya, Syria and Yemen until the Arab regimes responded with force against the protesting public. The Mubarak regime's violent tactics did not intimidate the Tahrir Square protesters. Hence, Indian understanding, support or empathy for the protesting Arab public would have been natural and even inevitable.

However, this did not happen. The Indian government and civil society, in general, approached the Arab Spring through a national security paradigm. In the words of one former diplomat India "should accord the highest priority to considerations of national interest rather than moral and ethical principles" (Gupta, 2013, p. 147). A large Indian community and its strategic economic interest prevented India and its civil society from rallying around the Arab Spring protests. There was a deafening silence on events in the Gulf Arab countries, especially Bahrain, Saudi Arabia and Oman, which witnessed different degrees of protests since early 2011. The Left-wing intellectuals who are often at the forefront of raising human rights concerns vis-à-vis Israel have been silent on the Al-Khalifa's response to demands for reforms in Bahrain. The explanation has to be found in the large share of people from Kerala—the only major state ruled by the communists in 2021—among the Indian migrants in the Gulf. Drawing parallels with the Tahrir Square moment in Manama would have resulted in a mass exodus of returnees not only from Bahrain but also from the Kingdom of Saudi Arabia and UAE, still the most popular destination for Kerala migrants. Hence, the Indian elites and civil society community preferred realism to human rights concerns.

This approach was more palpable in the Indian response to events in Syria. The peaceful and non-violent Syrian demand for limited political opening and reform largely escaped Indian attention. If the Indian government continued its cautious approach, elites and policy circles securitised the Tahrir Moment in Damascus. Secular credentials of the Assad regime, Islamist composition of the anti-regime forces, the intervention of conservative monarchs, anti-Americanism and pro-Russian sentiments led to the coalescence of a securitised narrative of the Syrian crisis. The Indian civil society never presented or saw the Syrian crisis as an uprising seeking demands similar to the people of Tunisia or Egypt.

The enclosed picture was taken from the Jawaharlal Nehru University, the country's most politically active campus, reflects this dichotomy. Amidst the protests in Tahrir Square, one of the student union posters depicted Mubarak as Pharaoh (Figure 1); interestingly, during his trial in 1982, Khalid al-Islambuli remarked that he only killed a Pharaoh and justified his assassin of President Anwar Sadat. The expression 'Pharaoh' has a special meaning among conservative Islamists and denotes the leader of the pre-Islamic Jahiliya period. Even if one assumes this to be a reference to an aging and despotic ruler, there were no posters, protests or even marking of events in Syria. In the decade-long crisis, directly or indirectly, President Assad presided over the death of close to a quarter of a million Syrians and displaced another 11 million. If the Indian government could not express its judgment due to national interest calculations, the Indian elites never held Assad accountable for the human tragedy in Syria.

Figure 1: Poster of Mubarak Depicted as Pharaoh

Source: Picture taken by author.

UN Security Council: During 2011-12, India was a non-permanent member of the UNSC and this provided India with an opportunity to enunciate a position that would reflect its attention and concerns vis-à-vis the Arab Spring. Though it was an early stage, events in Libya and Syria dominated the Council's attention and compelled India to go beyond 'studied silence.' On 17 March 2011, the UNSC deliberated and adopted Resolution 1973, which endorsed 'No Fly Zone' in Libya towards protecting the civilian population from the Gaddafi regime. While ten members voted in favour, India joined Brazil, China, Germany and Russia to abstain. However, the general consensus and demand on the issue from the Arab League and Africa Union nudged India to give its tacit consent to 'responsibility-to-protect.'

Western powers, however, used Resolution 1973 as a carte blanche for a regime change in Libya, leading to two critical developments concerning Libya; the mass lynching of Gaddafi near his hometown of Sirte on 20 October and reopening the tribal divide and plunging the country into a spiralling civil war that has no signs of ending even after a decade. Despite this, on 4 October, India abstained during a UNSC vote on Syria that condemned "grave and systematic human rights violations' in that country and contemplated sanctions against President Assad. This resolution, however, could not be adopted due to the veto by Russia and China. In 2012, India voted for two UNSC resolutions on Syria; in February, the Council considered an Arab League-proposed UNSC Resolution that demanded all parties in Syria—both government and armed opposition groups—to stop all violence and reprisals; and in July debated sanctions against the Syrian regime. But both the resolutions could not be adopted due to veto by Russia and China. In August, India was part of the IBSA delegation that visited Syria and met Syrian officials, including President Bashar al-Assad, who "reassured the delegation of his commitment to the reform process, aimed at ushering in multi-party democracy, including through revision of the constitution" (India, MEA, 2012). Unfortunately, the general IBSA demand for all parties temporarily eschewing violence to facilitate negotiations did not materialise.

In short, on Libya, the Indian abstention eventually contributed to the West-inspired regime change, and on Syria, its support for prevailing

Arab consensus was sabotaged by the Russia-China duo. In both cases, the gains for India have been minimal.

Palestinian question: There were even suggestions that 'heightened attention to the Palestinian cause' would be one of the "key patterns that are likely to shape future dynamics' of the Middle East." (Abhyankar and Pourzand 2013, 29 and 30). Not only this did not happen, but the Arab Spring protests also undermined the Westphalian order and compelled the prioritisation of regime survival over Palestinian statelessness. Indeed, Bahrain which faced persistent protest normalised relations with Israel in September 2020 while a few others moved in the same direction following the unveiling of the Trump Peace Plan in January that year.

Some lament, though incorrectly that "India has received no appreciation either from the region or at home for its hands-off approach" (Abhyankar and Pourzand, 2013, p. 31). In their view, the criticisms within the country "centred on four important concerns: the rise of political Islam and Islamic governance; regional stability; India's confusing stand on the Arab uprisings in the UN Security Council; and India's role in the changed circumstances" (Abhyankar and Pourzand, 2013, p. 31).

Non-interference: Official statements and responses and positions at the UNSC underscore the resolute Indian position of non-interference in the internal affairs of other countries. Even if it sounded unethical and indifferent, India has resolutely avoided making a judgment on domestic developments of other countries, even if no vital interests are involved, which is not the case in the Middle East and the Gulf region. As a former diplomat reminded, "the principle of non-intervention in internal affairs has always been sacrosanct for India" (Gupta, 2013, p. 148). Indeed, it is worth remembering that Prime Minister Jawaharlal Nehru's confidant and later defence minister, V. K. Krishna Menon dismissed the marching of Soviet tanks into Budapest as 'internal affairs' of socialist states. Nor did it react to the assassination of former Lebanese Prime Minister Rafik Hariri in February 2005. Besides principles, this non-interference also has practical considerations. As Pakistan continues to internationalise the Kashmir issue, New Delhi does not wish to provide an alibi for other countries to comment on domestic Indian developments.

Assessment

Examining the Indian actions and statements, it is possible to draw some broad conclusions and assessments.

No regional policy: The Arab Spring did not result in India abandoning its country-specific approach to the Middle East and evolve a regional policy. At the same time, it could not escape from the regional problem posed by popular protests. Though the outcomes were not uniform, the popular demands across the Arab world were not different. New Delhi's position and stand vis-à-vis one country could not be divorced from others. This approach became useful and effective when India persisted with its policy of non-intervention. Even when protests spiralled into civil wars, India focused only on the welfare of its citizens in the warzones and their evacuation. As a non-permanent member of the UNSC, it followed the prevailing international consensus on the crises in Libya and Syria and did not make waves.

If distance and speed of events precluded any response on Tunisia, strategic calculations prevented India from commenting on protests in Bahrain. Likewise, evacuation delayed its responses to events in Egypt, Libya and Yemen. This pattern was followed in other Gulf Arab countries and Jordan. The situation in Syria rekindled the traditional Indian preference for secular Ba'ath nationalism and opposition to Salafi extremism, and both resulted in a non-committal stand that reflects the prevailing Arab consensus.

The response of the civil society also reflected an interesting pattern. Vociferous support for Tahrir Square protests was accompanied by the Indian elites adopting security logic for the Syrian crisis. The interests of the expatriate population, who are largely composed of Keralites, led to the civil society not responding to events in Bahrain, Saudi Arabia or Oman in the same vigour as Tahrir Square. Jordan, which saw popular protests, also did not evoke any response from New Delhi.

Evacuation: The evacuation of people from Egypt, Libya and Yemen does not indicate that the Indian government was prepared for a mass movement of migrant workers from the Gulf Arab countries. Exodus from one country would have pushed similar movements from other countries and created a humongous humanitarian crisis. From the materials available in the public domain, India did not develop a contingency plan for a possible evacuation of its citizens from Bahrain and Oman, which also witnessed public protests. If the Covid-related evacuation—or homecoming at its depicted officially—is an indication, the government did not visualise and hence did not plan for any large-scale evacuation following the Arab Spring.

Structure handicap: In terms of the organisational structure of the External Affairs Ministry, Iran and Turkey—the two non-Arab countries which stirred Arab Spring protests in Syria and the Gulf region, are not part of the West Asia and North Africa or WANA Division of the Ministry. If Turkey is part of the European Division, Iran is included in Pakistan-Afghanistan-Iran Division and hence their role in the Arab Spring protests, prolongation and hurdles in solving the crisis do not figure in shaping India's response to the Arab Spring. Indeed, the absence of Iran in the Gulf Division of the Ministry harms Indian understanding of the strategic concerns of the Gulf Arab countries. India's Gulf policy is formulated without India considering the Arab concern, if not paranoia about Iran and its hegemonic aspirations. While it is not necessary for India to get involved in the sectarian division—especially when it has a large Shia population—a meaningful understanding of the geostrategic reality of the Gulf would require placing Iran in the Gulf Division. The much-talked-about 'structural changes' introduced by External Affairs Minister S Jaishankar in the early 2020 did not address the Iran file. Moreover, following the initiation of the nuclear cooperation agreement with Washington, some of the sensitive decisions concerning Iran seemed to be taken by the US Division than by WANA or PAI Divisions.

Conclusion

Interests and not principles drive states and societies. Nations adopt moral high grounds and pontify human values when they suit—only when they suit—their vital national interests. This is a universal norm, and exceptions would result in national decline and irrelevance. Seen within the realist paradigm, India has handled the Arab Spring protests with finesse. Its policy of non-intervention served Indian interests well and functioned as a diplomatic cover for its interest-driven approach to Arab Spring. Given its limited political influence, the protesting Arab public also did not expect much from India or its elite. Thus, the strategic interest, especially concern over expatriates, became relevant to explain the Indian position.

Moreover, 'studied silence' also minimised the negative repercussions of an activist approach, and this is vindicated by the continuous flow of migrants to the region. On the eve of the COVID-19 pandemic, there were at least 8.5 million Indians in the Gulf Arab countries, including about 320,000 in Bahrain, which witnessed the maximum protest in the Gulf region. The less vocal policy became handy when India faced the GCC crisis over Qatar in June 2017 that lasted until January 2021. Indeed, the Arab Spring is perhaps one of the few occasions when talking less proved to be a blessing for India and its interests.

Note

1. Due to the larger theme of this volume, this chapter primarily focuses on the Arab countries while making passing references to the three non-Arab powers—Iran, Israel and Turkey—wherever necessary.

References

Abhyankar, Rajendra, and Azadeh Pourzand. 2013. *Protests and Possibilities: West Asia and India.* Mumbai: Gateway House. https://www.gatewayhouse.in/wp-content/uploads/2013/04/West-Asia-Online.pdf.

Dietl, Gulshan. 2013. "The 'Spring' Has Had a Contagious Effect Much Beyond." *Indian Foreign Affairs Journal* 8 (2): 134–41.

Gupta, Ranjit. 2013. "Fallout of the 'Arab Spring': Challenges for India." *Indian Foreign Affairs Journal* 8 (2): 142–55.

India, Lok Sabha. 2011. "Impact of Turmoil in Gulf, Unstarred Question, No. 2590, 17 August." http://mea.gov.in/lok-sabha.htm?dtl/16781/Q2590_Impact_of_turmoil_in_GULF.

India, Lok Sabha. 2016. "Unstarred Question No. 649, Indians Stranded in Libya." https://mea.gov.in/lok-sabha.htm?dtl/27064/question+no649+indians+stranded+in+libya.

India, MEA. 2011a. "Indians in Bahrain Safe, 18 February." http://mea.gov.in/media-briefings.htm?dtl/3319/Indians_in_Bahrain_safe.

India, MEA. "MOS Shri E. Ahamed on Safety of Indians in Bahrain, 14 March." http://mea.gov.in/Speeches-Statements.htm?dtl/319/MOS_Shri_E_Ahamed_on_safety_of_Indians_in_Bahrain.

India, MEA. 2011c. "Ambassador Calls on Prime Minister of Bahrain—Assured of Safety of Indian Nationals, 17 March." http://www.mea.gov.in/press-releases.

htm?dtl/643/Ambassador_calls_on_Prime_Minister_of_Bahrain__assured_of_safety_of_Indian_nationals.

India, MEA. 2011d. "Visit of Foreign Minister of Bahrain to India, 30 March." http://www.mea.gov.in/press-releases.htm?dtl/32/Visit_of_Foreign_Minister_of_Bahrain_to_India.

India, MEA. 2011e. "Transcript of Foreign Secretary Smt. Nirupama Rao's Speech at the French Institute of International Relations (IFRI), Paris." https://mea.gov.in/Speeches-Statements.htm?dtl/359/Transcript_of_Foreign_Secretary_Smt_Nirupama_Raos_speech_at_the_French_Institute_of_International_Relations_IFRI_Paris.

India, MEA. 2012. "IBSA Delegation Calls on President Assad to Discuss Situation." https://www.mea.gov.in/press-releases.htm?dtl/57/IBSA+delegation+calls+on+President+Assad+to+discuss+situation.

India, Rajya Sabha. 2016. "Unstarred Question, No. 101, Indians Residing in War-Torn Countries." https://mea.gov.in/rajya-sabha.htm?dtl/27677/question+no101+indians+residing+in+wartorn+countries.

Indian Embassy in Libya. 2018. "India-Libya Bilateral Relations." https://www.embassyofindiatunis.gov.in/india-libya-bilateral-relations.php.

Kumaraswamy, P. R. 2012. *Reading the Silence: India and the Arab Spring*. Jerusalem: The Leonard Davis Institute for International Relations. http://davis.huji.ac.il/sites/default/files/davisinst/files/readingthesilence.pdf.

Index